THE ART AND ARCHITECTURE
OF ENGLISH GARDENS

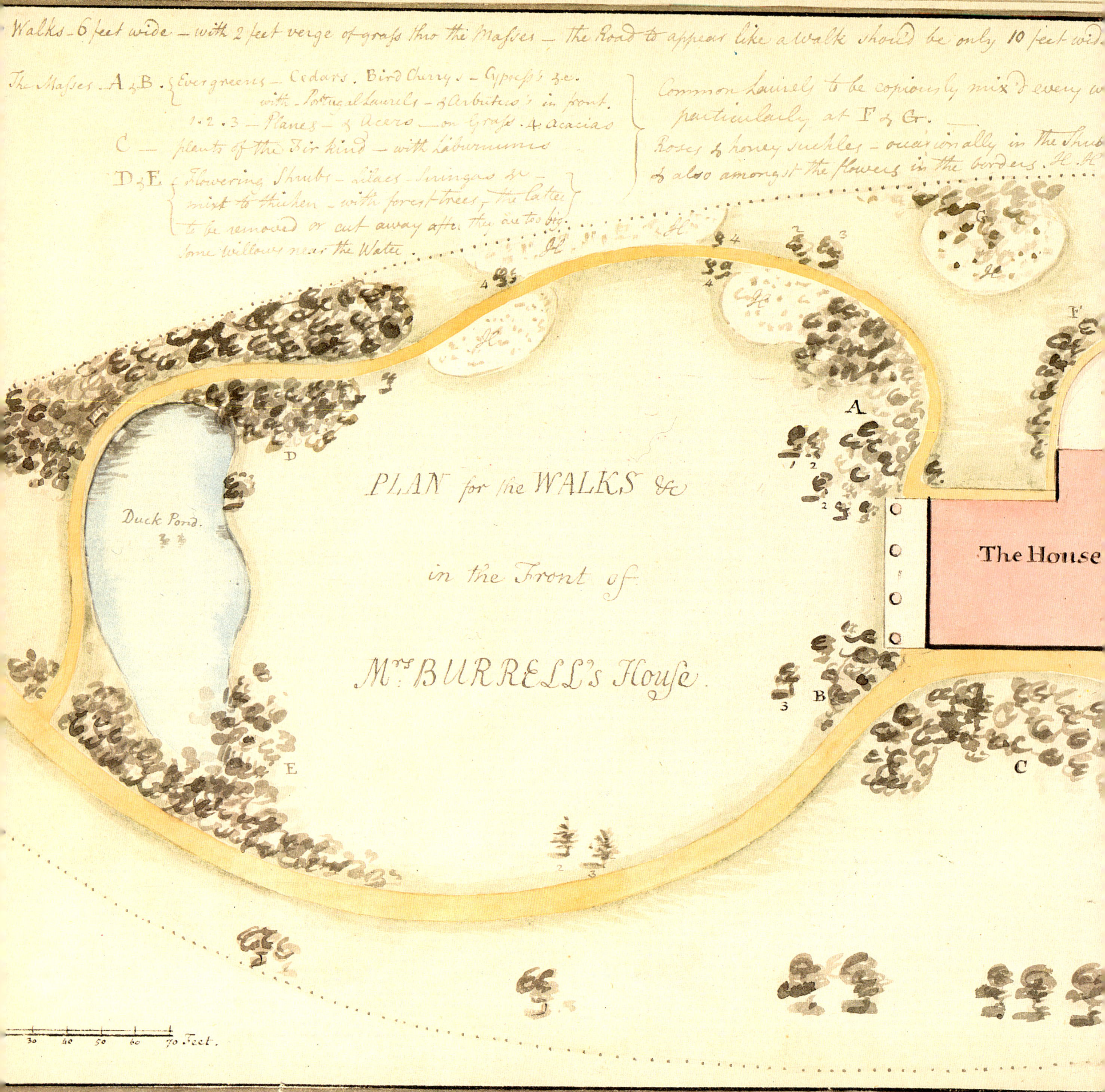

Walks - 6 feet wide - with 2 feet verge of grass thro the Masses - the Road to appear like a Walk should be only 10 feet wide

The Masses. A & B. Evergreens - Cedars. Bird Cherrys - Cypress's &c.
          with Portugal Laurels - & Arbutus's in front.
     1. 2. 3 - Planes - & Acers - on Grass. 4. acacias
  C - plants of the Fir kind - with Laburnums
  D & E { Flowering Shrubs - Lilacs - Syringas &c -
          mixt to thicken - with forest trees, the latter
          to be removed or cut away after they are too big.
          Some Willows near the Water -

Common Laurels to be copiously mix'd every w
particularly at F & G. -
Roses & honey suckles - occasionally in the Shrub
& also amongst the flowers in the borders. H. H.

Duck Pond.

PLAN for the WALKS &

in the Front of

Mrs BURRELL's House.

The House

A

B

C

D

E

F

30   40   50   60   70 Feet.

_____ *Jane Brown* _____

THE ART AND ARCHITECTURE
OF ENGLISH GARDENS

DESIGNS FOR THE GARDEN
FROM THE COLLECTION OF THE
ROYAL INSTITUTE OF BRITISH ARCHITECTS
1609 TO THE PRESENT DAY

WEIDENFELD AND NICOLSON LONDON

For my godchildren, Emily Watkinson and Benjamin Maggs

PHOTOGRAPHIC ACKNOWLEDGEMENTS
All illustrations are reproduced by kind permission of the RIBA Drawings Collection.
In addition we would like to thank the following: Fig. 5 Yale Center for British Art,
Paul Mellon Collection; Fig. 6 The Board of Trustees of the Victoria & Albert Museum;
Figs. 7 & 8 The National Trust Photographic Library; Fig. 9 The President and Officers of
The Royal Society; Fig. 10 The Trustees of the Tate Gallery; Fig. 11 John Chichester
Constable Esq.; Fig. 13 Devonshire Collection. Chatsworth Settlement Trustees;
Fig. 14 Norfolk County Library; Fig. 15 The Linnean Society of London; Figs. 16 & 17
The Royal Horticultural Society, Lindley Library; Figs. 18 & 22 National Monuments
Record; Figs. 23, 24 & 27 Country Life; Figs. 28 & 29 Erith and Terry Architects;
Figs. 32 & 33 Royal Horticultural Society, Lindley Library (photo. Hugh Palmer);
Cat. no. 255 Sir Geoffrey Jellicoe.

Frontispiece: Plan for the Walks for Langley Park, Kent, by Humphry Repton. See no. 30.
Picture facing page 6: A garden balustrade with urns by Alexander Roos. See no. 233.

George Weidenfeld and Nicolson Limited
91 Clapham High Street
London SW4 7TA

ISBN 0 297 79638 0

Phototypeset by Keyspools Limited, Golborne, Lancs
Colour separations by Newsele Litho Ltd
Printed in Italy by Printers Srl, Trento
Bound by L.E.G.O., Vicenza

CONTENTS

ACKNOWLEDGEMENTS

My first thanks are to Jill Lever for giving me this chance to explore the RIBA's treasure house, and for her continued help and advice. At both the drawings Collection and at the British Architectural Library in Portland Place I have been given help and encouragement by many people, but especially by Jane Preger, Neil Bingham and Andrew Norris; indeed, I owe something to almost everyone I have met at Portman Square around the most celebrated eighteenth-century kitchen table in London! My book owes a great deal to the skill and hard work of Geremy Butler, who has photographed all these drawings.

Tackling three hundred years of garden history has been a daunting task to one who inevitably only feels at home in this twentieth-century; I could not have attempted it without a galaxy of books on the various periods and I am in debt to many people's research, some of whom happily I may call my friends mentioned within.

Lastly, my thanks to everyone at Weidenfeld's, particularly Michael Dover, my book's designer Trevor Vincent, and most especially my editor, Suzannah Gough.

Foreword

The 350,000 or more drawings in the Collection of the Royal Institute of British Architects range from the Renaissance to the present day. Not all of them are designs for buildings and many show the architect in another rôle, perhaps as archaeologist or engineer or – garden designer. The *Oxford Companion to Gardens* has entries for more than seventy architects who are also garden designers and some of them will be met in this book. But land-owners, writers, painters, horticulturalists, plantsmen, plant collectors as well as professional gardeners, garden designers and landscape architects have all contributed to the design of gardens. The question of what was the architect's particular contri-bution is explored here, and the relationship between the design for a house and for its garden. This survey of the garden theme among the RIBA's drawings also allows for a comparison of the methods of conveying garden and landscape design; probably the most difficult to represent of all the art forms.

The publication of these drawings with Jane Brown's zestful and highly individual commentary will I know bring much pleasure to many new and old friends of the Collection.

Jill Lever, Curator, RIBA Drawings Collection
March 1989

Fig. 1] Humphry Repton's Trade Card, engraved by Thomas Medland after a design by Repton, 1788, from the Red Book for Langley Park.

INTRODUCTION
Architects in the Garden

The purpose and the pleasure of this book is to explore gardens through the Drawings Collection of the Royal Institute of British Architects. Along the way something of the relationship between architects and gardens and gardeners will be revealed, and hopefully some inspirations to present-day garden makers and designers will occur.

Edith Wharton coined a particularly good phrase for the role of flowers in the Italian villa gardens, she called them 'a parenthetical grace'; the garden drawings have a similar role in this great Collection.[1] The Collection dates from the founding of the Royal Institute of British Architects in 1834. At first, drawings came from private collections of architects and antiquaries but by the 1870s the Council of the Institute was making repeated appeals for drawings to be left in its care, and their appeals were well heeded. The foreseen purposes of holding these drawings were to provide an accurate basis for architectural history, as well as inspiration to young architects from the most eminent of their profession.[2] That the Collection does indeed hold the works of the greatest architects is a celebrated fact; it is one of the most distinguished Collections in the world. The published catalogue now runs to twenty volumes, (a complete list to date will be found in my Bibliography) and new treasures are continually being added.

The drawings are used, as frequently as is good for them, for exhibitions in London and all over the world. In 1986 John Harris, Jill Lever and Margaret Richardson presented eighty-two *Great Drawings*[3] in a New York exhibition of works by Palladio, Inigo Jones, Wren, Kent, Sir James Thornhill, the Adam brothers, Sir William Chambers, Bonomi, Decimus Burton, Barry, Pugin, Scott, Alfred Waterhouse, Norman Shaw, Lutyens, Voysey, Frank Lloyd Wright, Mies van der Rohe and James Stirling. Particular aspects of the Collection have been celebrated in books and exhibitions: John Harris on *The Palladians*, Gavin Stamp's *The Great Perspectivists*, David Dean on *The Thirties*, Margaret Richardson's *Architects of the Arts and Crafts Movement* and Jill Lever's *Architects' Designs for Furniture*. Thus research, publication and exhibition are the continual and continuing role and purpose of the Collection. As David Watkin has acknowledged in *The Rise of Architectural History* the Collection has become, in the last twenty years, 'the true centre of research into English post-medieval architecture', and this supremacy is largely attributable to the brilliance and generosity of John Harris, Curator of the Collection from 1962–86.[4]

Clearly John Harris's characteristic and delightful scholarship as a garden historian boded well for my exploration of the Collection. But I had the distinct impression that as far as garden history was concerned, the traffic through the door of the elegant Georgian building on the corner of Portman Square that houses the Collection, has in the past been rather one-way. John Harris has brought out a stream of contributions to garden history, but how many garden historians have gone in?

Not, I think, too many. The subject of garden history, which has been forwarded by leaps and bounds since the founding of the Garden History Society in 1965, has been predominantly based on literary and historical sources. (To be fair, there is such a vast amount of such material that it has been more than enough to fill the time of the small army of garden historians.) However, I feel this may have given a philosophical bias at the expense of the more visual, design element of the subject, and there are signs that garden history is changing, perhaps entering what may be called a second stage.

The achievements of the first stage must not be overlooked. Aspects of garden history are now quite usual as university thesis subjects, and 'a thousand years of British gardening' was celebrated in an elaborate and evocative exhibition at the Victoria & Albert Museum in 1979 with a subsequent memorable exhibition at Sotheby's in 1987 – called *The Glory of the Garden*. Ray Desmond's *Bibliography of British Gardens*, published in 1984, must rank high on the list; this mammoth achievement lists reference sources for five and a half thousand gardens in a vast array of books and archives. The political achievement has been in English Heritage's registration of gardens for their historical value, masterminded by Christopher Thacker, a founder member of the Garden History Society, in his appointment as Gardens Inspector at the Department of the Environment, from 1982–7.[5]

While not underestimating these achievements, the swing to a more design-orientated view of gardens does seem particularly exciting. Recent books – Brent Elliott's *Victorian Gardens*, Roy Strong's *Renaissance Gardens in England*, and David Jacques' *Georgian Gardens* make full and sound use of the plan and pictorial material available to them in harmony with their literary sources. John Dixon Hunt's revelatory *William Kent . . . an assessment and catalogue of his designs* made me realize for the first time just how Kent *saw* his gardens and landscapes. At the other extreme *The Oxford Companion to Gardens* is both boon-companion and a world-wide overview, edited by two landscape architects, Sir Geoffrey Jellicoe and Michael Lancaster, and a design historian, Patrick Goode. And, as I write, the latest development is a combined effort from a wide range of garden interests to form a national reference and resource for collections of garden and landscape design drawings, being co-ordinated by Peter Goodchild from the Centre for the Conservation of Historic Parks and Gardens at York University.

This shift of emphasis is timely. The purpose of garden history is not merely to indulge in fantasies of the gardens of the past, it is to foster and push forward the cause of restoration and conservation. Garden restoration is a more complex task than the restoration of a painting or a building, because a garden goes on living, and dying, and the question of time passing complicates every decision. Plans and working-drawings convey the most direct information as to the designed intention, far more realistically than pages of perfect prose. Perhaps too much prose and poetry on the subject of gardens has created a nostalgic image which causes a gulf of disillusion between the image in the mind's-eye, and the reality either restored – or more likely still derelict – on the ground. As it must be the conservation-trained architect or landscape architect who leads the restoration team, it is as well that the rest of us, who are deeply interested, understand his language and means of expression. But plans, sections and elevations are difficult to interpret, and there is often a sense in which the layman feels excluded. Perhaps meeting them here, through the centuries, often in quaint and fragile form, though

also often as exquisite and beautiful drawings, will remove some of their terrors.

This difficulty of understanding technical drawings has been approached by Jill Lever and Margaret Richardson in *The Art of the Architect*.[6] Their essay and comments on their chosen drawings provide a clear interpretation of the mysteries of technique, and perhaps a few of their points are worth repeating here. Two kinds of professional drawing offer little difficulty, the freehand sketch and the finished 'presentation' drawing, which is often a perspective. Sketches are often the most magical moment of invention; the outstanding example here is the Munstead Wood sketchbook by the young Edwin Lutyens (nos. 90–92). Lutyens, who was the son of a painter of horses and landscapes, Charles Lutyens, was an irrepressible sketcher, on the backs of envelopes, on menu cards and table-cloths or even shirt-cuffs, and somehow his sketches invariably contained the essence of the eventual design. Finished perspectives are at the other extreme, and they are the most easily admired representations especially of houses and gardens. Perspective drawing was developed in Italy in the fifteenth century, and came to England via two parallel methods. The two-point perspective came into English architecture via Inigo Jones, Wren and Lord Burlington; a second style went from Leonardo and Bramante to San Gallo and the Italian villa gardens and on to de Cerceau and his drawings of the chateaux and axially planned French gardens. This latter style influenced the engravers Knyff and Kip, in whose work the sight lines are moved up high to produce the 'bird's-eye' perspective. The famous Talman drawing of the Trianon for Hampton Court Palace of 1699 (no. 9) is a very early use of this bird's-eye view in a design drawing. Text books on perspective were fairly plentiful in the early eighteenth century, but 'it was not until the 1770s . . . that English architects made much use of perspective convention, and when they did it had evolved into a particularly English phenomenon – the watercolour perspective set in a pictorial landscape'.[7] *The Art of the Architect* attributes this phenomenon to two influences, that of Piranesi and Clerisseau at the French Academy in Rome, where both William Chambers and Robert Adam studied, and to the topographical watercolourists Paul Sandby and Thomas Malton, and the paintings of Canaletto. But it would be not unlikely, I think, that the English feeling for gardens was beginning to assert itself. William Kent drew his designs in perspective in landscape settings because he was interested in the 'arrangement' of the landscape around the buildings. With the Victorian architects and the design of formal gardens to match their houses, the perspective reveals them equally, and the seductive value of the technique in convincing the prospective client made it worthwhile employing a professional perspective artist; the impressive scheme which Charles Barry hoped to carry out for Drumlanrig Castle was painted by Thomas Allom. Though many of the Arts and Crafts architects were accomplished artists – Charles Voysey often painted his own superb perspectives – the perspectivists were employed to invent gardens for the houses, as a 'selling-point' for the design: Thomas Hamilton Crawford gave Ernest Newton's Fouracre a delightful garden with apple blossom, a well and yew enclosures, which the house never had in reality. There is no doubt that the garden became a very attractive motif for the architectural perspectivist.

The earliest forms of plans, called 'plattes' or 'platforms' are shown in the Robert Smythson garden drawings in Chapter one; Smythson's gardens are drawn essentially the same way as building plans – in a simple two-dimensional expression – and such plans for formal gardens have changed little over the centuries and have become accepted. Their patterns were derived from timeless symbols, the circle within a square, various forms of a cross, from geometric division and proportion, and occasionally from rather more ingenious sources. The latter undoubtedly include the concentric circles of the Copernican sun-centred universe which Jung says turned artists from 'imagination' to 'nature', and which Roy Strong identifies in the garden plan for Lord Bedford's house at Twickenham (no. 1); classical paving and ceiling designs have been adapted for gardens, and baroque decorative swags and swirls were laid out in coloured gravels for Victorian parterres. The 'rosary' garden was originally derived from the great rose windows of Chartres, Notre Dame and York Minster. But it is worth noting that these clever derivations do not last, and are rarely repeated, whereas the classical symbols and proportions come round time and time again.

In architectural drawing convention the plan is allied to an elevation, which is 'a directly frontal view of a building made in projection on a vertical plane', and a section, which represents the building 'as it would appear if cut through on a plane at right angles to the line of sight'.[8] In gardens of manageable size architects have tended to go on using elevations and sections; both are immense assets in judging the relation of vertical elements in a garden to each other and to a building, and in depicting the effect of changing ground levels on a design. Elevations and sections are at their best here in comparatively modern drawings, in the A.B.Pite drawings for Burton Manor (nos. 207–8) and the Jellicoe and Shepherd section for the spectacularly-sited Villa Medici at Fiesole (no. 173).

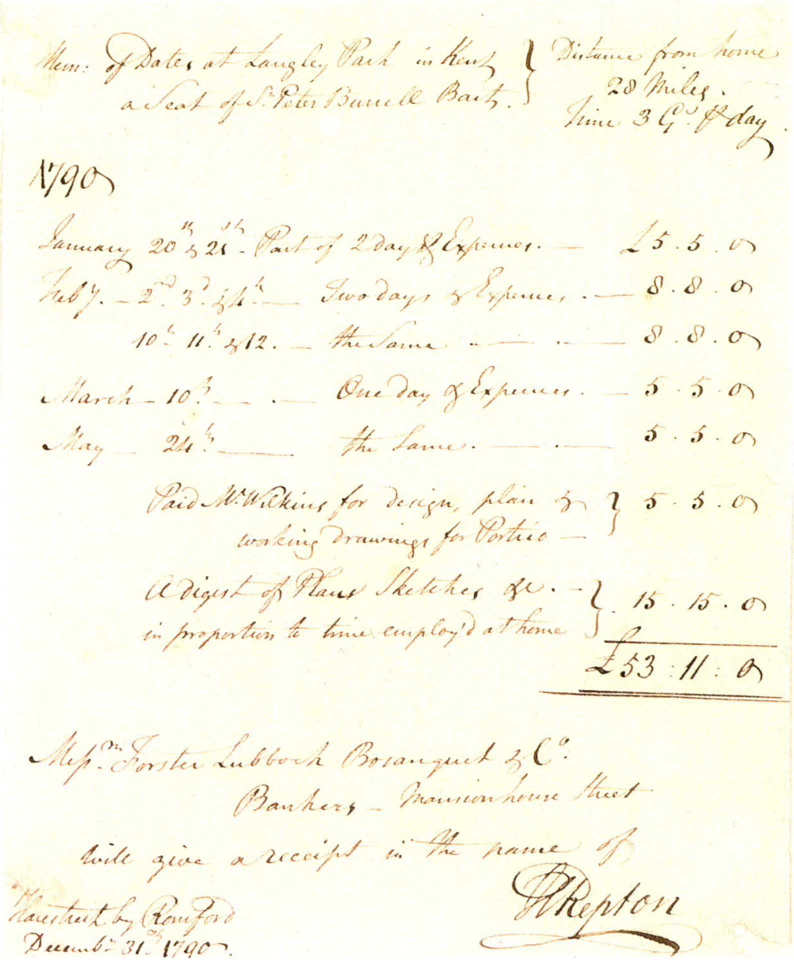
Mem: of Dates at Langley Park in Kent
a Seat of Sr Peter Burrell Bart. } Distance from home 28 Miles. Time 3 Qrs of day.

1790

January 20th & 21st. Part of 2 day & Expenses. — £5.5.0
Feby. 2d 3d & 4th Two days & Expenses, — 8.8.0
10th 11th & 12. the Same — 8.8.0
March 10th One day & Expenses — 5.5.0
May 24th the Same. — 5.5.0
Paid Mr Wilkins for design, plan & working drawings for Portico } 5.5.0
A digest of Plans Sketches &c. in proportion to time employ'd at home } 15.15.0
£53:11:0

Messrs. Forster Lubbock Bosanquet & Co.
Bankers – Mansion house Street
will give a receipt in the name of
H Repton

Hare street by Romford
December 31st 1790.

Fig. 2] Humphry Repton's account for work at Langley Park which is kept in the back of the Red Book.

But with the eighteenth century and the English landscape style, the elevation and section were discarded and the plan became the main expression of design. It is interesting that William Kent, who 'leap'd the fence' never used a plan; he was a painter and persisted in a painterly form of design. It was up to the remarkable Capability Brown to develop his style of landscape drawing from the techniques of the seventeenth-century map makers, with their wavy lines for roads and little windmills and trees drawn in elevation. The extent of his achievement is shown in the 'meander' (no. 23), a typical Brown feature, dramatized in the varied strokes of his sepia pen, and highlighted with red lettering. This has all the good qualities of a landscape drawing: clarity, sound information and a fluidity and softness that is in the mood of the natural landscape, and far removed from hard geometrical design drawing. William Emes' plan for Erlestoke (no. 26) is also a fine example of a large-scale landscape plan. Brown's and Emes' clients, the Whig landowners, were probably quite happy with these plans, as they were used to estate maps and surveys of their land. But nervousness about plans was to be avoided with newcomers, the *nouveau riche* like the Upchers and the Burrells, who were to be Humphry Repton's clients. Repton had more than a little sense of vocation to teach these newcomers how to live in the country in what he felt was the right tradition, so it was a stroke of genius to invent the *before* and *after* watercolour to make it perfectly clear to them what was right and what was not. Repton adopted the 'slide' or 'flap' across part of the painting, on which he painted the view as it existed; when the slide was removed, the transformation to what the view could be, was revealed. There is a fine example of this with the Sheringham drawings, where the undulating hills beside the sea are instantly replaced by Repton's garden with flower baskets, rose trellis and conservatory all full of flowers in bloom (nos. 39–40).

Repton is recognized by present-day landscape architects as the 'codifier' of their profession; his published theories do provide what may be called the 'ten commandments' for landscape beauty which are the guide rules for design. Most importantly he taught how to convey the message to the client, a client who was probably preoccupied, distracted, busy and fearful of what seemed like enormous expense involved in moving his land around; Repton's delicious watercolours and simple plans with colour added for clarity, allayed their fears. There was no one with Repton's ability to carry on, and the concept of *before* and *after* lapsed until used by landscape architects with photographs and photo-montage in very recent times. The Victorians resorted to plans, often rather boringly so, and the Papworth Leigham Court plan (no. 71) and Thomas Allason's plans (nos. 43–4) are fair examples of this plainness. John Claudius Loudon was a self-taught architect and his

drawing always had rather a 'cottagey' style; he was at his most professional in his standard for landscape design, especially late in his life when, unable to draw after he had his right arm amputated in his early fifties, he exacted fine standards from his draughtsman. The plan for Kiddington House (no. 67), echoed by those for Coombe Abbey (nos. 82–4) have a fine restraint, a very Victorian politeness about their treatment of the land, so very far removed from Brown and Emes's more sensual love of the landscape. Victorian gardens for the middle-class were polite, the paths around the lawn were afraid of curving too sensuously, respectability was tightly-corseted. They held the Victorian virtues against the opulence of Charles Barry's parterres for aristocrats on the one hand, and the contorted writhings of paths and amoebic flower beds that were put into the most characteristic Victorian garden achievement, the public park, on the other. These were designed by Loudon and his successors as landscape gardeners and not in the main by architects. The most notable park designer was Sir Joseph Paxton, whose park for Crystal Palace at Sydenham (no. 74) shows such an area of writhings and contortions which always seems like microscope-inspired design.

Sanity and skill returned to garden plan-drawing with the twentieth century, but with a few notable exceptions it was not now architects who were drawing the plans. The exceptions are here. Edwin Lutyens demanded exquisite architectural geometrics for garden details but did not bother much with 'soft' garden schemes. The outstanding examples of plan drawings in the Collection and this whole book are not for a working commission, but for an academic study, the Shepherd and Jellicoe drawings of the Italian villa gardens. The Collection holds the complete set of illustrations for their book *Italian Gardens of the Renaissance*, first published in 1925, and I have been unashamedly greedy in my selection. Shepherd and Jellicoe employed the full gamut of convention, plan, section, elevation and bird's-eye perspective to a high degree of skill; the watercolours have fine lines and subtlety of shading that almost gives, in the case of the plans, a dimension of depth, a feeling of the bulk of the hedges, their shadows cast and the sense of enclosure. The pen and ink perspectives have been highly influential on generations of landscape designers, for they demonstrate so clearly how the designed elements of the gardens sit in their landscape, and grow from it in return.

The date of the Italian villa garden drawings, 1925, is significant; the high standard they set influenced the complete vision of graphic representation that the newly-founded land-scape architecture profession (the Institute of Landscape Archi-tects was set up in 1929) had to aim for; since then examinations in drawing ability have played a great part in the education of landscape architects. Non-architect candidates for the profession have often found this difficult, sometimes too difficult to overcome, and the standards of drawing required have undoub-tedly contributed to the charge of exclusivity in the profession, and to the fact that now so much garden work is designed by practitioners who have learned their skills elsewhere. But that is another story. The lucid and informative drawings for the Festival of Britain gardens by Peter Shepheard (nos. 162–3) are fine examples of modern office practice. There are additional sections and elevations to deal with landform, though now, in the era of the mechanical digger, this is very much down to on-site supervision and a skilled driver. The careful and clear spacing of plants and the accurate use of Latin names are part of a landscape professionalism that contractors now understand. However, even as I write, I know that the richest period for plans and drawings like Peter Shepheard's was the sixties and seventies, and the art is on the wane, superseded by photographs, photo-montage and computer-aided print-outs, which will pass merely mechanical messages between the professional designer and his contractor on the ground.

These past and impending changes in the processes of garden design, and the roles of designers, seem to make it imperative that a sufficient record is saved. Except for the design of exquisite garden buildings, as in the work of architects like Clough Williams-Ellis and Quinlan Terry, the architect has now really left the garden scene. I have already mentioned that the identification and collection of a national record of garden drawings is in the planning stage. This mammoth task could only be contemplated in the computer age but it will still take a very long time, and in the meantime much will be lost. There may be a growing awareness that such drawings should be saved but there is simply so often just nowhere to store them as designers close their offices and retire. Thus the imperative message of this book must be to my readers, that if you have or know of garden drawings in need of a home, please contact the Drawings Collection at 21 Portman Square, London, or Peter Goodchild at The King's Manor in York.

If, as it seems, we are coming to the end of the architect's involvement in garden design, then my book becomes more

timely, for the evidence of his role during the last four centuries of English garden making becomes increasingly valuable. (I fear it is *his* role; with great joy I found Ethel Mary Charles (1871–1962), the first woman member of the Institute, but she did not appear to be interested in gardens.) And surely, like Miss Charles, some architects were interested, and some were not. Who was interested? Who was not? I approached the Collection on its own terms (which seemed only polite) by checking through the published alphabetical catalogue. My attitude was mainly that of a reasonably well-prepared explorer with an open mind; but I must admit to a touch of missionary zeal, secretly hoping that some new and preferably very distinguished architects could be identified for the garden cause. In working though from Abromovitz to Zucchi I attempted to pick up all the garden references; I added those from recent accessions and checked all of them in the card catalogue. In addition I tried to heed all the helpful suggestions of the Curator, Jill Lever, and her assistants, for they know this vast Collection in a way no stranger ever can.

My missionary zeal was soon on stalks; could the famous Adam brothers really be co-opted as garden designers? They certainly dabbled in 'romantic and imaginary landscapes' and the Collection has a list of flowers left by John Adam (1721–92). Fortunately, for my progress, the Adam drawings are mainly in the Sir John Soane's Museum, London. One glance at Robert Adam's drawings for the park at Kedleston though, assures me that to explore their interest in gardens would be to wander in a delightful grove.[9] It is disappointing that Thomas Archer (1668–1743) is only respresented by Chettle House and Hey-throp, and that the Collection does not have his designs for the pavilion and baroque garden at Wrest Park which seem not to have survived.

The 'B' volume produced great treasures; here is Sir Reginald Blomfield (1856–1943) author of *The Formal Garden in England*, who plays a great part in this book, and the little-known R. Shekleton Balfour's (d. 1910) drawings of the garden at Monta-cute in Somerset; he was doing exactly what Blomfield preached, that these 'old gardens' should provide the model for the Arts and Crafts architects' inspiration. Here also are Sir Charles Barry (1795–1860) and Edward Blore (1787–1879), two heavyweight Victorians both with a grand interest in gardens. Then, a fanfare! For Richard Boyle, 3rd Earl of Burlington (1694–1753), architect and gentleman of taste who made gardens the rightful concern of gentlemen and architects. Burlington was a modest architect, but in the realms of gardening and collecting drawings he ranks as a god; in the first for employing William Kent, and in the second for saving the Palladio drawings. The saga of the Burlington-Devonshire Collection can only be told at its briefest here, but it has the makings of a fine adventure story and bears upon several drawings in my book. It began with Inigo Jones visiting Italy from 1613–5 and acquiring a large collection of drawings by Palladio (1508–80), which he brought home and added to his own. Inigo Jones died in 1652, hardly less of a legend than Palladio, and this 'snowball' of precious drawings was left to his nephew John Webb, who carried on working in the Jones manner and added his own. The whole collection, or a significant part of it, passed on to William Talman (1650–1719) who used Palladian inspiration for his Trianon at Hampton Court (no. 9). Talman's son John, sold the drawings to Lord Burlington, who subsequently added William Kent's drawings to his collection, but not before he had been to Italy and found more Palladio drawings which he bought and brought home. This snowball-haul of architectural treasure, to which Lord Burlington continually added in his lifetime, was left to his daughter Charlotte, who was married to the 5th Duke of Devonshire. Eventually, in 1894, the 8th Duke gave half of his collection to the RIBA, while keeping his own share at Chatsworth.[10] So, for garden historians the direct line to Lord Burlington and Chiswick House and the birth of the English landscape movement is miraculously secure, and yet tantalizingly absent from this Collection: the RIBA's share of the 'snowball' concerning Chiswick House and garden are oddments detached from the very large number at Chatsworth.[10] Lord Burlington's handiwork is elusive as he so easily employed others to draw for him, and the pavilion by the lake (no. 192) and elevations for the orangery, drawn by Henry Flitcroft, are attributed to him and his garden. As to William Kent (1685–1748), John Dixon Hunt's recent catalogue of all his known garden and landscape drawings illustrates forty-one that are at Chatsworth, and the majority are of Chiswick's garden.[11] Another drawing from the Burlington-Devonshire collection has been slipped in, possibly attributable to Kent, of a rusticated obelisk topped by a sphinx (Fig. 3).

From this great moment in history when the matter of gardens had equal standing with the sister arts, I was plunged back into the harshly superior and prosaic world of architecture, the mistress art, on her high horse. The long entries for William

Fig. 3] Design for a rusticated gate pier topped with a sphinx by William Kent or Lord Burlington. A similar design was published by Isaac Ware in *Designs by Inigo Jones and Others*, 1735, and the gate piers at Temple Newsam, Leeds, are of this design.

Burn (1789–1870), architect of Scottish country houses, were endless: offices, conveniences and drains, with never a mention of a garden. Colen Campbell (1673–1729) seems to have been a Palladian purist, far from garden thoughts even though he knew both Studley Royal and Stourhead, and John Carr of York (1723–1807) was likewise, though the mood lightens with James Gibbs (1682–1754) designing some garden buildings and Nicholas Hawksmoor (1661–1736) showing a passing interest in what John Evelyn was doing at Wotton; a Hawksmoor sketch of the house with some garden is worth noting, but more appealing by far is the small, mellowed sheet bearing Evelyn's (1620–1706) broad pen strokes and sepia ink designing his own parterre (no. 13). This design most probably dates from the 1650s when John Evelyn, in tactful withdrawal from the Commonwealth government in London, was concentrating upon gardening and his own garden at Sayes Court in Deptford. The Restoration in 1660 was to bring gardens and John Evelyn back into their own; as gentleman, courtier, diarist, philosopher and scientist, author of his 'discourse on forest trees', *Sylva*, with its appendix on orchards, he single-handedly gave gardens their high profile in the eyes of the gentlemen of England. He revived the idea of paradise as a garden, which for a moment became entangled in the swags and topiary of Dutch William III's tastes (so splendidly illustrated by the William Talman drawings here, nos. 9–12) but then was caught and thrown into the fresh air and open landscape by Lord Burlington and William Kent. With Kent's inspiration succeeded by the one-man monopoly of Lancelot 'Capability' Brown, it does not, upon reflection, seem at all surprising that the Palladian giants, Inigo Jones, Campbell, Carr and Gibbs kept well inside their porticos and refrained from designing groves and green mounds; not only was the physical distance between house and park of considerable expanse, the intellectual gulf between unruly bushes and the *harmonic proportions* of Palladian beauty was likely to be too extreme for a single mind. But the Palladian mansions 'floating in their seas of grass' like heavenly gondolas, also exactly represented just that superiority that the mistress art can so readily assume.

It is rapidly becoming clear that the relationship between architects and gardens revolves, in time, upon two distinct planes, the imaginary and the physical. The architect, like Robert Smythson at the start of the seventeenth century, is perfectly happy with the tight formal, outdoor room of a garden, under complete control, and he is equally happy, like William Talman, when the formality expands over vast acreages, as at Hampton Court and Dyrham Park, under the Dutch influence at the very end of the seventeenth century. But with John Evelyn, and then Alexander Pope, and dreams of paradise involving large tracts of soggy greenery (it may have been sunlit, ferny greenery in the Italy of Poussin and Claude, but in England it was invariably soggy), the architects resorted to fantasy; – Inigo Jones painted 'landscapes' for stage sets and Robert Adam amused himself with romantic landscapes. I have a strong impression that even William Kent, whose recipe for paradise was to arrange fine buildings among green hills and groves, had very little to do with the messiness of nature. His drawings of trees and boskages are purely symbolic, he was not interested in the names of plants or how they grew, or even if they would grow in a particular place, but merely in the look of them. And with Kent, the architect of

imagination thus leaves the scene to the prosaic and practical Capability Brown and his successors, until intellectual control can be regained with the Picturesque.

Physical control of the garden was fought for during the nineteenth century, and this alternate theme soon emerged from my exploration. As houses and gardens were re-established into a relationship with each other, it was clearly desirable that harmony should result from the plan, ornament and materials being subjected to a single mind. We do not think of harmony as a Victorian virtue, but the ebullient, opportunistic Sir Charles Barry (1795–1860) comes charging through with his Italianate palaces of Trentham and Harewood and their matching gardens which are very virtuous in this respect. Perhaps Barry is under-appreciated as a designer of gardens, and it is worth remembering that Trentham, seen through the eyes of Benjamin Disraeli in *Lothair* was a very Victorian assemblage of paradisaical delight.[12] Barry though, is not really a fashionable Victorian, because admiration is reserved nowadays for the Divine Goths, Pugin, Scott, William Butterfield and George Edmund Street. They, naturally, have endowed posterity with paperwork as substantial as their buildings, and these, for the mere seeker of gardens and groves, are arid labyrinths of stone and gilt, tombs and reredos, workhouses, government offices, grammar schools and the London Law Courts. With the Smirkes, Robert and Charles, it was possible to weed out a balustrade for Haddon Hall somewhere after entry one hundred and eleven, but G.E.Street even kept on faithfully sketching only cathedrals and abbeys whilst he was on holiday. This was the stern face of Victorian ecclesiology, when the only justifiable work for an architect was in churches, philanthropic institutions or palaces of commerce, in that order. More painful than this claustrophobia of High Victorian obsession, was my observation of attempts to escape; naturally, with Ruskin and Morris preaching a love of nature, and her inspiration, the beginnings of the Arts and Crafts movement in the 1880s were a matter of opening casements, just a crack, to let in the fresh air. William Lethaby's (1857–1931) massive collection of drawings for every detail of Avon Tyrell in the New Forest, for the Manners family, is full of flowers. Going through them I could feel his mind being torn from the solid architectural Victorian tradition from which he has come, and his longing to go outside; he uses flowers for carvings and decoration, for 'a handrail with a trail of flowers', and he even refers to garden details that are firmly attached to the building.

None were garden drawings, merely the outside of his house. Lethaby, says Roderick Gradidge in *Dream Houses*, was restrained by his puritanism, and the same was true of Philip Webb, (1831–1915) who was to be Edwin Lutyens' hero, and who could be rescued for indulging himself in his sundial for Great Tangley Manor, and his collection of beautiful flower drawings, made from life, from which I have chosen the parrot tulip (no. 86). It was all a matter of flexibility, or of being young. Poor John Dando Sedding (1838–91) earns his place in garden history for *Garden Craft Old and New*, published after his sudden death. He was a distinguished church architect and craftsman (a reputation he would probably prefer) but wrote his garden book in secret. He is remembered here with a delightful coloured frieze-design of owls and poppies (fig. 19, Chapter 4) but that is the nearest to nature his drawings go; he was, though, the first architect to return to the seventeenth-century formal gardens for the inspiration of the young generation of Arts and Crafts architects. Further light on 'escape' is thrown by the example of Harold Peto (1854–1933); this talented, if autocratic gentleman architect was in partnership with Sir Ernest George (1839–1922) when Edwin Lutyens entered their office as a pupil in the late 1880s. Ernest George was a pioneer of the softer, vernacular approach to architecture (he was building Limnerslease at Compton near Guildford for the artist George Frederic Watts) but even that was too much for Harold Peto. He soon left the practice, turned completely to gardens and the Italian inspiration, and became famous for his own garden at Iford Manor in Wiltshire and for Buscot Park in Oxfordshire, now owned by the National Trust. Though drawings for the George practice came into the Collection, sadly there are no Harold Peto drawings here.

Reginald Blomfield, who was a type not to be baulked by fusty traditions, made gardens really acceptable with *The Formal Garden in England*, in 1892, which was wholly devoted to the architectural delights of the old formal gardens and really returned the garden into the architect's care. The time was right, for the best Arts and Crafts architects were now designing houses, and more moderately-sized houses which needed a close relationship with their gardens on a physical level. The rich involvement with architects of the Arts and Crafts period, here defined as 1890–1914, is one of the outstanding treasures of the Collection which I hope is reflected adequately in my book. From the arid if gilded caves of Victorian Gothicism, we plunge into sunny, scented gardens, perfectly confident of the architec-

tural integrity of it all, as were Reginald Blomfield, Charles Voysey, Edwin Lutyens, Ernest Newton, Charles Mallows and Oliver Hill. It was a fine flowering, and is often referred to as such, of houses and gardens that exactly caught the mood of that golden afternoon of Edwardian England. It was a period, as the drawings here reflect, when house and garden were really equal and inseparable, and have to be considered as a unit; this really applies to more Arts and Crafts architects than just Edwin Lutyens, who has been noticed by gardeners because his gardens were so properly and prettily dressed by his great gardening friend, Gertrude Jekyll. These drawings show that Charles Voysey, M.H.Baillie Scott and Oliver Hill had a real interest in the gardens of their houses and perhaps these further benefits of the Arts and Crafts Movement will soon be explored.

After the First World War architectural philosophy was mostly all about building for the brave new world. Gardens of elaborate design and great expense were no longer quite the decent thing, and even more definitely were rarely any longer affordable. One architect alone, H.S.Goodhart-Rendel (1887–1959) goes on designing a substantial number of gardens into the 1930s, but in the main the architect now assumes, or re-assumes, the role of designer of garden buildings and ornaments for gardens. Whereas other rich centuries have been treated in a single section, I have devoted two to the twentieth century. This is not so much a reflection of the amount of material in the Collection, the importance of the role of the architect, or even that this is the period in which I am most competent; it really reflects the confusion that I feel gardens have been governed by, as the art of the people, for the past sixty years. I feel this is a peculiarly English thing, and two World Wars (though not our burden alone) have not helped; the Modern Movement had such a brief fling here, truncated by the second War, that its gardens are hardly recognized. The Collection has an evocative record, in the drawings of Peter Behrens, Mendelsohn & Chermayeff, Raymond McGrath and Berthold Lubetkin of gardens 'as they might have been', without the War and without the ensuing necessity for architects and landscape architects to deal with the large landscapes. I felt this was well worth illustrating in isolation.

The Modern Movement in gardens really was isolated, almost as if it never happened. Our present revival of 'classical gardens' in terms of outdoor rooms, topiary triangles, Chippendale seats, pots from China or Pompeii, and French seventeenth-century trellis work, does seem a little *recherché* or unadventurous, and hardly needs an architect, even if we could afford one. And then, as I show in my essay on 'Continuing Classicism' in Chapter 6, the cool reason of classical revivals, their now well-mannered restraint, can lie heavily on a garden, and deaden the essential delight. The most well-known garden in England to successfully combine these elements is now that of Sissinghurst Castle in Kent, made by the definitively classical-romantic partnership of the would-be architect, Harold Nicolson and his poetical wife Vita Sackville-West. Their equal contributions – his strictly formal design, her luxuriantly blooming flowers – now seem the accepted recipe for both discipline and delight.

In many ways the frivolity and delight that Geoffrey Jellicoe noted as a quality of the Italian Renaissance gardens – was not only the casualty of two wars, but also more systematically destroyed in the professionalism fostered by both the RIBA and what is now the Landscape Institute since the 1920s. Architects now rarely see themselves as artists, and garden-making cannot be turned into a slick science – at least, not in these understood traditions of the English garden, and in the forseeable future. But all is not lost; two people, both architects, have hinted that the earthly paradise, for the individual or collective consciousness, may be more readily within our grasp than ever before; but these are surprises I wish to leave until later in my book.

A word about 'Englishness'; this has been used both in the title and in writing of 'the English garden' as a stylized term, adopted a very long time ago, as in '*le jardin anglais*' or '*das englischer garten*' and now happily used in the United States. It relates more to characteristics than any confidence in a national achievement that outshines that of any other part of the British Isles, and in fact the very essence of this book is that what may be called 'Englishness' is made up of influences from far and wide. Through many of these drawings it is possible to watch the English garden being distilled from Indian, Chinese, Dutch, Spanish or French sources, but all-pervasively, from Italy, Italy all the time: from a precious little sketchbook from James 'Athenian' Stuart with shaky images, brown with the dignity of age of a garden house at Villa Pisani, to the wonderful array of John Shepherd and Geoffrey Jellicoe's drawings of the *Italian Gardens of the Renaissance*, which have had such an enormous influence on modern designers. From an architect formerly unknown to me, David Moccata (1806–82), designer of fine Victorian railway stations who slipped off on sketching holidays to the gardens of Villa Capra

and Villa Albani, to a repeated fascination with Villa d'Este which echoes from different hands down the years. If it were not for the vast and indeterminate differences in our climates, there would perhaps be no English gardens at all, merely Italian gardens moved over.

And finally, I want to highlight the two particularly special qualities that these drawings have, above any other means, of beautifully illustrating a book. Firstly, that they are all miraculous survivors. Architectural drawings, whether first sketches or full of painstaking mathematical details, are working drawings; they get spattered with rain, shunted from hand to hand then pushed in a drawer when the job is done. They are never, like paintings, mounted and framed and treasured. As I have written elsewhere, regarding the distinguished company of seventeenth-century drawings, each of these drawings must have a tale to tell, and many are travel-stained and fragile. Much detective work is often needed to track their provenances; the story of the Smythson Collection is related by Mark Girouard in *Robert Smythson and the Elizabethan Country House*, that of the Burlington–Devonshire Collection is detailed in the published catalogue and both have been briefly re-told here. But individual drawings have their fascination too, though perhaps none more so than the shattered (now carefully restored) wreck illustrated as figure 4, which is by Daniel Robertson. Robertson was a mysterious character, who died about 1844/5 and whose great claim to gardening fame is as the designer of the upper terrace at Powerscourt in County Wicklow for the 6th Viscount Powerscourt in 1843. He took the design from Villa Butera in Sicily. Robertson was related to the Adam brothers and probably their pupil; he did a little recorded restoration and some alteration work in Oxford before leaving for Ireland, under some mysterious cloud, in 1829. He continued to work as an architect, but this garden layout for Kilruddery House, also in County Wicklow of about 1840, and Powerscourt, are his only known garden designs. Perhaps the explanation lies in Lord Powerscourt's recollections, published in 1903: Robertson was 'given to drink, and always drew best when he was excited with sherry. He suffered from gout, and used to be driven about in a wheel-barrow with a bottle of sherry; while that lasted he was ready to direct the workmen, but when it was finished he was incapable of working any more'.[13] The damaged but precious drawing was found at Kilruddery by the architect Claud Phillimore, when working there in the 1950s, and it came into

Fig. 4] *Garden layout for Kilruddery House, Co. Wicklow, c.* 1840
by Daniel Robertson. This drawing was found at Kilruddery
by Claud Phillimore and came to the Collection with his papers.

the Collection with his drawings. This squirrel tendency of architects has always brought in many drawings besides their own; it largely happens because they have gone on returning to the same places, for the same families, over and across the years. This kind of connection, if it could ever be tracked, must have brought another precious if vague watercolour, that of the Brompton Nursery (no. 14), into the company of the Smythson drawings in the early years of the eighteenth century. The connection here would seem to be the Cavendish family, and their ownership of both Bolsover and Welbeck, where the later Smythsons, William Talman and London and Wise can conceivably be connected through this one fragile piece of paper.

Such surmises are legion and the possibilities are the fascination of architectural and garden history. But the chief and most potent charm of all these drawings is their immediacy. They catch, in a simple bright flash or complicated stream, the ingenuity and invention of the artist. He may have concentrated for a moment or slaved patiently for hours, but the essence of the first-hand idea is there. The magic of these drawings is in being able to count the blotches made by John Evelyn's pen more than three centuries ago, in seeing over Charles Voysey's shoulder as he paints flowers on a wall or hearts on a lawn, to hear the failing John Claudius Loudon nagging at his draughtsman to get it right. Here, to hand and at a glance, is the breathtaking dream of Barry's most elaborate garden for Drumlanrig, the curious detail of John Hungerford Pollen's Claude glass made out of antique wood for a wedding present, and William Newton's changing ideas on the advantages of a greenhouse for an eighteenth-century gentleman. Such drawings as these are the purpose and pleasure of this book; they are for looking at, perhaps reading for a while for curiosity's sake, and then returning to and looking again for new discoveries every time.

1

THE SEVENTEENTH CENTURY
Masons, Gardeners and Gentlemen 1609–1714

These first fifteen drawings are of two types, observations (in the main careful surveys) and designs. Since in no case does anything substantial survive of what they represent they are rare and miraculous relics from an age so very far away, and rather like those priceless bottles of claret from an ancient cellar or recovered food-rations after fifty years in the Antarctic ice, they are curious treasures but of little real use.

The first eight drawings are by Robert Smythson and his successors, then there are four by William Talman, a glimpse of George London and Henry Wise's famous Brompton Park nursery garden and a sketch from the hand of John Evelyn. They cover a period of gardening that we know little about; the Robert Smythson surveys of Wimbledon and the other London gardens date from his trip south in 1609, and thus they actually illustrate gardens of Elizabeth I's England. In some cases these gardens lasted well into the seventeenth century, but there is still a wide gap in shadowy time until William Talman is working for King William III and Queen Mary at Hampton Court in the 1690s. The only mid-century glimpse is over the shoulder of John Evelyn as he works on his great unpublished garden book, *Elysium Britannicum* in the 1650s. We are used to our garden images from the whole of this period coming via highly stylized paintings, and those distant bird's-eye perspectives by Leonard Knyff and Johannes Kip. These are much more practical images, of a workday freshness and spontaneity that makes them truly magical survivors from across the centuries. Each one of them must have a traveller's tale to tell; in some cases some of their background is known and I offer it here to present the drawings in their context.

The Smythson Collection is one of the great treasures of the RIBA; the four boxes holding 153 sheets of varying sizes marked in brown ink are a unique and long lost source of knowledge about the building of great Elizabethan houses, including Longleat, Hardwick Hall and Bolsover. That such drawings had survived was first noted in 1725; they were owned by Lord Byron 'who got them from the family who liv'd at Bolsover'.[1] When the 5th Lord Byron's belongings at Newstead Abbey were sold in June 1778 the Smythson drawings were Lot 344; they were bought by the Revd D'Ewes Coke of Broke-Hill Hall, Pinxton in Derbyshire. The good Reverend thought them mainly of local interest and showed them to local historians, but then put them safely away. They next appeared on 25 February 1907 when Colonel Coke of Broke-Hill Hall lent them to be shown at the RIBA President's at-home; two papers on the contents of the drawings were delivered in the following years, 1907 and 1908, as an article and lecture respectively, and the drawings were catalogued by J.H.Gotch. They then returned to their Derbyshire home until 1922, when the Coke family again lent them to the RIBA; after that they were left on permanent loan and finally given to the Collection.[2] But it was not until 1962 that they were really revealed and celebrated, when a young architectural historian named Mark Girouard carefully studied and re-catalogued them. His discoveries about the Smythsons were put into his book *Robert Smythson and the architecture of the Elizabethan era*.[3]

Robert Smythson (1535–1614) was a remarkable man, 'a pioneer, a man of vigorous and enquiring mind', says Girouard, and 'without doubt one of the heroes of the national Elizabethan and Jacobean style'.[4] In an age when the profession of architect was unrecognized,[5] he became one of the professional artificer-class, having worked his way up as a master mason and then transferred his time to surveying, plan drawing and organizing the building task. In this way he played his parts at Longleat, Wollaton, Worksop, Hardwick and Bolsover; in tracking him through these wonderful buildings Mark Girouard has written a thrilling detective book of architectural delights.

Robert Smythson died in 1614, aged seventy-nine; it seems perfectly in character that he never stopped looking for new ideas, and his journey to London in 1609, when he was aged seventy-four, saw him busily surveying and drawing gardens –

'indeed he seems, to judge from his drawings, to have been more interested by gardens than by houses' writes Mark Girouard (perhaps with some amazement!). It is the very end of his life which endears him to garden historians, and these survey drawings, of which five appear here, offer us a unique insight into gardens that Queen Elizabeth I knew.

Pride of place, as the first drawing of the book, is given to Robert Smythson's drawing of Lord Bedford's garden at Twickenham for purely romantic and literary reasons. Lucy Harington, Countess of Bedford, was rich, extravagant, undoubtedly beautiful, beloved by John Donne and, has been revealed by Roy Strong, an enthusiastic and talented gardener. However, it is Donne who takes the bow here, for wishing himself a mandrake or a fountain in his agony of unrequited love, in his 'Twicknam garden', from *Songs and Sonnets*, quoted in no. 1. Whether the forlorn poet, Robert Smythson and us are actually looking at a garden made to the taste of Lucy Harington seems uncertain; she does sound like a lady of action and determination so may well have ordered her planting of circles of rosemary and fruit trees in the manner of the pre-Copernican universe with the earth in the centre of the planetary spheres, all within two years of taking possession. However, the house was leased, up until 1606, by an even greater gardener, Sir Francis Bacon, and it would be all the more intriguing to think this was his work.[6]

The two plans for Wollaton Hall in Nottinghamshire (nos. 2 and 3) are not surveys but designs. Robert Smythson first went to Wollaton in the spring of 1583, and he stayed there until his death; his monument is in Wollaton church and reads 'Here lyeth ye body of Mr Robert Smythson, gent, Architector & Survayor unto the most worthy house of Wollaton with diverse others of great account. He lived in ye fayth of Christ 79 yeares & then departed this live XV October ano DNI 1614'.[7] Sir Francis Willoughby, Wollaton's builder, was a man of considerable talents, extravagant dreams and frenetic activity, just the kind of courtier who would go to these extreme lengths for one approving glance from Gloriana; some of Wollaton's splendour, though not exactly as Smythson designed it, is conveyed by a painting of 1697 by Jan Siberechts (fig. 5); the house survives almost unchanged externally and its siting and Smythson's layout make it the supreme example of the late seventeenth-century imposition of order upon the English landscape – 'so that house, gardens, courtyard and outbuildings were combined in one scheme of complete four-way symmetry'.[8] The orchard plan (no. 3) is by Robert's son, John, who died in 1634; much of his life was spent at Wollaton and he married a local girl, Margaret Newton in 1600. He apparently finished his father's works at Wollaton and then moved to work for the Cavendishes at Bolsover, Welbeck and Slingsby.

The drawings of Worcester House, Wimbledon, Ham and Somerset House were all carefully observed by Robert on his 1609 expedition to London. I have chosen them because they represent some of the most important gardens of the period.

Wimbledon, as Roy Strong reports, was begun the year Wollaton was finished. It was built by Thomas Cecil, Lord Burghley's eldest son, later Earl of Exeter, and Queen Elizabeth I paid several visits in the last years of her life. The indomitable Queen would have taken her carriage into the Outer Court, but then because of the steeply rising ground, she would have had to walk up the semi-circular stair to the Inner Court and the house; if lunch was first on the agenda, as was likely, she would progress through the house and on up the steps to the Banqueting House, in the centre of an eighty-five-foot square surrounded by high hedges.[9] The alternative approach was to turn to the left from the house, to the walled flower garden with a pillared loggia along the east side of the house; from there the steps led up to the greater square, where Robert Smythson has marked the central 'piller' – Roy Strong says 'In the atmosphere of Queen-worship that pervaded the last decade of the reign surely a pillar set up in the centre of the garden of a great house built to receive her and her court on progress could only ever have had one significance, homage to the Queen?'[10]

Gloriana would only have gazed at the terraces of blossoms that are ranged up the hill of the farther garden; these were the latest fashion by the time Robert Smythson saw them, so much so that when the great French gardener, Daniel Marot, came to modernize Wimbledon for Queen Henrietta Maria in 1642, he retained the fruit terraces though swept away the enclosures around the house.[11]

Somerset House in the Strand, where Robert Smythson had recorded the garden made for James I's Queen Anne of Denmark, is thought to show some of the earliest work in England of another great French gardener, engineer, master of garden automata, Salomon de Caus (c.1576–1626). If so, the indefatigable Robert Smythson has identified yet another great moment of gardening history. Saloman de Caus worked in Italy and Brussels before he was tempted to England in 1607, to work for the Royal family and for Robert Cecil at Hatfield House. His speciality was in designing and engineering elaborate garden waterworks; he was to write a book on hydraulics, *Les Raisons des Forces Mouvantes*, which was first published in 1615. Roy Strong believes that one of de Caus's specialities, a giant pile of rock with many water spouts and statues, which he called Mount Parnassus, was built at Somerset House, on the octagonal base in the smaller garden enclosure.[12]

The final Robert Smythson drawing here could be a design rather than a survey (no. 8). It is for the garden of Ham House by the River Thames at Petersham, and when Robert came south in 1609 the house was just being finished. In this plan, house and garden are closely related, with the main axis of the house extending out to dictate the layout of the garden. Ham was built by Sir Thomas Vavasour, Knight Marshal to James I, but quickly went through several owners and masters in the next forty years before it found a remarkable mistress in Elisabeth Dysart, heiress and Countess in her own right, and eventually – when the course of true love straightened itself – the Duchess of Lauderdale. The Lauderdales and their story are fascinating and much of their fascination seems to have rubbed off onto their house.[13] They made Ham splendid, both house and garden, in the 1670s, and at that time the garden was laid out to a plan by a German engineer John Slezer and a Dutch artist, Jan Wyck, who were both working there. This layout, with straight gravel paths, squares of grass, a wilderness of hornbeam hedges and small trees of strictly geometrical form, an orchard and a parterre of box-edged beds filled with lavender cotton and other scented herbs, has been restored to Ham by its owners, the National Trust, in the past ten years. The remnants of the Lauderdales' garden, in many areas undisturbed for three hundred years, were recognized as the basis for this very important restoration, and the care and skill that has gone into the project has virtually made Ham's garden new again, as though we were seeing it three hundred years ago. This is the essential magic that good garden restoration can work; Ham's garden is now the best of those that Robert Smythson drew for conveying his distant world, the orderly look of the raked gravel and clipped plants, the neat prettiness of the blossoms, nature well and truly under control as it would please his Elizabethan mind. Ham has also retained a very particular atmosphere from its past and the ghosts of the mutually-adoring Lauderdales are very happily present in their house.

The Lauderdales' garden at Ham was seen by John Evelyn (1620–1706), who was to be chiefly responsible for persuading English gentlemen into their passion for gardens and growing things. When Evelyn visited Ham in 1678, he was seeing it through the eyes of his experience of the great gardens of Europe, and found its splendours 'inferior to few of the best Villas in Italy itself; the Flower Gardens, Orangeries, Groves, Avenues, Courts, Statues, Perspectives, Fountains, Aviaries & all this at the banks of the Sweetest River in the World, must needs be surprising'.[14]

John Evelyn was a conoisseur of gardens, and carried his interest and enthusiasm to the Restoration court of Charles II where he was highly respected. His influence on gardeners throughout the ages stems from his philosophical belief in a garden as an 'idea of Paradise', which gave the subject a standing in the eyes of his fellow founders of the Royal Society, as well as in the science of silverculture and horticulture. Evelyn's *Sylva, or a discourse of Forest Trees* with its appendix, *Pomona, or an Appendix concerning Fruit Trees* was published in 1664, and *Sylva* remained a standard textbook on tree propagation and planting and forester's lore well into the nineteenth century. Evelyn was famous in his own time for three gardens; his first effort at garden design was for his brother at the Evelyn country home at Wotton in Surrey. The house, still the home of the Evelyns, is set in a beautiful and well-watered valley among sandstone hills, and John Evelyn created a great multi-level mount, grottoes and an elaborate fountain. A little farther west in Surrey, at Albury Park, the forms of the long canal, the great terraces and the tunnel – inspired by an Italian 'Crypta' which allowed two coaches to drive abreast underground – that he made in 1667 for Henry Howard still remain. The small drawing (no. 13) from the Collection is Evelyn's sketch for a parterre in his own garden at Sayes Court, Deptford, where he lived and gardened quietly during the Commonwealth years. He also worked on a book about all aspects of gardening which he called *Elysium Brittanicum*, for which this plan was probably made, but which was never published in full in Evelyn's lifetime. Part of the manuscript survives with John Evelyn's papers, and hopefully will eventually see the light of day in an edited form.[15]

If John Evelyn's little sketch brushes the coat-tails of great gardening history, then the drawings from the Collection by William Talman (1650–1719) come from the very heart of it. The Glorious Revolution of 1688 brought England a Dutch king, William III, with two particular passions, his army and his

gardens; his English Queen Mary was an enthusiastic and knowledgeable botanist, and this Royal pair were largely responsible for the influence of Dutch garden design on England. Hampton Court Palace was their favourite home, enlarged for them by Sir Christopher Wren, with King William's Great Fountain Garden designed by Daniel Marot with scrolls of *broderie* in box, and coloured gravels, pyramids of yew, globes of bay and holly and thirteen fountains, arrayed on Wren's new east front. The present-day Hampton Court, unbelievably splendid in many ways, is only a ghost of what William III intended; the newly restored Het Loo, from which he brought his Dutch ideas, has much more of the splendour of that age. Queen Mary died of

smallpox in 1694, and the King carried on his garden schemes in her memory; Talman worked in Holland, at the Château de Voorst, in 1695, and thus knew all about Dutch taste by the time he designed the Trianon for the King in 1699. The spectacular bird's-eye view of the Trianon (no. 9), a palatial hideaway to be built far across the park, at the end of the Ditton avenue on the other side of the River Thames, is one of the great drawings of the Collection.[16] Was the sad King trying to recall both his Queen and their youth, for this is such a romantic building; a place to gallop to on a balmy evening, taking only amusing friends, hallooing for those gates to open, for the candles to be lit and the music to begin. The whole miniature paradise is walled, but the

Fig. 5] Left: Wollaton Hall and Park, Nottinghamshire, 1697 by Jan Siberechts (1627–c. 1700). The painting shows how effectively Wollaton and its garden were conceived as a single architectural unit, and features that survived from the Robert Smythson survey drawing of 1609 (see no. 2).

Fig. 6] Ham House, the South Front from the Wilderness, 1675, by Henry Danckerts. This is the garden front in the time of the Duke and Duchess of Lauderdale, who elaborated the design by Robert Smythson (see no. 5).

inner 'walls' around the court are actually hedges, with alcoves and arches clipped to invite games of tag and blind man's buff, and ornamented with live obelisks, figurines and shell-backed seats. The whole concept of this garden seems to invite fun and games, a release from the stiff parades of palace life. Surely it was a lonely king's dream? And it was never built; King William's horse stumbled over a molehill in the park and threw him, and he died in 1702. Queen Anne, his successor, did not approve of his Dutch garden ideas.

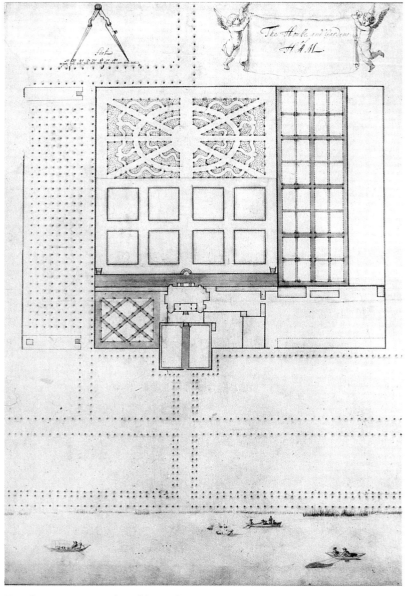

Fig. 7] *Ham House, plan of the garden*, 1671, attributed to John Slezer and Jan Wyck; this is the Lauderdales' garden and the National Trust's restoration of the layout and planting is based on this plan.

William Talman also worked on another famous Dutch-inspired garden; the fragile and delicate sketch for the cascade for Dyrham Park in Gloucestershire is another reminder of this fantastic period. (no. 12) The owner of Dyrham, by virtue of marrying its heiress, was William Blathwayt (c.1649–1717), sometime Secretary to Sir William Temple while he was Ambassador in Holland, and King William's hard-working servant in a number of minor offices. Blathwayt has been rather dismissed by history as a 'colourless underling',[17] (probably simply because his chief interests were in gardens, flower paintings, Delft china and tapestries, and because he spoke Dutch). At Dyrham William Blathwayt had the wit and substance to make a most amazing garden, only now to be seen via Kip's engraving in Sir Robert Atkyns' *The Ancient and Present State of Glocestershire* of 1712 (fig. 8). The house sits in a valley, with formal canals and gardens back and front, and rising to cover the slopes of the hills; the water features, and the giant carp and perch that occupied the pools were the great wonders, and the greatest of all was farthest from the house, where the water was brought down the hillside in a cascade '. . . you come to a noble Cataract or extended Cascade of Water; this Cascade is on a line with the Octagon Fountain, and the Canal, and all exactly fronting the Door of the Green-house; it has, as I remember' writes Stephen Switzer, 'near-two-hundred-and-fifty Steps to the Top, and as many falls for the Water to descend, and it is so high, that you have several Seats erected for Resting'.[18] Only the statue of Neptune in the park at Dyrham, now owned by the National Trust, and this Talman drawing survive to prove that this fantastic garden ever existed. Dyrham's formal Dutch garden was swept away, along with so many other formal gardens, with the taste for the English landscape style in the eighteenth century; it seems rather too ambitious a project for even the National Trust to restore.

The final drawing from Talman's colourful career[19] comes to us carrying Margaret, Duchess of Newcastle's note for posterity 'A scrach of a Garden by Mr Tollman'. Her Grace's use of the word 'scrach' might indicate a rough drawing, with catches and blots (which it has) or that she was simply tired of the sound of Mr Talman's pen. This is one of a series of six drawings in the Collection, all but one presented by the Duke of Portland in 1970, and therefore of direct provenance from Welbeck archives, and several were inscribed by the Duchess, though only the scratching on the garden plan seemed to annoy her. Talman was

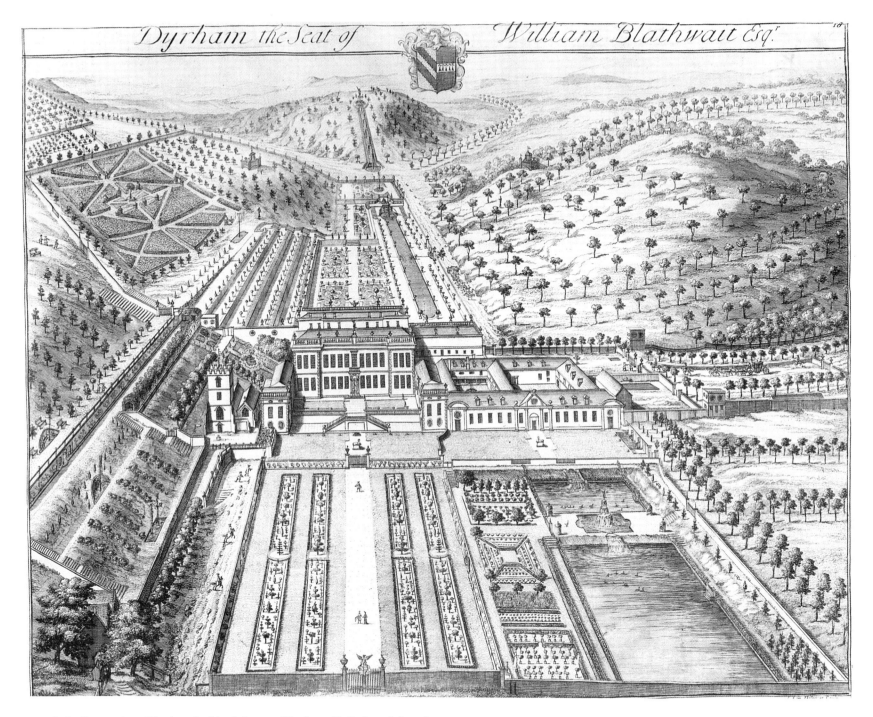

Fig. 8] Bird's-eye view of Dyrham Park by Johannes Kip from Sir Robert Atkyns'
The Ancient and Present state of Glocestershire, 1712.
The cascade is on the hillside farthest from the house

at Welbeck in the summer of 1703 making tentative plans for a rebuilding of the house, for which the Duke had also consulted his arch-rival, Sir John Vanbrugh; all such plans were brought to nought by the Duke's death. But the Welbeck plan, with the Duchess's reminder, has just that great force of immediacy that these fragments of paper splotched with brown ink carry so vividly from the distant past.

Both Robert and John Smythson had made plans for Welbeck[20] which were only partly carried out, so the drawings in this chapter have come full circle. There is also an intriguing similarity between the semi-circular pool with a canal that William Talman designed for Welbeck (no. 11) and a feature in the sketch inscribed *Carpenters Garden at Bronton by Kensington* (no. 14). This pale and unfinished watercolour is one of a few miscellaneous and unidentified drawings found with the Smythson Collection. Tracking a possible link in gardens and inspiration from the Smythsons and Bolsover, the Cavendishes and Welbeck to William Talman and George London and Henry Wise, is an intriguing prospect but can find no place here; I will be content with suggesting that 'Carpenter' is in fact Joseph Carpenter, who with William Smith took over London & Wise's famous nursery at Brompton Park in 1714. The nursery, on a site now occupied by the Victoria & Albert Museum in Kensington, was set up by George London in 1681; London was a designer in the French manner, and he made plans and supplied the plants for Longleat, Chatsworth and Melbourne Hall. The large nursery at Brompton, on a forty-hectare site, became the most famous (and expensive) in the land: 'They have a very brave and noble assembly of the flowery and other trees' approved John Evelyn. Brompton Park was very much the Harrods, or perhaps Hilliers, of the day, and Stephen Switzer actually wrote that it would be 'hard for posterity to lay their hands on a tree' anywhere in Britain that did not owe something to the nursery's care. But memento of great gardens as it may be, this drawing shows Brompton at the moment of decline. George London died in 1714 and Henry Wise retired from his interest to concentrate on his role as royal gardener and his work at Blenheim. Carpenter and Smith were not of the same calibre as their distinguished forerunners and could not justify the high prices that Brompton Park had to charge for carrying trees half way across England; the nursery's great reputation declined and it became a prey to builders.

Though I have ascribed the date 1714 to the Brompton Park sketch, the name 'Carpenter' could have been added after the sketch was made, or indeed, the nursery may have been known as Carpenter's before the official lease to him was signed in 1714; Henry Wise had moved to Blenheim in 1705, and though George London was nominally in charge he was perhaps less involved in the years before his death in 1714. Whatever the exact date, the sketch was clearly a late addition to the miscellanea of the Smythson Collection, and has come a long way in time from Robert's trip to London to look at houses and gardens in 1609. As has been noted, he was already an old man then, and he died at Wollaton in October 1614. He was succeeded by his son John, who also took an excursion to London in about 1618, and his drawings of the garden of Arundel House in the Strand are in the Collection, but he did not have his father's interest in gardens. John died in 1634, and his son, the rather shadowy figure of Huntingdon Smythson (by now calling himself Smithson) carried on the family profession, working at Bolsover where he died in 1648 and is commemorated by a plaque in the church there.[21] John the Younger, Huntingdon's son (1640–1717) lived and worked at Bolsover, and a few drawings of garden buildings, a water pavilion for Welbeck Abbey, and a fountain for Bolsover, possibly the original Venus Fountain which was a great feature of the Castle garden, are credited to him. It was John the Younger who also made designs for Bulwell in Nottinghamshire, a Byron house, so this is how the Byrons became entitled to the Smythson Collection, presumably collected from John's house after his death in 1717.[22] This is the background of time for the garden drawings from this precious Collection; some idea of their worth in providing information about the gardens of the first Queen Elizabeth and the early seventeenth century may be gathered from the large part they now play in garden histories of the period, notably Roy Strong's *Renaissance Gardens in England*. But they also leave us with riddles and unanswered questions; if only the good Robert Smythson could tell about what he saw at Longleat and Hardwick, especially the latter, for is there any reason to suppose that Bess, Countess of Shrewsbury's garden there was any less spectacular than the 'supreme triumph' of her house.[23]

Brushing the coat-tails of history seems to be the prerogative of these distinguished old drawings, and there is a further example of this in the Collection which is not illustrated here. There exists a modest-looking, chunky volume, bound in brown leather, containing the drawings of Jacques Gentilhâtre. The name is probably unfamiliar; little is known about him, other than he was a Huguenot, born in north-eastern France in 1578, and earned his living as a master mason (as did the young Robert Smythson). The Gentilhâtre volume has been thoroughly researched and catalogued by Rosalys Cooper;[24] Gentilhâtre drew almost exclusively architectural features, but his drawings are of the Chateaux at Fontainebleau, Charleval and Verneuil-sur-Oise, each a particular name in French garden history. In her research, Rosalys Coope has discovered that the young Gentilhâtre worked in the *atelier* of the du Cerceau family during the early years of the seventeenth century; Jacques Androuet du

Cerceau I, to whom the gardens of Charleval and Verneuil are attributed, and whose volumes *Les plus excellents batiments de France* of 1576 and 1579 are such an important source for sixteenth-century gardens, had died about 1584. His son Jacques II and grandson Salomon de Brosse however were there, and the Gentilhâtre volume contains drawings copied and drawn for them as well as copies never used for engravings by the great Jacques I. These images of fountains and pavilions for Charleval and Fontainebleau seem to symbolize the fascination of these early drawings, and the fragile connections that can be drawn across the centuries.

Fig. 9] Portrait of John Evelyn (1620–1706) *by Sir Godfrey Kneller* (1646–1723).

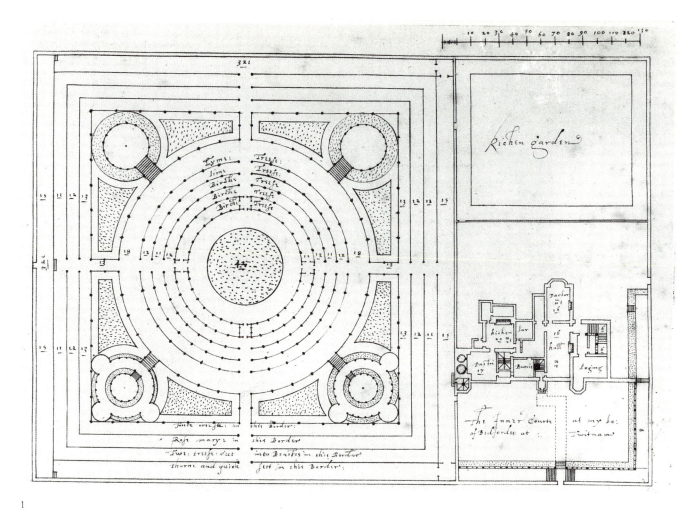

1

TWICKENHAM, MIDDLESEX

1] ROBERT SMYTHSON *c.*1535–1614

Plan of ground floor and garden of Lord Bedford's house

Twickenham, Middlesex, 1609
Sepia pen
185 × 260 mm. /$7\frac{1}{4}$ × $10\frac{1}{4}$ in.

This is a survey drawing rather than a design and has been dated to 1609 by Mark Girouard;[25] though several of the drawings that follow were also made on Smythson's trip to London in that year, this one takes pride of place for the simple delight of the square garden and because this is the garden referred to by John Donne in his poem 'Twicknam garden' from *Songs & Sonnets*:

> *. . . Love let mee*
> *Some senslesse peece of this place bee;*
> *Make me a mandrake, so I may groane here,*
> *Or a stone fountaine weeping out my yeare.*

Lucy Harington, Countess of Bedford, lived here from 1608 to 1618, but the house had been leased previously to Sir Francis Bacon from 1595 to 1606. Mark Girouard thinks it most likely that this is therefore a plan of Bacon's work in the garden as the Countess would not have had time to change things so much in a year. The use of circles within a square will find many echoes in this book, but perhaps most notably across three hundred years to Edwin Lutyens' design for the sunken rose garden at Folly Farm. In Lady Bedford's garden the concentric circles of dots indicate rings of birch and lime trees. The outermost border of the square is planted with *Thorns and quicksett*; inside this he has marked *Fwr* (fir) *trees cut into Beastis in this Border*, with a border of rosemary inside that. The innermost border has more trees but their description is difficult to read – possibly it is fruit. In a contemporary plan, for Lord Worcester's garden at Nonsuch (no. 5), the dots in the beds indicate flower plantings, but here it is tempting to suppose this an early use of the present-day symbol for grass.

WOLLATON HALL, NOTTINGHAMSHIRE

2] ROBERT SMYTHSON *c.*1535–1614

Plan for ground floor, garden and outbuildings

Wollaton Hall, Nottinghamshire, 1609
Sepia pen, the garden tinted green
335 × 350 mm. /13¼ × 13¾ in.

The owner of Wollaton, Sir Francis Willoughby, had entertained Queen Elizabeth and, expecting further visits, he prepared by building himself this new hall between 1580 and 1588. The hall was designed on an elevation to be seen hopefully by the approaching Queen as well as lesser mortals; it was observed from the roof of Nottingham Castle by Celia Fiennes. In *The Renaissance Garden in England*[26] Roy Strong cites Wollaton as 'the unique Elizabethan instance' of a house and garden conceived as a single unit. The orientation of the plan would appear to be at the entrance, i.e. with *The Gatte House* on the north side and the formal garden laid out below a terrace to the south; the ornamental buildings, *The Deayrie and Landre* close the north-south axis and the east-west axis is bounded by *The Stabell* and *The Bakehouse and Bruehouse* respectively. However, there is no evidence that these were ever completed.

The story of Robert Smythson and Wollaton Hall is related by Mark Girouard in *Robert Smythson and the Architecture of the Elizabethan Era*[27]. Wollaton was one of his most important commissions, though there were other versions of the garden. There is a view of the house and garden by Jan Siberechts dated 1697 (fig. 5) which shows the arrangement of parterres on the south front to be very similar to Smythson's plan. In the painting the enclosure on the east of the house has been extended to semi-circular terraces to fit the slope of the land; these terraces are planted with concentric semi-circles of neat trees.

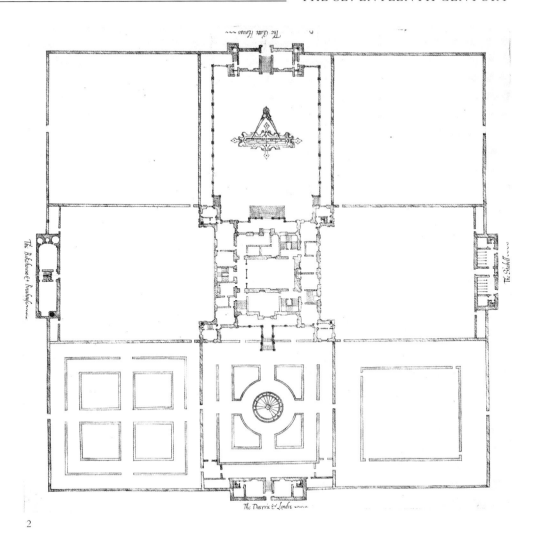

2

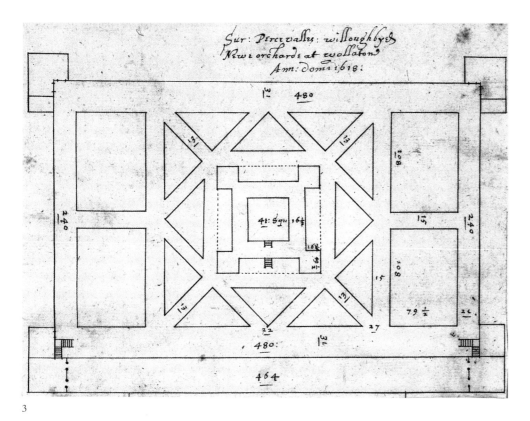

3

WIMBLEDON HOUSE, LONDON

4] ROBERT SMYTHSON *c*.1535–1614

Plan of ground floor and garden

Wimbledon House, London, 1609
Sepia pen
285×350 mm. $/11\frac{1}{3} \times 13\frac{3}{4}$ in.

This is another of Smythson's survey plans made on his southern tour in 1609. Wimbledon House was built by Thomas Cecil, later Earl of Exeter, and dated 1588. This plan is dated, by Smythson, 1609 and shows the complexity of this famous garden: Roy Strong calls this plan 'the most important and complete we have from the Elizabethan period'.[28]

Smythson's inscription at the bottom reads *The Platforme of my Lo: of Exceters house at Wymbellton 1609*—but his notes on the rest of the garden layout are of greater interest. There is a small Privy Garden, walled and set with flower parterres, immediately next to the house; on the garden front elaborate steps lead up to a paved terrace and a small *Banketing house*. To the right, beyond another small hedged square, *Gardens for Earbes* are set out. To the left of the banqueting house is the largest garden, half walled, half hedged with thorn, divided into squares and planted with flowers, hedge knots and topiary. Pride of place in the centre of this space, Smythson has noted the *Piller*, a device of Queen Elizabeth I, and an emblem frequently set up in her honour.

From the placing of the steps on this plan, it is clearly seen how this great house and garden were set into rising land. The rest of the garden is terraced into orchards and walks: Robert Smythson has carefully varied the spacings of his tree 'dots', presumably to indicate the size of the trees. The smallest orchard might have held large bushes or cordons with roses, with larger fruit trees in the next enclosure – apples, pears, quince and medlar. Then the slope is cut by a lime walk *both for shade and swetness*. The largest enclosure is hedged and densely planted, perhaps with fruit trees and vegetables and salads beneath them; he has marked climbing roses on the walls at either end of the enclosure. Finally, the highest level is planted with vines—Wimbledon's garden must have been wonderful indeed at blossom time, and at harvest.

3] JOHN SMYTHSON d.1634

Plan for an orchard

Wollaton Hall, Nottinghamshire, 1618
Sepia pen
125×170 mm. $/4\frac{7}{8} \times 6\frac{3}{4}$ in.

The plan is inscribed *Sur Percevalles: Willoughbyes New Orcharde at Wollaton Anno Dom. 1618*. There is no evidence that the orchard was ever laid out; it does not appear in either Kip's view (*Britannia Illustrata*) or Siberechts' painting. But the plan has historical value for the pattern and measurements of an early seventeenth-century orchard. There is a central mount, surrounded by gravel paths with plots for the fruit trees and bushes. Robert Smythson, John's father, was at Longleat while Sir John Thynne was planting his orchard with 'cherry stones, abrycocks and plum stones' brought from France, and such an interest in fruit growing was perhaps the inspiration for this design.

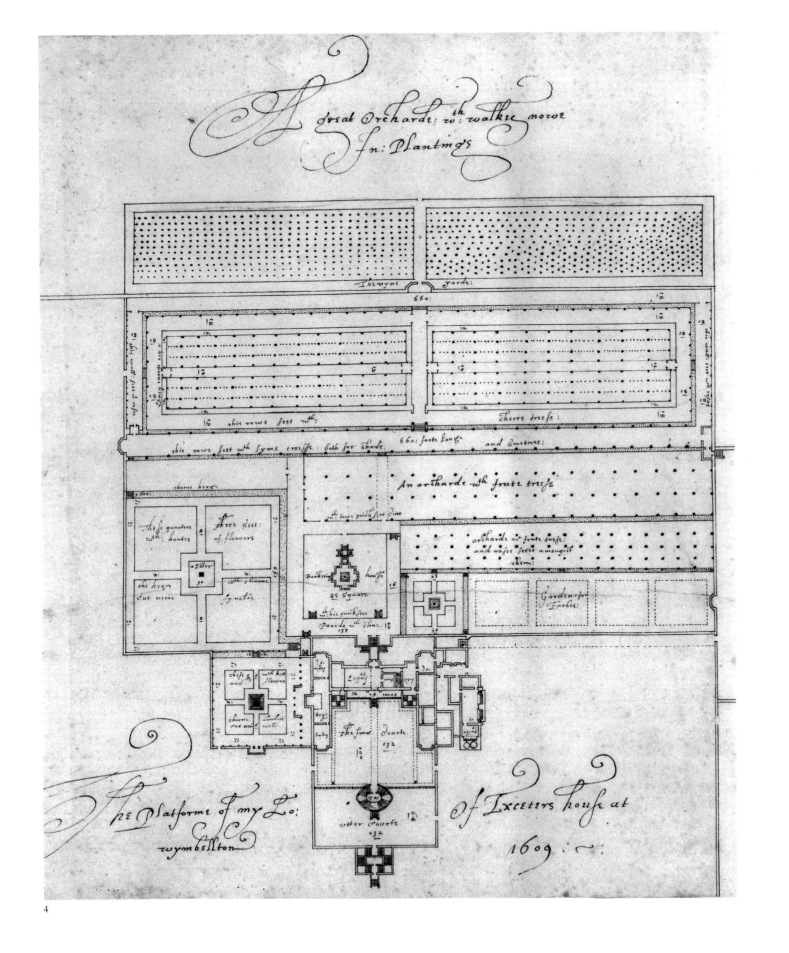

A great Orcharde: to: walkre noror
In: Plantinges

The Platforme of my Lo: of Ixceters house at
wymbellton
1609

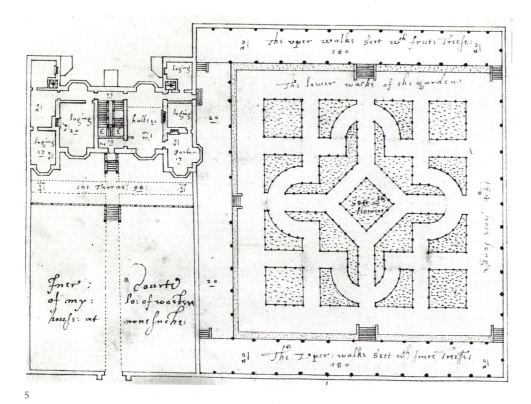

5

HAM HOUSE, SURREY

6] ROBERT SMYTHSON *c*.1535–1614

Plan of ground floor and garden

Ham House, Richmond, Surrey, 1609
Sepia pen with pencil shading
195 × 185 mm. /7¾ × 7⅞ in.

This survey drawing is inscribed *The Platforme: of sur Tho: vavesers house: at Peterson: in Surrey:* Ham was finished at the time of this drawing (the date on the house is 1610) by Sir Thomas Vavasour, Knight Marshall to James I.

The house is approached from the banks of the river Thames, and the courts, with the stables, are on the river front. The walled 'platforme' and the long terrace on the garden front remain, but this first version of Ham's garden was enlarged and remodelled by the Duke and Duchess of Lauderdale in the 1670s. The house is now the property of the National Trust; it was handed over by the Tollemache family in 1948. In three centuries of living here the family had changed little of the Lauderdales' work, so it has been possible for both house and garden to be restored to its mid-seventeenth-century style. In this garden of gravelled walks and flower parterres, and in the geometric wilderness (added by the Lauderdales) of hornbeam hedges and small trees, it is now possible to see the kind of gardens that Robert Smythson knew.

NONSUCH, SURREY

5] ROBERT SMYTHSON *c*.1535–1614

Plan of ground floor and garden

Worcester House, Nonsuch, Surrey, 1609
Sepia pen
125 × 155 mm. /5 × 6⅛ in.

This is a survey drawing, again dated by Mark Girouard to Smythson's 1609 trip to London. The inscription in the left hand corner reads: *Iner: Courte of my: lo of wosters house: at nonesuch.* The 4th Earl of Worcester was keeper of Nonsuch Great Park.

The square garden has raised perimeter walks inside the wall marked *The uper walke sett with frute treese:.* The central 'diamond' is marked *sett wth flowers* which would seem to indicate that the dots in the rather unusually shaped parterre were all for flowers.

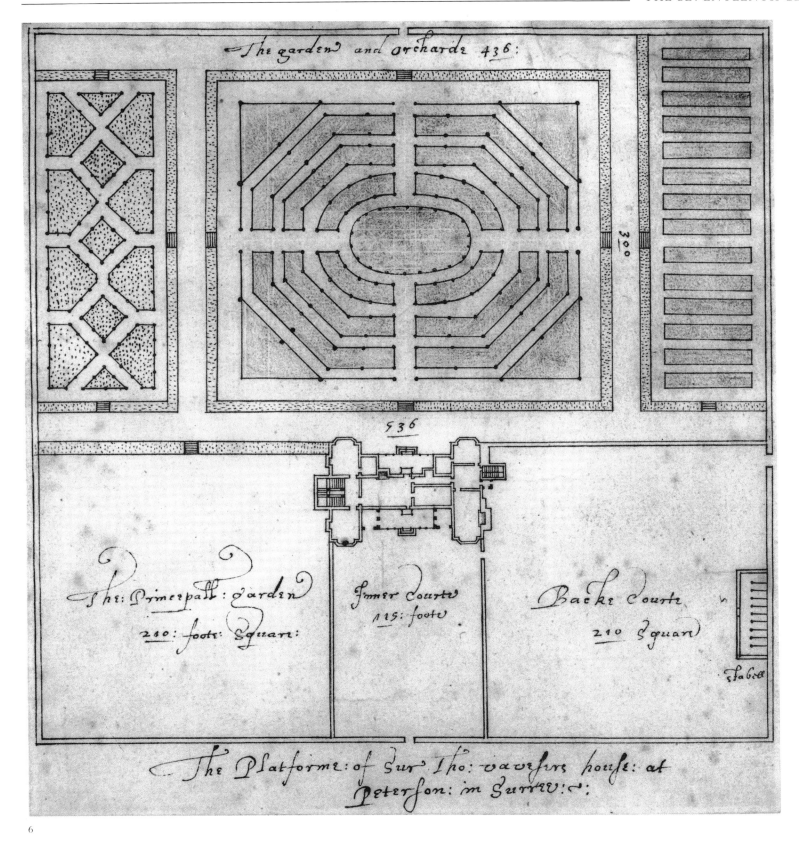

The garden and orcharde 436:

300

536

The Princepall garden
210 foote Square

Inner courte
115 foote

Backe courte
210 Square

stable

The Platforme of Sur Tho: vaurseus house: at
Peterson: in Surrey:

6

7

UNIDENTIFIED DRAWING

7] JOHN SMYTHSON THE YOUNGER 1640–1717
Terrace garden steps

Design inscribed 'Dean Tarras', undated
Pen, sepia pen and brown wash
190 × 325 mm. /$7\frac{1}{2}$ × $12\frac{3}{4}$ in.

This small design for terraced garden steps with an alcove is a
mystery, but an interesting one. It seems to show the artist
struggling with levels, perspective and Italian inspiration that
he perhaps does not quite understand, and offers an insight
into the way design ideas are transmuted. Was he designing
for Dean (a mystery place or person) a version of Palladio's
facade for the Palazzo da Porto Festa, which was published in
Quattro Libri in 1570? This great drawing, one of the treasures
of the RIBA Collection, is reproduced below.

SOMERSET HOUSE, LONDON

8] ROBERT SMYTHSON *c.*1535–1614

Plan of ground floor and garden

Somerset House, Strand, London, 1609
Sepia pen
280 × 265 mm. /11 × 10½ in.

The plan is inscribed on the house terrace *The Platforme: of Somersett garden/the Queenes house* and in the court at top right: *The newe adition at/Somersett house*. The Queen was Anne of Denmark, who began to remodel her house and garden by the Thames in 1609. Roy Strong suggests that Smythson recorded the very first stages of garden work by the French Mannerist wizard, Salomon de Caus, who

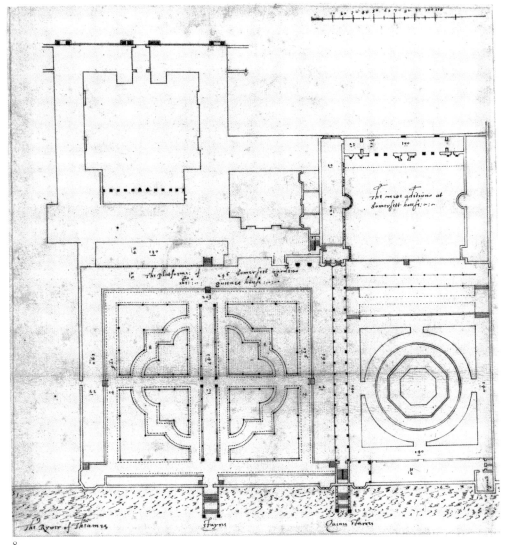

8

worked for Queen Anne from 1607–13.[29] It was previously thought that the design was the work of Simon Basil.

Smythson notes two garden rectangles divided by an avenue of trees leading to a water-gate for the Queen's use. The larger west garden has a raised walk around it, and is divided in half by another tree-lined walk to a secondary set of water stairs. This garden has a quatrefoil laid onto a divided square for its geometrical basis, though this was merely the preliminary to what became a complex arrangement of knots, beds and emblematic devices. The east garden has an octagon set within a circle; Roy Strong confirms this as the site for an elaborate grotto fountain representing Mount Parnassus. De Caus had published his design of a great rock, surmounted by figures representing rivers, spouting water and set in an octagonal pool.[30]

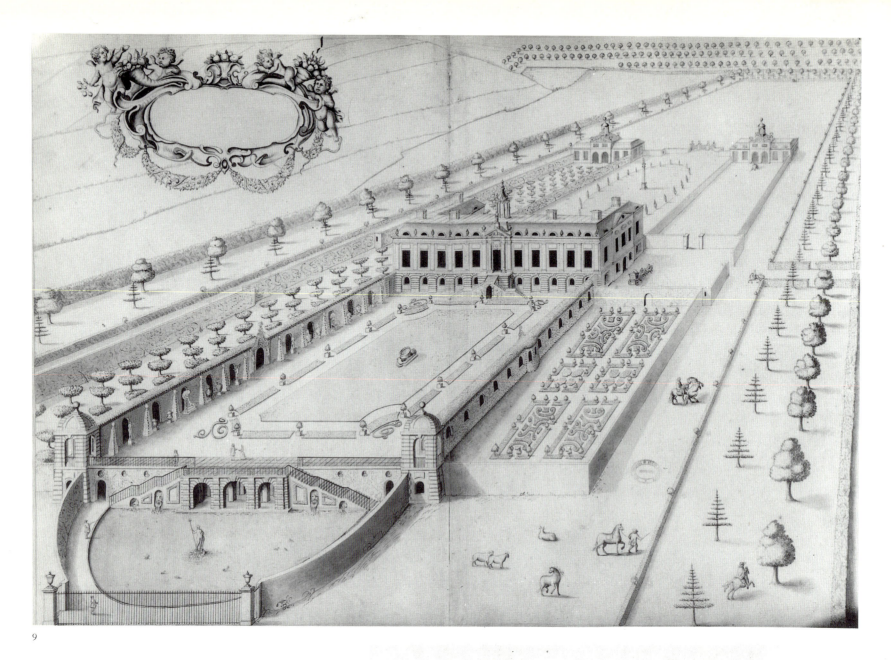

9

10

HAMPTON COURT PALACE, SURREY

9] WILLIAM TALMAN 1650–1719

Design for a Trianon

Hampton Court Palace, Surrey, *c.*1699
Pen and wash with faded brown pen
515 × 735 mm. /20¼ × 28⅞ in.

Talman was the most fashionable architect to William III's court and was the King's Comptroller of Works when he designed this retreat which was to be sited far from the palace, across the river at Thames Ditton. As the King died in 1702 the Trianon was never built. This splendid and justly famous drawing represents the highest sophistication of Dutch inspired formality, especially in the treatment of the hedges closing the court on the east and west sides into which windows and alcoves are clipped. The twin domed pavilions each have a grotto beneath, thus giving access on the upper or lower levels to the semi-circular pool in which Neptune presides over both ducks and fishermen. Much of the impact of this drawing is in the surprise of the bird's-eye technique, highly unusual for this date and not to become an architectural drawing convention until the nineteenth century.

10] WILLIAM TALMAN 1650–1719

Elevation of the Trianon's garden enclosure

Hampton Court Palace, Surrey, 1699
Pen and wash
Detail: 515 × 360 mm. /20¼ × 14⅛ in.

This detail shows the highly stylized treatment of the hedge and its attendant pillars and how the most complicated trelliswork, statues, vases, arches and seats were used to ornament the living greenery.

WELBECK ABBEY, NOTTINGHAMSHIRE

11] WILLIAM TALMAN 1650–1719

Design for proposed garden

Welbeck Abbey, Nottinghamshire, *c.*1703
Pen and wash
270 × 225 mm. /10⅝ × 8⅞ in.

This drawing is inscribed on the back *A scrach (sic) of a Garden by Mr Tollman* by Margaret, Duchess of Newcastle. In 1703 both Vanbrugh and Talman were competing to rebuild Welbeck for the Duke; it was not rebuilt in his lifetime, and thus Talman did not make his garden. However, this strange and rather naive drawing, with patterned parterres and rows of neat trees, has a spontaneity that more finished drawings lack; one can almost hear *Mr Tollman's* pen scratching across the centuries, imagine him trying to humour the Duke with his sketches, perhaps hear the Duchess tut-tutting as she gathered up the drawings and neatly labelled them knowing that such fine schemes were only dreams.

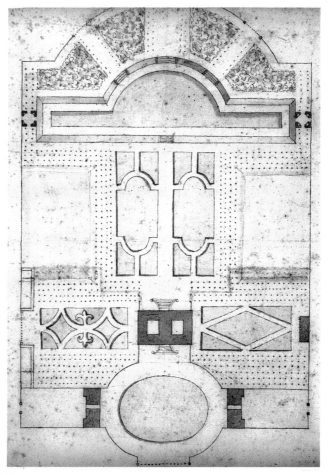

11

DYRHAM PARK, GLOUCESTERSHIRE

12]   WILLIAM TALMAN 1650–1719

Design for a cascade

Dyrham Park, Gloucestershire, *c.*1698
Pen and pencil
300 × 460 mm. /12 × 18 in.

The drawing is inscribed in Talman's hand *for Mr Blathwayt.*
William Blathwayt learned his gardening as Secretary to Sir
William Temple, maker of a famous seventeenth-century
garden at Moor Park, Farnham in Surrey, while Sir William
was Ambassador in Holland. Blathwayt married the heiress
of Dyrham and made an extensive and elaborate, Dutch-
influenced, formal garden and great water cascade there;
Talman designed this baroque cascade as a grand finale to the
garden making, but it may never have been built in quite
such an elaborate form.

Dyrham Park is now owned by the National Trust and the
Neptune statue shown on the drawing remains in the park:
the formal gardens became very dilapidated by the late
eighteenth century and were 'landscaped' away as in so many
other parks. (See also fig. 8.)

12

DEPTFORD, LONDON

13] JOHN EVELYN 1620–1706

Design for a parterre

Sayes Court, Deptford, London
Sepia pen and pencil
203 × 190 mm. /8 × 7½ in.

The inscription, by William Upcott, reads: *Sketched by John Evelyn of Wotton for 'Elysium Brittanicum' not printed.*

Wotton in Surrey is the Evelyn family estate, and the garden that John Evelyn made there for his brother in the early 1650s is well documented and known. However, from 1652 John Evelyn spent much of his time at his own house, Sayes Court, where he made a garden in the French style. This plan was intended for his great work on all aspects of gardening called *Elysium Brittanicum*, which was never published in full during his lifetime; part of the manuscript survives in the library of Christ Church, Oxford.

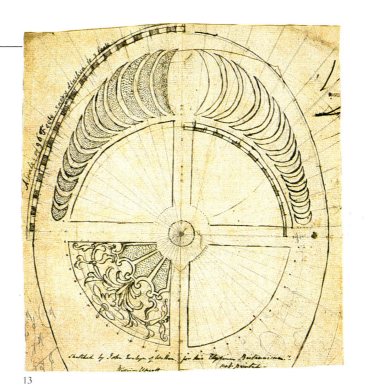

13

BROMPTON PARK, LONDON

14] SMYTHSON COLLECTION

'Carpenters Garden at Bronton by Kensington'

Early 18th century
Pencil and green wash
273 × 384 mm. /10¾ × 15⅛ in.

This rather tentative sketch, found with other miscellaneous drawings among the Smythson papers, offers a glimpse of gardening history. It is of a rather formal part of Brompton Park Nursery, the famous nursery founded in 1681 by George London and Messrs Lucre, Field and Cooke. In 1688 London took Henry Wise into the partnership, and in 1714, Joseph Carpenter and William Smith took the nursery over from London and Wise. Carpenter continued to work on the royal gardens with Wise for the next ten years, but he never made a success of the nursery and died, in debt, in about 1725.

This view down a grass vista to a semi-circular bay in a wall, flanked by statues in niches, possibly depicts a rather similar feature which can be identified near the main entrance of the nursery in a plan published in David Green's *Gardener to Queen Anne: Henry Wise 1653–1738 and the Formal Garden*.[31] Apart from supplying trees for Blenheim, Hampton Court and Bushey, Wise's nursery grew treasures of it own, including lemons, jasmines, bays, fruit and rare shrubs.

14

2
THE EIGHTEENTH CENTURY
Art and Nature

The eighteenth century opened on an English countryside innocent of fashion. The word 'landscape' had not entered the language.[1] No shadow of taste had been cast over the natural greenery; there was still a great and widespread fear of the dark woods and tracts of pathless wastes, where one could become lost as in any desert of sand or ice, and nature was to be feared, respected and conquered, never courted and embraced. The drawings in this chapter offer vivid insights into the practical creation of the change of heart and mind that was to be called the English landscape movement. These drawings are the fragile surviving visions from the minds of men such as Lancelot Brown and Humphry Repton who were to change the face of, and even more potently, the image of England, for ever.

The enormity of this green revolution, which gave the soft, sleepy and dank countryside an emotive power to match that of Classical Greece or Renaissance Italy, can only be realized by an appreciation of what was there already. Each image of the particular that follows needs to be set against a general background. If I were Humphry Repton I could now draw the *before* image of England, paint it in watercolour, and present it on a paper flap, but – not being so – I have to juggle some words of description and call the indispensable Professor Hoskins to my aid. In *The Making of the English Landscape* he presents the facts: 'Over large tracts of the country, especially in the west and the north, and to a considerable extent in the south-east also, the pattern of field and hedgerow, hamlet and farm, road and lane, had established itself pretty much as we know it. But over millions of acres between Yorkshire and the Dorset coasts, the country scene was still largely medieval. Farming was carried on in open fields that had not changed basically since the thirteenth century, and beyond the arable fields and their meadows lay great tracts of common pasture, much of it covered with gorse and furze, rising in places to moorland and mountains'.[2] This is a prosaic description totally in keeping with its subject. To the working men and women of this countryside their horizon was

set by the limit of the fields they worked all day, and extended once in a blue moon to the market town in the next valley. To the gentleman in his manor house the vision was extended by the stamina of his horse. For him, and everyone who could afford it, the function of rural England was as a hunting ground, and any management ploys in the way of planting or felling, fencing or hedging, were for the benefit of fox, partridge and wild boar. The really great lords, who owned most of England, journeyed from Whitehall to their country houses with the blinds down, for what was the point of looking at land if it belonged to someone else. When they arrived home, to those great houses built in Elizabethan England or converted from doomed monasteries, they looked with critical, altruistic but purely practical eyes on their miniature kingdoms. These houses – Knole, Chatsworth, Ragley and Burghley, which the early eighteenth-century engravers captured in their panoramas of England – were surrounded by neat and functional gardens. To feed a household of two hundred the gardens had to be well organized for producing fruit, vegetables and salads and herbs, with only the smallest spaces allowed for 'my lady's rosy bower' or even emblematic topiary tributes to royalty that may deign to visit. Beyond the pales, the greatest lords had conquered their countryside with avenues vaunting pride, in the French manner, a signal of wealth and power over nature, but never planted with any of those effete and foreign artistic intentions.

Into the Englishman's phlegmatic view of his home tumbled the coffee shop gossip and the power of the pen; in the *Spectator* of 25 June 1712 (revolution has such exact beginnings) Joseph Addison threw down the velvet glove: 'Our English Gardens are not so entertaining to the Fancy as those in France and Italy, where we see a large extent of Ground covered over with an agreeable mixture of Garden and Forest, which represents everywhere an artificial Rudeness, much more charming than that Neatness and Elegancy which we meet with in those of our own country . . . why may not a whole Estate be thrown into a kind of Garden . . . Fields of Corn make a pleasant Prospect, and if the walks were a little taken care of that lie between them, if the natural Embroidery of the Meadows, were helped and improved by some small additions of Art, . . . a Man might make a pretty Landskip of his own Possessions'. Addison's was a powerful pen, and in league with Alexander Pope, he planted the idea of 'Beauty in the Landscape' into the minds of the Whig landlords. The Royal gardener, Charles Bridgeman, was already exploiting the Picturesque attributes of the settings of Blenheim and Stowe, to the delight of noble clients who could not bear to contemplate that their acres were any less lovely than the romantic landscapes painted by Claude and the Poussin brothers. A former apprentice of the Brompton Nursery (see no. 14) Stephen Switzer, had produced the textbook of the age, three volumes of *Ichnographia Rustica* which tackled the practical points of a sympathetic treatment of the natural landscape, most importantly the secrets of the ha-ha, purloined from France, the device which kept the cattle out of the garden, without actually appearing to be there at all.

The popular idea of 'leaping the fence' and of 'all Nature as a Garden' is so seductive, that it is usually carried forward by the momentum of great names: Bridgeman, Switzer, Kent and Brown, so that it is easy to forget that it did not, nor could not, happen overnight – or even in a direct line of progress. The drawings shown here in relation to Gopsall Park present one of the many oblique images of this book, a surprising and not quite quantifiable images of the realities of history: Gopsall seems to be a place where a perceptive and interested owner was groping for something he did not quite understand.

Charles Jennens, known as 'Solyman the Magnificent', was Handel's librettist and so inevitably one of Lord Burlington's coterie. He inherited Gopsall Park in Leicestershire in 1747, at the age of forty-seven and just at the time when the *Messiah*, first performed five years earlier, was becoming appreciated. Jennens at first employed a local builder-architect, John Westley (1702–69), to alter his house to his liking, but sometime in the later 1750s the work was taken over by William and David Hiorn, the leading architects in the Midlands, based in Warwick. The Hiorns had learned their craft from their father's involvement in the building of Ditchley Park in Oxfordshire by James Gibbs, and Gopsall was to be a fine work, 'one of the most significant contributions to provincial domestic architecture in England' in the Palladian style.[3] Even so, the house became

derelict and was demolished in 1951. But the papers, seventy-three drawings, that the Hiorn brothers amassed while working on the house came into the Collection, and the drawings shown here allow a glimpse of what was happening in the garden and park.

The survey of 1749 by John Grundy of Spalding (no. 15) shows the gardens on the west side of the house to be traditional and functional. But on the south and east there appears that embryonic kind of levelling, rolling and mowing that attempted to integrate the garden surroundings into the larger landscape. There is still firm formality and control, but the view is *outwards*, and the long banks of grass are on the verge of becoming a ha-ha, as 'The Hanging Lawn', at least in spring, resembled Addison's embroidered meadow. The Great Pond has such an awkwardness about it that it can only be a formal shape in uncomfortable transformation into a serpentine lake. Gopsall gives all the impressions of being, in 1749, a garden and landscape in the process of change. The Hiorn brothers were keen on designing garden buildings and their best designs are included here. It is interesting that when Charles Jennens' requirements went beyond their experience, they resorted to the pattern book of the day, Thomas Chippendale's *The Gentleman and cabinet maker's director* (1754) for Chinoiserie and Gothic designs; can a certain impatience with his sound, provincial men be discerned from Jennens' commission to the most fashionable architect of the 1760s, James Paine, for a temple to commemorate Edward Holdsworth? It was clearly one of those spontaneous contracts, made at a dinner table at a club or country house, for the architect did not even note his client's name (no. 17). But the various styles of the buildings and features indicate that Gopsall was being moulded to take them, and Woolfe & Gandon record that a delightful park was then being laid out 'at a great expense'.[4] But that far these drawings do not go; Gopsall poses many unanswered questions but opens the mind to the great landscape revolution and the certain achievements to come.

Apart from changing the image of England, the landscape movement forged a new profession, that of landscape architect or landscape gardener, names available according to preference. The new profession had to formulate a way of presenting ideas on paper as the necessary preliminary to executing them on ground. The Hiorn drawing of the plan and elevations for the summerhouse and railing beside the Square Pond at Gopsall (no. 16) is one of the most exquisite drawings in this book, but it

Fig. 10] *View of Box Hill, Surrey*, 1773 by George Lambert (1700–65) – a rare impression of the open, 'champion' landscape of England before the concepts of enclosure and improvement of the English landscape style.

is a purely architectural presentation, confined to straight lines and geometrical principles: if there was to be a change in the landscape clearly a new way of drawing had to be found.

The honour of being the first to make the quantum leap 'from the twilight of imperfect essays' to see that 'all nature was a garden' is accorded to William Kent (1685–1748) by Horace Walpole and posterity.[5] Kent, a sometime coach painter and interior decorator, who became Lord Burlington's architect and garden designer, may thus be forgiven for remaining as a draughtsman in the familiar bounds of landscape painting. Alexander Pope taught him that gardening *was* painting, but with different media; Kent's surviving landscape drawings, for his famous creations at Rousham, Holkham and Claremont, are the roughest of preliminary sketches as for a painting, with buildings, clumps of trees and water disposed in a picturesque

composition, light and shade indicated, and all having primitive perspectives and an almost nursery simplicity. These sketches gave purely picturesque information; there is little evidence that Kent knew anything about trees or shrubs or even the construction of a pond. Once the 'finished painting' was on the ground the sketch was dispensable. Also, his patron, Lord Burlington, was a great connoisseur of fine drawings; it was, of course, his ownership of the Palladio drawings that advanced his patronage of architecture and landscape design, but with the treasures of Palladio and Inigo Jones he is hardly likely to have valued these cursory sketches of the fledgling landscape art; he did keep Kent's architectural drawings and garden buildings which are in the Burlington-Devonshire Collection, the provenance of which is explained in my Introduction. Here, Kent's place in history is acknowledged through the eyes of James 'Athenian' Stuart and his drawing of the Praeneste at Rousham, no. 190.

Apart from the drawings' dispensability, other reasons may explain the comparative rarity of drawings by Lancelot 'Capability' Brown (1716–83), of which there are two in the Collection, both of great importance, nos. 23 and 25. Brown began work as a gardener in his native Northumberland at the age of sixteen; seven years later he came south to work for Lord Cobham at Stowe in Buckinghamshire, where he taught himself about architecture and learned to draw plans. By 1751 he had set up on his own account, working from his home by the Thames at Hammersmith, and from then until his death he fulfilled over two hundred landscape commissions, mainly for the Whig landowners, covering thousands of acres of England and Wales with smooth mounds, curving clumps of trees and sinuous lakes. He died, in 1783, aged only sixty-six, greatly mourned – the immortal Brown, 'Dame Nature's second husband' and a legend in his own lifetime.[6] Though he left behind a copious correspondence and detailed account books, no office copies of his drawings seem to have been made and the originals were despatched to his clients. From this scattering they have, especially in the twenty-five year period between the first edition of Dorothy Stroud's biography of 1950 and her revision in 1975, come to light in muniment rooms and local record offices.

However, the two that appear here are worth a great deal of celebration. Brown was no great artist, indeed Christopher Hussey describes his concept of drawing as more of literary than visual composition, 'setting a comma here, a full stop there',[7] but his concentrated ability did convert landscape drawing into an art. Brown began by adopting the conventions of the map-makers, the cardboard cut-out trees and prosaic curves familiar from the estate maps of places where he worked. The anonymous survey drawing of Lord Milton's estate (no. 24) is of the clear but gawky standard of his day, full of intrinsic interest and information but devoid of art. How much more intriguing is the plan for the garden layout around the ice-house (no. 25) which is good enough to be in Brown's own hand. The design conveys a smoothness and delicacy of form in this small landscape which were two of the essential attributes of Beauty, as defined by Edmund Burke; that this is possible on paper, as well as in the landscape itself, is a mark of Brown's genius.

But the full-blown achievement of his drawing style is in the 'mysterious meander' illustrated no. 23. The subtle sepia, the shading, the hint of red, the clustering, toy-like trees and erotic, even intestinal writhings of the river, reveal the extremes of appeal that landscape can make to our senses. This drawing aptly illustrates what Edmund Burke analyzed – 'that all emotion is sensation with a physical basis, and that all physical phenomena were divisible into the Sublime and the Beautiful according as

Fig. 11] Burton Constable Hall, Yorkshire, the East Front, 1777 by George Barret (1732–84). Capability Brown was working here improving the park when William Constable commissioned this painting, but Brown being behind schedule, the intended lake had not yet been dug.

they aroused sensations of danger or appealed ultimately to the sexual emotions'.[8] Here, both in drawing and in landscape, are the phenomena producing Beauty – 'Smallness, Smoothness, Gradual Variation, and Delicacy of form . . . the physical basis of the "waving" and "serpentine" forms felt by Hogarth to constitute the "line of beauty" and pre-dominant in the lines of Chippendale's furniture no less' than in the paths and rivers of Brown's landscapes.[9].

By one of the quirks of history (in which the Collection abounds) this is the appropriate place to introduce a drawing of the 1890s, for a Claude glass, the instrument by which connoisseurs of the phenomena that produced beauty viewed both Brown's landscapes and the wild. The Claude glass, named after the landscape painter Claude Gellée, born in Lorraine in 1600, who spent all his adult life in Rome and painted Italian landscapes, was a slightly convex mirror which gave a picturesque effect to the view through its distortion. For fine day viewing the mirror was smoked, but a silvered mirror was to be used on grey days; travellers carried small folding versions, but the drawing by John Hungerford Pollen (fig. 12) is rather more for an ornamental version – a symbol of the fine taste of its owner when displayed on a hall table – or meant for travelling by carriage.

John Hungerford Pollen (1820–1902) was a cultivated and well-travelled watercolourist, a descendant of the Cockerells of Sezincote, who feature later in this chapter. He designed this Claude glass as a wedding present for Henry Somerset on his marriage in 1896; at the time Pollen was working designing stained glass windows, a fireplace and plasterwork for Lady Henry Somerset, mother of the bridegroom, at Reigate Priory in Surrey. He notes the glass to be *reflecting from surface*, indicating that this one was silvered, and records the further details of its making as follows: *The stem and frame is of black oak, taken from the roof of the Old Priory, Reigate. The mounting etc. are of silver. The wooden part was carved at the School of Art, South Kensington.*

Pollen's Claude glass is a delightful object and a presentation of some genius, even more beneficial than the proverbial rose-coloured spectacles for viewing the landscapes of Edwardian England. Its mid-eighteenth-century predecessors, especially when used on lowering days in the English Lake District, had inspired terror and excitement, most luridly described by the poet, Thomas Gray,[10] which was to gradually diminish the regard for Brown's smooth and sinuous hills.

Capability Brown's genius had several emulators and successors, notably Samuel Lapidge, Richard Woods and William Emes, or Eames, (1729–1803). The latter is the most rewarding, largely because of Keith Goodway's patient detective work on his career, and the single Emes drawing in the Collection (no. 26) has a spacious clarity and fine professionalism. According to Goodway, most of the sixty-five commissions he has traced are in the north Midlands and North Wales, reflecting the fact that Emes lived near Derby for most of his life. He obviously came south to work on Erlestoke in Wiltshire in 1786, and his plan was carried out, though the park is now largely derelict. In 1789, upon the death of his wife, Emes moved to Elvetham Hall near Hartley Wintney in Hampshire, where he seems to have been under the wing of the Mildmay family, for whom he landscaped Dogmersfield Park. By 1802 he had returned to London, where he died the following year.[11] By that time the tide had turned, and the immortal Brown and all his works were out of favour; he was scorned for sweeping away the old formal gardens and for covering England with lookalike landscapes. It was time for another change.

It is one of the truly English paradoxes of the so-called national style, that it encouraged a taste for all things foreign. There is no finer example of the exotic settling itself into the English countryside than that of Sezincote House in Gloucestershire. The onion domes, the 'Chajjahs and chattris made of amber stone' that so enchanted the young John Betjeman[12] in his Oxford days, adorn the house that the Cockerells built in the early nineteenth century; the Collection is rich in material pertaining to Sezincote, and I have chosen the most fascinating in connection with the garden to tell its marvellous tale.

On returning from Bengal in 1795, Colonel John Cockerell bought the estate of Sezincote to be near his friend Warren Hastings at Daylesford. Less than three years later the Colonel died, leaving his estate to his brother Charles, who had been with him in the East India Company and shared a passion for Indian art and architecture. A third brother, Samuel Pepys Cockerell (named in honour of his ancestor, the diarist) was a clever and established architect, who had built Daylesford between 1790–96, so it was quite natural that he should help his brother with Sezincote, built in the style of the Moghul Akbar with a deliberate mix of Hindu and Muslim detail, and finished in 1805.

In the early 1800s the brothers sought help with their garden and naturally approached Humphry Repton, who was at the pinnacle of his power and well-known locally as working for the Leighs at Adlestrop and William Blathwayt at Dyrham Park. Repton's one known drawing for Sezincote is reproduced here (no. 32), having been bought for the Collection in 1957 with eighteen drawings for the house and garden by S.P. Cockerell and three letters from Thomas Daniell to Sir Charles Cockerell. This Repton drawing is a fascinating example of his use of flaps or slides to denote the before and after of his recommendations, and has more than an element of the comic cartoon about it, with the magical vanishings of the pigs and washing lines. The hilly slope in the background of the drawing indicates that what Repton was doing was removing the domestic vestiges of the old Sezincote house from what is now the formal Indian garden on the south front; he was doing Sir Charles Cockerell the greatest service.

There is no Red Book known for Sezincote, and Repton's involvement apparently ended here; well, almost, for he records that while he was at the house, admiring the Indian inspiration for the architecture and proposed garden buildings, that he 'even assisted in the selecting of some of the forms from Mr T.Daniell's collection'. There is a note of regret as he goes on to realize that

Samuel Pepys Cockerell is quite capable, 'has displayed as much correctness as could be expected'[13] with such a new style and was to oversee the garden work. However, the present owners of Sezincote, Mr and Mrs David Peake, believe that they have a Repton 'feel' to their park and to the sweep of their lake.

The drawings by Thomas Daniell that Repton saw are now in the Collection; there are 261 catalogued drawings and water-colours plus some 100 sketches made on a tour of northern India between 1786 and 1793 by Thomas Daniell (1749–1840) and his nephew, William (1769–1837). They are a treasure house of Indian landscapes, temples, tombs, forts and palaces, and formed the basis of six volumes of *Oriental Scenery* published by the Daniells between 1795 and 1808. In addition, there are the ten designs for Sezincote, three of which are illustrated here (nos. 33–5) for the Temple of Surya, the wall of mossy crevices and the Indian bridge, which are all part of Sezincote's garden today.

The additional Sezincote drawings (nos. 36–7) are by Samuel Pepys Cockerell; the working details of the Indian bridge show his skills as an architect, for these had to be made up from his own experience, having only Daniell's sketch as his guide. As to his garden design abilities, awkwardly illustrated in the plan for flower beds to the north of the house, perhaps it would have been better if Humphry Repton's involvement had continued!

Repton's experience of Sezincote made a lasting impression; inspired by the Indian designs, he sang their praises to the Prince of Wales, who was contemplating his Royal Pavilion at Brighton. The Prince visited Sezincote in 1806, and plumped for his own onion domes, and though the Pavilion was built by Repton's ex-partner, John Nash, it was Repton who made the royal garden.

It is also to Humphry Repton that modern landscape architects turn, as to their first master, or, as Sylvia Crowe has called him, the 'codifier' of their profession. Repton, through his published writings, notably his *Observations on the Theory and Practice of Landscape Gardening*, 1803,[14] his *Fragments* on the same theories, published two years before his death in 1818, and in his Red Books, has presented the new profession with its commandments and office practice methods. Repton, born in April 1752 in Bury St Edmunds, Suffolk, and apprenticed to the textile business at the age of sixteen, had to fight for his chosen career; despairing of bombazines and worsted satins he tried farming, illustrating (for he was always keen on drawing), speculating and being a private secretary until, aged thirty-six, he made the conscious and right

decision to fill the void left by the death of Brown in 1783, by announcing himself in business as a landscape gardener in 1788. He soon discovered a difficulty, which remains the chief obstacle of his profession to the present day, that though he could clearly imagine the way a place could be improved, he wanted the means for making his ideas equally visible and intelligible to his client. How Repton came upon the idea for his Red Books is not recorded, but he conceived them as beautiful and prestigious documents – not without advertisement value – in which he recorded in words and pictures his proposed recommendations and works. He was careful to extoll the virtues of the place the wisdom and felicity of his clients as well as the greater benefits they could attain by employing him. His first book was for Lady Salusbury at Brandsbury in Middlesex in 1789, and he charged her ladyship ten guineas for it.[15] Number one was followed by some 170 others in the years up until 1816, when the ageing Repton made a special effort for his son, Rev. Edward Repton and his project at Crayford Workhouse, in Kent. About half of this number have disappeared; of the remainder, scattered in private and public collections and occasionally exhibited, some are truly red, bound in red morocco, but an equal number appear in brown calf.[16] The volume for Langley Park from the Collection and illustrated nos. 27–31 is one of the small brown examples (215 × 295 mm. /8 × 12 in.); the Sheringham Red Book, truly red and of a larger format, is similar to those made for Repton's grandest commissions, such as Longleat, Magdalen College, Oxford, and the Royal Pavilion at Brighton.

Repton's watercolours are an obvious delight, but his Red Books also gain from his essential humanity. His life was not easy; he had many disappointments and dead-ends before the calm certainty of his decision to become a landscape gardener; his eldest son, John Adey, was born completely deaf; he was always concerned over his family and friends, and when he seemed to reach a peak of success, in 1800, he was only forty-eight and had years of disillusion and financial worries ahead of him. But he always retained a belief in his work, a certain canny snobbishness and human warmth that he was not afraid to put before his clients; he was confident enough to preface the Red Book for the Royal Pavilion at Brighton with aesthetic warnings to the Prince of Wales: quoting Edmund Burke on the frontispiece – 'Designs that are vast only by their dimensions, are always the sign of a common and low imagination. No work of art can be great but as it deceive, to be otherwise is the prerogative of nature only'.[17]

He was politically Conservative, and did not flinch from saying so to the *nouveau riche*; he felt they needed his advice in order to understand the English countryside in which they now proposed to live – in the Red Book for High Legh he observes: 'A large red house close by the side of a turnpike road, can seldom possess much dignity of appearance, it is apt to convey the idea of those Mansions which spring up like mushrooms near great Cities, and which are more the habitation of sudden Affluence, than the Ancient dwelling of Family Inheritance.'[18] He was considerably

concerned that the new lords of the countryside should be of the right attitude, which is why he cared so much about Abbot Upcher, the client for Sheringham, whom he believed would do much good. The background to this commission was typical of Repton's involvement in his work: it began at the end of 1808 when Charles Abbott, Speaker of the House of Commons, asked him to look out for a suitable property which a grateful nation could bestow upon the surviving brother of Horatio Nelson, in honour of Trafalgar's hero. Repton found Sheringham via his son William who was the estate steward and knew it was for sale. However, Sheringham was merely a pretty site and not grand enough for the nation's honours, so Repton, anxious for the opportunity to work this lovely site, persuaded the young Abbot Upcher to buy the estate and that it was a bargain at £50,000

Fig. 12] Design for a Claude glass, *c.* 1890 by John Hungerford Pollen (1820–1902). This was made as a wedding present for Henry Somerset out of black oak from the roof of Reigate Priory, where Pollen was working for Lady Henry Somerset.

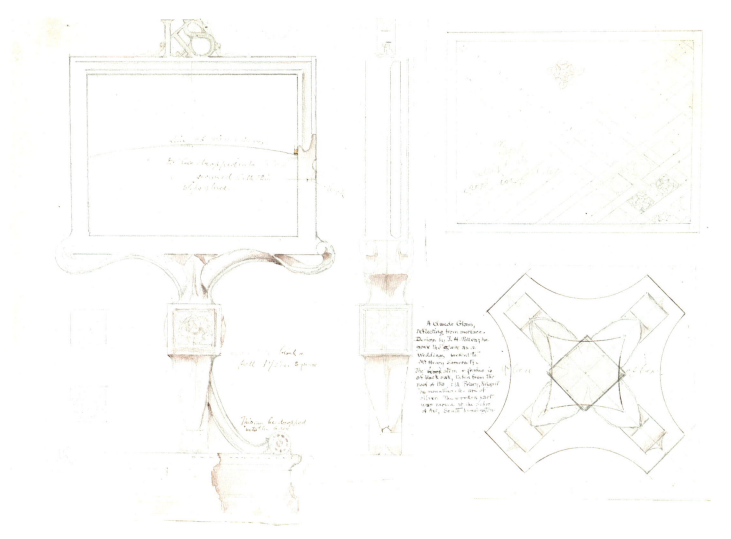

Fig. 13] *The Orange Tree Garden, Chiswick House, Middlesex*, by Pieter Andreas Rysbrack (1684–1748). Lord Burlington's garden was the inspiration for the English love of orange trees in tubs, which were set out in the garden in summer and preserved in the orangery in winter.

guineas. Repton and John Adey duly prepared the Red Book (nos. 38–42) and their schemes; Mr Upcher faltered, afraid of the additional expense involved, and decided to sell. Repton tried to rescue him – 'my first object is to serve poor Upcher, whom you know I Lov'd almost at first sight – as another myself . . .' he wrote, as he tried to persuade the Government that Lord Nelson should have Sheringham after all! Lord Nelson was being settled at Stanlynch Park in Wiltshire (hardly as appropriate as the Admiral's native Norfolk) but the crisis was over, Upcher recovered and Repton's Sheringham – his 'favourite and darling child in Norfolk' became a reality.[19]

Repton was kind and reasonably honest, – 'It has been a rule with me this Life, my dear boy – never to make an enemy – particularly of a friend – tho' he may have behaved ill' he wrote to William in 1807[20] about his friend William Windham; he was vulnerable, a man of the world of Gainsborough, Zoffany and Stubbs in that age of such apparent elegance but truly of 'violence and agression, with coarse language and gross manners' – which belongs to the 'savage pictures of Hogarth and the brutal squibs of Rowlandson and Gillray' – as J.H.Plumb so effectively described the paradoxes.[21] This is why it is so appropriate that the final illustrations of drawings in this section illustrate the bitter controversy that marked Repton's declining years, the pictures of Deepdene that symbolize the assertion of the Picturesque.

Thomas Hope, aesthete and collector, bought The Deepdene at Dorking in Surrey in 1807, a year after his marriage. The Deepdene was intended to become his expression of the new Picturesque theories of Payne Knight and Uvedale Price – what

David Watkin so nicely calls 'an "excited" version of a Capability Brown park on the very grandest scale'.[22] Knight and Price's attack on Repton had begun early in 1794 with the former's poem *The Landscape, a Didactic Poem addressed to Uvedale Price* containing an accusation, addressed to Brown and Repton, that they had produced boring landscapes of 'many a tedious round' and 'lawn that never Ends'.[23] They felt that Repton's works were not half as exciting as the paintings they proposed to emulate; Repton loyally defended Brown's reputation and argued that there were five considerable differences between the ways in which a painter and a gardener saw any place: the painter could pick his view with detachment, whereas the gardener was *in* his garden; a painter's view was confined whereas the real view is usually far greater; a painting could not represent a view down a hill – often the most rewarding view in a garden; the painter could fake the light whereas in reality it is changing with the time of day; and a painter can introduce a rotting tree trunk or bunch of docks to emphasize his foreground, but no real garden owner would allow such things space. These were part of a wordy and bitter argument that soured Repton's last years, and Thomas Hope's Deepdene was to become the most praised and fashionable example of all Payne Knight's and Price's charges.

John Britton (1771–1857), the author of The Deepdene volume, was a distinguished antiquarian and topographical writer; in 1827 he published a book on Sir John Soane's London house in Lincoln's Inn (now the Sir John Soane's Museum) titled the *Union of Architecture, Sculpture & Painting* representing the house as a triumph of the Picturesque for city living. The two Deepdene manuscript volumes were prepared to honour Thomas Hope's country house as the equivalent achievement of the Picturesque in a country setting. But they were never completed; the two volumes were found in the library of Bedgebury House in Kent, this one was presented to the RIBA Collection, the second was auctioned and bought by the Minet Library for their Surrey Collection. This volume, because it is incomplete, as is explained in the captions to the illustrations nos. 45–9, is less well-known; it contains the watercolours by the young artist William Bartlett, which are, says David Watkin, 'in their own right a work of the Picturesque'. 'Deliberately but subtly they heighten the effect of all that they chose to depict'[24] – they make the Surrey hills even steeper, the plants and flowers more luxuriant, the disposition of objects more artistic and the trees and foliage more effective. In fact, they do exactly as Repton said a painter could do; the question is, do they convey really what The Deepdene was like? That we shall never know, at least not by being there. The Deepdene's garden stayed splendid until the early years of this century, but now it has long gone back to the wild and the house, of which Thomas Hope was so proud, fell into disrepair and was demolished in 1969.[25] Though Hope died in 1831, his son, Henry, carried on his traditions. David Watkin suggests that the best evocation of what The Deepdene was like is in the pages of Disraeli's novel *Henrietta Temple* of 1834. He reminds us that the Young England movement was founded there – 'if ever there was a political movement deserving the title of Picturesque, then it was Young England'[26] – the last colourful fling before the Victorians settled into sedate virtues. Only a few years would pass before John Claudius Loudon was defining the Gardenesque from the 'festive impermanence' of Deepdene's faded Picturesque, and architecture and gardens were moving into the grandest of Barry's Italianate fantasies. And so, The Deepdene makes a fitting and evocative end to this Collection of wonderful drawings that chronicle a time when the English wanted to make the views outside their windows as carefully balanced and artistic as the prospect paintings they hung on their walls. It was an expansive and subtle art movement; looking at this primary material only makes me wonder if, despite paintings and Red Books and even the survival of such places as Blenheim, Stowe and Sheringham, we can ever really understand.

In his last published work, *Fragments* 1816, Repton hoped that his new profession had a future; Patrick Goode assesses this. 'Looking back from the troubled and threatening world of 1816, his theoretical conflict with Knight and Price, however acrimonious verbally, must have seemed like a distant echo from a vanished age when aesthetic questions could be the subject of a leisurely discussion between gentlemen. Repton must have realized that the picturesque controversy marked the end of an era, and that the aesthetic problems of landscape gardening were now inextricably involved with complex social and political issues.'[27]

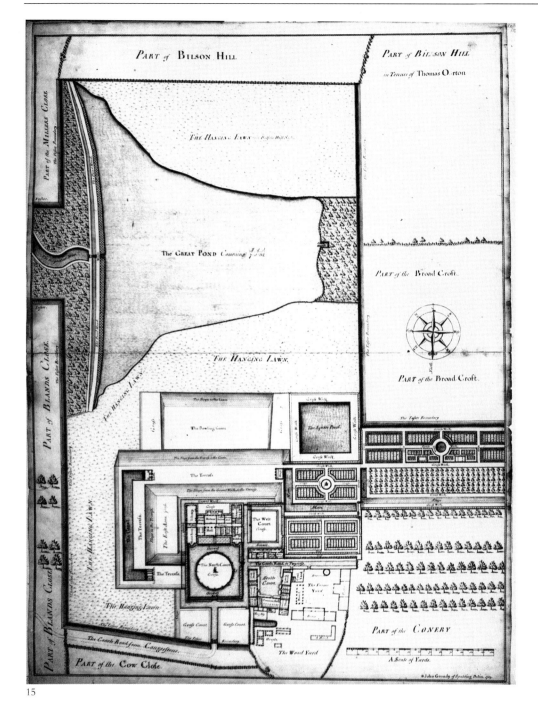

15

GOPSALL PARK, LEICESTERSHIRE

15] JOHN GRUNDY *fl.* 1749

Survey plan of a park

Gopsall Park, Leicestershire, 1749
Sepia pen and wash
735 × 530 mm. /28⅞ × 20⅞ in.

The Gopsall estate was inherited by Charles Jennens (1700–73) in 1747: he was a friend of Handel's and the librettist for several of his oratorios, including the *Messiah*, and known as 'Solyman the Magnificent'. Jennens started work immediately to modernize and enrich his house and garden and the Collection holds a large number of drawings relating to work at Gopsall between 1747 and 1770. The builders and architects were in the main provincial men, and throughout the drawings there are many obvious pattern-book derivations, even though they are of the highest quality. It seems that Jennens' fine and aware mind would have missed neither architectural nor garden innovations and this survey of 1749, by a surveyor from Spalding in Lincolnshire named Grundy, seems to illustrate a garden in the first stages of transition from the old formality to the new feeling for the natural landscape. Capability Brown was not to start working at Stowe for another two years, but Batty Langley's *New Principles of Gardening*[28] had been in existence for twenty and Jennens seems to have cleared out his fancy parterres, emblems and ornaments as Langley suggested, and started to look outwards to his landscape. On the west side of the house the functional, productive gardens remain in the traditional style, but on the south and east there is a remarkable layering of gravel walks and grass terraces, with enormously steep banks of steps. Even for one so magnificent, to have these steps built of stone would have been impossibly extravagant, and they must be fine examples of grass steps, a most delicious feature of English gardens now far too rarely created or preserved. In 1749 the grass steps and 'The Hanging Lawn' were on the verge of becoming the ha-ha and rolling parkland, and this survey seems to convey that last moment before the light dawned.

The Great Pond, kept in existence by an enormous and presumably costly dam, is clearly a feature of some considerable pride; its ugliness, as well as its precariousness, somehow intimate just why the landscape style was to become so popular, and how much more sensible and practical it would be to work with the English landscape rather than against it.

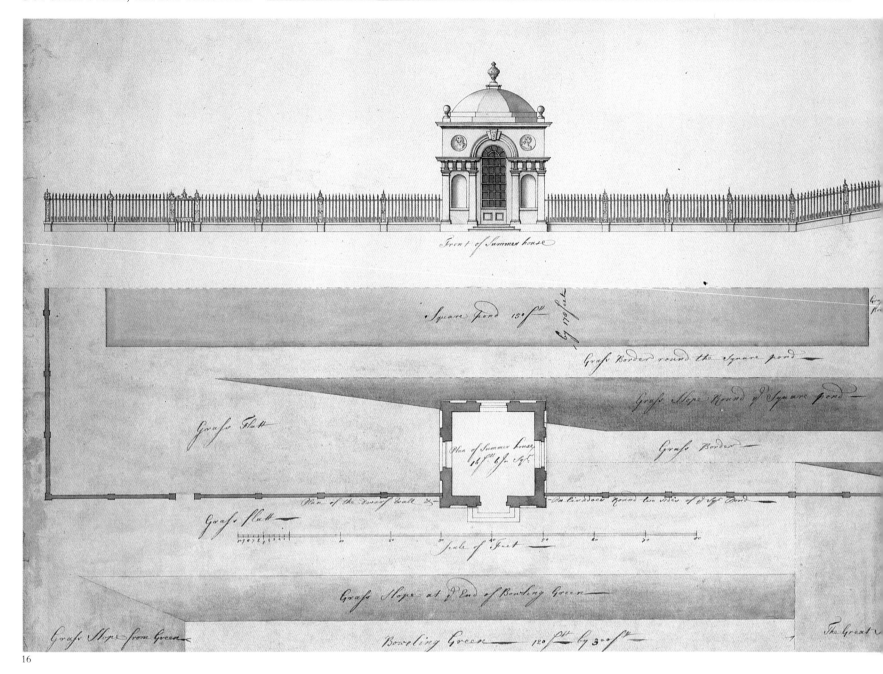

Front of Summer house

Square Pond 150 ft

Grass Border round the square pond

Grass Slope Round ye Square pond

Grass Flatt

Grass Border

Plan of Summer house 16 ft by 16 ft

Plan of the dwarf wall &

Palisddoes Round two sides of ye Sqre Pond

Grass flatt

Scale of Feet

Grass Slope at ye End of Bowling Green

Grass Slope from Green

The Great

Bowling Green 120 ft by 300 ft

16

16] WILLIAM HIORN 1712–76 and
DAVID HIORN d.1758

Plan and elevation of a summerhouse and rail

Gopsall Park, Leicestershire, before 1758
Pen with grey, green and brown washes
315 × 545 mm. /12⅜ × 21½ in.

This is undeniably the most beautiful of the Gopsall drawings, largely because of the elegance of the plan-drawing on the lower half of the sheet, which shows how the summerhouse is sited to look down upon the bowling green one way and the square pond in the opposite direction.

Like so many of the Gopsall drawings it is unsigned and undated, but is thought to belong to the main period of development in the garden of the 1750s and 60s.

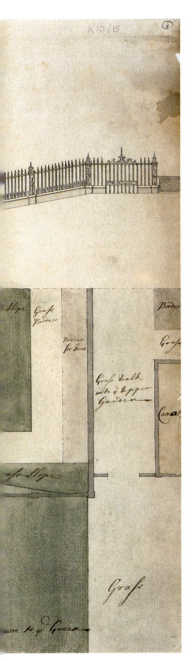

17

17] JAMES PAINE *c.*1717–89
Elevation of an open temple

Gopsall Park, Leicestershire, before 1758
Pen and sepia wash
365 × 264 mm. /14⅜ × 10⅜ in.

The drawing is signed by James Paine, who has left a space for the initial of his client, Charles Jennings (*sic*). The octagonal, domed temple was built on a hill (and still survives) in the park at Gopsall, dedicated in memory of Jennens' friend, Edward Holdsworth. It was also illustrated in Paine's *Plans, elevations and sections of Noblemen and Gentlemen's Houses* published in 1767.

18] WILLIAM HIORN *c.*1712–76 and
DAVID HIORN d.1758
Plan and elevation of an open temple

Gopsall Park, Leicestershire, before 1758
Pen, pencil and wash
465 × 255 mm. /18¼ × 10 in.

This temple by the Hiorn brothers for Charles Jennens is octagonal with a stepped dome topped with Roubiliac's

18

statue depicting *Religion*. This drawing, like so many of the Hiorn drawings, is undated; it appears to be an alternative to the temple by James Paine (no. 17). Jennens' idea was to build a classical temple in his park to commemorate his friend Edward Holdsworth. Whether he simply did not like this design, or whether he felt his friend warranted the work of a highly fashionable architect such as Paine, rather than his own good provincial men, we shall never know. But Paine's temple was built.

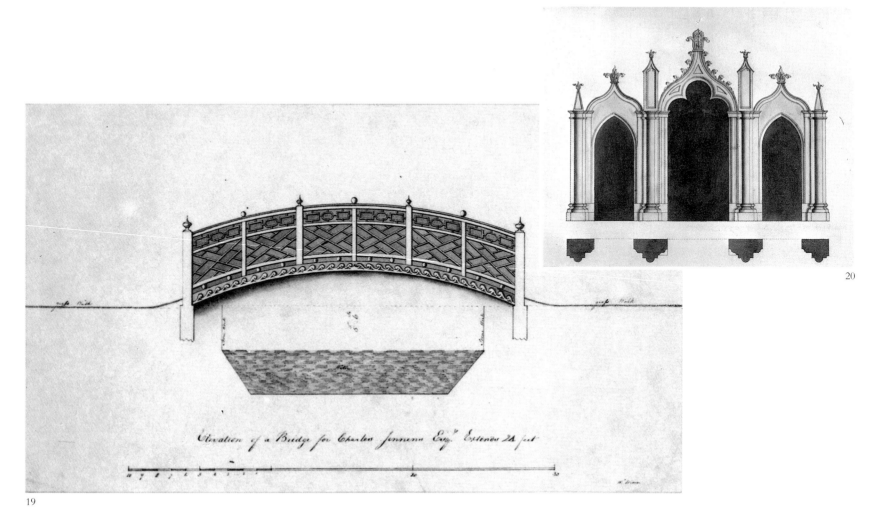

19

20

21

19] WILLIAM HIORN *c.*1712–76 and
   DAVID HIORN d.1758

Elevation of a bridge

Gopsall Park, Leicestershire, before 1758
Pen and wash
200×355 mm. $/7\frac{7}{8} \times 14$ in.

The bridge, above, extends twenty-four feet; its design, like the rail, is directly from Chippendale's *Director*. The use of pattern books for ideas is of course the reason for 'styles'. This Chinese Chippendale bridge design for Gopsall, a place out of the mainstream of design, offers a fresh insight into the spread of features we associate with the 'English landscape style'. In a countryside of isolated enclaves among rutted tracks and impassable woods, the emergence of what we so blithely call a national style was a miracle of perseverance and determination.

20] WILLIAM HIORN *c*.1712–76 and
   DAVID HIORN d.1758

A garden seat

Gopsall Park, Leicestershire, before 1758
Pen and wash
254 × 305 mm. /10 × 12 in.

A design from the last phase of the Hiorns' work at Gopsall,
this Gothick seat shows the influence of Batty Langley's *New
Principles of Gardening*. From this theorist and practitioner of
the 'Irregular' and the Gothick, both Jennens and his
architects would have learned of the value of surprise in the
garden. To come upon this fanciful structure in an evergreen
grove would certainly have been a surprise to Leicestershire
country squires and their ladies, whose eyes had only just
become accustomed to domed temples and pillared porticos.

21] WILLIAM HIORN 1712–76 and
   DAVID HIORN d.1758

Elevation of a Chinese rail

Gopsall Park, Leicestershire, before 1758
Pen, sepia pen and wash
155 × 385 mm. /6⅛ × 15⅛ in.

This drawing seems directly derived from Chippendale's
Director,[29] described as 'Chinese Railing . . . very proper for
gardens and other places . . .' Provincial architects, and busy
ones, like the Hiorns, could never travel or take time off to see
fashionable innovations. The pattern books, like
Chippendale's *Director*, enabled them to keep up with the
desires of perceptive clients like Jennens.

CIRENCESTER HOUSE, GLOUCESTERSHIRE

22] GEORGE HERBERT KITCHIN 1870–1951

Pope's Seat

Cirencester House, Gloucestershire, August 8 1908
Pencil sketch in sketchbook no. 19, England 1908
145 × 230 mm. /5¾ × 9 in.

Alexander Pope (1698–1744), prophet and pioneer of the
English landscape style, first visited Cirencester to advise his
admired Lord Bathurst, inspirer of *An Epistle*, in 1718. To
commemorate the friendship this classical temple was sited
next to the avenue they planted and named in the poet's
honour. The honour was mutual:

Oh teach us, Bathurst! *yet unspoil'd by wealth!*
That secret rare, between th' extremes to move
Of mad Good-nature, and of mean self-love.

22

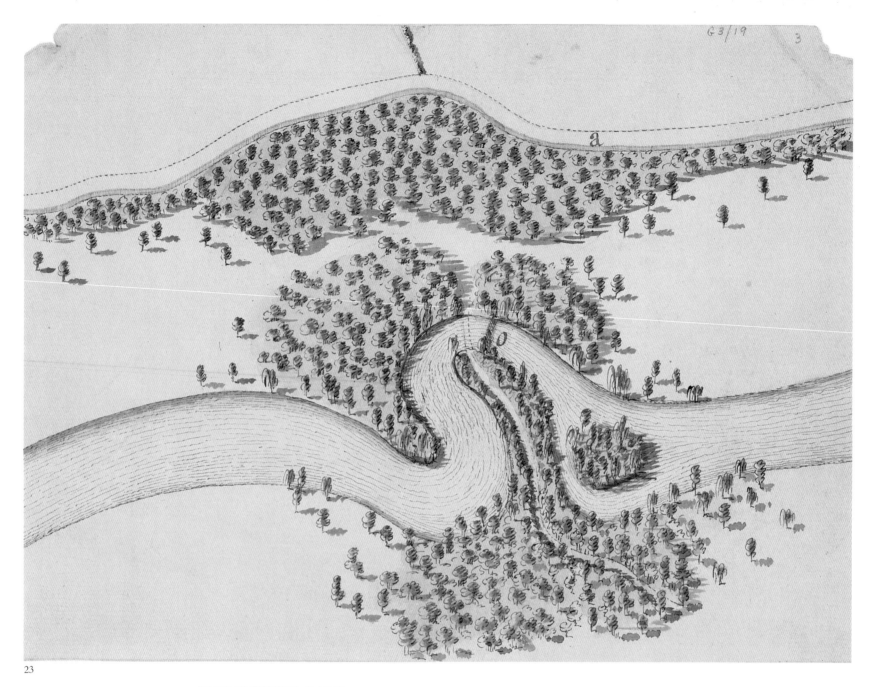

G3/19 3

23

UNIDENTIFIED PARK

23] LANCELOT 'CAPABILITY' BROWN 1716–83

Design for planting a river meander
c.1764

Pen and brown/grey wash
203 × 260 mm. /8 × 10¼ in.

This typically Brownian detail has strayed from his surviving known drawings. The letter *a* in red ink defines the fence line,

which was to be screen planted. The letter *o* in the river seems to mark a waterfall or dam, as well as the site for the proposed bridge.

The provenance of this drawing records its sale by the Earl of Bute in 1951, from where it came into the Collection. The 3rd Earl was Brown's patron and client, which suggests Luton Hoo in Bedfordshire as the site.[30] The bend of the river is distinctively extreme, but Brown rather liked to do this for dramatic effect; Blenheim and Rothley are other possible locations.

MILTON ABBAS, DORSET

24] Anonymous artist

Plan of Lord Milton's estate

Milton Abbas, Dorset, 1763
Pen and wash
400 × 330 mm. / 15¾ × 13 in.

This survey plan relates to Capability Brown's first visit to Milton Abbas in May 1763. The estate had been bought by Joseph Damer who had married a daughter of the Duke of Dorset and been created 1st Baron Milton in 1753. He had bought the remnants of a flourishing medieval township, with its streets, cottages, gardens, an inn and a school clustered around the ruins of the former abbey. Brown's first work was to make large plantations on the rising ground west and east of the stream valley, on the borders of this plan; the trees marked may be a surveyor's idea of such plantings (but certainly not Brown's).

The further value of the plan is as an illustration of the noted tendency of the eighteenth-century lord to oust mere ordinary mortals from his view. Lord Milton first employed, and unhappily, William Chambers, and then James Wyatt to build his new house on the site marked *The Abbey*. Then he wanted to clear out the villagers in his valley and allow the dammed waters of the stream to spread into a lake, as Brown had planned for him. Evidence from Brown's visits in the early 1770s suggests that he designed the picturesque, thatched model village that Lord Milton intended his cottagers to inhabit: at the bottom right corner of this plan there is a line marked *Stone Park Wall – Way to the New Town*. The reluctant cottagers, Messrs Harrison, Hams, Bingham, Martin et al still did not want to move, so Lord Milton enters the corridors of infamy as one of the lords who unleashed the pent-up waters by opening his dam to wash them away. The villagers had the last laugh; at first the lake did not work and the waters seeped away, though a large and impressive lake is there now. And, of course, everyone goes to Milton Abbas these days to admire the 'New Town' rather than his lordship's park.

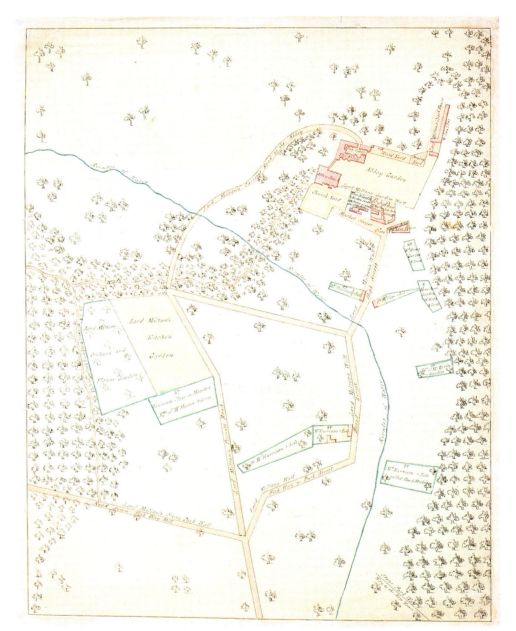

24

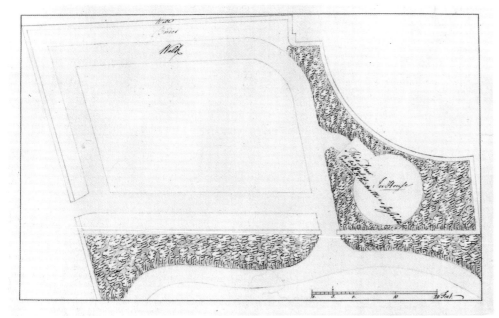

25

26] WILLIAM EMES (or EAMES) 1729–1803

Design for a park layout

Erlestoke, Wiltshire 1786.
Pen on vellum
635×641 mm. /$25 \times 25\frac{1}{4}$ in.

This drawing is inscribed *A Plan of the Park and Demesne Lands at Earlstoke the seat of Jos(hua) Smith Esqr with some Alterations by Wm Emes 1786.* The scale is in chains and the numbers refer to the following:

1. House and Offices.
2. The Church.
3. Kitchen Garden.
4. Flower Garden and Green House.
5. Farm yards.
6. Small Banqueting Room for Fishing.
7. Walk leading to –do.–
8. The Park.
9. Cow Pasture.
10. Arable Lands.
11. Remaining part of the Village with Gardens and Orchard.
12. Shrubbery walks around the Sheep pasture.
13. Approach Roads with small lodges.
14. The Improvements.
15. Temple.
16. Paddocks.
17. Nursery for Trees and common Garden Stuff.

Emes is now regarded as one of the most successful of the designers who continued the English landscape style after Capability Brown's death. Some sixty-five of his commissions are known, including Tixall, Staffordshire, Hawkstone Park, Shropshire, and the park at Powis Castle in Wales. This is the only drawing by Emes in the Collection and it seems that no great number of his drawings has survived. Dr Keith Goodway, who has made a study of Emes' works, thinks that his suggestions for Erlestoke were mostly carried out, though the park is now neglected and spoiled.[31]

25] LANCELOT 'CAPABILITY' BROWN
(attributed to) 1716–83

Plan of a garden layout and ice-house

Milton Abbas, Dorset, 1763
Pen and wash
241×381 mm. /$9\frac{1}{2} \times 15$ in.

Brown began working for Lord Milton at Milton Abbas in 1763, and made further visits ten years later. This finished and exact detail for the location of the ice-house would appear to be near the house; the inscription reads: *This Door to be put as much to the north as possible.* The ice, brought from the lake, would be packed for storage in the round part of the building, and the neck of the entrance packed with straw for insulation.

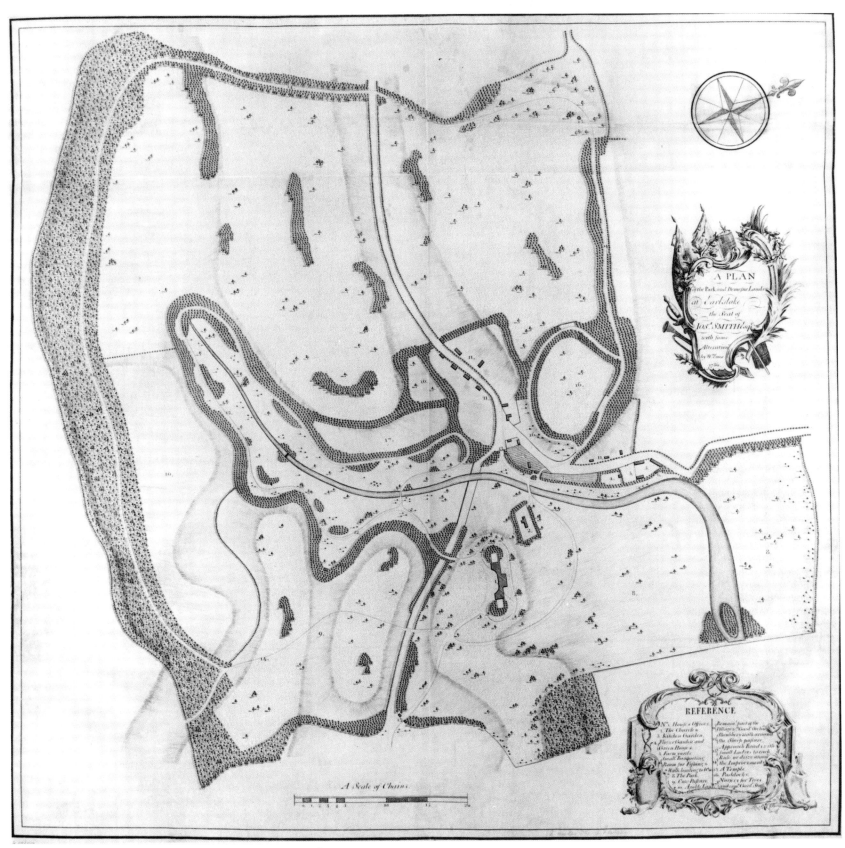

27

LANGLEY PARK, KENT

27] HUMPHRY REPTON 1752–1818

Prospect towards the river

Red Book for Langley Park, Beckenham, Kent, 1790
26 leaves bound in brown calf; watercolour
215×295 mm. /$8\frac{1}{2} \times 11\frac{5}{8}$ in.

This is one of Repton's early Red Books. Like many of its fellows it is actually bound in brown calf rather than red morocco, though the more glamorous name that he applied to the larger volumes has remained. This volume contains Repton's trade card, with his address—Hare Street, Romford, Essex—and the engraving of two surveyors at work beside a beautiful lake—which is to be made yet more beautiful by the band of improvers who are starting earthworks (fig. 1).

This first watercolour in the book (f.8) shows Langley Park with its river, a simple bridge and a classical temple; this illustration accompanies Repton's discussion of the *Situation, Advantages* and *Additional Advantages* which he puts before Sir Peter Burrell, Bart.

28] HUMPHRY REPTON 1752–1818

Agricultural landscape

Red Book for Langley Park, Beckenham, Kent, 1790
26 leaves bound in brown calf; watercolour
215 × 295 mm. /8½ × 11⅝ in.

This is folio 20 of the Red Book and illustrates the area of the park north of the avenue as agricultural landscape, i.e. as Repton found it. The outline of the flap of cartridge paper can be clearly seen. In Repton's day these flaps were called 'slides' (as some worked that way) and the guiding principle was revelation: first one saw the familiar view, as here, and then, in a trice, the mist cleared and the boring and old-fashioned, distasteful landscape disappeared.

29] HUMPHRY REPTON 1752–1818

Pastoral landscape

Red Book for Langley Park, Beckenham, Kent, 1790
26 leaves bound in brown calf; watercolour
215 × 295 mm. /8½ × 11⅝ in.

The same view, with the flap or slide lifted, reveals arable fields turned to pasture, planted with random groups of trees, and the lake – made by damming the river – has filtered into the lower ground. The pleasures of sailing have been introduced. The element of sleight of hand in Repton's use of the slide incited criticism from others, notably William Mason, the Rev. William Gilpin and John Claudius Loudon, but it is hard to read these criticisms without feeling that a tinge of envy weighted them: 'SLIDES, though used with the utmost possible accuracy and fairness,' wrote Loudon, 'are still liable to deceive', and, said William Mason, 'he alters places on Paper and makes them so picturesque that fine folks think that all the oaks etc. he draws on Paper will grow exactly in the shape and fashion in which he delineated them'.[32]

28

29

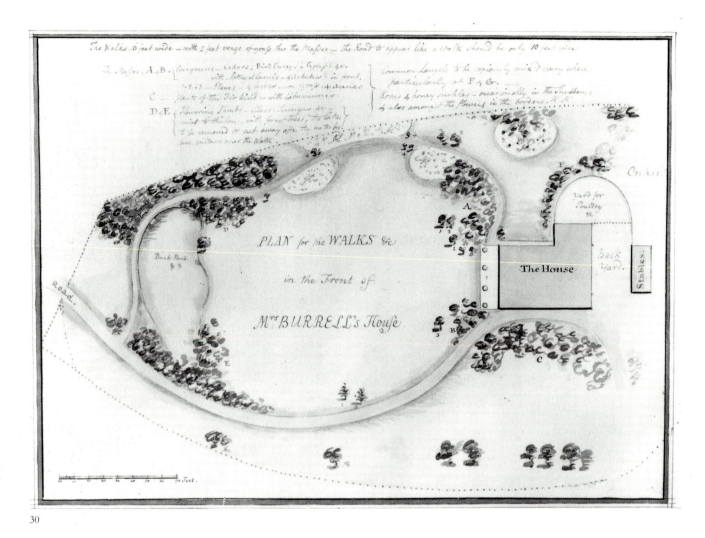

30

30] HUMPHRY REPTON 1752–1818

Plan for the walks

Red Book for Langley Park, Beckenham, Kent, 1790
26 leaves bound in brown calf; watercolour
215 × 295 mm. /8½ × 11⅝ in.

This is folio 11 of the Red Book and inscribed: *Plan for the Walks etc. in front of Mrs Burrell's House*. The key, written at the top, describes the evergreens that will frame the house, cedars, 'Bird Cherry', cypresses and Portugal laurel and Arbutus. *C* is a group of firs with laburnums. The *D* and *E* groups around the pond were to be scented lilacs mixed with forest trees, the latter to be felled when they grew too large. Repton wanted Common laurel 'copiously mixed' everywhere, and roses and honeysuckles occasionally combined with shrubs as well as in flower beds.[33]

31

31] HUMPHRY REPTON 1752–1818

The avenue

Red Book for Langley Park, Beckenham, Kent, 1790
26 leaves bound in brown calf; watercolour
215 × 295 mm. /$8\frac{1}{2}$ × $11\frac{5}{8}$ in.

A sepia washed oval vignette on folio 14 shows the avenue at
Langley Park, which already existed, well grown, when
Repton started work. His attitude to avenues was 'much
more liberal' than Brown's;[34] the latter swept them all away,
but Repton retained this one, as well as others at Nacton,
Tatton Park and Cobham. But he did recommend that it be
broken, i.e. certain trees removed to allow cross-views of
naturalistic planting within the park. This vignette shows
that even with the removal of some trees, the vista from the
garden would be retained.

32 a

SEZINCOTE HOUSE, GLOUCESTERSHIRE

32] HUMPHRY REPTON 1752–1818

Proposals for a view towards the south

Sezincote House, Gloucestershire, c. 1802
Pencil and grey wash
430 × 580 mm. /$16\frac{7}{8}$ × $22\frac{7}{8}$ in.

This fascinating drawing was found in the Sezincote Collection, purchased in 1957. It is known that Samuel Pepys
Cockerell was looking for a garden designer in the late 1790s,
and Repton wrote that he was at Sezincote just before
attending the Prince Regent at Brighton in 1805. Hence my
approximate dating of this drawing. It is inscribed: *View
towards the South – from the House*. The drawing is illustrated
in all its stages:

a] With both flaps down the house looks out on to the
   washing-line and the pig styes.
b] The left flap is lifted, and an ugly wing of the house, or
   outbuilding, removed; a glimpse of the pastoral park is
   revealed.
c] The right-hand flap is here removed and both washing-
   line and pigs have vanished, to be replaced by a flower
   garden and the clear view of the park. The farm buildings
   on the horizon have been castellated overnight!

32 b

32 c

33

Elevation of the Temple of Surya

Sezincote, Gloucestershire, *c*. 1810
Pencil, sepia pen and wash
203 × 324 mm. /8 × 12¾ in.

Thomas Daniell and his nephew William arrived in Calcutta in 1786 and travelled and sketched until they eventually returned to England in late 1793 or early 1794. On their return they spent thirteen years making 144 aquatints for six volumes on *Oriental Scenery* published between 1795 and 1808. 261 of their original drawings of temples, tombs, forts and landscapes are catalogued in the Collection and also to these ten designs by Thomas Daniell commissioned by Sir Charles Cockerell for his Indian garden at Sezincote. The special joy of these drawings, exquisite in their own right, is the additional knowledge that the reality of the Temple of Surya (Souriya) still graces the garden at Sezincote.

34

34] THOMAS DANIELL 1749–1840

Wall of mossy recesses

Sezincote, Gloucestershire, 1810
Pencil and coloured washes
133 × 229 mm. /5¼ × 9 in.

The mossy recesses were built on either side of the Temple of Surya and hold ornamental urns, of a funerary inspiration. The drawing shows how the earth was banked on top of the wall; it now grows ferns in abundance, bergenias and shrubs thus keeping the recesses dark, damp and grotto-like. Surya was a sun god, a minor Hindu deity, prayed to to stimulate the intellect of the worshipper.

35

35] THOMAS DANIELL 1749–1840
Frontal perspective of the Indian Bridge

Sezincote, Gloucestershire, 1810
Pen and coloured wash
216 × 311 mm. /8½ × 12¼ in.

The bridge is the subject of the first of three letters from Thomas Daniell to Sir Charles Cockerell, dated 12 December 1810. Thomas feels he is going to be 'a bore' and continues: 'I must mention a circumstance which unfortunately was omitted in my last – At Sezincot, I recommended, I still strongly recommend, the planting of Irish Ivy against the butments of the bridge and perhaps it may have escaped your memory. I write now in the hope of a little open weather, which would enable you to do in this season, thereby taking time by the forelock. The loss of a Season in vegetable concerns is a very serious thing you will readily allow'.

Sir Charles was clearly not too offended for Thomas records receipt of a turkey and hare 'in good order' at Christmas and on January 14 1811 congratulates him on his 'boldness in planting' and on the ivy which 'must turn out well'.[35]

A white Brahmin bull, Nandi, 'the happy one' and Shiva's favourite, can be seen sitting on the centre stone of the bridge parapet. Sir Charles Cockerell was particularly interested in the bulls, which were originally built of Coade stone, and of which there were several in the garden. There seems to have been some dispute between Sir Charles and Thomas Daniell about the siting of the bulls, especially on the bridge, and there are actually a pair on each parapet existing today. The Coade stone disintegrated so the present-day guardians of Sezincote are of cast iron.

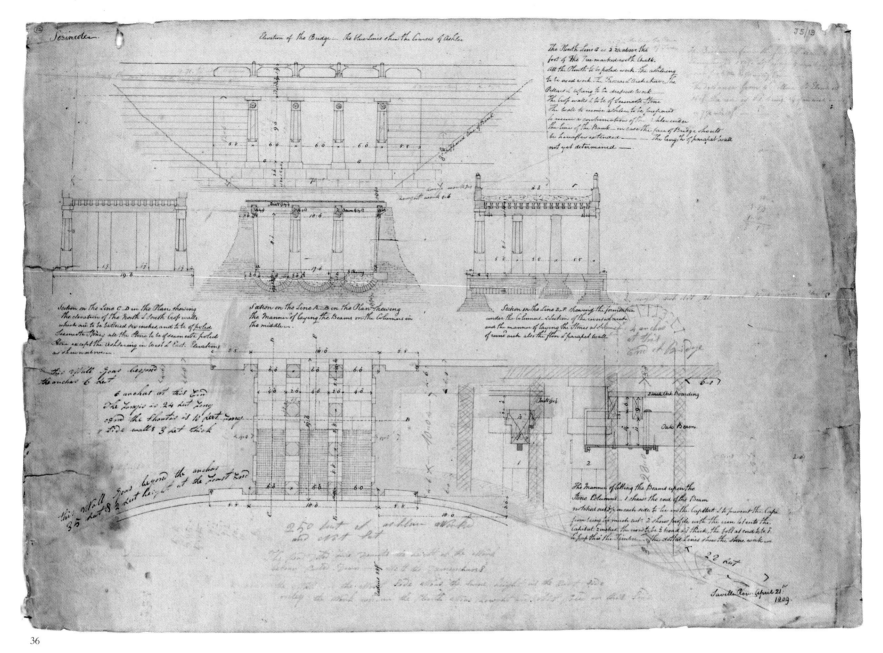

36] SAMUEL PEPYS COCKERELL c.1754–1827

Plan, section and elevation for an Indian bridge

Sezincote, Gloucestershire, 1809
Pen and wash
533 × 737 mm. /21 × 29 in.

This detailed and informative drawing shows well how the practical architect turned the artistic ideas of his nabob brother, Sir Charles Cockerell and his artist Thomas Daniell, into a well-constructed reality. The elevation at the top of the drawing is particularly striking as the bridge was drawn by Daniell (see no. 35). The sections and plan, minutely detailed, with full dimensions in feet and inches and notes on structure, turn the concept (a strange one for an English builder) into a working reality.

All the Sezincote material illustrated here (by Thomas Daniell, Humphry Repton and S.P.Cockerell) was purchased together by the RIBA in 1957. It is only a fraction of the design material for this Indian palace and its garden that must have once existed, but the range of material, illustrating the differing minds at work, offers a delightful insight into the creative processes of design.

37] SAMUEL PEPYS COCKERELL 1753–1827

Plan of a garden

Sezincote House, Gloucestershire, 1810
Pen and pencil
545 × 685 mm. /21½ × 27 in.

This pattern for flower beds for the north lawn at Sezincote is the clearest of three such sketches. Samuel Pepys Cockerell was a noted and capable architect; he built Daylesford, near Sezincote, for Warren Hastings, and converted his brother's Indian dreams into a well-constructed reality. Humphry Repton, who sketched garden ideas for the south front of the house (no. 32), noted that Samuel Pepys Cockerell was perfectly capable of dealing with the garden. Here he seems to be attempting an arrangement of beds, to be thickly planted with roses entwined with jasmines and honeysuckles, in the style of the designer of the latter part of the eighteenth century, Thomas Wright, who persisted with this garden-esque treatment around the house instead of the rolling greenery of the landscape style.

38

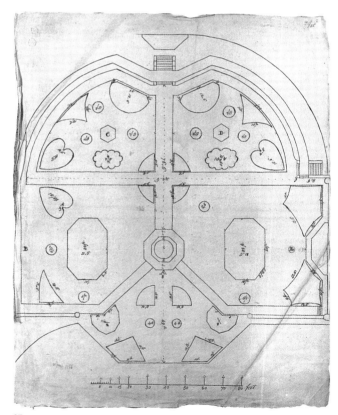

37

SHERINGHAM, NORFOLK

38] HUMPHRY REPTON 1752–1818

Prospect towards the sea

Red Book for Sheringham, Norfolk, 1812
36 leaves bound in red morocco; watercolour
450 × 340 mm. /17¾ × 13½ in.

One of the larger format volumes, with thirty-six leaves bound in red morocco. The inscription reads: *the Property of Abbot Upcher Esq. by H. Repton assisted in the Architecture by his son J. A. Repton* MDCCCXII. Sheringham is now thought to be Repton's masterpiece: he was very enthusiastic about the scheme, about working with his son, and about the kind of life he imagined that Mr and Mrs Upcher would lead in their delightful and romantic new park and garden. He begins: 'I cannot express the degree of satisfaction I have experienced while engaged in the digestion and arrangement of the following pages relating to Sheringham.'

This is the opening image of the book, the landscape-gardener's view of his client's land, with the sea beyond. His labourers are already on site and the transformation is about to begin.

View from the proposed Site looking towards the East.

39

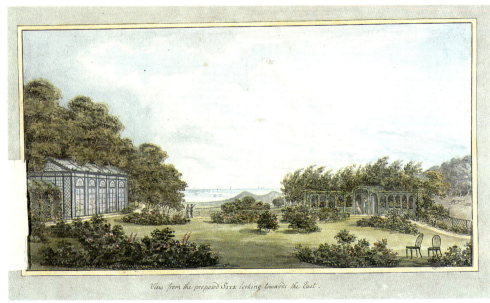

View from the proposed Site looking towards the East.

40

39] HUMPHRY REPTON 1752–1818

View from the proposed site

Red Book for Sheringham, Norfolk, 1812
36 leaves bound in red morocco; watercolour
450 × 340 mm. /17¾ × 13½ in.

Inscribed: *View from the proposed* SITE *looking towards the East.*
This is the view from the would-be house in its natural state,
before improvements, another of Repton's famous before
and after drawings, which he contrived by painting on the
flap of cartridge paper which can be seen in outline. As a note
on the previous Red Book, Langley Park (nos. 27–31)
records, some of Repton's contemporaries felt that the flap or
'slide' created false illusions and was misleading. But his
invention has been blessed by succeeding generations of
garden designers and landscape architects, because the task of
making a client understand and visualize the difference that
landform and planting can make, on any scale, has always
been the most difficult part of any commission.

40] HUMPHRY REPTON 1752–1818

The flower garden

Red Book for Sheringham, Norfolk, 1812
36 leaves bound in red morocco; watercolour
450 × 340 mm. /17¾ × 13½ in.

This is the same view as no. 39 with the flap raised to find that
Repton has painted in the transformation into the Upchers'
flower garden. Here he has included his most delightful
features, the basket-edged flower beds (as designed for the
Royal Pavilion in Brighton), an orangery and treillage
arbour, decked in flowers and carefully shelterd from the sea
breezes.

41] HUMPHRY REPTON 1752–1818

View of the house

Red Book for Sheringham, Norfolk, 1812
36 leaves bound in red morocco; watercolour
450 × 340 mm. /17¾ × 13½ in.

A closer view of the house proposed for Mr and Mrs Upcher,
inscribed: *South front with East front in perspective, an elevation,
a little richer.* Sadly, the house was not finished when Abbot
Upcher died in 1819, a year after Humphry Repton. The
interiors were finished in the 1840s and have been restored
and renovated in appropriate style within the last twenty-five
years.

South Front, with east front in perspective, an Elevation a little rich

41

Scene near the Temple, with a hint of the house on the site proposed distant about ¾ of a Mile.

42

42] HUMPHRY REPTON 1752–1818

Scene near the temple

Red Book for Sheringham, Norfolk, 1812
36 leaves bound in red morocco; watercolour
450×340 mm. $/17\frac{3}{4} \times 13\frac{1}{2}$ in.

Inscribed: *Scene near the Temple, with a hint of the house on the site proposed distance about* $\frac{3}{4}$ *mile*. Humphry and John Adey Repton designed the Upchers' house and began building it in 1813, while work in the park and gardens progressed concurrently. One of Repton's reasons for enjoying Sheringham so much was that Abbot Upcher shared the traditionally paternal and egalitarian attitude to the local community that Repton felt was disappearing from the English countryside. He recommended that the Upchers should receive the poor at the house and let them gather wood, that they should improve the local workhouse and organize community fishing matches on the beach.

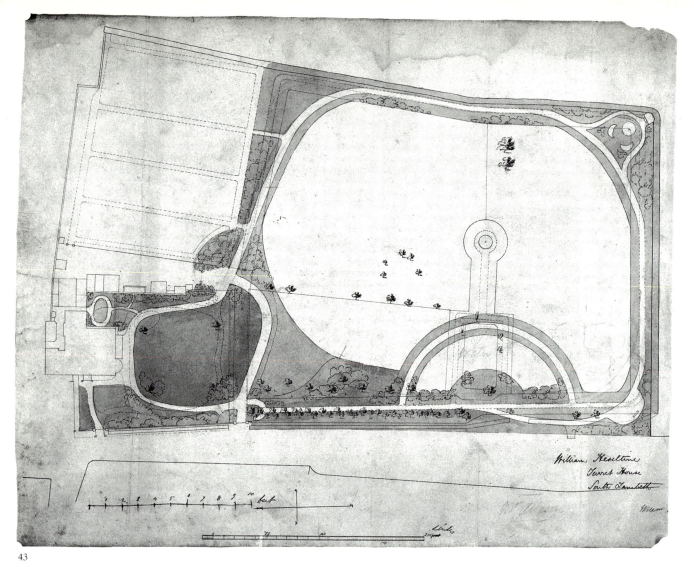

43

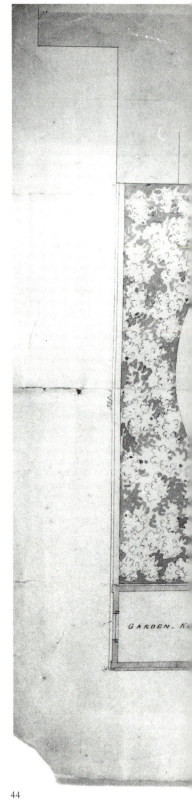

LAMBETH, LONDON

43] THOMAS ALLASON 1790–1852

Alterations to the garden

Turret House, South Lambeth, London
for William Heseltine, *c.*1830
Pen and wash
375 × 470 mm. /14¾ × 18½ in.

The house is on the left, with kitchen garden plots ranged
along inside the road wall. Allason is introducing serpentine
walks and shrubberies to soften a stilted and pedestrian layout
and these are shown by dotted lines. Whether the old
rectangular pool is to be replaced by the elegant semi-circle
of water is not clear, but the vast improvement in the quality
of design can be clearly seen.

RICHMOND, SURREY

44] THOMAS ALLASON 1790–1852

Plan of the Pleasure Grounds

Mr Irving's Mill at Richmond Gardens,
Richmond, Surrey, 1824
Pen and watercolour
349 × 495 mm. /13¾ × 19½ in.

A rather pleasing design in the transition from natural design
for large landscapes to the high formality of the coming
Victorian age. Thomas Allason had a busy career, was
sometime Surveyor to the Stock Exchange, and he designed
houses, furniture and gardens. His most notable garden
commission was to help the Earl of Shrewsbury lay out his
famous garden at Alton Towers between 1814 and 1827.

44

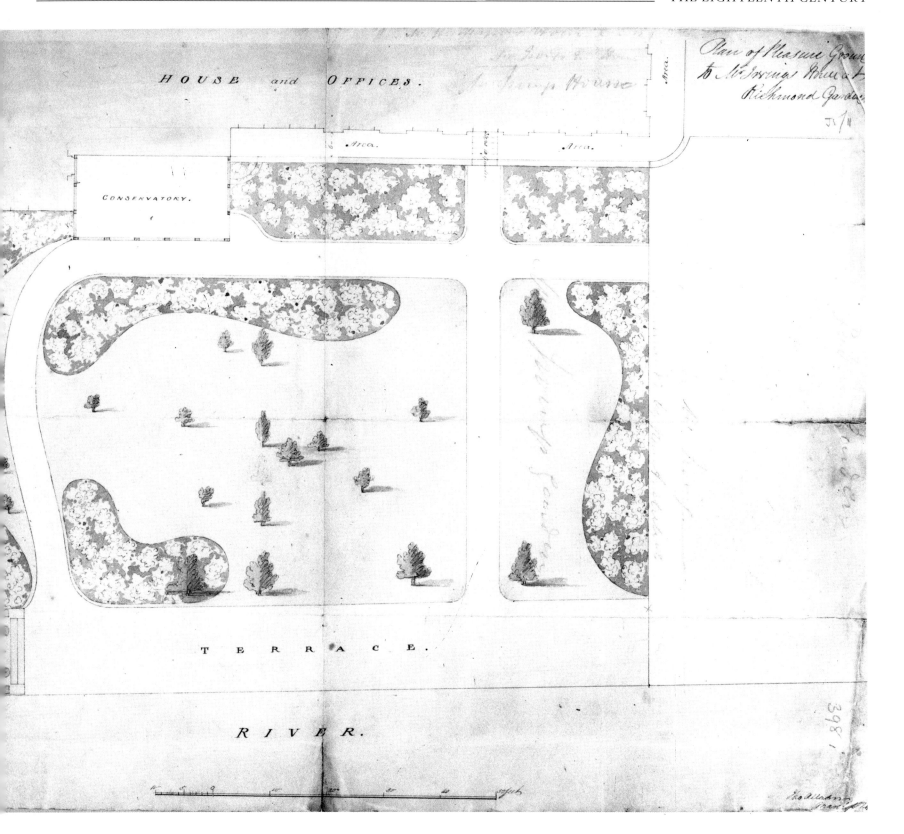

HOUSE and OFFICES.

CONSERVATORY.

Area.

Area.

Area.

Plan of Pleasure Ground
to Mr Irving House at
Richmond Garden

T E R R A C E.

R I V E R.

Bartlett del.   Deepdene Approach entrance

THE DEEPDENE, SURREY

45]   JOHN BRITTON 1771–1857

Approach Entrance

For 'Historical and descriptive account of The Deepdene',
Dorking, Surrey, 1825–6
Pencil and watercolour sketch by William Henry Bartlett,
1809–65
f.129 of bound volume
155 × 270 mm. /$6\frac{1}{8}$ × $10\frac{5}{8}$ in.

The Deepdene, in a naturally romantic setting of sandstone
hills just south of Dorking, had a mid-seventeenth-century
garden made by Charles Howard and admired by John
Evelyn. Thomas Hope (1769–1831), rich, aesthetic and a
collector of distinction, bought the estate in 1807 and made
his elaborate alterations and additions between 1817 and
1823. John Britton thus visited and recorded Deepdene's new
glory, taking with him the young artist William Bartlett on
his first major commission. The bound volume containing
Britton's hand-written *Historical and descriptive account* has
thirty-five of Bartlett's drawings tipped in, and five of these
of particular garden interest are reproduced here. This sketch
of the *Approach Entrance* emphasizes the dramatic setting of
the house, and shows Thomas Hope's neo-classical taste
which was much celebrated and talked-about.

46

46] JOHN BRITTON 1771–1857

View through a parapet

For 'Historical and descriptive account of The Deepdene',
Dorking, Surrey, 1825–6
Pencil and watercolour sketch by William Henry Bartlett,
1809–65
f.131 of bound volume
160 × 250 mm. /6¼ × 9⅞ in.

The neo-classical parapet around the roof of The Deepdene
allowed the views from 'the leads' of the surrounding
countryside to be framed in an interesting way. Britton's
hand-written description, dedicated to Mrs Hope, opens
with the words: 'Madam, if contrasts and novelties constitute
some of the most attractive charms of life, it must be
admitted that the Scenery and location of the Deepdene
afford these in an eminent degree'.

Britton continues to praise the country in contrast to 'the
ball-room glare and crowd', 'the busy hum of men' and the
paved streets of London. He devotes Chapter One to the
scenic charms of Surrey, which then included a rural
Clapham, Tooting and Epsom, with The Deepdene as almost
its farthest outpost of cultured society. His second chapter
was to contain his description of the scenery and presumably
the garden at Deepdene, but large parts of both Chapters
One and Two were never written. Chapter Three is on the
early history of the site and Chapter Four sings the praises of
some notable owners, mostly Howards of the Norfolk
family. Unfortunately neither Chapter Five on the house and
its contents, nor the final chapter on Dorking and the
surrounding places, were written. Despite Mr Britton's lapse,
The Deepdene is well documented (very little except the
natural beauty remains), and the full story has been told by
David Watkin in *Thomas Hope and the Neo-Classical Idea*.

47

47] JOHN BRITTON 1771–1857

The kitchen garden

For 'Historical and descriptive account of The Deepdene',
Dorking, Surrey, 1825–6
Pencil and watercolour sketch by William Henry Bartlett,
1809–65
f.133 of bound volume
135 × 220 mm. /$5\frac{1}{4}$ × $8\frac{5}{8}$ in.

John and Jane Loudon visited The Deepdene in August 1829
and extracts from their journal make up in part for Britton's
unfinished text. The Loudons expressed their agreement
with the prevailing opinion of Deepdene with their opening
sentence: 'This is a place which presents but little food for the
critic, since it contains so much beauty'.[36] The one place they
did criticize was this kitchen garden, it was 'in want of high
keeping' and its paths of sand and gravel would be better
paved because of the heavy wear and 'incessant' rain. It rained
for the whole of their visit. Perhaps the rain and disarray also
caused William Bartlett to lose his enthusiasm for this sketch,
in which the trees appear to be windswept and the garden has
the blowsy touch of late summer.[37] This is the only sketch of
the kitchen or fruit gardens in the Britton volume and it gives
a glimpse of the delights that the Loudons enjoyed – a fine
specimen of Mr Barclay's scarlet thistle, American and
English cranberries 'doing remarkably well in beds of dry
peat', peaches in 'low Dutch pits' being harvested between
the hothouse and open air varieties, and forty-nine species of
Hibiscus in a special botanic stove house, which may be that
sketched here.

48

48] JOHN BRITTON 1771–1857

Design for a conservatory

For 'Historical and descriptive account of The Deepdene',
Dorking, Surrey, 1825–6
Pencil and watercolour sketch by William Henry Bartlett,
1809–65
f. 149 of bound volume
155 × 225 mm. /6⅛ × 8⅞ in.

John and Jane Loudon describe the conservatory as follows:
'The conservatory is highly ornamental from the style of its
architecture, the free growth of the plants, the fine disposition of the climbers, the exterior approach through a
terraced garden of orange trees and exotics . . . In front of the
conservatory is a plantation of orange trees in pots sunk in the
ground; and of different descriptions of green-house plants,
chiefly from the Cape of Good Hope and New Holland,
turned out of the pots into the soil, in order to grow and
flower freely during the mild season . . .'[38]

49] JOHN BRITTON 1771–1857

View from the entrance

For 'Historical and descriptive account of The Deepdene',
Dorking, Surrey, 1825–6
Pencil and watercolour sketch by William Henry Bartlett,
1809–65
f. 155 of bound volume
190 × 270 mm. /7½ × 10⅝ in.

This final view is of part of the conservatory and one of the
sculpture galleries with more of their terrace gardens and
beds of exotics taking the summer air. John Claudius Loudon
recommends this Deepdene practice to all gardeners with
hothouses, saying that turning-out and bedding-in the
acacias, and other exotic plants, makes them more likely to
survive the winters. He adds a note on a less attractive aspect
of the garden: 'Snakes and adders are occasionally seen in the
ground here; but Mr Woods (the head gardener) has nearly
extirpated them, by giving 3d for each of the former, and 6d
for the latter, to his men'.[39]

49

3
THE NINETEENTH CENTURY
Victorian Formal Gardens

The English find it very difficult to love Victorian gardens. It is as if the last resentment of those harsh Victorian virtues laid on with such a heavy hand lies hidden in dusty shrubberies of laurel and bamboo and gaudy beds of heliotrope and picotees. And it is in part that the Victorian garden arose, like some pampas-cockaded phoenix from the ashes of rebellion against the eighteenth-century landscape park: the Victorians destroyed our dream of rural life in Capability Brown's England and supplanted it with their smoky cities. The fact that we have to go on using their railways, sewage systems and conservatories only makes it rankle more. But these are vestigial ghosts, and perhaps the most real reason for Victorian gardens being out of fashion is that, until very recently, they lacked a champion. The two best books on the subject have a gap of thirty-four years between them. The first of these, is Geoffrey Taylor's *The Victorian Flower Garden* of 1952; at the same time as John Betjeman was teaching love through laughter for Victorian buildings, his friend Geoffrey Taylor was doing the same for gardens, with this delightful small volume, another on nineteenth-century gardeners and with talks on the BBC's *Third Programme*. Unfortunately he died soon after his book was published, aged only 55,[1] and Victorian gardens have had to wait until 1986 for a new protagonist's study of the subject. Brent Elliott, most appropriately Lindley Librarian to the Royal Horticultural Society in London, had probably the richest source of all for primary and published material on his subject to draw on, and his book *Victorian Gardens* is indispensable to a new understanding. But the RIBA is a thoroughly Victorian institution in foundation too, and the architects of the day played a characteristically assertive role in garden-making, so the Drawings Collection is also rich in this period. Some of them are presented here to elicit some additional understanding of the kind of English gardens that reigned supreme after the death of Humphry Repton and before the enlightenment of the Arts and Crafts Movement.

Fairly early in the introductory chapter to *Victorian Gardens*,

Brent Elliott adopts his motto: 'Gardens are works of art rather than of nature'. He further explains, 'No theme is more important, no sentiment so regularly expressed in the Victorian literature on gardening, than this affirmation of the artistic and unnatural character of the garden'.[2] The sentiment was originally Humphry Repton's, so it will be both interesting and appropriate when following it down these Victorian decades, to begin with one of his last and favourite commissions.

When Repton paid his first recorded visit to the Earl of Bridgewater's Ashridge in Hertfordshire in March 1813 he found James Wyatt's Gothic palace rising from the remains of a thirteenth-century monastery, set in a large and splendid Capability Brown park. The Earl wanted gardens immediately around his new house, and Repton planned several small enclosures on virtually flat ground, including a rosary in a circle of rose-covered trellis, which was illustrated in his last book, *Fragments* of 1816. Repton presented his Red Book later in 1813, and the architect James Wyatt died in the same year. The consequent delay meant that Repton was unable to supervise his garden; he became seriously ill in March 1815 and did little travelling afterwards, dying three years later. Just at this time Jeffry Wyatville, James Wyatt's nephew, who had taken over the building at Ashridge, was beginning on the garden, and the drawings here are his.[3]

The Wyatt family drawings in the Collection merit a volume of the published catalogue to themselves; in his introduction, Derek Linstrum says that 'at a conservative estimate' the family produced twenty-five architects, eleven surveyors, eight builders, five sculptors and three painters.[4] (A typically Victorian enterprise!) Ashridge was an important commission, James Wyatt's best surviving Gothic building, though it was to be eclipsed by Windsor Castle in Jeffry Wyatville's career; the Collection has over four hundred drawings for the house and garden, and these garden drawings are typical of the attention to detail they contain.

Wyatville put Repton's rosary on the ground almost as he designed it and surrounded it with a yew hedge; it remains there today. It was probably originally planted with the 'old' Victorian favourite roses, moss, centifolia and damask strains, sweetly scented, with camellia-like flowers, such as the little Portland Rose. Repton had intended a central fountain and the Wyatville drawings, fine watercolours, are illustrated here. The orangery, for which Wyatville's plan shows details of the pipe runs for the heating, was built as part of the private east wing of the house, where the 7th Earl and his family slept, leaving the main house free for weekend parties of thirty guests or more. They would all have been fascinated by the Monk's Garden, which Wyatville built to the south-west of the house in the angle of the walls between the Monk's Barn and the dairy yard; it is interesting that Repton proposed the site for this garden farther east, but Wyatville wanted to avoid digging up some of the monastic ruins and so chose his site. In doing this he came up against the problem of the dairy yard (which Repton had probably foreseen, and knowing of his attitude at Sezincote (no. 32), he would probably have swept away) and had to devise the elaborate Gothic details for the wall, gateway and seat (nos 56–7), to deflect the minds of those in the garden from such bucolic happenings. The gate in the wall has a pull for opening on the garden side only, absolutely *no* access for dairymaids!

Wyatville entered greatly into the monastic spirit of the garden at Ashridge. The Monk's Garden was set out in four square plots with a central 'martyr's cross' type of monument; the box edged beds were crammed with cannas, heliotrope, fuchsias, iresine, pelargoniums and tropaeleums, and the arcades hung with wisteria, clematis and ivies. On special days, the gardeners were on duty in monastic garb.

Further additions to the garden at Ashridge were made throughout the nineteenth century. Sir Matthew Digby Wyatt built the Fernery, for which some of the drawings are illustrated, for Lord Brownlow in 1854; the puddingstone hillocks which were covered with ferns and mosses still survive around it. Fern-hunting was a mid-century Victorian craze so the Brownlows were well in the van. The Gothic palace and its garden stayed splendid into the twentieth century, becoming particularly attractive as one of the homes of the 3rd Lord Brownlow and his lovely wife, formerly Lady Adelaide Talbot, who was one of the coterie of Souls. After the First World War Ashridge was bought by Urban Broughton as a gift to the Conservative Party; it is now Ashridge Management College, and though new buildings and gardens have been added and the extent of the gardens is reduced from its heyday, many of Repton and Wyatville's features remain.

Before going any farther into the nineteenth century it is important to stop for a moment, and consider the effect of the death of Humphry Repton upon the world of garden and landscape design. Ashridge, like the Royal Pavilion at Brighton, both important commissions at the peak of his eminence, were for large enclosed gardens, and this was the way his work was moving when he became finally ill and died in March 1818. Repton's great skill had been both his understanding of the larger landscape, and especially his artistry at painting it, before and after, to represent his proposed improvements. As the nineteenth century grew older, not only were there less great park areas to be 'improved', but the taste in change had become much more romantic, as at Deepdene, or even wildly exotic, as at the 15th Earl of Shrewsbury's Alton Towers being made between 1814–27. There was no one to succeed Repton's combined skills as artist and landscape gardener, and, as he had feared, the art of expressing design intentions over large areas of land, as he and Brown and Emes had done, would not be perpetuated. Large-scale design was now to be done straight-from-the-shoulder, on the ground, as the imaginative Earl was doing it at Alton Towers, standing at the head of a valley and dictating where the trees should be felled and rhododendrons or alpine meadows planted, and siting his buildings, his three-storey pagoda-fountain and Swiss cottage for a blind harper, by pushing his toiling gardeners carrying wooden mock-ups this way and that. The scale of design now drops to large gardens, with the architect mostly used to design buildings in the romantic landscapes.

This is borne out in the way Thomas Allason (1790–1852), not a notable figure in the garden world, is represented in the Collection. His two drawings illustrated, for Turret House at Lambeth and Mr Irving's Mill at Richmond, show pleasure ground gardens of serpentine walks around lawn and shrubberies following firmly on from Repton's plan for the surroundings of Mrs Burrell's house at Langley Park (no. 31). Allason had trained in the office of William Atkinson, the architect employed by Thomas Hope at Deepdene; perhaps he had visited Deepdene and seen 'romantic designing' in progress there? He was also to help the Earl of Shrewsbury at Alton Towers but as this is only a known-fact, and not supported by drawings, Allason slips out of

THE ROSARY AT ASHRIDGE

London·Published Feb. by J.Taylor

Fig. 14] The Rosary Garden for Ashridge, Hertfordshire,
designed by Humphry Repton and published in
Fragments on the Theory and Practice of Landscape Gardening, 1816.

gardening fame. He probably did a great deal at Alton Towers, but *not* great drawings, and I feel his case is a salutary reminder of how architects, like so many working gardeners, are often overlooked and underacknowledged.

The Papworth Collection provides another illustration of our all-too-easily distorted impression of early nineteenth-century design. John Buonarotti Papworth (1775–1847) as his name implies, was a colourful figure, sometime architect to the King of Württemburg who came to England to work for merchant princelings like the club-owner and wine shipper John George Fuller, for whom he designed Leigham Court at Streatham. The drawings for Leigham Court, nos. 70–71, represent Papworth here, but I do not feel they do him justice. The fault is partly mine; faced with 'the Papworth cabinet, its eight drawers crammed with (over two and a half thousand drawings) many of them brittle, dirty and badly-damaged'. These heart-felt words belong to the editor and cataloguer of the Papworth Collection, George McHardy, expressed at the outset of his 'daunting task'; there is really no excuse for my sentiments, except that the Papworth drawings are fragile and difficult, and it would clearly take long hours to achieve a full assessment of their gardening implications. However, George McHardy's introduction to his catalogue volume, reads like an adventure story, ripe inspiration for a novel on the sub-culture of leghorn hat makers, wine merchants, Members of Parliament and railway lords who were building Victorian England.[5] Papworth's commissions for Basildon Park, the splendid John Carr home of the Morrisons; for Cally House, Kirkudbrightshire and his fountain designed for Kirby Hall, deserve careful study. His published works on *Rural Residences*.[6] of 1812, and most importantly, *Hints on ornamental gardening: consisting of a series of designs for garden buildings &c*, of 1823, could be related to his real work for a much greater understanding of middle-class Victorian taste and design; perhaps now that Victorian gardens are returning to favour some faithful pilgrim will undertake this journey?

At least there is no chance of underestimating Papworth's almost exact contemporary, John Claudius Loudon (1783–1843); his staggering output, 'a monumental pile of first-rate books' says Geoffrey Taylor, and the devoted eulogies of his much younger wife Jane, have seen to that. Loudon *was* early Victorian gardening; no writer on the subject can avoid including him and a short paragraph here cannot do him justice. He was the son of a farmer, trained in horticulture, and he

Fig. 15] *Portrait of John Claudius Loudon* by John Linnell (1792–1882).

amassed a knowledge of all kinds of gardening and landscape planning; he was a workaholic, continually dogged by ill-health but he never lost his passion for botany and flowers, his curiosity about new plants, nor his belief in his own tastes and methods. In his writings and opinions he was highly critical, generous in his praise – as of Deepdene – and equally certain of his distaste – he called the Earl of Shrewsbury's Alton Towers the work of a 'morbid imagination' in his *Encyclopaedia of Gardening* of 1822. Reading the vast Loudon literature is a life's work, so that it was with some relief that I found only one commission, an exceptionally fine one, in the Collection. His drawings for Kiddington House were almost his last effort, done with the help of a draughtsman, and accompanied by a characteristically schoolmasterly set of instructions. Largely though, the instructions are sound good sense and for the health of the plants; his first priority was for flowers and scents, with roses everywhere, pillar or climbing centifolias on an arcade of hoops, with plenty of light and air for the flowers, bushes of tiny moss roses packed into flower baskets, and standard-roses set into beds of sweet-smelling mignonette, an annual which allowed the beds to be thoroughly 'cleaned' and fertilized each season. Kiddington shows his interest in the plant hunters' trove, for American kalmias, azaleas and *Magnolia acuminata* (the Cucumber Tree, after the shapes of its young fruit) and *Magnolia tripetala* (the Umbrella Tree) with scented cream-coloured flowers, all his special suggestions. But perhaps the plant-hunters did not always supply full information: when planting a Cedar of Lebanon and Deodar Cedar in the *same* circle, or even the Deodar surrounded by its fence, did he really realize just how big they would grow?[7]

The Loudon plans for Kiddington House (nos. 67–9) promise Mortimer Ricardo a delightful garden; with the growth and luxuriance of the roses and mignonettes, some hollyhocks and lilies added, this could be Corisande's garden, the flowery retreat of Disraeli's heroine in *Lothair*.

As a contrast to such romance, Edward Blore (1787–1879) is represented here by the working part of the gardener's estate. His only garden design drawings in the Collection are in two volumes of 460 sheets of details for the house and garden of Worsley Hall near Manchester, for Lord Francis Egerton, 1st Earl of Ellesmere, between 1839–45. This is one of the earliest instances in the Collection of the architect dealing with every detail of what may be called 'the domestic back-room' design, for stove houses, the melon pits and the gardeners' living quarters. They are included to emphasize the importance, that was to grow with the century, of the new breed of Head Gardeners, who ruled this cockpit of their kingdom, as well as the garden in general, with all the power embodied in the supplier of the necessities of life; grapes and nectarines, asparagus and strawberries. The Victorians were practical and hedonistic enough to see domestic design as money well spent.[8]

Edward Blore was a romantic figure, introduced to fame by being 'discovered' by Sir Walter Scott and commissioned to build Abbotsford in 1816. He went on to even greater things, working at Lambeth Palace, Hampton Court and Buckingham Palace, and his garden work was often taken care of by William Andrews Nesfield (1793–1881). It is with Blore in the back-ground that Nesfield comes forward as the designer of the spectacular, but sadly not executed, gardens for Buckingham Palace as it was re-modelled for Queen Victoria and Prince Albert in the late 1840s. Nesfield began as a soldier, serving with Wellington in the Peninsular War, then turned watercolour artist and painter of cascades; thus his scroll patterns, *broderie* in box hedges and coloured gravels were subject to his purely painterly design skills, and were as effective on the ground as on paper. He had designed some elaborate parterre patterns for Blore's Worsley Hall, (see fig. 16), and with the help of Blore, and on the evidence of his designs for vistas and parterres around the Palm House at Kew Gardens, that he was working on with Decimus Burton, it was quite natural that he should go to the Palace. Nesfield's written submission to HRH Prince Albert and the Commissioners for the Improvement of Buckingham Palace accompanies the lovely watercolour drawings, and provides an interesting background to the design. The proposed gardens were to stand right and left, i.e. south and north, on the new east front of the Palace, with the dividing road in the centre leading directly from the Mall. The gardens, two large *parterres de broderie* aligned to two canals with cascading fountains, exactly represented the best of Nesfield's artistic skills; in his 'Remarks concerning the Gardens' he adds history and allegory: 'The most requisite features however are Fountains, which should be on the largest scale admissable, in order to avoid the common-place character so frequently observed both in public and private gardens. The intention is to introduce such artistic designs, as will create a National interest; hence the Sculpture on the South garden might represent the Navy, and that of the North, the Army, and each of the great divisions of the Garden might be occupied by Statues of the Sovereigns of England'.[9]

The South or Queen's Garden has Queen Victoria's initials in box, with further box scrolls, on a background of Derbyshire spar chippings, pounded red bricks and Kensington gravels. Prince Albert's North parterre would match. The trees were to be limes, though 'Cedars of Lebanon would be more desirable but none of these conifers will thrive in the climate of London'. Undoubtedly Nesfield meant the smoky, polluted air. And, as he had indicated, the fountains were symbolically important, set in oblong basins, 425 feet long on pedestals 'for semi-colossal statues of British Sovereigns [arranged chronologically with the Queen's pedestal having the earlier sovereigns] attached to the kerb of the Basin at intervals'.

The fountains themselves have a monumentality only the Victorians could achieve: 'Fountains, 35 ft high, to represent Britannia on the apex of a rock directing Plenty to diffuse her gifts over the Globe, which rests on the shoulders of Atlas, attended by Commerce and Neptune'. Prince Albert's Fountain was to represent St George and the Dragon, with Father Thames below flanked by Fame and Victory. The rocks were to be rough-hewn grey granite, the figures of bronze and the animals in red granite for 'a desirable variety of colour'. The final touch to each garden was a seventy-foot-high obelisk surmounted by a 'burnished gilt ball' to provide perspectives from St James's Park. Victoria's obelisk was to be engraved with naval victories and Albert's with land victories.[10]

Nesfield's intentions, obviously fulfilling his brief from Prince Albert and the Commissioners, were for a garden to outshine anything in Europe or even Elizabethan England in Mannerist homage to the Monarch and her Nation. But in this instance the Monarch did not agree with her beloved Consort and preferred to see the groves of St James's Park from her windows, and so the gardens were not made; the Victoria Memorial stands on their proposed site now.

These are the only drawings by William Andrews Nesfield in the Collection; they were presented by the Architectural Association in 1953, having come from the Ministry of Works, where presumably they had lain for a hundred years after the Queen's rejection. Nesfield's influence will be seen in the later drawings for Coombe Abbey (nos. 82–4).

Nesfield's name has been commonly linked with that of Charles Barry (1795–1860) in the context of Victorian gardens, but Brent Elliott dismisses this 'partnership' as a myth and Nesfield's name certainly does not occur in connection with the Barry drawings.[11] Charles Barry made an extensive Grand Tour of the Mediterranean countries when he was in his early twenties which inspired his taste for Italianate architecture. He began practice as a Gothicist and was knighted by the Queen in 1852 for his work on the Houses of Parliament, but he is most famous for his Italianate Pall Mall palaces, the Traveller's Club, 1830, and the Reform Club, eight years later, and these buildings set the style for his gardens. Barry, in the words of John Betjeman, sounds likeable, unselfconscious and expansive, 'in the old architectural tradition—self-educated, a demon for work, an artist and a visionary'.[12] His gardens rather conform to these personal qualities, and it seems likely that Barry was steady and consistent too, for his gardens are; whether on the flat, like Trentham, or on a hill, as Shrubland Park, (see fig. 17), they are unmistakeably his gardens. They all have the direct symmetry, the echelons of heavy balustrades topped with vases, the stately stairs and their every level space embroidered with circles and segments of water, coloured gravels, flowers and sentry-like evergreens.

The Barry drawings in the Collection are mostly for his great buildings. His expansive personality seems to have affected his office management, and he allowed his assistants to take sketches and tracings of commissions they had worked on away with them; one also feels that his heavy workload and his generosity led to the dispersal of drawings, as with his alterations and gardens for Dunrobin Castle for the Duke of Sutherland; there his preliminary designs of 1844 were found to be based on inaccurate survey work, and they were corrected and the work supervised by a seemingly self-appointed *locum*, a Mr Leslie of Aberdeen. Though Barry approved work done in his name, sheaves of drawings obviously went northwards and never returned. In two cases the hauls of two of his assistants have been returned by their families, and many of the garden drawings in the Collection are actually tracings made by James Murray or Octavius Barrett when they worked in Barry's office.[13]

Under these circumstances the coverage of Barry's work is patchy and not a little perverse. There are no drawings for his great terraces at Cliveden, and the magnificent scheme painted for Drumlanrig Castle was not carried out. There are no drawings for Shrubland Park, one of his best gardens, and the scheme he planned for Clumber Park was not carried out. (Barry was frequently dismissed as being too expensive). The thirty drawings of ornamental details for Trentham: for balustrades, vases, pavilions and gates – even the house for the guardian of the ornamental birds – are tracings made by James Murray, but at least the balustrade detail for Kingston Lacy (no. 230) is an office tracing which has been signed by Barry himself. Eleven of the twelve Harewood House garden drawings are tracings by Murray, and the twelfth is by Octavius Barrett.

Perhaps Barry's inability to sit patiently in his office and draw and then look after his drawings, is balanced by his ability to build well, and to last. Cliveden, Shrubland Park, Trentham (now devoid of its house), Kingston Lacy and Harewood House still show their Barry gardens off, largely to his credit, and they are as apt expressions of their exuberant age as the Albert Hall or Tower Bridge.

Brent Elliott reveals how well Barry got on with three great Head Gardeners, George Fleming at Trentham, John Fleming at Cliveden and Donald Beaton at Shrubland Park. Cool heads were required, for this is where Victorian gardening takes off: George Fleming arrived at Trentham in 1841 to carry out Barry's designs and his first task was to design and install a drainage system for the flat parterre terraces between the house and the lake. Over the next ten years he turned the parterres into dazzling demonstrations of the art of bedding out: harmonies, contrasts, 'the graceful blending of the trailing with the erect species' with thousands upon thousands of little lobelia, petunia, verbena, calceolaria, *Salvia splendens*, nemophila, alyssum, clarkia, snapdragons, and candytufts. The 'ribbon border' was a *tour de force*, long and thin and occupied with three continuous rows of colour for their whole length: 'The first on each side of the walk is blue; the second yellow; and the third, on one side is scarlet, and on the other, white . . . the following are the plants: *Nemophila insignia*, for blue; *Calceolaria rugosa* for yellow; and the Frogmore geranium, for scarlet'.[14].

At Shrubland Park, George Fleming's great rival, Donald Beaton, was creating striking effects beside Barry's great staircase; the balustrades were topped with hundreds of pots of scarlet pelargoniums, and the slope was planted as a kind of evergreen wilderness, with pyramidal evergreen forms rising from masses of box with a 'curious effect'. The parterre beds on the round terrace at the bottom of the staircase were wreaths and scrolls of yew, turf, silver-sand and flowers, 'but the most striking feature consists of a large double-headed serpent, laying lazily across the back of each bed, formed of variegated box, twisted over, among, in and through the Yew'.[15]

Finally, at Cliveden, George Fleming's brother John, was filling Barry's broderie beds below the great terrace with anemones, pansies, tulips, hyacinths in scarlets, red, yellow, white and blue for the spring bedding. Barry would have loved it all; he was no gardener and when he designed his *broderies* he thought no farther than filling them with coloured gravels; even William Robinson's only criticism of Barry's work was the penchant for coloured gravels, and when the parterres were filled with real flowers, he too found them splendid.

The other great gardening architect and knight of the Victorian age, Sir Joseph Paxton (1803–65) is represented here and in the Collection, by James Duffield Harding's painting of the Crystal Palace at Sydenham (no. 74), which was exhibited in the Royal Academy in 1854. The Paxton archive remains chiefly at Chatsworth, where he rose to fame as Head Gardener to the 6th Duke of Devonshire and remained until the Duke's death in 1858. The garden at Chatsworth, his public parks (notably Birkenhead Park) and his great glasshouses are his claim to fame. His Crystal Palace, tremendously successful as the home of the 1851 Great Exhibition in Hyde Park, was moved to its permanent home at Sydenham, and re-opened there by Queen Victoria in the summer of 1856. Paxton designed the garden, if that is an adequate word, which gives the impression of being Repton's Ashridge, Nesfield's Buckingham Palace designs and Barry's Trentham all rolled into one. There are, in the painting, monumental terraces, pavilions, miniature palaces, fountains galore, a rosary, shrubberies that hide statues of prehistoric monsters and a kind of water-park refuge for the living contents of Noah's Ark. The whole design is held together by a broad central avenue rather reminiscent of The Mall, and what must be miles of serpentine gravel paths. It is a public theme park on the grandest scale, and was conceived and made as a homage to Victorian enterprise and Empire. The Crystal Palace itself, as a revolutionary house of glass, was the inspiration to conservatories, greenhouses, ferneries, stove-houses and the whole future of growing plants indoors; its setting did not live up to Harding's painting for long, being a drain on public money to maintain, quite apart from what it must have cost to build, needing thousands of visitors and a national holiday and sunshine to make it live, all of which were rarities.

In a way the Crystal Palace, which William Robinson was to castigate as ugly, costly rubbish and 'the greatest modern example of the waste of enormous means in making hideous a fine piece of ground',[16] was the spur to the rejection of Victorian gardens by the Arts and Crafts Movement. But, happily, my story of Victorian gardens need not end there, but with the delightful gardens of Coombe Abbey, just outside Coventry, which survived in a way not too different from their designed intention.[17] The fine watercolour plans credited to the little-

Fig. 16] *Opposite above: The Terrace Garden, Worsley Hall, Manchester,* as designed by Edward Blore, painted by E. Adveno Brooke, for *The Gardens of England*, 1856.

Fig. 17] *Opposite below: View from the Upper Terrace, Shrubland Park, Suffolk,* as designed by Sir Charles Barry. Painted by E. Adveno Brooke for *The Gardens of England*, 1856.

known William Miller make a more intriguing and positive transition to the new age than William Robinson's outbursts.

Coombe Abbey was the home of the Cravens since the early seventeenth century; they actually bought it from the same Lucy Harington, Countess of Bedford, whose garden drawn by Robert Smythson is the first drawing in this book. She is said to have sold it to settle her gambling debts. The generations of Cravens made Coombe splendid in keeping with the times; it is drawn by Knyff and Kip in *Britannia Illustrata* with a great compartmented formal and functional garden; in due time it acquired a Capability Brown park, and in another hundred years the 2nd Earl of Craven commissioned Richard Norman Shaw's young partner, William Eden Nesfield, to restore its medieval appearance. Young Nesfield (in deference to his eminent father of Buckingham Palace fame, William Andrews Nesfield, in his seventies by this time) dug a moat around the south front and used the excavated soil to make the level terrace between the house and the lake. Brent Elliott records that Nesfield senior designed a parterre for this level terrace at this time (1864) which would have been in his particular style and, then, at the height of fashion.

Nesfield senior died in 1881 and William Eden Nesfield died in 1888; by this time fashions had changed, but here in quiet Warwickshire, another ten years on in 1898, well into the time of the Arts and Crafts Movement, and five years into the partnership between Edwin Lutyens and Gertrude Jekyll, William Miller quietly perpetuated the high fashions of the 1860s. William Miller (1828–1909) now comes into focus as a latter-day member of the breed of great Victorian head gardeners. He seems to have been at or near Coombe all his life; he was Head Gardener to the 2nd Earl of Craven, who started Nesfield's building work then died in 1866, then carried on for the 3rd Earl and did a great deal of planting in the larger garden and park during the 1870s. At this time he made most of the drives and walks through these forty acres of pleasure grounds and supervised the enormous kitchen garden with its vast ranges of greenhouses and stove-houses which supplied pineapples, grapes and bananas for the house. The 3rd Earl died in 1883, by which time William Miller would have been fifty-six; was it at this time that he took a kind of semi-retirement and set himself up as a landscape gardener, as the drawings are stamped from his home in Berkswell, nearby?

The new owner of Coombe, the 4th Earl, brought his American heiress bride to settle at Coombe in 1893. Presumably it was Lady Craven's idea, in keeping with the golden-age taste of her homeland society, to have the prettily-patterned parterre? Perhaps William Miller, now nearing seventy, had treasured William Andrews Nesfield's design all those years in the hope of carrying it out. If so, his proud assertion on his drawing of *the first and Accepted plan of the Coombe Abbey Parterre Flower Garden – I planted this garden in 1897 and in 1898*, then is the happy ending to the story.

Coombe Abbey, for all its charm, was a late, late bloom of the High Victorian garden style, and by this time the fashion had already changed. The definitive Victorian garden seems to belong to Sir Charles Barry, in partnership with the heroic Head Gardeners, John Fleming at Cliveden, Donald Beaton at Shrubland Park and George Fleming at Trentham. This last, thinly disguised as 'Brentham' by Benjamin Disraeli in his novel *Lothair* (1869), the home of the amiable Duke and Duchess as well as of his adored Lady Corisande, was a place where 'all was Art and Art of a high character'. Disraeli wrote of the 'Italian palace of freestone; vast, ornate, and in scrupulous condition . . . rising . . . from statued and stately terraces. At their foot spread a gardened domain of considerable extent, bright with flowers, dim with coverts of rare shrubs, and magical with fountains'.[18] *Brentham* keeps re-appearing through his long novel in ever more glorious guise, the garden always colourful and charming . . . especially in the lustrous effulgence of a glorious English summer'. The happy ending among the roses, heliotrope, stocks and lilies of Corisande's retreat, shows that she will be a true Arts and Crafts kind of gardener, but the novel enshrines Victorian Trentham as a perfect period piece.

ASHRIDGE, HERTFORDSHIRE

50] SIR JEFFRY WYATVILLE 1766–1840
Plan for the arcaded flower garden

Ashridge, Hertfordshire, 1818
Pen and wash and pencil
545 × 745 mm. /$21\frac{3}{8}$ × $29\frac{3}{8}$ in.

Humphry Repton presented his Red Book of designs for fifteen different kinds of garden for Ashridge to the Earl and Countess of Bridgewater in 1813. Some of Repton's designs were carried out, but upon his death in 1818, Wyatville took over the garden design tasks for the Countess. The Red Book for Ashridge is not in the Collection (it is privately owned), but these drawings represent Wyatville's chief excursion into gardens and illustrate well the character of this great Victorian garden.

The architect's notes on this drawing read: 'Set out a perpendicular line from the centre of the Arcade at A.

Make the centre of the Trellis Walk at B opposite the middle of the Buttress C and make the Walk parallel to the line of the Arcade A. Place a post on each side the Walk D, and from D to E divide the space into seven or nine equal parts so as to have an opening in the centre at F.

If the centre line F is carried on to G it will cut the line A–B at H and give a point for the middle of the principal compartments of the garden.

The Center being thus determined the beds for flowers may be set out with regularity.

The Beds in front of the Arcade to have the angles cut off or to remain square as in Mr Long's plan. The beds on the eastern side may be similar or only sunked (*sic*) by the grass divisions and box borders.

The Octagon marked I to be paved and at each angle a foundation to support pedestal with vases or Flower pots

A foundation also at each of the places marked K for similar purpose.' A note at the foot of the drawing reads: 'The Arcade to have diagonal piles (and not strait ones) in order that the creepers may form groins.'

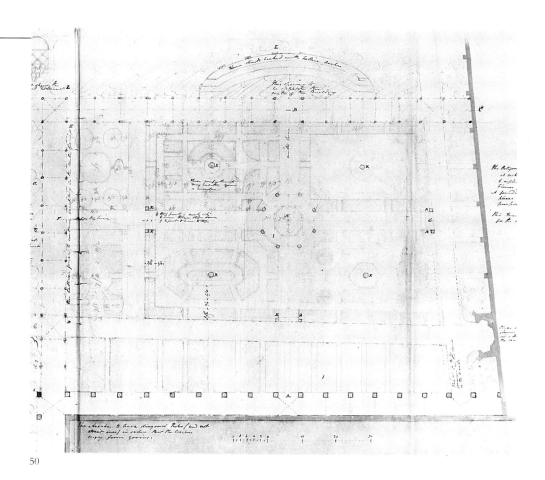

50

51] SIR JEFFRY WYATVILLE 1766–1840
Trellis detail for arcaded flower garden

Ashridge, Hertfordshire, 1818
Pen and wash and pencil
Detail from drawing 51

This detail has been enlarged from the top left hand corner of the plan drawing, 50. The inscription reads: *These divisions to be formed by pieces three 3 inches square so that the outside width will be equal in width to the posts of the Arcade.*

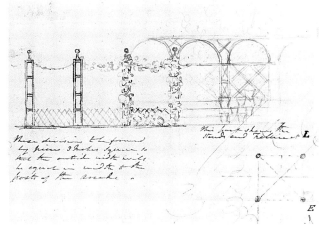

51

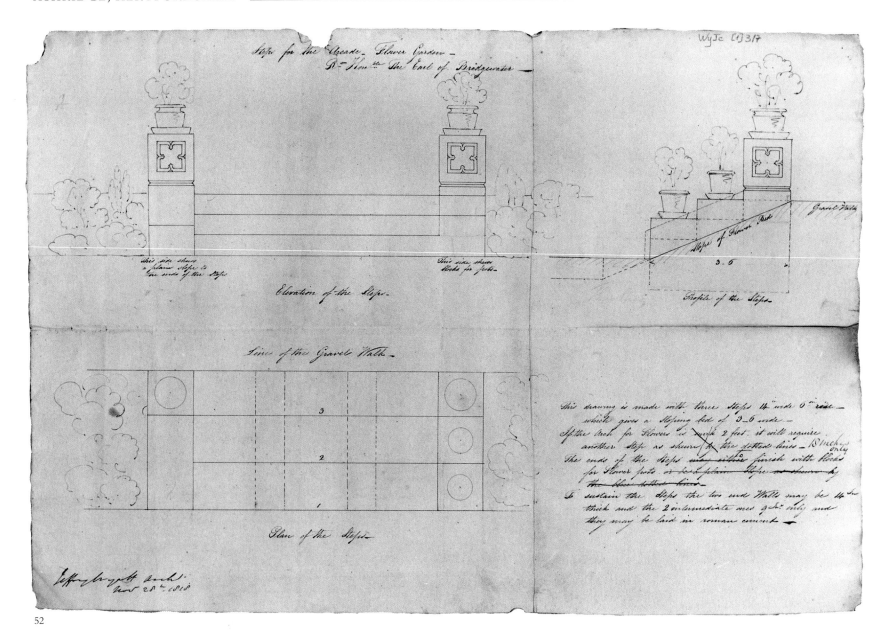

52]   SIR JEFFRY WYATVILLE 1766–1840

Steps for the arcaded flower garden

Ashridge, Hertfordshire, 1818
Pen
370 × 540 mm. /14⅝ × 21¼ in.

This clear and careful drawing is a credit to the office of a grand and fashionable architect, who is prepared to take pains with garden details, realizing that standard details for interior

steps will not do for out of doors. Small details, such as this leisurely scale for steps, mark out the architects that understood their garden work.

Though this drawing and the preceding plan are marked for the *Arcade* garden, it seems that they relate to what became the Monk's Garden. Repton planned the Monk's Garden farther east, but Wyatville realized that this would involve destroying genuine monastic remains, and transferred his Monk's Garden to the site adjoining the dairy yard.

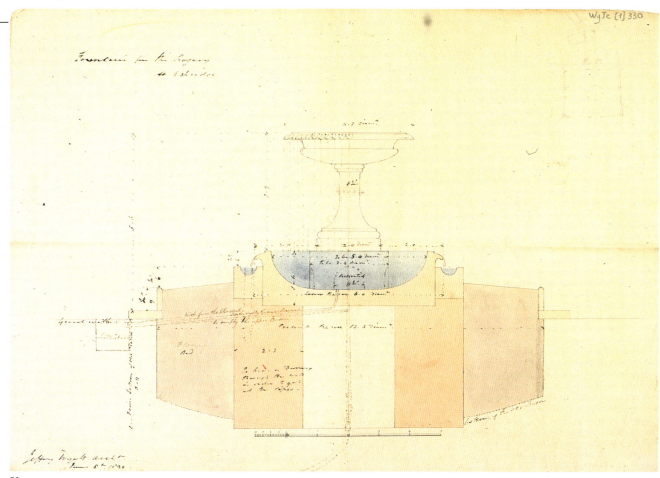

53a

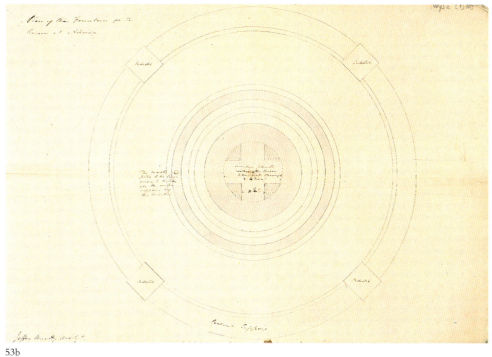

53b

53] SIR JEFFRY WYATVILLE 1766–1840

Fountain for the rosary garden

Ashridge, Hertfordshire, 1820
Pen and wash
(a) Section 375 × 535 mm. /14¾ × 21 in.
(b) Plan 375 × 535 mm. /14¾ × 21 in.

The rosary was one of the most important of Repton's designs for Ashridge. It was illustrated in the Red Book and in his book *Fragments of the Theory and Practice of Landscape Gardening, 1816* (see fig. 14). The illustration shows a circle of rose arches and a low trellised fence surrounding and enclosing teardrop shaped beds of roses, with basket edgings, radiating from a central round fountain. The fountain has a plain bowl and a single high spout of water; this drawing is therefore Wyatville's construction of the fountain Repton had imagined.

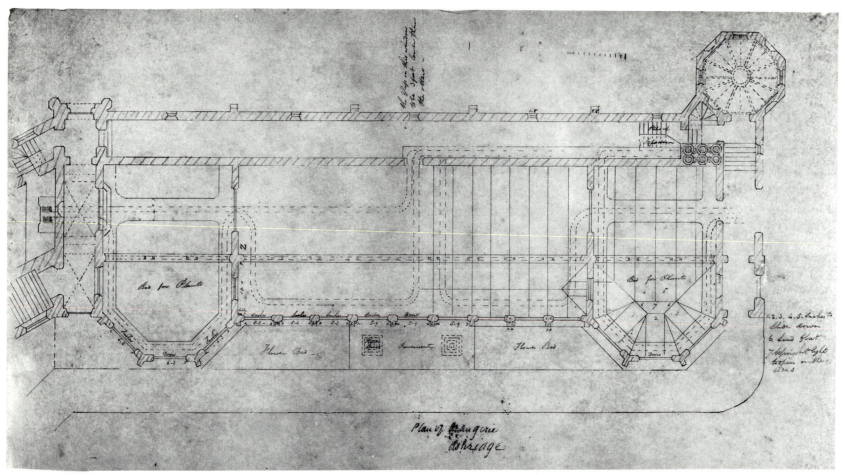

54

54] SIR JEFFRY WYATVILLE 1766–1840

Design for an orangery

Ashridge, Hertfordshire, *c.*1817
Pen and pencil
370 × 525 mm. /14⅝ × 20⅝ in.

Wyatville took over from his uncle, James Wyatt, as the architect to the Earl of Bridgewater for his house, which was completed in 1817. This orangery was one of the last buildings, designed as a wing of the house. Details of the pipe-runs for the heating and for the opening sashes to alleviate summer sun can be clearly seen.

The scents of oranges and lemons, and their jewel-like colours and shapes, rather than their culinary qualities, had entranced rich English garden owners for two centuries. To have a room built to the plant's requirements and where they could be over-wintered and enjoyed in winter, was the height of luxury.

55] SIR JEFFRY WYATVILLE 1766–1840

Design for an orange tub

Ashridge, Hertfordshire, *c.*1817
Sepia pen
530 × 325 mm. /20⅞ × 12¾ in.

Orange and lemon trees were kept in movable tubs, to allow for cleaning the orangery and to facilitate moving them out of doors in the summer. It went without saying that the precious plants were worthy of tubs of special design, in matching sets. The tub was made of wood, ideally painted in the armorial colour, and had a metal liner. This simple design has sloping sides to make it just a little different from the classic straight-sided Versailles tub, which was a copy of those that held the orange trees at Versailles, the original inspiration for the fashion. In summer these tubs would be ranged along the terrace or set out in an enclosed garden.

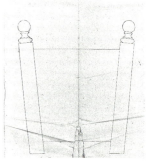

55

56] SIR JEFFRY WYATVILLE 1766–1840

Elevation of the flint wall and garden seat

Ashridge, Hertfordshire, 1818
Pen and buff and grey washes
375 × 540 mm. /14¾ × 21¼ in.

The inscription on this drawing reads: 'This garden seat is supposed to be an old doorway closed up with small stones – or it might be a real door if the cowshed within were formed with neatness. If the flint wall is not to be carried on to the new Stable but only the battlement continued the whole of the Gateway or Seat should be stone without flints.

The parts coloured yellow to be stone. The Buttresses and Cornice to be the size of those to the flint wall. In addition to the fixed niches each of which will form seats for two persons a loose seat may be placed against the blank door.'

57] SIR JEFFRY WYATVILLE 1766–1840

Garden gateway

Ashridge, Hertfordshire, 1818
Pen
540 × 370 mm. /21¼ × 14⅝ in.

The elaborate Gothic details of the garden seat and of this gateway, illustrate how fully Wyatville entered into the spirit of the Ashridge garden. Both seat and gateway were part of a scheme to screen the Monk's Garden, a theatrical re-creation of a monastic bower, from the all too earthly sounds and smells of the dairy yard. Presumably the scheme was successful, for many famous photographs of the Monk's Garden, complete with robed monks, appeared in late nineteenth-century gardening books.

The note indicates that the gateway was to be of stone or ashlar *but not made smooth* and the door was to be studded oak, with a bell pull on the garden side only.

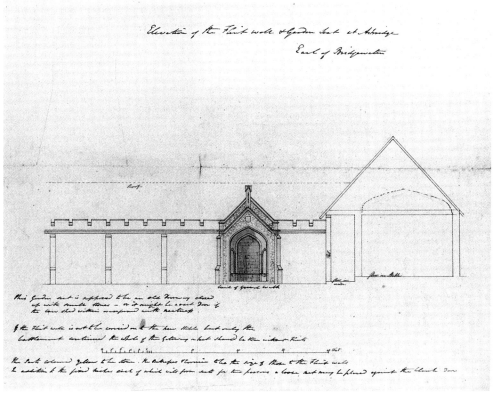

56

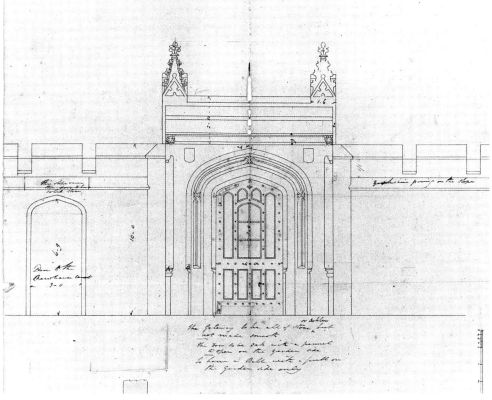

57

VILLA D'ESTE, TIVOLI

58] CHARLES TYRELL 1795–1832

Plan of the garden

Villa d'Este, Tivoli, Italy, 15 June 1821
Pen, pencil and watercolour
465 × 375 mm. /18¼ × 14¾ in.

Tyrell was a surveyor and he made this drawing of Cardinal Ippolito's famous garden on a visit to Italy with Henry Parke and T.L. Donaldson in 1821/2. It is interesting to note that in terms of geometry and proportions, this drawing closely resembles an engraving of the garden made in 1573 when the Cardinal was adding the final touches. However, in the early nineteenth century, the garden was in poor repair and one wonders if Tyrell saw the tumbling, spouting, gushing waters and curious plantings that adorn the garden, or whether it was as bland and bare as his drawing indicates. This is a quiet moment in the long-lasting passion, nurtured by English artists, for the Renaissance gardens of Italy.

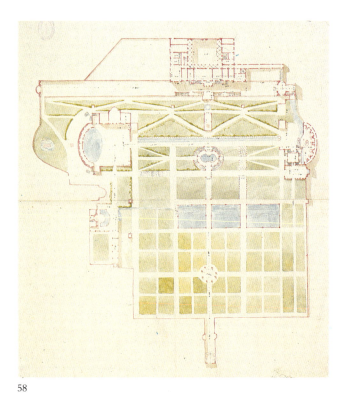

58

DRUMLANRIG CASTLE, DUMFRIES

59] SIR CHARLES BARRY 1795–1860

Perspective of the house and garden

Drumlanrig Castle, Thornhill, Dumfries and Galloway, Scotland, 1840
Watercolour
635 × 1016 mm. /25 × 40 in.

A grand perspective showing the most ambitious Italianate terrace gardens as Barry thought fit for the Duke of Buccleuch and Queensbury at Drumlanrig. The scheme was not carried out. The castle remains as built in rosy pink stone in the sixteenth and seventeenth centuries, with modest gardens. The grand perspective was a convention of the Barry office, but this is the only one with such detailed treatment of the gardens. It gives the best idea of the scale and architectural force of the Italianate Revival garden, as Barry created at Shrublands in Suffolk, Trentham, Staffordshire, and Harewood, Yorkshire, and shows us just what William Robinson was to oppose. This is what he was to call 'the railway embankment' phase of gardening, with lifeless terraces and complicated and paltry beds that gave no thought to the welfare of real flowers and shrubs.

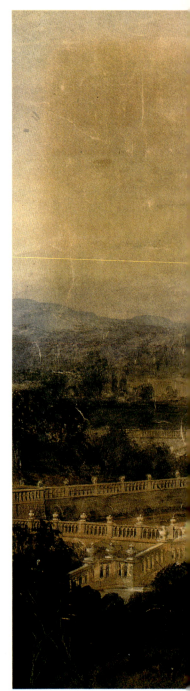

59

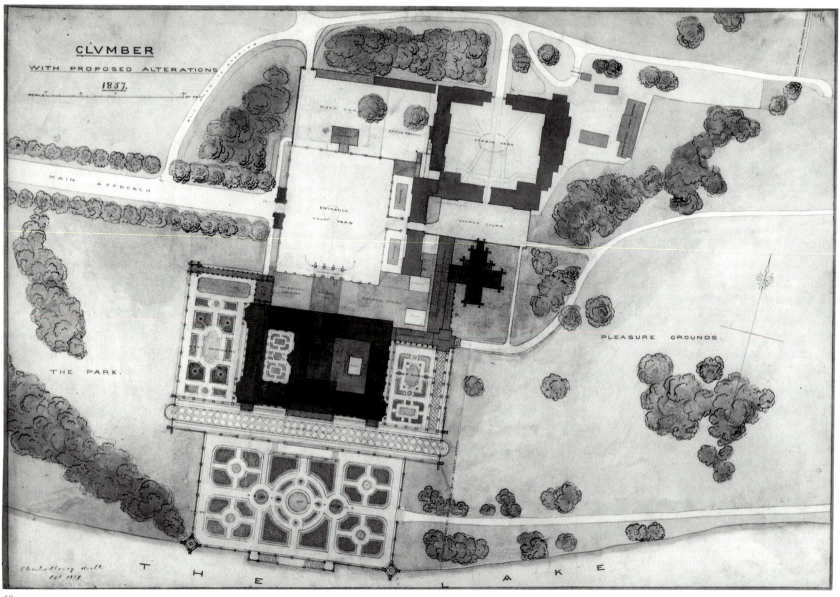

60

CLUMBER PARK, NOTTINGHAMSHIRE

60] SIR CHARLES BARRY 1795–1860

Proposed alterations to the park

Clumber Park, Nottinghamshire, 1857
Pen and wash
673×952 mm. $/26\frac{1}{2} \times 37\frac{1}{2}$ in.

The drawing is signed *Charles Barry Archt Oct 1857*: Barry's proposals included the elaborate east and west parterres as well as the terrace across the south front of the house (a house of 1770 by Stephen Wright which was to be altered and added to), and the large south parterre terraced to the lake's edge as at Trentham. The work was not carried out.

SHRUBLAND PARK, SUFFOLK

61]   SIR CHARLES BARRY 1795–1860

The great staircase

Shrubland Park, Suffolk, 1854
Print

Shrubland Park was Barry's greatest Italianate garden, largely because of the dramatic site of the house which gave him the chance to build terraces connected by this flight of 137 steps. The slopes were planted with evergreens and exotic shrubs and became known as 'the wilderness'. The view from the house-terrace is centred upon the lower circular terrace with a round pool (just visible in this print) which was surrounded by a circle of flower parterres set in grass. This highly stylized garden terrace seems to float in the rolling landscape beyond; it was much admired and painted, notably by E. Adveno Brooke for *Gardens of England* in 1856.

Shrubland Park was built by James Paine in 1772; Barry altered and added to the house and planned the garden for Sir William Fowle Middleton Bt. between 1849–54.

61

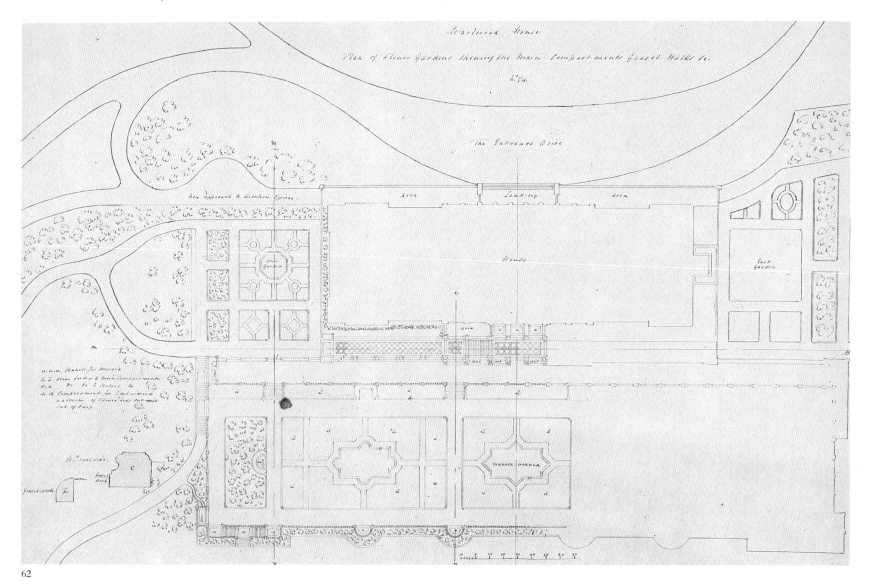

62

HAREWOOD HOUSE, YORKSHIRE

62]   SIR CHARLES BARRY 1795–1860

Plan of the gardens

Harewood House, Yorkshire, 1843
Pen and wash on tracing paper
495 × 743 mm. /19½ × 29¼ in.

This is a tracing made by James Murray of the plan, scale 1″ to 20′ for the gardens, and it is annotated in Barry's hand: *Harewood House Plan of Flower Gardens shewing the Main Compartments, Gravel Walks etc.* The rectangular block of the house faces the sweep of the entrance drive on the north; there is an elaborate west garden, and the east garden is outlined, and was intended to be equally elaborate in layout.

The south front appears to have a path or narrow terraces of encaustic tiles, then a grass or gravel terrace overlooking the patterned beds, marked as '*Embroidered parterres*' to be cut from the turf. Here the patterns sketched in the following drawing were laid out.

63] SIR CHARLES BARRY 1795–1860

Design for the flower garden

Harewood House, Yorkshire, 1843
Pencil and watercolour
127×311 mm. $/5 \times 12\frac{1}{4}$ in.

This is almost certainly a sketch from Barry's office (rather than the architect himself), for the flower parterre at Harewood. Barry worked for the Earl of Harewood between 1843 and 1850, making alterations to the house and laying out the Italianate formal gardens which largely survive today. As with the design for Trentham's parterre (no. 64), the colouring of this plan has nothing whatever to do with planting, it merely produces a pretty effect, which would have been transferred to the garden by the use of coloured gravel chippings with some bedding plants in summer.

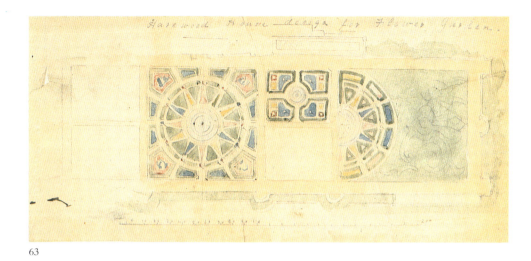

63

TRENTHAM HALL, STAFFORDSHIRE

64] SIR CHARLES BARRY 1795–1860

Design for flower beds

Trentham Hall, Staffordshire, 1834
Pen and wash
311×540 mm. $/12\frac{1}{4} \times 21\frac{1}{4}$ in.

One of the four segments and part of the central circle for the parterre garden layout on the lake terrace at Trentham; the drawing also shows the profile of the moulding around the central pool. Barry made the great Italianate garden at Trentham for the 2nd Duke and Duchess of Sutherland between 1834 and 1842. Photographs of these gardens in about 1900 show the parterre beds patterned in grass and bedding plants and the design enhanced with coloured gravels. Barry's approach to these designs was in graphic terms (he was certainly not interested in the flowers), and as long as the patterns were clearly defined, the plants suited their purposes. The great gardens at Trentham, now minus the house are maintained as a public park.

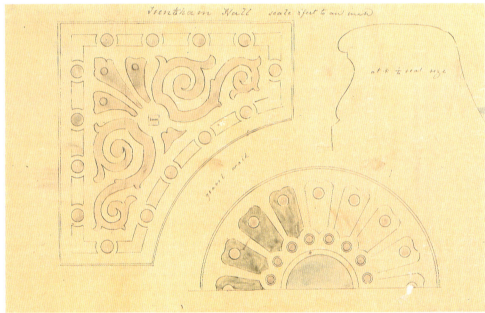

64

WORSLEY HALL, near MANCHESTER

65]   EDWARD BLORE 1787–1879

The kitchen garden

Worsley Hall, near Manchester, 1841
Pen and wash
Sheet from a bound volume
698 × 540 mm. /$27\frac{1}{2}$ × $21\frac{1}{4}$ in.

The key for the kitchen garden layout reads:

1. Open Shed (for carts, barrows etc.)
2. Potting Shed
3. Mushroom House
4. Under-gardener's living room
5. Under-gardener's sleeping room
6. Stoke hole (for Vinery boilers)
7   and 8 are the Stoke Holes for the Pine Stoves
9, 10, 11 and 12 are Asparagus forcing pits

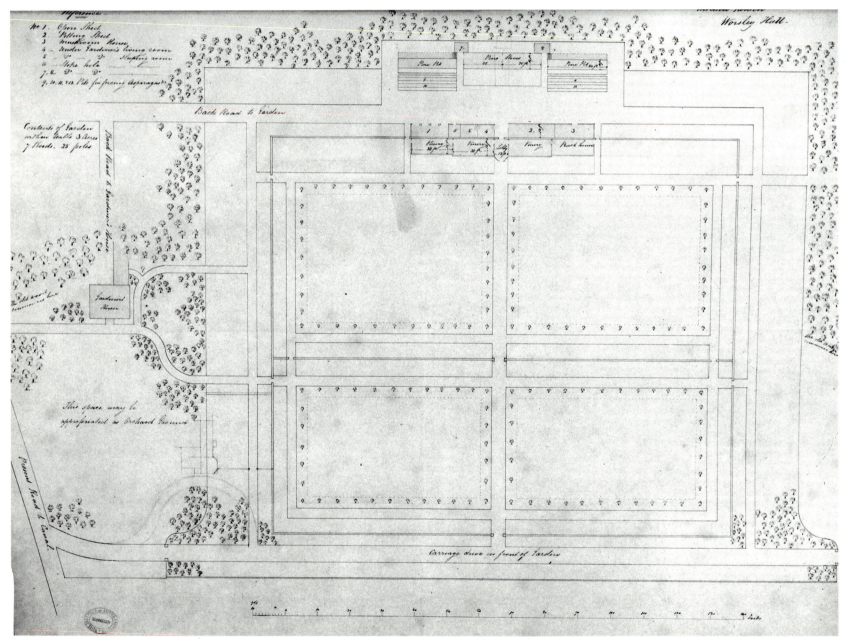

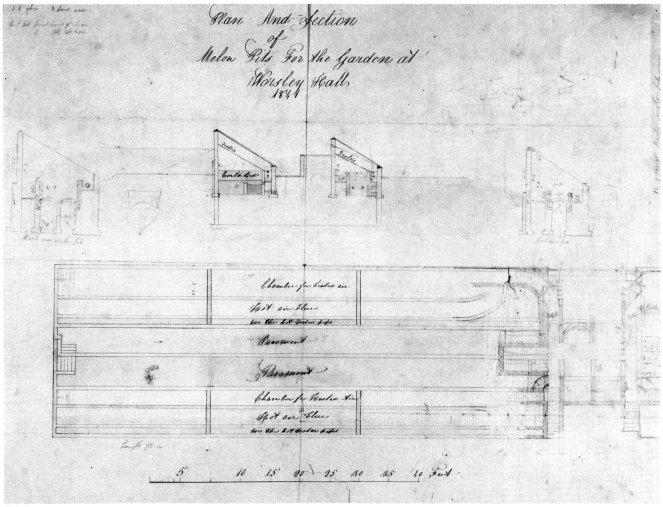

66

The complete designs for Blore's work at Worsley Hall come in two bound volumes, 460 sheets in all, and the work was carried out between 1839 and 1845. Edward Blore was not an exciting garden designer but this drawing shows the thoroughness that was the mark of his prosperous and royally-favoured practice.

The kitchen garden of a Victorian mansion was a fine and private world, ruled by the Head Gardener from his house in the shrubbery, outside the wall, and maintained by the constant presence of an under-gardener who slept in the boiler houses.

66]   EDWARD BLORE 1787–1879

Melon pits

Worsley Hall, 1841
Pencil, pen and wash; from bound volume
698 × 540 mm. /$27\frac{1}{2}$ × $21\frac{1}{4}$ in.

In the nineteenth century melons were a highly-desirable fruit, but the plants were sprawling and ugly and therefore confined to the kitchen garden. Stephen Switzer's *The Practical Fruit Gardener* of 1724 gave some of the earliest advice on melon-growing, either by planting them next to a heated wall or by growing them in pits, covered with a frame, as here. The base of the pits was filled with a mixture of tanner's bark and horse manure, which combusted, so making them 'hot beds'.

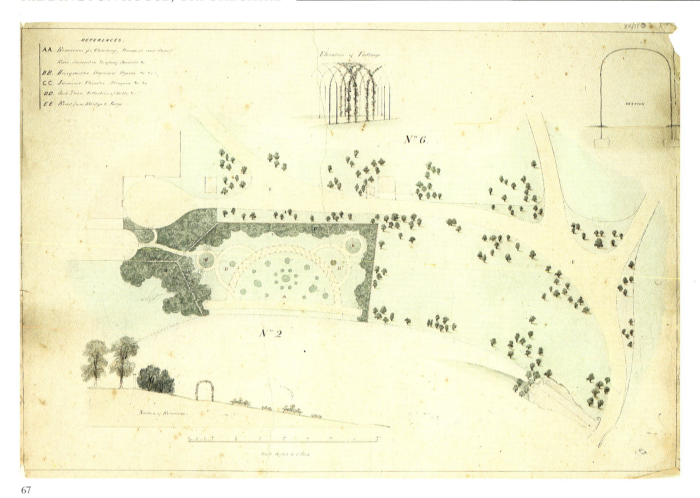

67

KIDDINGTON HOUSE, OXFORDSHIRE

67] JOHN CLAUDIUS LOUDON 1783–1843

A garden design

Kiddington House, Enstone, Oxfordshire, 1843
Pencil, pen and watercolour
722 × 489 mm. /$30\frac{3}{8}$ × $19\frac{1}{4}$ in.

This is an alternative treatment for the garden at Kiddington
for Mortimer Ricardo, designed by Loudon, with the help of
a draughtsman, in the last weeks of his life. The references are
as follows:

A, A   Rosarium for Climbing, Standard and dwarf roses,
      disposed in Ironoko Baskets
B, B   Honeysuckles, Bignonias
C, C   Jasmines, Clematis, Atrogenas
D, D   Dark Trees, Collection of holly etc.
E, E   Road from bridge to lodge

68

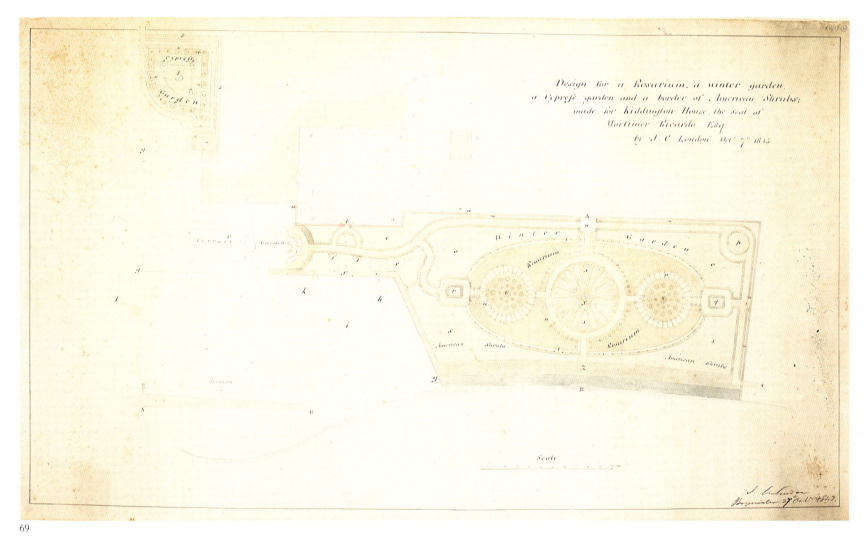

69

68] JOHN CLAUDIUS LOUDON 1783–1843

A wall trellis

Kiddington House, Enstone, Oxfordshire, 1843
Watercolour
199 × 714 mm. /7⅞ × 28⅛ in.

Elevation and enlarged section to illustrate the construction
of a squared, wooden trellis to carry wall plants for the
garden at Kiddington. This is on an untitled sheet, but signed
by David Ramsay, with the two previous presentation
drawings. Loudon demonstrates his endless ideas for en-
couraging climbing plants as vertical features in his gardens,
with the circular arcade for roses, marked U, U on no. 68,
and the criss-cross treillage drawn on no. 69. This drawing
however, is not for roses, as he says in his note, because a wall
trellis does not allow them enough light and air. Clematis,
jasmines and honeysuckles would be planted here.

69] JOHN CLAUDIUS LOUDON 1783–1843

Design for a rosarium

Kiddington House, Enstone, Oxfordshire, 1843
Pencil, pen and coloured washes
580 × 987 mm. /22⅞ × 38⅞ in.

The full inscription reads:
*Design for a Rosarium, a winter garden, a Cypress garden,
and a border of American shrubs; made for Kiddington House,
the seat of Mortimer Ricardo Esq. by J.C.Loudon
October 27 1843.*

A long hand-written key to the drawing is in the
Collection and provides the following information:

A, A Proposed wall for separating the entrance court from
the garden scenery and protecting the terrace from loose
dogs and horses . . . and strangers
B Private entrance to the garden scenery

C, C Terrace flower garden, already existing

D, D Two small dug circles for standards of curious shrubs, such as *Cotoneaster buxifolia* or *Calopheaca wolgarica*, as terminating objects to the two small walks from the entrance B

E, E Shrubs with some trees; the ground to be dug for a few years, the plants gradually thinned out and grass introduced so that the shrubs ultimately stand on their own, hardly touching, in mown grass

F Grass terrace, which ought to have a low parapet on the top of the sunk wall as far as G

G, G, G Proposed parapet on top of the sunk wall, the flower border at present within to be made a grass walk

H Site for a Deodar cedar, to be enclosed in a circular wire fence

I Site for a Cedar of Lebanon

K Site for an *Arancaria imbricata*

L Site for a Cedar of Lebanon and a Deodar Cedar in the same circle

M, M, M Border for winter flowering bulbs at the base of the wall

N Arbour of trellis work

O, O Junipers, cypresses, yews and *Arbor Vitae* planted at such a distance apart so that they do not touch for five or six years, when they are to be thinned – 'and the ground turfed up to their decumbent (*sic*) branches' as at E, E

P Aransaria imbricata

Q Arbutuses

R Variegated hollies

S, S American shrubs with one or two standard magnolias in the widest part of the plantation

T, T 4 foot high fence of large poles with the bark on, or of strained wire, to be covered with sweetbriers mixed with honeysuckles

U, U Arcade of roses of what are called climbing or pillar kinds. Care must be taken not to confound this arcade with a trellis of roses; as the latter does not display the flowers to advantage for want of light and air

V, V Baskets of roses

W, W Dug circles with a standard rose in each and a ground covering of mignonette

X Beds of grass

Y A circular seat, which will form an object from the arbour, N, and the broad terrace, Z

Z Broad terrace

At the time Loudon wrote out his suggestions for Mr Ricardo he was weak from bouts of pneumonia. Jane Loudon records that he visited Kiddington at the end of September 1843, and was so weak that he had to be taken round in a wheel chair. When he left, he appeared to be so ill that Mr

Ricardo tried to persuade him to take one of his servants to help on the return to London. John Claudius, determined to the last, refused. He arrived back at his house in Bayswater on 30 September, and Jane persuaded him to seek medical advice. He persisted in working on these drawings and other projects, including his *Self-Instruction for Young Gardeners*, though he was confined to his bedroom and a drawing-room after 16 October. He had the help of a draughtsman, and though the design for the Rosarium etc. at Kiddington is signed by Loudon, the other drawings are not. As the only Loudon work in the Collection they are a fitting tribute to the bravery of a remarkable man.[19]

STREATHAM, LONDON

70] JOHN BUONAROTTI PAPWORTH
1775–1847

Walled garden and shrubbery

Leigham Court, Streatham, London, *c.*1840
Sepia pen and wash
600 × 450 mm. /$23\frac{5}{8}$ × $17\frac{3}{4}$ in.

Papworth was a competent and versatile designer of everything from a new town (with gardens) in America to every kind of garden ornament. His book, *Hints on ornamental gardening*, full of designs for pavilions, seats, trellis etc., was published in 1823.

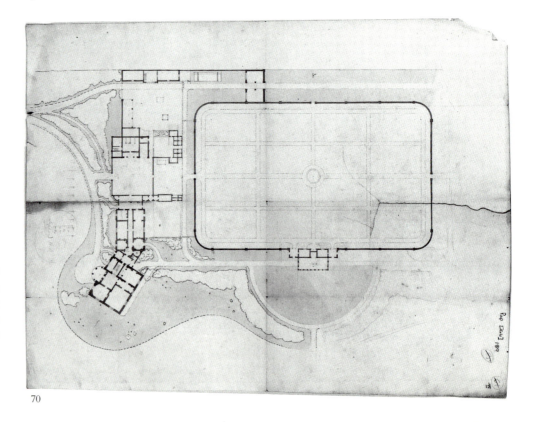

70

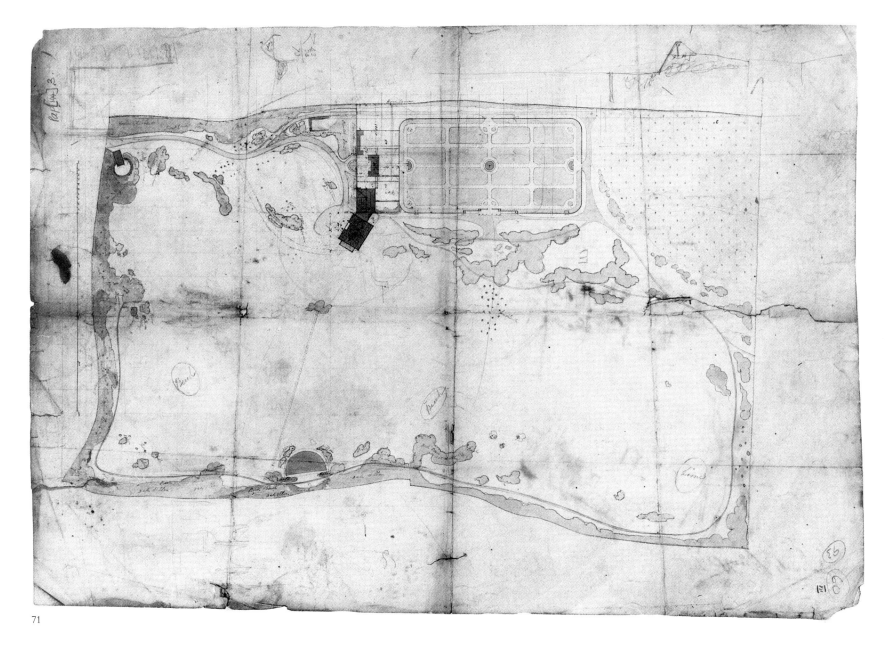

71

71] JOHN BUONAROTTI PAPWORTH
1775–1847

A house and garden

Leigham Court, Streatham, London, *c*.1821
Sepia pen and coloured washes
630 × 440 mm. /$24\frac{3}{4}$ × $17\frac{3}{8}$ in.

Leigham Court, for John George Fuller, a wine merchant and half-owner of Boodle's in London, was one of Papworth's major commissions, where he worked from 1820–46, the year before his death. The commission began with a small house, which was converted to offices for a second house, built at an angle to the original; the complete building is on this plan, while the garden design is shown in some detail in the preceding drawing and shows a fine contrast between the discipline of the traditional kitchen garden and the flow of the Victorian shrubbery walks.

There are 212 drawings for Leigham, including designs for melon pits, an apiary, flower stands, seats and a pond, but (like the majority of the 2,600 drawings in the Papworth Collection) they are brittle, dirty and difficult to read. They are a treasure house of Victorian garden design that has never really been explored.

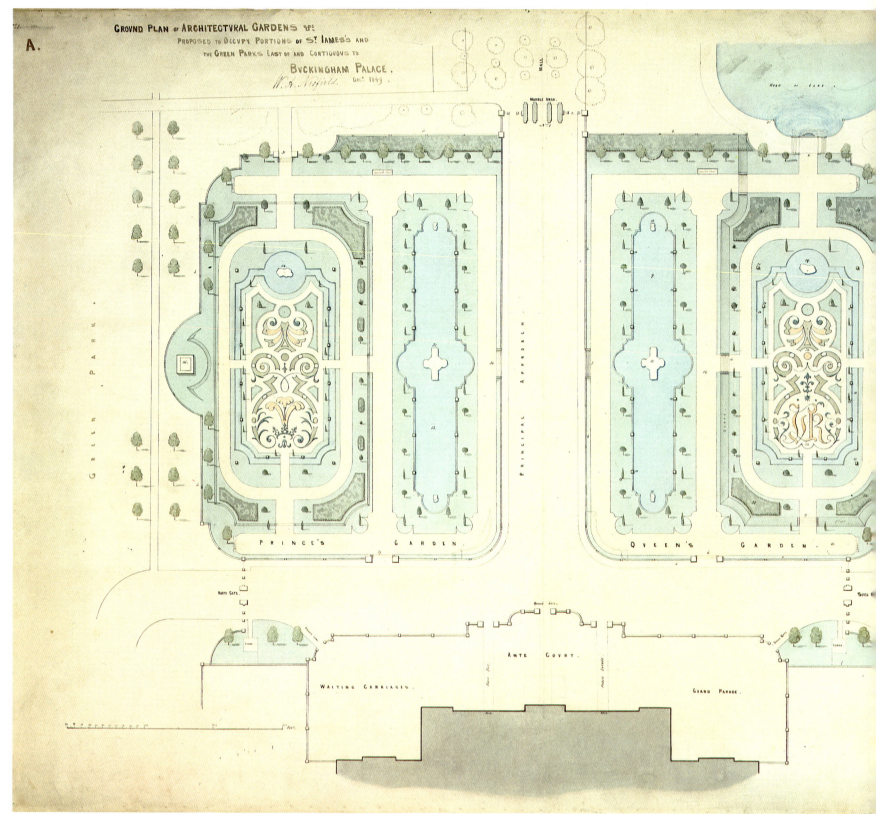

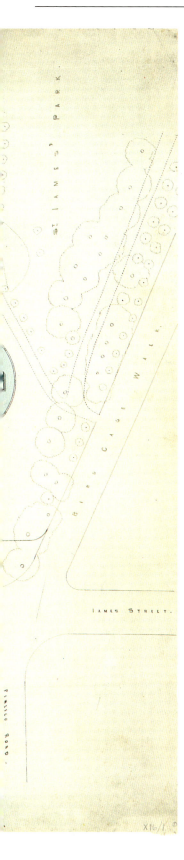

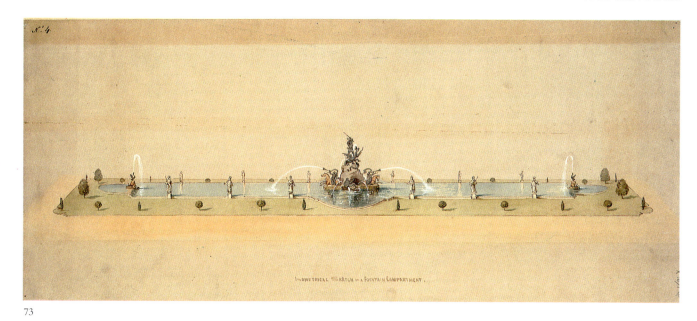

73

BUCKINGHAM PALACE, LONDON

72] WILLIAM ANDREWS NESFIELD 1793–1881

A formal garden

Buckingham Palace, London, 1849
Pen and coloured washes
720 × 1000 mm. /28⅜ × 39⅜ in.

The drawing is inscribed: *Ground Plan of Architectural Gardens to occupy portions of St James's and the Green Parks east and contiguous to Buckingham Palace.*

The gardens were planned for the area where the Victoria Memorial now stands; Birdcage Walk can be seen on the right and part of Green Park on the left. The Marble Arch is drawn in as the main entrance to the Palace from the Mall, but was to be moved to its present site north of Park Lane by Nesfield in 1850. The formal gardens were designed to complement Edward Blore's new East Wing of the Palace, completed in 1847. Nesfield's garden scheme, illustrated in four watercolour drawings (of which two are shown here) was presented to Prince Albert at the very end of 1849. The drawings were accompanied by Nesfield's handwritten report describing his proposals and this, with all four drawings, is in the Collection. It is interesting to note that he has signed himself as a 'Landscape Architect' – a term hardly used in England before this date.

73] WILLIAM ANDREWS NESFIELD 1793–1881

A fountain for the architectural gardens

Buckingham Palace, London, 1849
Pen and watercolour
295 × 695 mm. /11⅝ × 27⅜ in.

Nesfield made three sketches of the fountain compartments, two in perspective (not shown) and this aerial version. The figures on the fountain are St George and the Dragon on the rock, with Father Thames lying below surrounded by Fame and Victory.

W. A. Nesfield was, as this commission would indicate, a notable garden designer of his day. He began as a soldier, serving with Wellington in the Peninsular Campaign and then turned to watercolour painting. In 1852 he resigned from the Society of Painters in Watercolour and became a landscape architect. W. A. Nesfield had two sons: William Eden Nesfield (1835–88) became an architect and some of his architectural projects and sketchbooks are in the Collection. He worked on additions to Coombe Abbey in Warwickshire, 1860–66 and the garden designs there (see nos. 82–4) have definite Nesfield characteristics. The second son, Markham Nesfield, was a landscape gardener, and one of his formal gardens survives at Doddington Place in Kent.

74

CRYSTAL PALACE, LONDON

74] SIR JOSEPH PAXTON 1801–65

Design for gardens and park

The Crystal Palace, Sydenham, London
Exhibited at the Royal Academy 1854, by the artist
James Duffield Harding (1798–1863)
Pencil and watercolour heightened with white
920×1940 mm. / $36\frac{1}{4} \times 76\frac{3}{8}$ in.

Paxton's Crystal Palace, designed for the Great Exhibition of 1851 in Hyde Park, was re-erected and surrounded by terraces, wilderness walks and waters on its permanent site at Sydenham, then still countryfied and outside of London. It was re-opened by Queen Victoria in the summer of 1856, so there may be a fair deal of artistic licence in this scene.

Paxton's designs for the grounds of the Palace were part of his significant contribution to the Victorian park movement, but was this extreme and fantastic design justified? Certainly William Robinson did not think so and in 1889 wrote that: 'There are . . . a great many ugly gardens in Europe, but at Sydenham we have the greatest modern example of the waste of enormous means in making hideous a fine piece of ground'. He attacks Paxton's creation as outdated – 'the fruit of vulgar ambition to outdo another sad monument of great means put to base uses – Versailles' – and goes on to question its relevance, workability and lack of respect for the laws of nature. But Robinson, in full spate, should not be paraphrased!

'Our means for garden adornment have increased a hundredfold since Versailles was designed, and our modern illustration of a barbarous style has none of the excuses which might be urged for Versailles. As Versailles had numerous tall water-squirts, the best way of glorifying ourselves was to make some taller ones at Sydenham! Instead of confining the geometrical gardening to the upper terrace, by far the greater portion of the ground was devoted to the baser features of a stony style of garden design, and nearly in the centre were placed the vast fountain basins with their ugly pipes. These water basins are more hideous than the crater of a volcano. The contrivances to enable the water to go downstairs, the temples, the statues, the dead walls, all add to the distracting elements of the central region. This costly rubbish was praised by the gardening papers as the marvellous work of a genius – Paxton!'[20]

And so this wonderful painting comes into gardening history not so much for the grand design it displays as for the change of attitudes that it inspired.

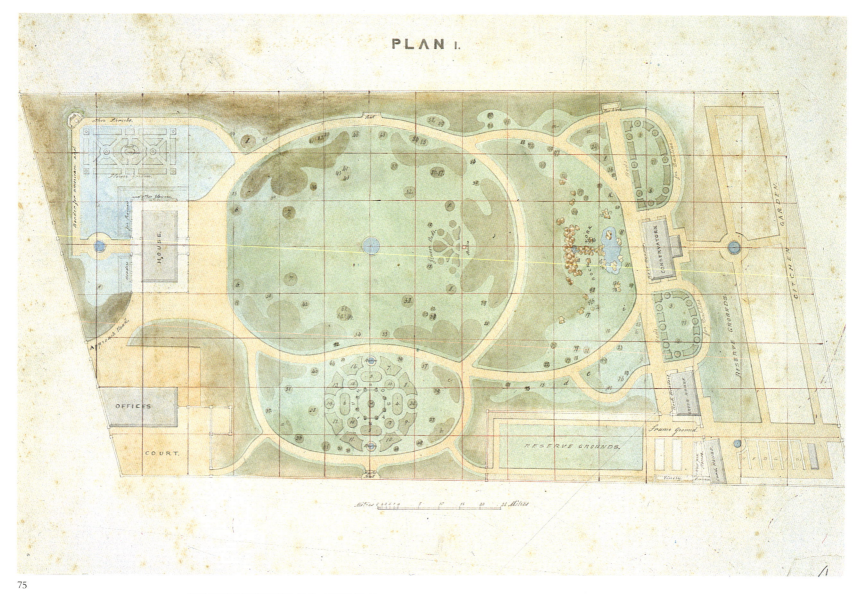

PLAN I.

75

75] THE PUGIN COLLECTION

Design for a garden

Unidentified, *c.*1870
Pencil, pen and coloured washes
390 × 590 mm. / $15\frac{1}{2}$ × $23\frac{1}{4}$ in.

This is the first of a set of three plans in a sequence found loose among the five volumes of drawings by A. W. Pugin for Scarisbrick Hall in Lancashire.

Plan I has a pattern of grid squares, each representing ten metres. It is a highly sophisticated design and drawing, equal in qualities to the drawings of the best Victorian designs of Nesfield and Loudon. The spelling of 'Citchen' garden is odd, but does not, I think, justify the French attribution given in the RIBA catalogue of his work; this French origin is additionally inspired by the inscription *Corbeille of Dahlias* on plan II, but *corbeille*, meaning a basket of flowers, was a common term used by Humphry Repton and his successors.

Though the drawings are very definitely numbered, in Roman numerals, there is no plan III in the Collection. Plan II (not illustrated), only varies from this plan I in that the trees and flowerbeds are shown in different colours but without numbers. No key to the numbering has survived.

PLAN IV.

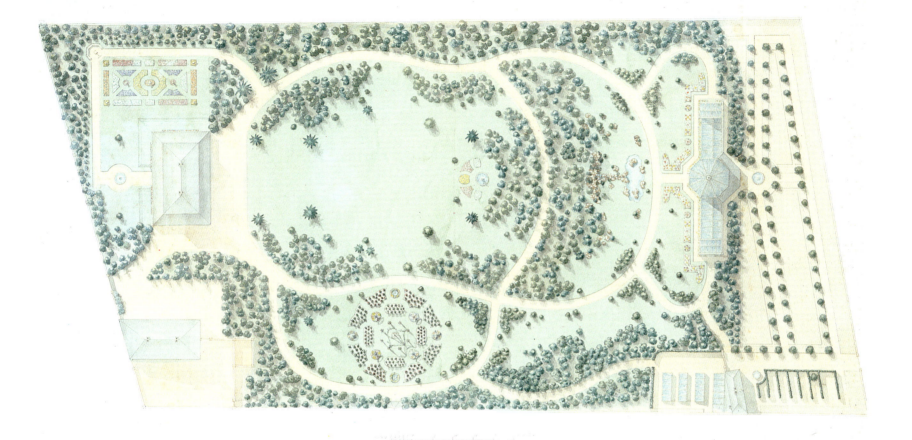

76

76] THE PUGIN COLLECTION

Design for a garden

Unidentified, *c.*1870
Pencil, pen and coloured washes
390 × 590 mm. /15½ × 23¼ in.

Plan IV differs from I in that the flowers and trees are coloured, and, most importantly, the conservatory is of a larger and different design, and the *Reserve Grounds* are eliminated, leading to several changes in the layout of the end of the garden. This conservatory, a long glass building with a domed centre, compares interestingly with one designed by A. W. Pugin for Scarisbrick Hall, no. 199.

These two drawings are also worth comparing to the Loudon designs for Kiddington (nos. 67–9) and the unidentified French garden (nos. 75–6). The whole concept is of a delicacy and delight that seems to intimate the perfect Victorian villa garden.

ASCOTT HOUSE, BUCKINGHAMSHIRE

77] GEORGE DEVEY 1820–86 (Office of)

A garden plan

Ascott House, Wing, Buckinghamshire, *c.* 1880
Pen and wash on linen
587 × 852 mm. /$23\frac{1}{8}$ × $33\frac{1}{2}$ in.

This is not an inspiring drawing but it does lead to interesting garden connections. Ascott was bought in 1873 by the Baron Meyer de Rothschild of Mentmore, and taken over as a hunting lodge by Leopold de Rothschild.

The latter employed George Devey, an eminent and established country house architect, famous for romantically elaborate Tudoresque buildings such as those he had added to Penshurst Place and village in Kent during the 1850s. Devey was trained as a painter with John Sell Cotman and James Duffield Harding, and while he made Ascott into a free Tudor rural palace he retained painterly instincts, and modest ones, in this layout for the garden. Thus, though the Ascott garden, now owned by the National Trust, is credited to Leopold de Rothschild, clearly Devey must take some credit for the original design, though he is not an architect normally associated with gardens.

78] GEORGE DEVEY 1820–86 (Office of)

Design for trellis

Ascott House, Wing, Buckinghamshire, *c.* 1880
Pencil on tracing paper
442 × 550 mm. /$17\frac{3}{8}$ × $21\frac{5}{8}$ in.

A loose sheet of designs for treillage pavilions at Ascott for which Devey used the grandest of French inspirations, probably from Le Nôtre and other early eighteenth-century sources. The idea of balustrades, pillars and roundels is much more sophisticated and substantial than those fragile trellises returned to English gardens by Repton and Loudon.

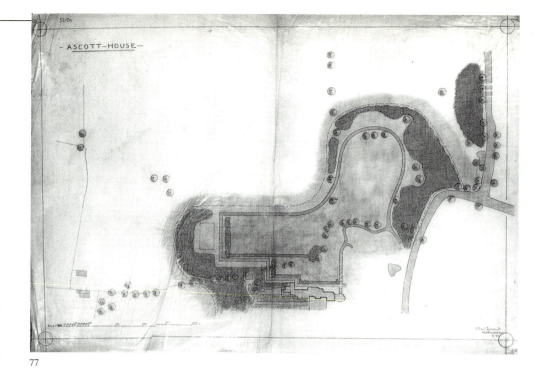

77

78

79] GEORGE DEVEY 1820–86 (Office of)

A sundial

Ascott House, Wing, Buckinghamshire, *c.* 1880
Pen and wash
271 × 315 mm. /$10\frac{5}{8}$ × $12\frac{3}{8}$ in.

A hasty sketch included with the Ascott drawings, the kind of thing that is done on the spur of the moment when the rich client expresses a need. Devey's sundial has the appearance of a first recollection of a familiar Victorian style to be seen in many gardens, rather than a carefully thought out individual design, such as those by Philip Webb (no. 253) and Edwin

79

Lutyens (no. 254). The idea of the 'romance of time', the Victorian love of moralizing, made sundials boom in popularity in the 1880s. An edition of Mrs Gatty's *A Book of Sun-dials* appeared in 1889, with her collection of suitable mottoes in the *sic vita fugit* (so life flies) vein.

80] GEORGE DEVEY 1820–86 (Office of)
Plan for gardens

Ascott House, Wing, Buckinghamshire, *c.*1880
Pen and wash on linen
562×757 mm. / $22\frac{1}{8} \times 29\frac{3}{4}$ in.

It is difficult to date this plan, but a photograph of the 1880s in the Collection shows the garden to be substantially laid out as drawn here. In the 1880s the ageing Devey was a hero and inspiration to young Arts and Crafts architects and his work at Penshurst, and perhaps Ascott, was studied and admired by Antony Salvin, Richard Norman Shaw, William Eden Nesfield and Charles Voysey. In her book in the RIBA Drawings Series on the Arts and Crafts Architects, Margaret Richardson gives Devey pride of place as the first of the 'Precursors and Masters' of the movement, simply because of his thorough knowledge of vernacular building and country life, especially horse-orientated life, that went with them.

Ascott was a large and long-standing commission for the Devey Office; these drawings appear to be subsidiary designs, possibly supervised by Devey's partner James Williams. But the main interest lies in the office succession after Devey's death in 1886, when the partnership devolved down to Edmund Wratten and Walter H. Godfrey, as the latter was to become a noted garden architect.

81] EDMUND WRATTEN 1877–1925 and
WALTER H. GODFREY 1881–1961
Sketch plan for the garden

Ascott House, Wing, Buckinghamshire, *c.*1890
Pencil, pen and wash

The formal garden outside the Billiard and Drawing Rooms at Ascott were elaborated by Walter H. Godfrey. The formal parterres, planted with bedding plants in season, were surrounded by a low yew hedge with clipped triangles of topiary equally spaced around the Billiard room garden, and rounded topiary used on the Dining Room corner. A *Country Life* photograph published in 1904 shows the garden elaborately planted. This plan was illustrated in Godfrey's *Gardens in the Making*, published in 1914.

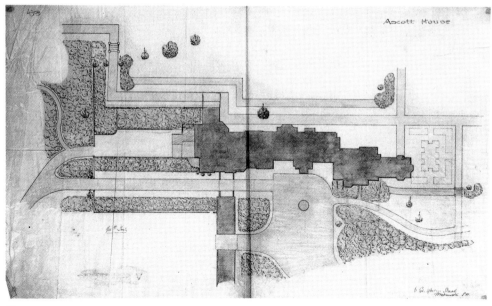

80

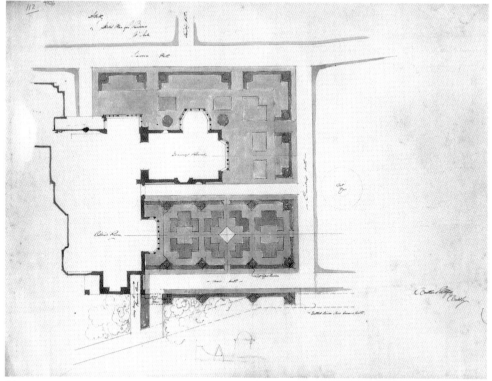

81

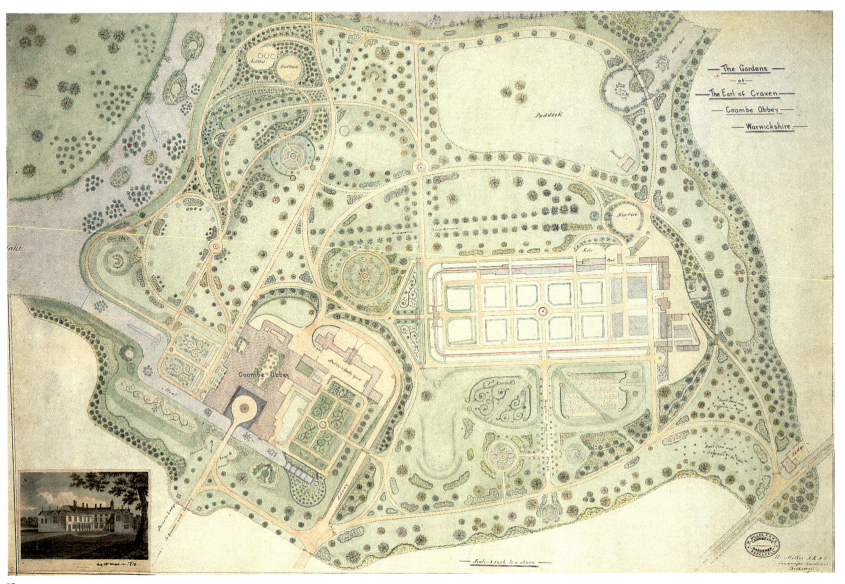

82

COOMBE ABBEY, WARWICKSHIRE

82] WILLIAM MILLER 1828–1909

Plan of the formal garden

Coombe Abbey, Coventry, Warwickshire, 1897
Pen and watercolour
676 × 1010 mm. /26⅝ × 39¾ in.

The formal garden layout around the Abbey, especially the way the Moat is brought along the entrance front, was designed by William Eden Nesfield for the 2nd Earl of

Craven, who died in 1866. The gardens were then in the care of a head gardener, William Miller, who apparently planted Nesfield's designs and made walks through the park, planting many fine and exotic trees, including Wellingtonias, for the 3rd Earl during the 1870s.

If he was a very young head gardener, it is possible that Miller left the Earl's employ and trained as a landscape gardener; alternatively these plans are the work of his son, also named William. They are stamped *William Miller*

F.R.H.S. Landscape Gardener, Berkswell, Coventry, and whether he was a former gardener or a gardener's clever son does not detract from the quality of their design and workmanship.

In 1893 the 4th Earl of Craven brought his American bride, an heiress, back to settle at Coombe; the gardens were to enjoy a heyday that lasted until the First World War. William Miller appears to have used the bones of Nesfield's layout to create this wonderful arrangement of parterres and formal beds around the house; to clarify the walks through the woodland and design new gardens among the walks, and to create a whole new and enormous kitchen and fruit-garden.

83] WILLIAM MILLER 1828–1909
Vegetable and salad beds

Coombe Abbey, Coventry, Warwickshire, 1897
Pen and watercolour
513 × 740 mm. /20¼ × 29⅛ in.

This drawing shows the details of the vegetable and salad beds, the orchards and the croquet ground. The quality of the design is of the highest; the almost living, amoebic writhings of the shrubberies express the cherished tastes of Victorian England to perfection.

84] WILLIAM MILLER 1828–1909
Detail of beds for the west garden

Coombe Abbey, Coventry, Warwickshire, 1897
Pencil, pen and wash
495 × 540 mm. /19½ × 21¼ in.

The inscription in William Miller's hand reads: *This was the First and Accepted plan of the Coombe Abbey Parterre Flower Garden, afterwards slightly altered and improved – a plain border was substituted for the Chains pattern.* The drawing is stamped and also signed and dated 21 February 1897; he has added: *I planted this garden in 1897 and in 1898. WM.* A photograph of 1909 shows the gardens well-planted. Lord Craven was drowned from his yacht at Cowes in 1921 and Coombe was subsequently sold. Today it is a Country Park owned and managed by the City of Coventry; a well maintained box parterre occupies the site of this design.

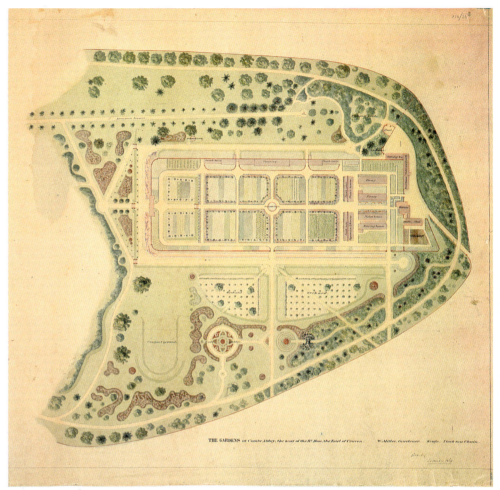

83

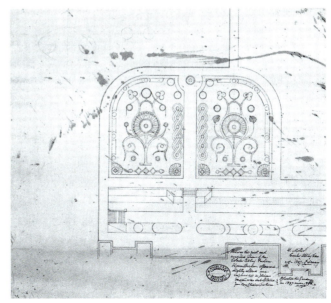

84

Fig. 18] The Water Garden, Moor Close, Binfield, Berkshire, as designed by Oliver Hill; photographed in 1924.

4

THE ARTS AND CRAFTS GARDEN
1890–1914

The ideal Arts and Crafts garden surrounds its Edwardian vernacular house, and is laid out so that straight paths and vistas spring from the house doors and windows. Both house and paths are bordered with flowers, and the paths are of stone and brick, sprouting thrift and thymes, leading to yew-walled rooms furnished with a sundial or a pool, and a seat for contemplation. Somewhere one walks beneath a pergola, dripping with wisteria or laburnum, to a small square summerhouse, and, if the garden is large enough, on through a walk of hazelnut trees to a copse with wild roses, honeysuckles and ferns,

Certain words and phrases in this description need a little further explanation from the standpoint of 1890 as the beginning of the Arts and Crafts garden movement. It was the first premise of William Robinson's *The English Flower Garden*, published in 1883, that the garden should not be set apart from the house, limited by soil and aspect and confined to being visited as 'the old and general rule' of the Victorians; the acceptance of the garden *surrounding* the house was his first victory. The strange word *vernacular* (which I discover has its root in the latin *verna*, a home-born slave) was the cachet of the bright young architects of the 1880s, whose common aim was to throw out the pattern-books and styles and go on sketching expeditions to study the construction methods of old English buildings, and so renew their art. They also shared William Morris's respect for craftsmen – plasterers, masons, painters, carvers and sculptors – who could build and ornament their work with inspiration from nature. Their highest ideal was the artist-craftsman, who could both design and create, and many Arts and Crafts architects were competent craftsmen of one kind or another. The ultimate, and most secret yearning, was to also be a good gardener (which does not come easily to architects) and this was the deepest motivation for the fact that there came to be Arts and Crafts gardens at all. The element of being in touch with nature, as well as in touch with the past, that Ruskin and Morris had inspired, gave young architects the confidence to feel that the garden was their rightful territory; hence the introduction of so many built features – pergolas, summerhouses, steps, pools, into these gardens. But there would have been no magic without wonderful planting, and so the essence of these gardens remains that supreme harmony of design and flowers, a harmony for which the time just happened to be right.

Many horticulturalists are suspicious of Arts and Crafts gardens and this is because they grew out of an architectural movement. There must have been something in the air of the 1860s that gave birth to such a crowd of talented young architects who spilled into and out of the London offices of the 1880s. That their yearnings for the vernacular traditions became a Movement was largely because of the way they were trained, by being articled to a successful master. The office network has been described in every fascinating detail by Margaret Richardson in *The Architects of the Arts and Crafts Movement*[1] and my story, as well as our whole recognition of this movement in gardens, owes much to her knowledge of the drawings of this period. Some of the architects whose gardens appear on the following pages are connected thus: the office of Richard Norman Shaw, architect of Cragside, Northumberland (now National Trust) and New Scotland Yard, produced Ernest Newton and Gerald Callcott Horsley; the office of Ernest George (Batsford Park, Gloucestershire and Claridge's Hotel) and Harold Peto (the gardens of Buscot Park, Oxfordshire and Iford Manor, Wiltshire) sheltered Herbert Baker and Edwin Lutyens; Charles Voysey was a law unto himself, but Charles Mallows and Oliver Hill were both in William Flockhart's office; Flockhart was a less well-known architect than the others, but he built, in best old-English style, Pasture Wood at Abinger in Surrey where Gertrude Jekyll made one of her earliest large, wild rock gardens. Finally, John Dando Sedding's office produced Ernest Gimson and Ernest Barnsley, both of whom were to play important roles in the Cotswold Arts and Crafts Movement which encouraged so many wonderful gardens, and perhaps the most purely Arts and Crafts house and garden of them all, Rodmarton Manor in Gloucestershire[2].

A second contributory factor to the welding of the Movement was the craze for societies. William Morris's Society for the Protection of Ancient Buildings, founded in 1877, was a great attraction; then, in 1884, five pupils from Shaw's office (Ernest Newton, W. R. Lethaby, Gerald Horsley, Mervyn MacCartney and Edward Prior) formed the Art Workers' Guild to enourage artist-craftsmen, largely in the face of the Royal Academy's single-minded interest in oil painting which ignored all the crafts. Out of this mood, in 1888, the Arts and Crafts Exhibition Society was formed, fixing the name of the Movement, and creating a showcase for everyone's work.

This then was the architectural basis of the Movement, but, for all these brilliant young men and their talents, there would have been no gardens but for one remarkable woman. Gertrude Jekyll, born in 1843, was nine years younger than William Morris, and in many ways he was her guiding star. She grew up, a country child in energies and interests, with a determination to be a painter. She studied at Henry Cole's Kensington School for two years (as did many of the architects) and then travelled, painted and encountered painters with a characteristic verve and dedication. By her mid-twenties she had met both Ruskin and Morris, and widened her efforts into a steady, and highly-talented, pursuit of many arts and crafts. She became accomplished and well-known for her embroidery, decorative painting, carving, repoussé work, silver jewellery, wrought ironwork and most delicate inlay of mother-of-pearl and ivory. She did not marry and her lifestyle was gregarious and indefatigable; in a less balanced person it might have been called frenetic.

Unfortunately, though fortunately for gardening, this super-woman did have one weakness, in her myopic and poor-sighted eyes. By the time she was thirty she was suffering severe head-aches from overstrain, and she eventually heeded the specialists' advice and concluded that she would have to change her lifestyle and give up most of the interests she loved. In 1878, her widowed mother settled into her last home, a house that was built for her on Munstead Heath, just south of Godalming in Surrey. Gertrude joined her mother, came home to the beloved Surrey of her childhood and took to writing and gardening. Her dedication and energy were soon revived, if they had ever left her, and she made as thorough a passage through the gardening world as she had done through the world of Arts and Crafts. She also targeted William Robinson, and was soon writing for his journal *The*

Garden and also contributed the chapter on colour to *The English Flower Garden*; as a contributor she was in the company of her new gardening friends, Canon Ellacombe, Dr Michael Foster, the Dean of Rochester and George Frederick Wilson among them.

At home in Surrey she bought her own garden plot which she called Munstead Wood, and took up photography to record the making of it; she pursued her own interest in the country ways and traditions in *Old West Surrey*,[3] and became a familiar figure in her pony trap, driving fearlessly along the narrow sandy lanes to visit her friends. On a particular visit, to the rhododendron grower Harry Mangles at Littleworth Cross near Farnham, to see his garden at its best in May of 1889, she was introduced to the young Edwin Lutyens as a likely architect for her own house.

The friendship that grew between this twenty-year old, callow architect and rather distinguished spinster of forty-five was based on a shared interest in the old buildings and craft traditions of west Surrey, which they explored together in preparation for ideas for her house. Along the way they discussed gardens, and talked themselves into a partnership which was to produce some of the most beautiful houses and gardens that England has ever known. A few of them can be illustrated in this context, but in the main the story has to be found elsewhere, in my book *Gardens of a Golden Afternoon*.[4]

Two particular points are relevant here; firstly, that Miss Jekyll was writing on gardening for *Country Life* magazine and she introduced Lutyens to its owner Edward Hudson. Hudson became one of Lutyens' most generous patrons and the magazine carried lavish pictures of his houses and their Jekyll gardens which gave the partnership all the free advertisement they could desire. Secondly their work was seen, not only by future clients, but by all the other architects (*Country Life*, in its infancy, was just as much a cult magazine as it is now) and they were drawn to Miss Jekyll's garden writing, both in the magazine and in her books, which were being published in a steady stream during the 1900s. She was the link between architecture and gardens for the single reason that architects felt she could understand them; as well as coping with her maverick-genius, Lutyens, her artistic education, her travelled knowledge of the gardens of Renaissance Italy and Moorish Spain, and her expressed allegiance to the 'old' i.e. sixteenth- and seventeenth-century gardens of England and Scotland, were exactly in line with their own sympathies. She could clearly be trusted to know just how those mysterious

Fig. 19] Design for a fireplace frieze with owls and poppies by John Dando Sedding. This depicts symbols of night and sleep, and represents the nearest form of garden inspiration that Sedding allowed himself in his design work.

things called plants should be rightly kept in their places in formal gardens. Aside from her partnership with Lutyens, for which she was involved in over one hundred gardens, she kept up a busy private practice as a consultant for the rest of her life. She inspired and advised on gardens by Charles Voysey, Oliver Hill, M. H. Baillie Scott, Herbert Baker, Robert Weir-Schulz, Robert Lorimer, Forbes & Tait, Harold Falkner and L. Rome Guthrie. Her artistic theories of planting and sound practical knowledge of plants, her wisdom and her energy really welded these houses and gardens together, and no part of this heritage in Arts and Crafts gardens is without her influence.

There is no doubt that these architects enjoyed designing gardens, but it was an enjoyment dearly won, and not without that tinge of secret yearning to have a garden of their own, in the midst of a frantic professional life.[5] In the 1880s gardens were hardly a fit subject to waste the time of such a noble profession; the rightful business of architects was church work, and failing that highest of callings, the monuments to commerce or public service were allowed. John Dando Sedding (1838–91) was a distinguished church architect with a profound knowledge of Gothic decoration and love of building crafts. As far as I know he never designed a garden or garden feature, and so the little frieze of owls and poppies (fig. 19) must stand for his love of such things. He practised his gardening at home during the weekends and in the last years of his life he studied the gardens of seventeenth-century England for his book, *Garden Craft Old & New*, which was published posthumously after his sad and sudden death in 1891.

Sedding was therefore the first to alert the young architects to the old gardens, much to the fury of the urbane, articulate and far from secretive, Reginald Blomfield, whe was researching the same subject simultaneously. Blomfield's *The Formal Garden in England* was published the following year; his sketches of the garden at Montacute in Somerset, from his sketchbook no. 11 dated 1889, are the most direct evidence of his researches that I could find (nos. 85–87). His book, illustrated with fine pen drawings by F. Inigo Thomas was highly influential. In it he gave gardens back to the architects; he revived the interest in the built features and ornaments – walls, gates, sundials, garden houses, bridges and terraces – and in the architectural treatments of living hedges i.e. topiary, in the gardens of Levens Hall, Canons Ashby, Brympton d'Evercy, Montacute, Melbourne, Penshurst and Wrest Park. In doing so he opened up a battle with William Robinson, who hated topiary as much as he hated architects, which raged for several years, but it was largely a duel over the interpretation of words, for it was well known that Robinson agreed that a formal layout and good stonework had its place, as his own garden at Gravetye Manor in Sussex demonstrated; he also summoned Edwin Lutyens to discuss architectural ideas, possibly even for the Gravetye garden, but the only design from that meeting is for the circular garden seat to go around a tree (no. 248). The battle 'of the styles' as it was called, just increased the sales of both Blomfield's and Robinson's books, and sent more and more young architects out to learn about old gardens.[6] The rather uninspired drawings by R. Shekleton Balfour of Montacute (nos. 88–90) and the splendid works of John James Joass of Edzell, Balcaskie and Barncluith (nos. 93–99) are the evidence of all these young men out with their sketching pads. While Balfour's sketches are interesting for the view they give of Montacute at that time, the Joass drawings are full of the technical design information that was to be recycled for Arts and Crafts gardens. These great old Scottish gardens were very unspoiled; the buttresses and balustrades and little conical roofs of Balcaskie, the chequered walls and summerhouse at Edzell and the patterns of the flower beds at Barncluith, the sense of enclosure, of orderly paths and terraces in all three gardens, all such ideas would be turned to again and again during the next twenty years.

Having looked back to the seventeenth century, it is time to go forward. Edwin Lutyens made his first garden with a great deal of help from Gertrude Jekyll (who introduced him to the client,

Adeline, Duchess of Bedford) at Woodside, Chenies in Buckinghamshire in 1893. It was a simple terraced walk from the house down to a small stone court with seats and flower borders beside the River Chess. The sundial he designed for this garden is illustrated (no. 254). Few of Lutyens' drawings for work in the 1890s have survived his several moves of office and the London blitz. His sketchbook for Munstead Wood is one of the great treasures of the Collection (nos. 90–92), and his sensitivity to gardens, in particular to Miss Jekyll's own garden in which he was allowed no formal part, comes clearly from the three sketches to please her, for her entrance gate, and the north and south fronts of her house, which was eventually completed the way *she* wanted it, in 1897. From these beginnings they went on to make their most famous gardens – Deanery Garden at Sonning, Berkshire for Edward Hudson (1901), Folly Farm, Sulhamstead, near the Kennet & Avon Canal on the opposite side of Reading (1901–12), Marsh Court, Stockbridge in Hampshire for Herbert Johnson, and Hestercombe in Somerset for Lord Portman, both in 1904. The Collection has no drawings of value for any of these gardens, and ironically, the most relevant drawings survive with Miss Jekyll's papers in Berkeley, California[7] because Lutyens always sent her surveys and outline designs and she has always kept duplicates of her own planting plans. The Lutyens drawings are difficult in garden terms; the collection is vast, occupying a volume of the catalogue to itself[8] and came directly from the architect's last office in Mansfield Street, London W1.[9] Unless a commission carried on over a number of years, as with Ashby St Ledgers where Lutyens went on working for Lord Wimborne after the Great War (no. 102), or unless the drawings, of which there was usually only one set, ended up in the house rather than the office, the material from his early, pre-War garden-making period, was cleared out due to lack of space. Of the drawings for gardens that have survived, many are badly faded, or on a cheap tracing paper that the years have dried to a yellow brittleness which crumbles almost at the touch. The Buckhurst garden drawings (nos. 104–6), which survived because they were at the house, show these signs of age. Fortunately they also show the brilliance and invention of Lutyens' games with geometry in a garden setting.

If Lutyens' reputation as a garden architect survives despite his drawings, then the opposite is true of Charles Francis Annesley Voysey (1857–1941). He is best known as an architect and graphic designer but his drawings reveal how his solemn reverence for nature and his designer's ability to stylize its flora and fauna, lead him into his garden. Voysey's gardens are dreams, not real at all; his watercolour presentation drawing for Oakhurst (no. 128) is of a house no client could resist, for it comes with a magical garden where scillas, hollyhocks and roses and sunflowers are all in bloom at once beneath a chilly-looking sky, and even the trees look like the decorative motives on his wallpapers. The garden plan for Dixcot (no. 129) is equally irresistible, suggesting the design for a bedspread with appliquéd hearts and flowers.

There seems to be a definite Voysey style of garden which can be pursued and put into reality, with considerable restraint in planting; after all, if gardens could be made to emulate a landscape painting by Claude, how much more appropriate for our time are these finely balanced, spare and exquisite inspirations from a superb graphic designer? The RIBA's Voysey Collection of drawings is also large and catalogued in a single volume.[10] Besides the watercolours of dream-gardens, most of his houses – including four of his Surrey masterpieces, Lowicks in Frensham, Greyfriars on the Hog's Back, Littleholme in Guildford and New Place in Haslemere, have carefully ordered terraces and vistas. All his gardens have the details that he loved to design – summerhouses, seats and tables, gates, sundials, pigeon-cotes, a bird bath, and he also designed a playground for Kensal New Town with a sandpit. Many of his other designs have a garden theme: an embroidered bedcover called 'Squire's Garden' (fig. 21); a textile design, 'My Garden'; there are garden scenes on painted furniture, and endless flowers and trees, butterflies and birds on wallpapers and fabrics.

Charles Voysey was a purist, even a puritan, kindly but autocratic. He qualified in 1879, aged twenty-two, spent a short time in George Devey's office then set up on his own. For his whole career he maintained a modest office, with only two pupils at a time and no other staff. He executed all his own designs and drawings, even wrote his own letters, and only allowed his pupils to copy drawings and read the letters; unsurprisingly none of them became inspired architects! He believed in simplicity at all costs, made as few drawings as possible and reworked his standard details introducing subtle changes. These economies are rather clearly illustrated in the drawings for gates (nos. 217–20), where the sheets are carefully crowded and colour is used to clarify details.

As Voysey was not interested in how his gardens were laid on the ground, they are not really 'his' any more. At Littleholme in Guildford he designed the terraces and retaining walls for the sloping site, but as Gertrude Jekyll describes in *Gardens for Small Country Houses*, the garden was taken over by one Thomas Young, to whom, even she, gives the credit for an immaculate layout of angled vistas, flower beds and parterres and orchards on differing levels. I suspect that the bones of the layout are Voysey's and Mr Young merely supervised the contract and the planting and took the credit. At New Place, Haslemere, which Voysey designed for Sir Algernon and Lady Methuen in 1901 it was Miss Jekyll herself who took over. The plans for New Place garden are in the Collection; this is another terraced site, with paved vistas to a summerhouse, flat-topped retaining walls and lovely iron gates, all in the Voysey manner, and a small parterre laid out with his favourite heart-shaped beds, echoing the heart motif which fills the house in woodwork and iron details. The architect wanted the borders and beds filled with rue, undoubtedly for its lovely bluish-haze (which matched the blue-green slate tiles on the roof rather well) but perhaps also because he had observed the young leaves to be heart-shaped. Lady Methuen, who with her husband, was a keen and knowledgeable gardener, was adamant: no rue, she could not stand the smell! She resorted to Miss Jekyll, who lived not far away, who covered Voysey's rather severe walls with jasmines, clematis and climbing roses and decreed beds of roses with standards, *Viscountess Folkestone, Madame Abel Chatenay, Madame Lambard and Grace Darling* planted amongst scented bushes, *Marquise de Salisbury, Camoens, Little White Pet and Gruss an Teplitz* respectively. Voysey would have undoubtedly approved, for he has drawn standard roses for Oakhurst's garden (no. 128) and standards amongst bushes were very much in vogue. But it remains a tempting prospect to restore one of his gardens faithfully and ease his garden dreams into a reality.

Charles Edward Mallows (1864–1915) was a less distinguished architect but an equally attractive artist, who was influential in his own time and still has enormous appeal in ours. Mallows originated in Bedford, and most of his work was done in the swathe of counties around London from there to Middlesex. His drawings, for over forty projects, mostly topographical ones of churches and cathedrals, and his sketchbooks and diaries were presented to the Collection by Miss S.D.M. Mallows in 1947. He was very interested in garden design and some of the drawings illustrated were made for a series of articles on 'Architectural Gardening' that were published in *The Studio* 1908–11. These were influential, as was the generous coverage of his work and high praise, given to him by Gertrude Jekyll and Lawrence Weaver in *Gardens for Small Country Houses*, when it appeared in 1912. Mallows had undoubtedly learned much from the town planner and garden designer, Thomas Mawson, for whom he had illustrated *The Art and Craft of Garden Making*, which had been published in 1900. In a way, I feel, Mallows stands surrogate here for Mawson, who is the most notable absentee of this period from the Drawings Collection.[11] However he came by them, Mallows' virtues are many, and may be outlined as follows: he had a fine, and graphic sense of harmony in garden plans, balancing his space division well and making fine contrast between the thrust of paths of movement and the enclosed, static spaces. He exploited 'architectural greenery' and gave generous spaces to flowers and other plants; where this balance is not maintained an aridity creeps in, which is a common pitfall among architects. He handled pavings with sensitivity, raising them from the overly-rustic and aptly-named 'crazy' variety (usually beloved for its cheapness) to the realm of respectable good order, not too harsh and softened with plants. Finally, he is good on details; his plain pool for his father-in-law's garden, Compton House (no. 112) has been filled to the right level for reflections, his garden buildings are substantial and not too fanciful, and his steps have a leisurely human scale.

The work of L. Rome Guthrie (1880–1958) was also praised by Jekyll and Weaver, and Miss Jekyll executed planting plans for one of his gardens, Caenwood Towers, Highgate, London (1920) for which her drawings survive, and some of his are in the Collection. However, his garden work would have been unknown to me and to the Collection had not Hampshire Gardens Trust been concerned over his garden for Townhill Park, Southampton (which survives but is in need of repair) and the Trust's interest revealed these drawings for South Stoneham, Townhill and Chelwood Vetchery in Sussex (nos. 124–7, 130–31 and 133–4). They are a remarkable series of drawings and they have an intrinsic interest and fascination, in differing ways, that has nothing to do with their 'style' or influence on others. They show how the architect, who was a distinguished and well-known figure in RIBA circles, understood both the sites he was working on and the essential garden mood of the time. There is a distinct impression that the architect was learning as he went along, and by the time he had consulted Gertrude Jekyll's books he was competent to design a very fine garden for Townhill

Fig. 20] House and garden, Higham, Woodford, Essex, 1904 by C. F. A. Voysey for Lady Henry Somerset: a fine example of how the architect painted the harmony of house and garden to please his prospective client.

Fig. 21] Opposite: Design for a bedspread, *Squire's Garden* by C. F. A. Voysey.

Park, the formal garden with the surrounding pergola and small summerhouse, which survives today. That the drawings were discovered because of a local interest in the garden, and then in turn become a valuable tool in restoration work is especially important with gardens of this period, which are now becoming recognized and valued.

Edward Maufe (1883–1974) and Oliver Hill (1887–1968) are architects we think of as making their reputations in more modern times, Maufe above all for Guildford Cathedral, begun in 1932 and the Cooper's Hill Royal Air Force Memorial (1953), and Oliver Hill for his International Modern buildings, but they both began in the Arts and Crafts period. Maufe, who changed his name from Muff, was inspired to architecture by living in the Red House at Bexley, built by Philip Webb for William Morris, when he was in his late teenage years; he was articled for five years in William A. Pite's office, and Kelling Hall in Norfolk (nos 135–7) was his first major commission, coming as a stroke of luck – out of a dinner-table conversation with his client, H. W. Deterding, director-general of Royal Dutch Petroleum. Possibly the point on which they clinched the deal was the fashionable and rather exciting butterfly plan, which Mr Deterding could have seen at Home Place at Holt nearby (as built by Edward Prior) and which the young Maufe was willing to supply. He did an extremely thorough job; the house was beautifully crafted down

to every small detail and all the drawings are in the Collection. The garden drawings are no less carefully made, and Maufe has kept detailed faith with the splayed wing layout in the way he has divided the garden. He has also gone to great trouble with the planting, devising spring bulb schemes in honour of his client's Dutch connections, a bed of blue lupins, delphiniums and anchusa with white hollyhocks, foxgloves, snapdragons and lilies, and long borders of hollyhocks, pyrethrums and day lilies, campanulas and verbascums. Kelling Hall, built in 1912, is one of the last truly Arts and Crafts houses and gardens; Christopher Hussey pronounced it 'a thoroughly vernacular work, never putting undue strain on the King's architectural English.'[12] There is a hint, perhaps, that the home-grown was becoming a little in-bred and that when too much money was thrown to tradition, it became quaintness?

Oliver Hill, on the other hand, could handle any tradition, and with such enthusiasm and flourish as to be totally convincing: as David Dean has written of him 'he was more than literally style-ish; there was an aplomb, a dashing elegance running through all his work'.[13] Hill's most important Arts and Crafts work was the outstanding garden creation for C. Birch Crisp at Moor Close, Binfield in Berkshire (nos 143–5). Though it was designed in 1913 after King Edward VII's death, this garden is everything that is conjured up by the word 'Edwardian'; Hill has taken those earnest aspirations of Morris and the young architects for honest tradition and good craftsmanship, and played them to the limit. This garden, layered and inlaid with stone, brick, pebbles, black marble, white marble, tiles on edge and coloured chippings has twice the number of differing materials than even the bumptious young Lutyens would have dared use: it has steps and stairs, loggias and garden gazebos, drooping walls and sunken pools, sundials, plant boxes, pergolas and seats, plants and patterns and foibles crammed in, rather like a gargantuan, over-blown Edwardian dinner; it comes bustled and heavily-bosomed, as did the most alluring of the King's mistresses. But, as the photograph taken in 1924 cannot hide (fig. 18), in a few short years it was touched with a tattered poignancy and out of place, almost seeming to retreat into its veil of greenery, ashamed of its flamboyance, because the new world was seeking different charms.

After designing Moor Close, Oliver Hill, aged twenty-seven, went off to the Great War and won himself a Military Cross.[14] The idea of the Arts and Crafts garden was to be completely destroyed by the War, even of the love of vernacular buildings limped on. It was not just that there was no money for gardens, nor even that so many of the young men who might make them or want them made, were killed; it was essentially that the pure enjoyment of a garden that was beautifully built and planted was no longer possible. Gardens are a luxury, even if of the most soulful kind, and a luxury England no longer deserved.

Apart from the stillborn Modern Movement, the Arts and Crafts gardens mark the last forward progression the English were to make in the art of gardening. We have been regressing, going over old ground, ever since. The Arts and Crafts Movement is constantly lauded as a flowering of English art, even equivalent to the English landscape movement. Hermann Muthesius first perceived the perfect expression of the English qualities of independence and naturalness as expressed in house-building in *Das Englische Haus* in 1905; Roderick Gradidge has passionately celebrated them in *Dream Houses*, and most recently, Gavin Stamp's *The English House 1860–1914* has re-assessed a

remarkable achievement that not even he, an astute critic, can fault. It was, as David Watkin has pointed out at length in a brilliant chapter in *The Rise of Architectural History*[15] rooted in a love of England and all things English. Nationalism was, as we know, something the Edwardians expressed rather well. That the RIBA Drawings Collection has such a supreme record of this English movement is thus right, and appropriate, and, even in this heyday of worldwide-market collectors for such drawings, it seems likely that it will always be so. The Collection is the best source from which to assess, firstly, the importance of gardens as part of the Arts and Crafts Movement, and secondly, the importance of these gardens in the context of garden history.

Even in a holistic philosophy such as this, gardens make considerable extra demands upon an architect. The taste for highly-built gardens was not unconnected to the percentage chargeable on the building contract. But, even so, to design and build a garden with the house took extra time and trouble; garden building techniques i.e. the kind of foundations and drainage had to be investigated, an immense survey carried out, extra and different kinds of labourers and craftsmen employed and the right kinds of materials and ornaments tracked down. All these imponderables came to the fore, and the nightmare of

Fig. 22 The Sundial Terrace for Moor Close, Binfield, Berkshire, designed by Oliver Hill and photographed in 1924. This flamboyant motif, made of tiles set on edge, was characteristic of Hill's early Arts and Crafts work.

having actually to deal with plants was always in the background. Edwin Lutyens' supremacy as the first architect who comes to mind in a garden connection was not just because he was so brilliant and worked so hard; his 'secret weapon' – his 'Aunt Bumps' down at Munstead Wood, who constantly advised him and drew up all his planting plans – was no mean asset. But what of other, Jekyll-less architects? Charles Voysey clearly loved designing gardens as he did everything else, and if he had had a gardening amuensis there would be many wonderful Voysey gardens. I think the same could be said for both Ernest Newton and Reginald Blomfield. As things were, both of them were interested in the surroundings of their houses, and designed them well, but could not carry through to complete real gardens. Blomfield, after his first flourish with *The Formal Garden in England* designed all manner of tradition-inspired gardens, most notably that for Mellerstein in Berwickshire (no. 108). Ernest Newton, who brought to perfection the design of the medium-sized, substantial Edwardian family villa, clearly knew that the garden was important to his clients, but either did not know enough, or did not have time enough, to make his gardens work. I know of no Newton house where the garden is exciting, which is a pity. Herbert Baker, who worked a lot in South Africa and then became Lutyens' 'Bakerloo' at Delhi[16] knew Miss Jekyll well enough but he was not interested in gardens. He consulted her over Cecil Rhodes's garden at Groote Schurr and she did the planting for Winchester College War Memorial Cloister for him in 1923. Gerald Callcott Horsley was one of the key figures of the Movement; he was in Shaw's office, a founder member of the Art Workers' Guild, and an advocate of the 'union', which meant a merging of painting, decorating and carving with architecture, and most of his career was spent on church decoration. The Links at Hythe (nos. 138–141) is, as far as I know, his only garden, but he has designed and drawn it superbly well.

Even in such a marvellous collection of drawings, there are disappointments. My first was Harold Peto, Ernest George's partner, who left the practice in the early 1890s to concentrate on gardens. There seem to be no drawings (I suspect he did not bother with such things, being an autocratic designer) but his gardens for Buscot Park (now National Trust), his own Iford Manor in Wiltshire and Garinish Island, off the west coast of Ireland, add greatly to the score of the period. Robert Lorimer (1864–1929) was interested enough to consult Miss Jekyll over

High Barn, at Hascombe in Surrey and Brackenbugh in Cumberland, and he restored a number of Scottish gardens, but his drawings are in Edinburgh.[17] Those of his compatriot, Charles Rennie Mackintosh (1868–1928), are at Glasgow School of Art and as far as I know he did not design any gardens, which is a matter for great regret considering all those divine watercolours of flowers he painted. I also regret that Gertrude Jekyll is the only woman featured in these pages; my excitement was roused when I discovered Ethel Mary Charles (1871–1962) who qualified as the first woman member of the RIBA in late 1898, to be followed by her sister, Bess, two years later, but neither sister appears to have been interested in gardens.

But the greatest disappointment is that Charles Holden (1875–1960), dubbed 'austere and fine like his tower for the University of London'[18] and an architect of war memorials and underground stations, cannot be drawn into the garden ranks. Or can he? Holden's sketch for a seat in his own garden (no. 249) here represents a garden connection that is especially fine. Holden joined the practice of H. Percy Adams (1865–1950) in 1899 and was made a partner just over seven years later. The practice specialized in hospitals, and Adams and Holden's first job as partners was to adapt and build a competition-winning design for King Edward VII's Sanatorium for tubercular diseases at Midhurst in Sussex. This hospital with 'the look of a large country house', when 'cheerless' and 'repellant' were more usual adjectives, was a revelation.[19] It was built on the butterfly plan, with very long wings; the south-facing range, with balconies and green shutters, held the patients' rooms which looked across the downs to the sea, and the north wings were offices. Adams and Holden arranged small courts and sheltered gardens in and around these wings, with sunny south terraced gardens, so that the patients could have every opportunity of being out of doors, and even of a little gentle gardening. They asked Gertrude Jekyll to do the planting schemes, which she took on with great care and sympathy (it was one of her largest commissions and she made dozens of drawings) using scented herbs and flowers, masses of rosemary and roses. The gardens were made and planted by students from the Glynde School for Lady Gardeners.[20] The sheer weight of good intent and sympathetic design that went into this building and garden made it a very special place, gave it a kind of blessing of benevolence which can be strongly discerned there still. Though some of the courts have been built over, Miss Jekyll's terraces thrive as do her flowers; magnolias, foxgloves and her original hedge of *Madame Plantier* roses.

In the pages of *The Studio* and among exhibitors at Royal Horticultural Society exhibitions, the list of prominent names began with Thomas Mawson and his highly successful firm, Lakeland Nurseries; much of his work, especially for Lord Leverhulme (of which The Hill, Hampstead is an outstanding example) was equal to the best of the period. Percy Cane came a close second; he had studied art and horticulture, worked as a gardening journalist and was a successful designer immediately after the war. Cane had a very real talent for the manipulation of green, as opposed to built, spaces, of which his work at Dartington Hall is the best known example. He wrote several books on his work, but he has slipped out of garden history and deserves revival.

The other big names included Gilbert Jenkins (in partnership with Romaine Walker), who was to be a founder member of the Institute of Landscape Architects, well-known for the garden of Rhinefield House in the New Forest, which is at present being restored. Edward White, yet another founder member of the ILA, designed a finely crafted and elaborate garden for Lord Cable at Lindridge in Devon in 1912. Darcy Braddell and Humphrey Deane made a much illustrated garden at Melchett Court, Romsey, and were proudly exhibiting a folksy cottage and garden at Paston in Norfolk, which probably endeared them to gardeners. Walter Godfrey was a distinguished garden man, designer of Kidbrooke Park in Sussex; none of his garden drawings are in the Collection but he does appear in succession to George Devey at Ascott (nos. 77–81). Walter Cave, praised by Gertrude Jekyll for his garden at Ewelme Down, Oxfordshire, also worked at The Wharf, Sutton Courtenay, for the Asquiths.

These were the prominent designers, and with the exception of Mawson, Cane and White, they were all architects. Undoubtedly, the philosophy of Arts and Crafts had, by 1920, made garden design the rightful and desirable objective of the architectural profession. But it was too late. There was only one gardener who knew how to deal with architects, and Gertrude Jekyll was nearing eighty (though in 1917 she had completed an enormous commission for Barrington Court for the architects Forbes & Tait). Mawson, White and Jenkins were part of a break-away movement, which appealed to architects and garden designers, which led to the formation of the Institute of Landscape Architects in 1929, and these new professionals wanted to create more serious works than gardens. Also, the age of the great amateurs was dawning, and gardens such as Lawrence Johnston's Hidcote Manor were growing without architectural help; garden owners in general, in line with the popular gardening journalists' advice, preferred independence as well as freedom from high professional fees.

Perhaps the final reason that the spirit of gardening went out with the war, was that so many architects had to turn to designing cemeteries and memorials. Edwin Lutyens, Reginald Blomfield and Herbert Baker were appointed architects to the War Graves' Commission, and Charles Holden soon joined them. In hundreds of cemeteries Gertrude Jekyll's planting suggestions formed the basis of what is still the Commission's style. When Lutyens returned to gardens in the twenties, as at Gledstone Hall in Yorkshire, or at Blagdon in Northumberland, for his daughter Ursula Ridley, his designs were for staid and arid gardens, even if they are grand. Lutyens' resilient genius, it seemed, could no longer summon up the sense of delight, without which a garden cannot live.

My final architect, a name I have avoided so far, is represented by the drawing of Clobb Copse at Buckler's Hard in Hampshire (no. 132). This watercolour is dated 1937, painted by Mackay Hugh Baillie Scott (1865–1945) and it is the only drawing of garden interest in a small amount of his material in the Collection. Baillie Scott was one of the brightest and best of the Arts and Crafts young men, a brilliant designer whose houses were in the reach of people of moderate incomes and yet still wanted fine design. He concentrated on houses and their contents (his 'Blue Bell' bedstead and 'Daffodil' dresser come to mind) and he knew a great deal about gardens and gardening. His sensitive and practical book of his work, *Houses & Gardens*, with many of his fine watercolours, first appeared in 1906, but it is difficult to find and has never been reprinted. Both his book and his work seem largely forgotten, which is sad; but perhaps Clobb Copse, for all its 'keeping in keeping' with historic Buckler's Hard, is sadder, for I feel it represents just what those Pied Pipers, John Ruskin and William Morris, did to all those bright young architects, and so many of the rest of us – they danced us back into the past, and left us there.

85

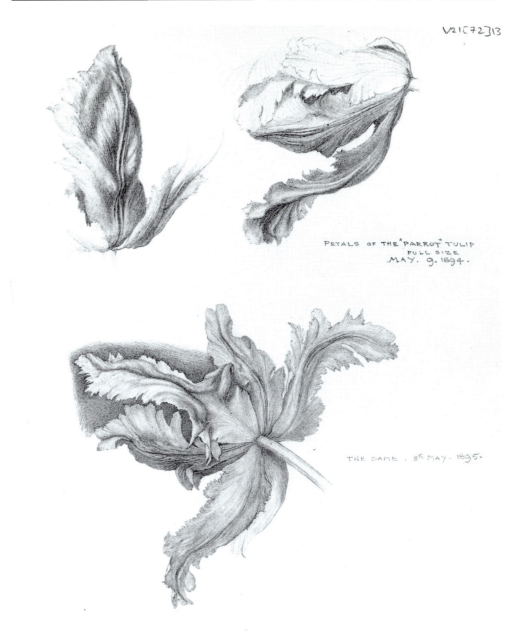

PETALS OF THE 'PARROT' TULIP
FULL SIZE
MAY. 9. 1894.

THE SAME . 8ᵗʰ MAY. 1895.

86

85]   ERNEST NEWTON 1856–1922

A study of a thistle

Pencil and watercolour
505 × 400 mm. /$19\frac{7}{8}$ × $15\frac{3}{4}$ in.

The Collection holds drawings of all Newton's works, over one hundred commissions that were in the main for comfortable country or suburban houses. This is the last drawing, and perhaps evidence of a single excursion into the living garden?

86]   PHILIP WEBB 1831–1915

Petals of the 'Parrot' tulip, 1894/5

Pencil with off-white wash
285 × 225 mm. /$11\frac{1}{4}$ × $8\frac{7}{8}$ in.

These sensitive pencil sketches exactly illustrate the susceptibility of the early Arts and Crafts architects to flowers, nature and gardens. This is one of twenty-three plant studies, which include drawings of lilies, spindle, aconite and peony, presented to the Collection by Miss Dorothy Walker in 1927. Webb was the arch-theorist and hard idealist of the Movement, the architect for William Morris's Red House at Bexley and also the artist for the oak leaves on his tomb at Kelmscott. The Collection has drawings for other Webb houses, including Coneyhurst at Ewhurst for a great gardener, Miss Mary Ann Ewart, and for Standen at East Grinstead, now owned by the National Trust. But he never became convinced about garden design and it took some younger architects of the Movement, namely Lutyens, Blomfield, Mallows and Hill, to transform the love of the flowers into an enjoyment of designing gardens.

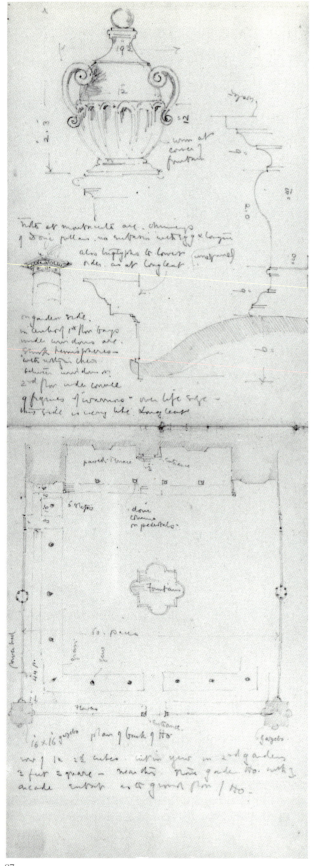

87

MONTACUTE HOUSE, SOMERSET

87] REGINALD BLOMFIELD 1856–1942

Details from the east garden

Montacute House, Somerset, 1889
Pencil sketches from sketchbook 11
125 × 180 mm. /$4\frac{7}{8}$ × $7\frac{1}{8}$ in.

These are the research sketches that Reginald Blomfield made for his book *The Formal Garden in England*, which was first published in 1892. These two illustrations form the open spread of the sketchbook.

a] shows measured sketches of one of the urns at the corners of the fountain, and the fountain plinth in profile. There are small additional details and notes on the Montacute chimneys.

b] is a plan of the east court garden with the fountain in the centre. This is the walled court which forms the principal entrance to the house today; Blomfield has marked the columns and steps of the entrance which he calls the back of the house, in deference to the splendid west front from Clifton Maybank which forms the 'state' entrance. He has noted the famous Montacute gazebos at the corners of the wall as measuring 16′ × 16′, and details of the yews spaced around the court. He has marked the positions of a 'pierced lantern' half way along each side wall, which he describes as 'a curious temple of stone; six pillars support a circular stone roof with projecting cornice on brackets, and an open cupola above, formed of three stone ribs joining at the top and terminating in an open ball formed of two intersecting circles of stone'.[21] These 'curious temples' and the gazebos are also shown sketched by R. Shekleton Balfour, no. 95.

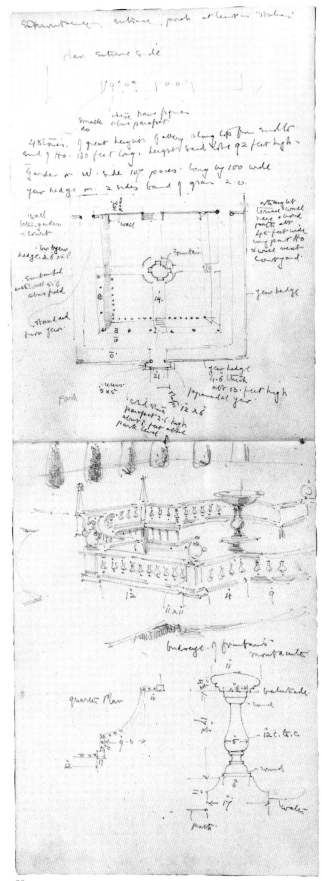

88] REGINALD BLOMFIELD 1856–1942

Details of the formal garden

Montacute House, Somerset, 1889
Pencil sketches from sketchbook 11
125 × 180 mm. /4$\frac{7}{8}$ × 7$\frac{1}{8}$ in.

This second spread of sketches from the same book show details of the formal garden to the north of the house, which is Elizabethan in origin.

a] is a plan of the garden surrounded by yew hedges, with clipped Irish yews beside the raised grass walk around the garden. The four gravel paths meet at the central pond and fountain, which is surrounded by a balustrade. The garden records show that this feature was new, thought to be of the 1890s but clearly there in the summer of 1889.

b] the second page of this spread of the sketchbook shows details of the balustrade, including measured details of a single baluster, which surrounds the fountain.

89] REGINALD BLOMFIELD 1856–1942

Yew and paving detail

Montacute House, Somerset, 1889
Pencil sketches from sketchbook no. 11
125 × 180 mm. /4$\frac{7}{8}$ × 7$\frac{1}{8}$ in.

A final page from Blomfield's sketchbook illustrates a clipped yew in the south garden at Montacute, a garden quaintly called 'Pig's Wheatie Orchard' and adjoining the kitchen garden to the west (where the National Trust car park is now). Yew hedges with clipped features were important here as screens to prevent the family from being disturbed by the gardeners at work. Blomfield had a major difference with William Robinson over topiary; Robinson detested it and Blomfield had discovered its delights: 'The *toparius*, or pleacher, was a very important person in the Roman garden, and the practice of cutting trees into various shapes was revived by the Italians of the fifteenth century'.[22]

The additional little detail here is of the paving of black marble tiles and Ham Hill stone in a chequer pattern on the floor of the gazebo.

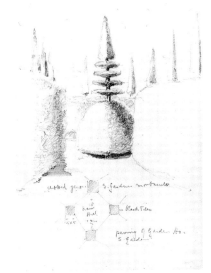

89

90

MUNSTEAD WOOD, SURREY

90] EDWIN L. LUTYENS 1869–1944

Design for an entrance

Munstead Wood, Godalming, Surrey, 1892–3
Pen and watercolour
From the Munstead Wood sketchbook
115 × 175 mm. /$4\frac{1}{2} \times 6\frac{7}{8}$ in.

Edwin Lutyens met Gertrude Jekyll in the spring of 1889: he had been practising as an architect on his own account for only a few months and was desperately looking for commissions. Miss Jekyll was forty-five, a distinguished artist-craftswoman and lady of independent means, and for six years she had owned Munstead Wood, a fifteen-acre plot of land which she was making into a garden. She was passionately interested in the buildings and traditions of the countryside of 'Old West Surrey' and their friendship blossomed with this shared interest. Eventually, that is three years after their meeting, Lutyens began to sketch for her the house she might like to build in her garden, and the sketchbook illustrates his ideas. His earliest sketches are for the Gardener's Cottage (1892) and The Hut, the small house he built for her in 1894.[23]

This is the first of his ideas for the main house (folio 1) marked 'Entrance'. He had already given a great deal of thought to the plan of the house, but to be able to begin, in an expeditionary kind of way, at the approach, demonstrates his remarkable ability to visualize the finished effect. Miss Jekyll, in her turn, was his ideal mentor, for modesty and a lack of pretension were strong traits in her practical personality; he was to design pillared and canopied entrances for future clients, but not for her. She gives her reasons for this sketch in the beginning of her book *Home and Garden*: 'My home is approached by a footpath from a quiet, shady lane, entering by a close-paled hand gate. There is no driving road to the front door. I like the approach to a house to be as quiet and modest as possible, and in this case I wanted it to tell its own story as the way in to a small dwelling standing in wooded ground'.[24]

91] EDWIN L. LUTYENS 1869–1944

North front

Munstead Wood, Godalming, Surrey, 1892–3
Pen and watercolour
From the Munstead Wood sketchbook
115 × 175 mm. /$4\frac{1}{2} \times 6\frac{7}{8}$ in.

91

92

This is folio 7 of the sketchbook, marked *Back Front* (with more than a touch of typical flippancy) and illustrating the first idea for the north front of Munstead Wood. Miss Jekyll wanted a formal court facing her garden walks and her workroom with its own door into the garden. Her architect was not possessed of her modesty and quiet taste – he loved tower rooms, with arrow slits, and clearly thought that a gardener should have a roof garden on top of her Moorish-looking workshop (he knew how she loved travelling in North Africa) and a double flight of steps for celebrity entrances into her garden! Not surprisingly he has pencilled *Bad* on the Moorish workshop, which was undoubtedly Miss Jekyll's verdict.

The north front, as built, has no gables, but a long straight eaves-line, a band of windows and the half-timbered overhanging-gallery below, with two projecting gabled wings. The right hand wing is the workshop, with a flower lobby, a modest oak door with two windows beside it, and a small flight of rough sandstone steps. The court between these wings was a precious achievement; paved in water-marked sandstone it was set with shade-loving plants and pots of lilies and hydrangeas in summer.

92] EDWIN L. LUTYENS 1869–1944

The south front looking towards the summerhouse

Munstead Wood, Godalming, Surrey, 1892–3
Pen and watercolour
From the Munstead Wood sketchbook
115×175 mm. $/4\frac{1}{2} \times 6\frac{7}{8}$ in.

Folio 9 verso from the sketchbook illustrates the *South Front Looking to Summer House*.

Miss Jekyll wanted the main entrance to the garden to be in the centre of the south front, leading directly out of her sitting room across the plain gravel terrace to the lawn and her most prized possession, her wide Green Wood Walk, the chief of her woodland garden paths. Lutyens has sketched, according to her dictum, greenery at the foot of the house (she planted rosemary bushes with some roses on the walls), and more greenery along the retaining wall of the gravel terrace (this was the hedge of Scotch brier roses).

The summerhouse was transformed into the entrance loggia – 'a kind of long porch, or rather a covered projection of a lean-to shape. This serves as a dry approach to the main door, and also as a comfortable full-stop to the southern face of the house'.[25]

MONTACUTE · HOUSE . 21ST· AUG . 1894.

93

MONTACUTE HOUSE, SOMERSET

93] R. SHEKLETON BALFOUR *d.*1910

A perspective of the garden

Montacute House, Somerset, 1894
Pen
380 × 535 mm. /15 × 21 in.

Little is known of Balfour's life and career, though he did exhibit his drawings of old buildings and some of his own projects in the Royal Academy between 1897 and 1902. He worked in Arthur B. Pite's office from around 1905 until 1910. His interest in the picturesque buildings of old England, i.e. the seventeenth century and earlier, was very much in keeping with the mood of young architects of the 1890s and the beginnings of the Arts and Crafts Movement. Montacute House, when he sketched it, was in the last years of the Phelips family ownership, with William Robert Phelips (1846–1919) only managing to stay on by selling the family silver to pay his expenses.

94] R. SHEKLETON BALFOUR *d.* 1910
A plan of the formal garden

Montacute House, Somerset, 1894
Pencil and green and blue washes
535 × 380 mm. /21 × 15 in.

This is the only garden plan which Balfour drew among a large collection of topographical sketches of old English houses and churches. He was recording the layout of the garden after nearly three hundred years of Phelips family ownership. This garden is Elizabethan in origin, with the raised walks around the sides; there used to be a mount in the centre which was demolished in the nineteenth century. The pool and balustrade, which are still there today, had just been built when Balfour made his plan.

95] R. SHEKLETON BALFOUR *d.* 1910
A perspective of walls, pierced lanterns and gazebos

Montacute House, Somerset, 1894
Pen on tracing paper
255 × 180 mm. /10 × 7 in.

TERRACE · AT · MONTACVTE · HOVSE.

R.S BALFOVR. DEL.
AVGVST 21st 1894.

95

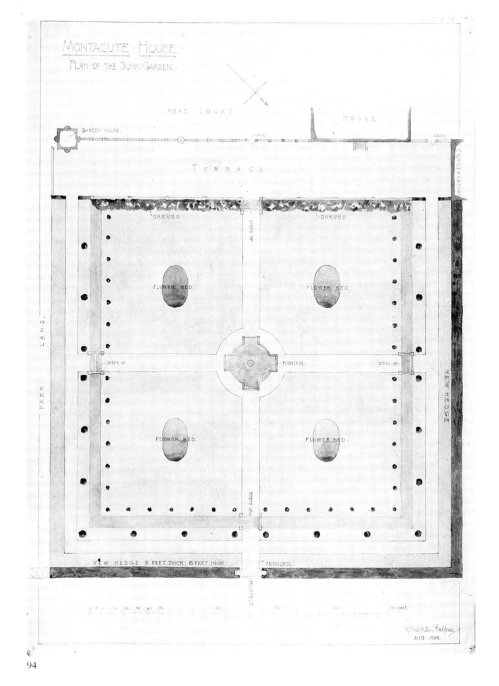

94

These are Montacute's most famous features, and they ornament the east court, the present (and only seventeenth-century) entrance front of the house. There is a lantern midway down each side of the court and a gazebo at each corner, farthest from the house. These were built at the same time as the house, i.e. 1601, and they add a Renaissance fantasy to the garden. The gazebos make an interesting comparison with one by Robert Smythson, no. 185. What Balfour's sketches do not show is the honey glow of the Ham Hill stone, which is the great joy of Montacute today.

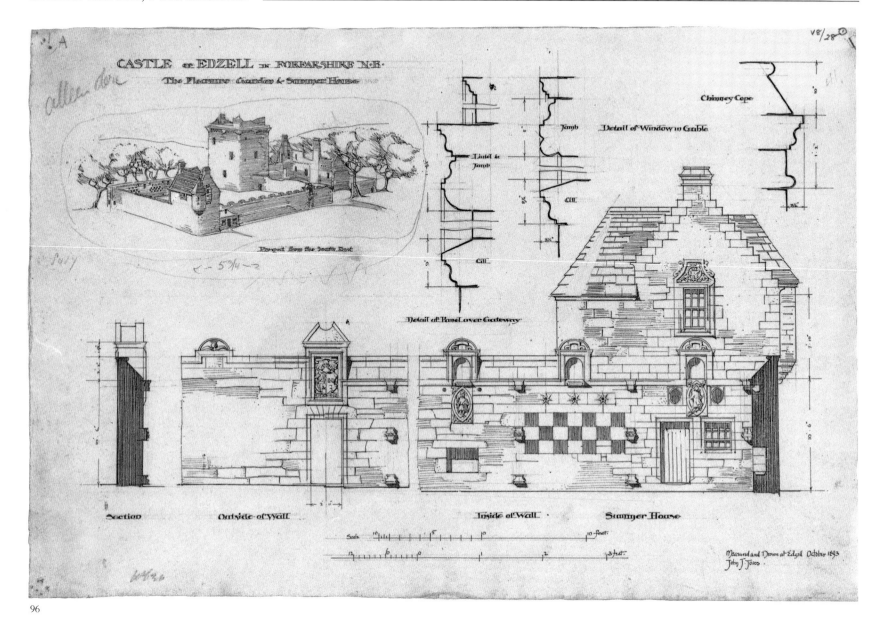

96

EDZELL CASTLE, FORFARSHIRE

96] JOHN JAMES JOASS 1868–1952

The pleasure gardens and summerhouse

Castle Edzell, Forfarshire, 1893
Pen and pencil
355 × 510 mm. / 14 × 20⅛ in.

The essence of the Arts and Crafts gardens – the love of an ordered, enclosed space, richly ornamented – derives from the 'old gardens' of England and Scotland. At the end of the

nineteenth century a number of artists and architects sought out these gardens and drew them as a source of inspiration for the new movement. Edzell, (now in Tayside Region) has this early seventeenth-century pleasance designed by the then owner of the castle, Sir David Lindsay, with the work carried out by his unknown stonemason.

The drawing is signed and annotated: *Measured and Drawn at Edzell, October 1893.*

97] JOHN JAMES JOASS 1868–1952

Plan of the pleasure garden

Edzell Castle, Forfarshire, 1893
Pen
355 × 510 mm. /14 × 20⅛ in.

Joass included this plan of the pleasure garden and elevation of the wall to show how the bas-relief sculptures were arranged. The date for the garden is 1604, which makes this structural feature one of the oldest surviving gardens in the British Isles. The carvings, some copied from mid-sixteenth century German engravings, are the philosophical emblems inspired by Sir David Lindsay, the garden's maker: the west wall carries the planetary deities, including Luna and Diana – who was included because of the ancient belief that the statue of Diana of Ephesus fell from the heavens. The east wall has the seven cardinal virtues – temperance, fortitude, prudence, faith, hope, justice and charity, and the south wall has the five liberal arts. The walls are further decorated with chequered patterns and flower boxes, which were traditionally to hold flowers in the Lindsay colours: blue and white against the pink stone wall. There are also nesting niches and boxes for birds and bees.

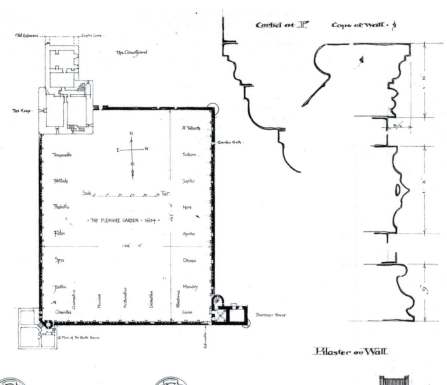

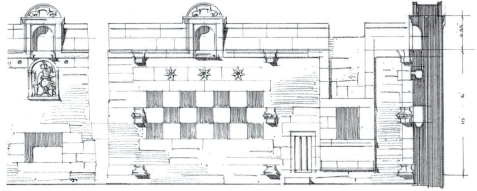

97

98] JOHN JAMES JOASS 1868–1952

Panels in the wall of the pleasure garden

Edzell Castle, Forfarshire, 1893
Pencil and green and brown washes
355 × 255 mm. /14 × 10 in.

The walls of the garden are divided regularly into panels of flower boxes, alternating with bas-relief sculptures such as these. As J.J.Joass has noted, the panels on the south wall depict the liberal arts (*Dialectica*), those on the west wall, the cardinal virtues (*Caritas*), and on the east wall, classical gods and planetary symbols.

98

BALCASKIE, FIFESHIRE

99]   JOHN JAMES JOASS 1868–1952

A view on the terrace

Balcaskie, Fifeshire, 1896
Pen
255 × 355 mm. / 10 × 14 in.

A perspective of the main terrace at Balcaskie with a dominating row of buttresses. The artist's view is from the staircase which makes a pair with that at the far end of the terrace, instead of the more usual central stair. The buttresses are structurally necessary, supporting the wall of the house terrace, but encouraged a fashion for yew 'buttresses' to break up the planting in a similar way in English gardens of the early twentieth century. These three Scottish gardens, drawn by Joass, well reflect the great interest in old formal gardens that Reginald Blomfield's *The Formal Garden in England* inspired.

99

BARNCLUITH, LANARKSHIRE

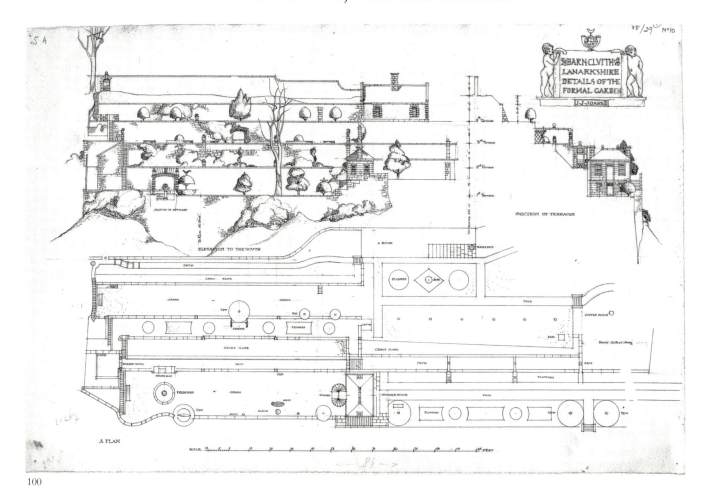

100

100]   JOHN JAMES JOASS 1868–1952

Elevation, plan and section of the formal garden

Barncluith, Lanarkshire
(Strathclyde Region), 1896
Pen
355×510 mm. / $14 \times 20\frac{1}{8}$ in.

This sheet of drawings further emphasizes the steepness of the
Barncluith terraces, and the strength of its definition via
walls, grass terraces, stone slopes and borders of flowers on
this Scottish hillside. It was no accident that architects
interested in old formal gardens rejoiced in Edzell, Barncluith
and Balcaskie, for Scotland had, of course, escaped the great
levelling of the English landscape movement which had
swept formal gardens away. Architects, such as Reginald
Blomfield, did not fail to capitalize on the destruction in the
cause of giving the architect back his place in the garden.
Blomfield had discovered Sir Walter Scott as advocate to his
cause in a paper he wrote in *The Quarterly* (1827) reviewing
Sir Henry Stewart's *Planter's Guide*: '. . . . Barncluith . . . an
old garden of the eighteenth century laid out by one of the
Millars "full of long straight walks, betwixt hedges of yew
and hornbeam, which rose tall and close on every side".'
With the recommendations of Scott and Blomfield, it was
not surprising that Barncluith became a goal for young artists
like Joass.

101]   JOHN JAMES JOASS 1868–1952

Perspective of the terraces

Barncluith, Lanarkshire
(Strathclyde Region), 1896
Pen
355×255 mm. / 14×10 in.

This bird's-eye perspective shows well the steepness of the
Barncluith terraces, on a hillside outside the town of
Hamilton. The garden is sixteenth century in origin, though
most of what John James Joass saw in the 1890s (and we can
still see today), dates from the seventeenth century. This
perspective shows the remarkable way the little stone garden
house is fitted into the terrace, with its steep double flight of
steps. Also remarkable are the sizes of the trees.

101

ASHBY ST LEDGERS, NORTHAMPTONSHIRE

102]   EDWIN L. LUTYENS 1869–1944

A house and garden

Ashby St Ledgers, Northamptonshire, 1903–4
Pen and watercolour
535 × 1010 mm. /21 × $39\frac{3}{4}$ in.

Lutyens made major additions to this house and designed a formal garden for the Hon. Ivor Guest (later Lord Wimborne), in the early 1900s. It was the beginning of a long association and patronage which lasted until 1924, in which the architect created an almost feudal enclave at Ashby and benefited from Guest family influence for other commissions. The house had Tudor and earlier origins (including a room where the Gunpowder Plot was planned), and Lutyens adopted a romantic 'Tudor idiom' for the house and made a grand manorial garden of long walks and borders, yew-walled rooms, terraces and a parterre of paved patterns and flower beds. This last, Miss Jekyll planted with roses and silver-leaved plants.

The Collection holds many drawings for Ashby St Ledgers but most are faded and creased, having survived many moves of Lutyens' office and the London blitz. The watercolour section and elevation through the house and garden, showing the east garden front of the house, is both delightful in itself as one of Lutyens' typically quirky early drawings, and shows the essence of Ashby's charm – the closeness of the church and other ancient buildings, and the garden filtering off into the romantic river landscape of its small park. Miss Jekyll went to great efforts to plan planting for the borders of the Church Quad, between the house and the church. Two attempts were necessary because Lutyens forgot to tell her that the Quad was heavily shaded by walnut trees (which don't appear here, either). Miss Jekyll's planting plans for the Ashby garden are with her papers in the Library of the College of Environmental Design, University of California, Berkeley.

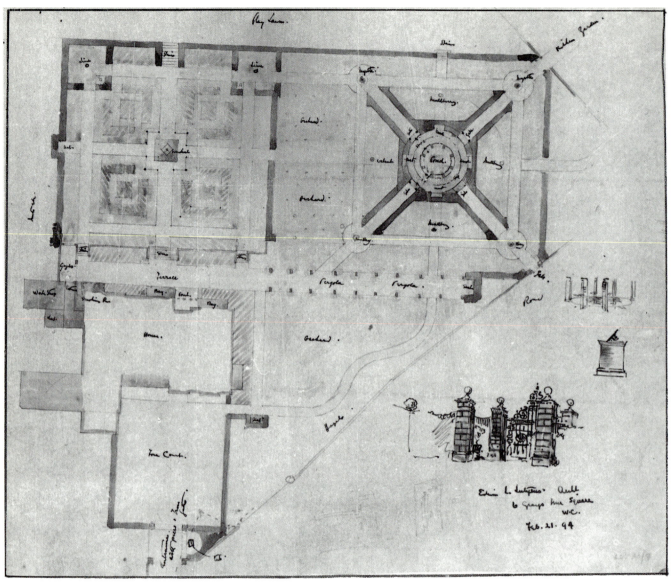

103

GREAT WARLEY, ESSEX

103]   EDWIN L. LUTYENS 1869–1944

Plan of a garden

Great Warley, Essex, 1894
Pencil, pen and wash
520 × 605 mm. /20½ × 23 in.

One of Lutyens' earliest garden drawings, done with the
encouragement of Gertrude Jekyll for her friend and fellow
gardener, Miss Ellen Willmott. It is of two formal garden
rooms, walled in yew, and separated by an orchard. There are

detail sketches of gates, a sundial and a circular arbour around
the pond. The entire drawing is in Lutyens' hand; No. 6
Gray's Inn Square was his first professional office, which he
used until he married and moved to Bloomsbury Square in
1897.

BUCKHURST PLACE, SUSSEX

104] EDWIN L. LUTYENS 1869–1944

A plan of pavement and upper terrace

Buckhurst Park, Withyham, Sussex, 1903
Pen and coloured washes on tracing paper
440 × 770 mm. /$17\frac{3}{8}$ × $30\frac{3}{8}$ in.

Despite the tears and creases of the brittle yellowed tracing paper, this drawing still shows how much Lutyens enjoyed playing with paving patterns, and how his joy infuses delight into a garden. It is no accident that Lutyens' best gardens belong to his youth and the Edwardian years, when he believed that architecture was a game 'to be played with gusto'. This pattern, using carefully cut stone (note the nicked circles), with two-inch-narrow bricks and tile insets, with the box hedging to the beds repeating the pattern, shows the same basic ideas as he used in many gardens, notably Orchards near Godalming, Surrey, Deanery Garden at Sonning, Berkshire, and Marsh Court, Stockbridge, Hampshire, in the turn of the century years. In none of these other cases have the early garden drawings survived: the RIBA's Lutyens Collection is large, but it came through several office moves and the London blitz. To these vagaries must be added that he was always economizing and drew on the flimsiest tracing paper, his offices were cramped and little thought given to posterity in those early days. The good, clear drawings are therefore miraculous survivors.

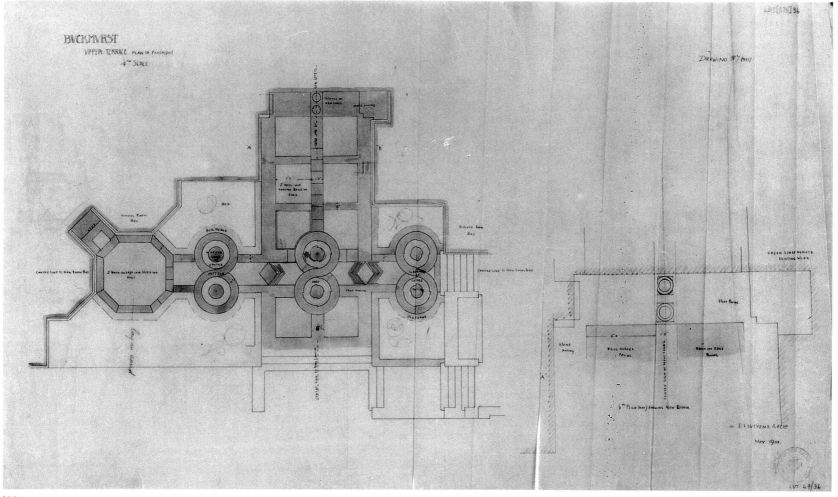

104

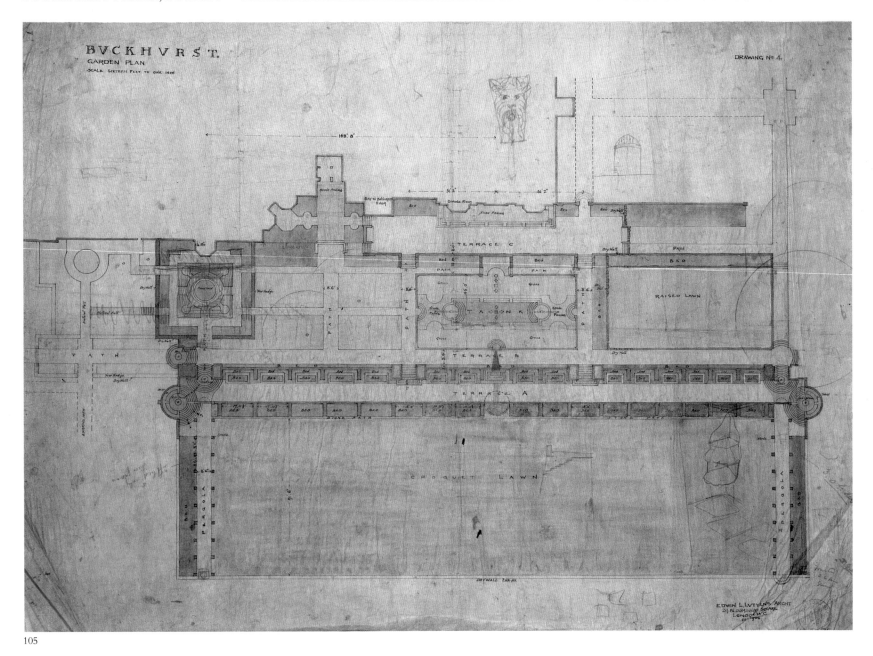

105

105]   EDWIN L. LUTYENS 1869–1944

Additions and garden design

Buckhurst Place, Withyham, Sussex, 1903–4
Pen, pencil and coloured washes on linen
605 × 785 mm./23⅞ × 30⅞ in.

Lutyens added a 'New Room' to Buckhurst Park for R.H. Benson (this wing has since been demolished), which gave him the opportunity for these large garden terraces which are typical of his best garden work. The house is outlined in red, with the new wing on the left; he has thoroughly integrated house and garden by making borders around the walls and extending the axial lines through his garden plan – all in accordance with his expressed dictum: 'A garden scheme should have a backbone – a central idea beautifully phrased. Thus the house wall should spring out of a briar bush – . . . and every wall, path, stone and flower bed has its similar problem and a relative value to the central idea'.[26]

The relative values and problems are beautifully expressed by his precise geometric games with concentric circles and divided proportions – all precisely built in stone or brick. But the most fascinating thing about this plan is that the geometry is not forced or aggressive. It has a fine delight and creates many opportunities in beds and over pergolas for the essential flowers. No plans by Gertrude Jekyll for this garden have been found and she was probably not involved, for Rex Benson came from a family of great gardeners.

106] EDWIN L. LUTYENS 1869–1944

Basin opposite the New Room

Buckhurst Park, Withyham, Sussex, 1903
Pen, pencil and coloured washes on linen
485×460 mm. / $19\frac{1}{8} \times 18\frac{1}{8}$ in.

This is a standard Lutyens detail, similar to one drawn for Orchards in 1899. The basin was to be sited in the yew-walled room (the space is marked *Fountain*) outside the New Room on the plan, no. 105. In the top right corner the N.B. (not in Lutyens' hand) reads: '*The water to discharge from the 4 Lions' Heads and overflow under the Lions' chins to the 4 Toads. The Toads to discharge into channel and the overflow of channel will run to tank in [. . .] Garden. No taps will be required. The water will always be running.*'

One wonders whether the office assistant who drew this plan knew what was happening to the water; it seems likely that, as it was taken to a tank, it was a re-circulating supply, or at least stored for garden-watering.

The Lion heads were probably the same as the one at Orchards, which was designed by Julia Chance, the client for Orchards with her husband William Chance, and a talented sculptress who made ornaments for several Lutyens gardens. A note on the Toad reads *Model to be seen at Architect's Offices*, implying the Lion to be readily acceptable while the Toad was perhaps a little unusual. Julia Chance designed tortoises for Heywood House in Eire for Lutyens and the Toad here was most likely hers as well.

The garden terraces at Buckhurst Park survive, but this garden room with its central fountain pool and rill does not.

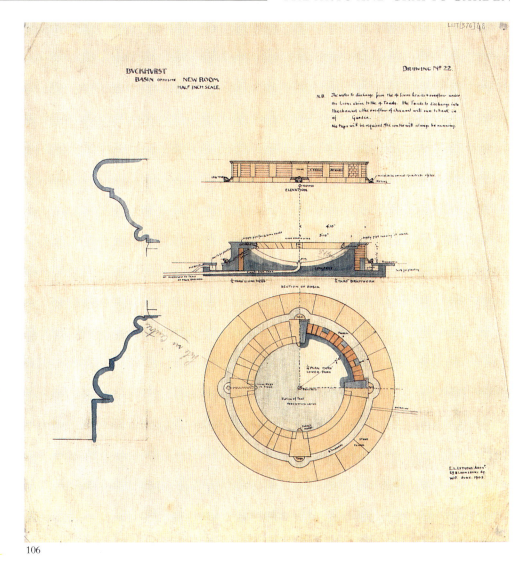

106

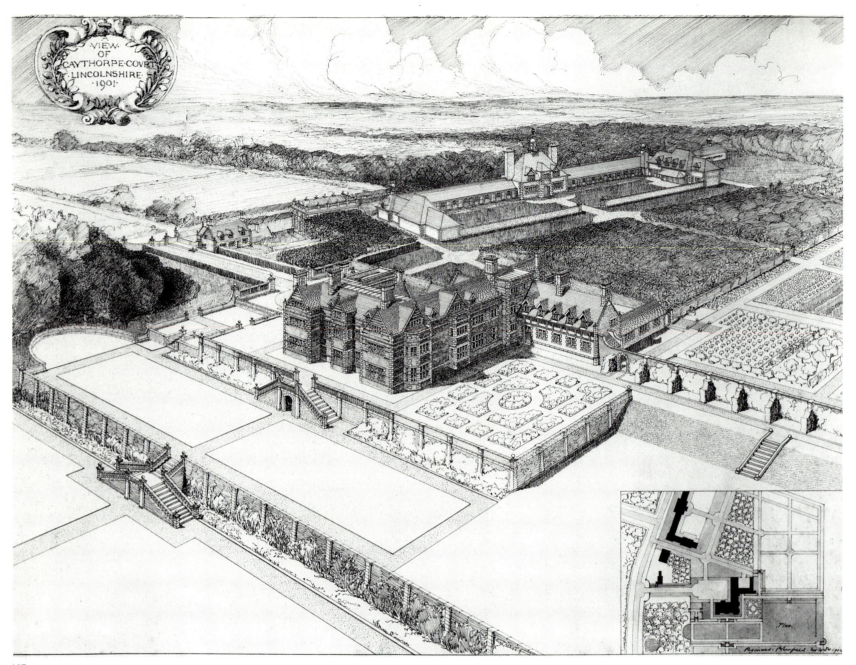

107

CAYTHORPE COURT, LINCOLNSHIRE

107]   REGINALD BLOMFIELD 1856–1943

Perspective

Caythorpe Court, Lincolnshire, 1901
Pen
521 × 650 mm. /$20\frac{1}{2}$ × $25\frac{5}{8}$ in.

A perspective that illustrates the scale of Blomfield's achievement at Caythorpe, where the house, gardens and stables
were all designed and built for a wealthy merchant banker,
Edgar Lubbock, between 1899 and 1901. At his client's wish,
Caythorpe was based on 'plain seventeenth-century Lincolnshire work' as far as the style of the house was concerned.
The garden, an expansive mix of enclosed formal gardens
and the functional spaces of a traditional, though fast
vanishing, garden establishment, demanded the confidence
and assurance of an architect like Blomfield. The scale is far
grander than the country house work of Lutyens or Voysey.

Caythorpe Court survives as an agricultural college.

MELLERSTEIN HOUSE, BERWICKSHIRE

108]   REGINALD BLOMFIELD 1856–1943

Garden perspective

Mellerstein House, Berwickshire, 1910
Pen
1017 × 682 mm. /40 × $26\frac{7}{8}$ in.

Undoubtedly the most impressive perspective of a design by
Blomfield drawn by Adrian Berrington: this twentieth-
century drawing echoes the work of Johannes Kip
(1653–1722) and Leonard Knyff (1650–1721) whose engravings of houses and gardens in *Britannia Illustrata* were exactly
to Blomfield's taste.

Blomfield designed these gardens to be seen from the first
floor and intended this perspective to be that of a distant
eagle's eye. Mellerstein originally had old terraces and a
formal garden but these had been swept away, and Lord and
Lady Binning wanted suitable but manageable replacements.

The strange feature of the design is the very steep sided
amphitheatre, which is partly masked by the cartouche and a
more distant view across a semi-circular pool. This lower
part of the design was not built, but otherwise Mellerstein's
garden is largely as Blomfield intended.

108

109

HARTLEY WINTNEY, HAMPSHIRE

109] ERNEST NEWTON 1856–1922

Perspective

Fouracre, West Green, Hartley Wintney, Hampshire, 1902
Pencil and watercolour, drawn by Thomas Hamilton
Crawford
250 × 370 mm. /$9\frac{7}{8}$ × $14\frac{5}{8}$ in.

Ernest Newton trained in the Norman Shaw office and started his own practice in 1879. He became the architect *par excellence* of the substantial Edwardian suburban house, but he was not interested in gardens, they appear only in professionally drawn perspectives of his houses, as contributions to the ideals of family life – the security and wholesomeness of the very life that could be lived in one of his houses.

This drawing of Fouracre was published in his *A Book of Country Houses*, 1903. A black-and-white version shows more clearly that there are fruit bushes and trees in the foreground, with hollyhocks peeping over the hedge. However, the 'planting' was artistic licence as the house never had a garden like this.

UNIDENTIFIED DRAWING

110] ERNEST NEWTON 1856–1922

Design for a house in Kent

Unidentified, *c.*1902
Pencil and watercolour perspective
drawn by Thomas Hamilton Crawford
395 × 540 mm. /$15\frac{1}{2}$ × $21\frac{1}{4}$ in.

One of several designs drawn for Ernest Newton by different artists for reproduction in *A Book of Country Houses*, 1903. It represents beautifully the solid desirability of Newton's houses; the lady emerging onto the terrace to consult her gardener about three newly-bought plants, possibly clematis, adds a further sense of well-being. Ernest Newton's houses, Buller's Wood in Bickley, Kent (decorated by William Morris), Redcourt in Haslemere and Fouracre (no. 109) played an important role in establishing the supremacy of the 'Edwardian' country house, but he seems to have been singularly uninterested in gardens. They were, however, added by the artists to give a desirable impression.

110

THE GREENWAY, GLOUCESTERSHIRE

111]   ERNEST NEWTON 1856–1922

A house and garden

The Greenway, Shurdington, Gloucestershire, 1912
Pencil and watercolour
390 × 530 mm. / $15\frac{3}{8}$ × $20\frac{7}{8}$ in.

This delightful watercolour by Alick G. Horsnell was exhibited at the Royal Academy in 1912. It seems to be the exception to the rule that Newton did not take much trouble with his gardens, for he merely altered this seventeenth-century house, obviously with a gentle touch, and did design this elegant little formal garden, which catches the Cotswold tradition to perfection. There is only one other drawing, a plan of house and garden, for this commission and it seems odd that such a modest work should have appeared in the architects' most prestigious showcase. The sensitivity applied to both house and garden, as well as to the watercolour perspective, is intriguing, and it seems a pity that neither the name of the client nor the circumstances of the work are known. Newton himself seems forgotten; the Collection has over one hundred folders of his commissions, his complete works, but no study of his marvellously stylish houses seems to have been undertaken.

111

COMPTON HOUSE, BEDFORDSHIRE

112] CHARLES EDWARD MALLOWS 1864–1915
Garden shelter and lily pond garden

Compton House, No. 17 Biddenham Turn, Biddenham,
Bedfordshire, 1900–1
Pen perspective by Frederick Landseer Griggs
360 × 290 mm. / $14\frac{1}{8}$ × $11\frac{3}{8}$ in.

Mallows designed Compton House and its garden for his
father-in-law. H.J.Peacock. This perspective was drawn for
exhibition at the Royal Academy in 1903 as no. 1474 *Pond
Garden at Bidenham (sic)*. The idea of this enclosed contemplation garden, with reflecting water, was that it divided the
tennis lawn on one side from the kitchen garden on the other.
It was a common Arts and Crafts device to create a 'still' space
between two areas of activity, which contributed to the
number of garden rooms and to the variety of garden
atmospheres.

The house and garden were built in 1909, but this
sophisticated part of the design was not carried out.

GARDEN SHELTER & LILY-POND at BIDDENHAM, C.E.MALLOWS & GROCOCK
112

113

144

UNIDENTIFIED DRAWING

113] CHARLES EDWARD MALLOWS 1864–1915
A design for a house and garden

Kent, 1909–10
Pencil
280 × 205 mm. /11 × 8⅛ in.

A vivid illustration of Mallows' understanding of fitting a garden into a landscape. This is one of three illustrations for a theoretical scheme chosen by Gertrude Jekyll and Lawrence Weaver for illustration in *Gardens for Small Country Houses* in the chapter 'Yew and Other Hedges' which celebrates the patience, protection and effectiveness of yew, of which values 'our architects' are well aware – 'A drawing by Mr Mallows shows, next below a raised terrace, two square garden courts, the terrace steps between them descending to a long green walk, with flower borders backed by yew hedges, leading to a circular fountain court, paved and brick-walled.'[29]

SHERBORNE, DORSET

114] CHARLES EDWARD MALLOWS 1864–1915
A house and garden

Near Sherborne, Dorset, 1907
Pencil on board
460 × 585 mm. /18⅛ × 23 in.

Exhibited in the Royal Academy in 1908 as no. 1557. This was almost certainly an exhibition design only, and never a real project, but it illustrates Gavin Stamp's description of Mallows as 'one of the finest architectural draughtsman of his generation'.[30]

Simply because he was so skilful, Mallows' projects were well publicized; he wrote and illustrated his own series on 'Architectural Gardening' for *The Studio* in 1908–10 and his influence was therefore much greater through his published drawings than through his actual work. This design appeared in *The Studio*[31] and the RIBA *Journal*.[32]

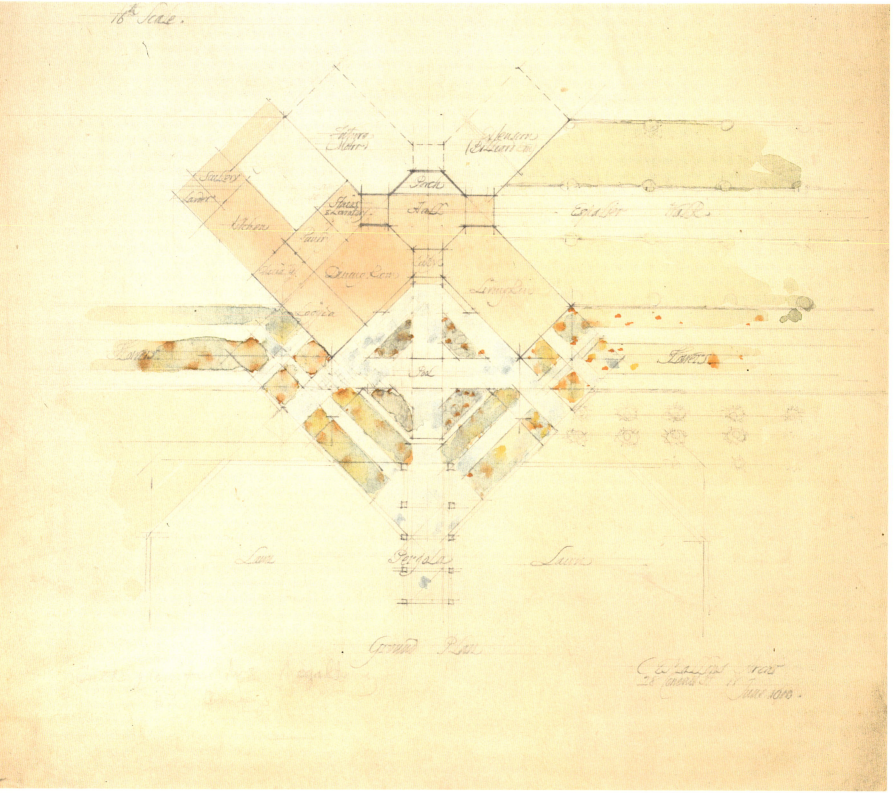

HIGH CHIMNEYS, BERKSHIRE

115]   CHARLES EDWARD MALLOWS 1864–1915

A preliminary design for a house and garden

High Chimneys, Sunningdale, Berkshire, 1910
Pencil and coloured washes
370 × 290 mm. / $14\frac{5}{8}$ × $11\frac{3}{8}$ in.

The 'butterfly' plan was all the rage at this time and offered ingenious gardening possibilities for fitting garden rooms into the framework of diagonals to which this is one of Mallows' solutions. It is one of several designs for a Captain and Mrs Macgildowny, and inscribed *as built* on the reverse.

EATON HALL, CHESHIRE

116]   CHARLES EDWARD MALLOWS 1864–1915

A preliminary design for a rustic bridge

Eaton Hall, Cheshire, 1905
Pencil and watercolour
390 × 565 mm. / $15\frac{3}{8}$ × $22\frac{1}{4}$ in.

Mallows designed a formal Dutch garden for the Duchess of Westminster in 1905 and this bridge was drawn for her at the same time. There is no drawing for the garden in the Collection, though it was made; a bridge of Japanese style was built, though not to this design.

117

TIRLEY GARTH, CHESHIRE

117] CHARLES EDWARD MALLOWS 1864–1915

A house and garden

Tirley Garth, Willington, Cheshire, 1906–12
Pencil
185 × 220 mm. /$7\frac{1}{4}$ × $8\frac{5}{8}$ in.

Tirley Garth was Mallows' *magnum opus*, for which the Collection holds twenty-seven drawings of which sixteen show some part of the garden or garden building designs. The house was started in 1908 for Mr Leesmith, a director of Brunner, Mond & Company, and the company took over the house in the following year when building was almost completed. It was leased to a Mr R.H.Prestwich in 1912 and Mallows did additional work, including a cloister court, for him.

This perspective, of part of the east front from the octagon garden, shows the house in 1908 with the garden hedges and borders as they would be with time.

118

119

118]   CHARLES EDWARD MALLOWS 1864–1915
Sundial court and pergola

Tirley Garth, Willington, Cheshire, 1908
Pencil on board
370 × 290 mm. / $14\frac{5}{8}$ × $11\frac{3}{8}$ in.

There is no overall plan or perspective of Tirley Garth's garden and it is difficult to imagine the idea of the layout. This is one of several ideas for different garden features, a paved court with a sundial in the centre and a pergola leading off into the distance. There is far too strong a perspective element in this sketch, a little reminiscent of a hall of distorting mirrors. There is no doubt that some architects, and Mallows was among them, brought too much 'architecture' into the garden, with the result that Arts and Crafts gardens were largely unappreciated for most of the twentieth century. The horticultural lobby sided with William Robinson's suspicion of architects[33] and it has taken the revival of Gertrude Jekyll's reputation, dating from Betty Massingham's biography (published in 1960), to restore the appreciation of architectural gardens.

UNIDENTIFIED DRAWING

119]   CHARLES EDWARD MALLOWS 1864–1915
Design for a garden

Unidentified, 1910
Pencil on board
280 × 370 mm. / 11 × $14\frac{5}{8}$ in.

A perspective of a long grass walk through wide herbaceous borders to an octagonal brick summerhouse, with a weathervane on the top. This is another of Mallows' skilful theoretical designs for his articles on 'Architectural Gardening' in *The Studio* in 1910. These drawings were highly influential; in particular this idea was surely caught up and used to great effect by Ernest Barnsley at Rodmarton Manor in Gloucestershire, where a lovely double-border walk, full of flowers, leads to a small summerhouse in just this manner.

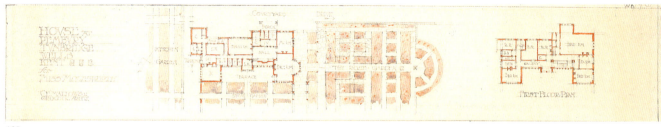

120

PEMBURY, KENT

120]   CHARLES EDWARD MALLOWS 1864–1915

A house and garden

No. 8 Tonbridge Road, Pembury, Kent, 1904
Pencil and coloured washes
95×525 mm. $/3\frac{3}{4} \times 20\frac{5}{8}$ in.

There is also an F.L.Griggs' perspective of this house, looking across the stone garden (an arrangement of rectangular beds with wide paved paths) to the terrace, flanked by the kitchen and the drawing room on the right. The drawing room has an additional covered way from which the pergola springs. The house is roughcast with steep Voysey-like gables and with romantic half-timbering in the centre section giving it a 'naturalness and purposely aged look',[28] to which Mallows added his highly architectural garden.

The house and garden were built for the Rev. R.F.W.Molesworth and his daughter in 1904–5 and Miss Molesworth lived there until 1914. It was a private house until after the Second World War and is now converted into local authority offices.

CRAIG Y PARC, GWENT

121]   CHARLES EDWARD MALLOWS 1864–1915

A house and garden

Craig y Parc, Pentrych, Cardiff, Gwent, 1913–4
Pencil and watercolour wash
365×545 mm. $/14\frac{3}{8} \times 21\frac{1}{2}$ in.

A typical Mallows design for an integrated house and garden, for Thomas Evans, a director of mining and railway companies. The house has an 'open air room' as well as a conservatory and a pergola leading to the 'garden studio'. The garden spaces include a rose garden, cloister court, lily pool and servants' garden as well as the terraces and orchard.

121

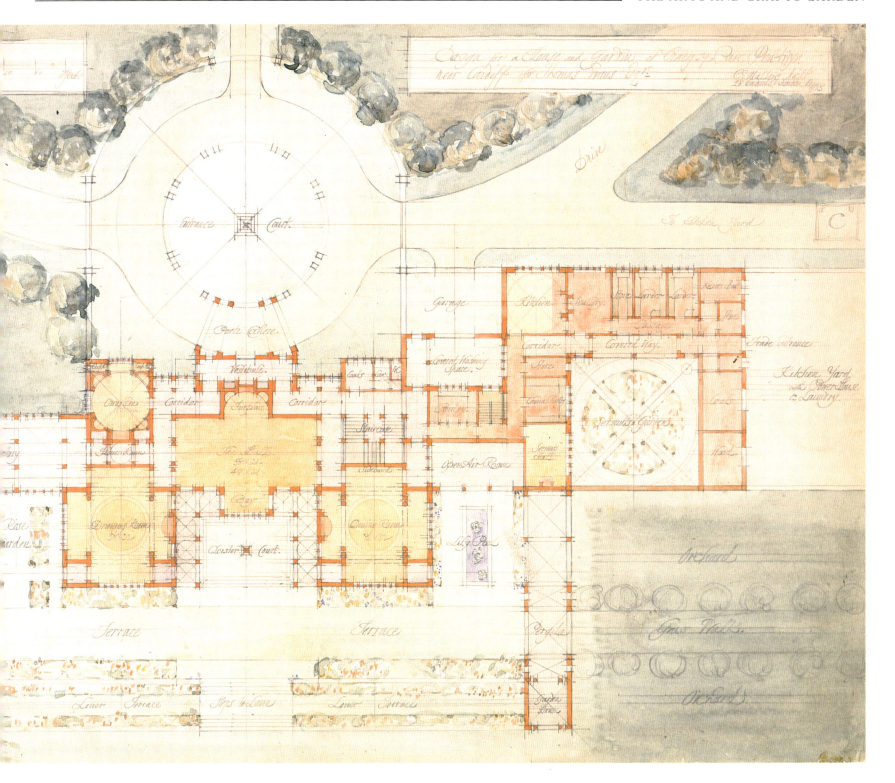

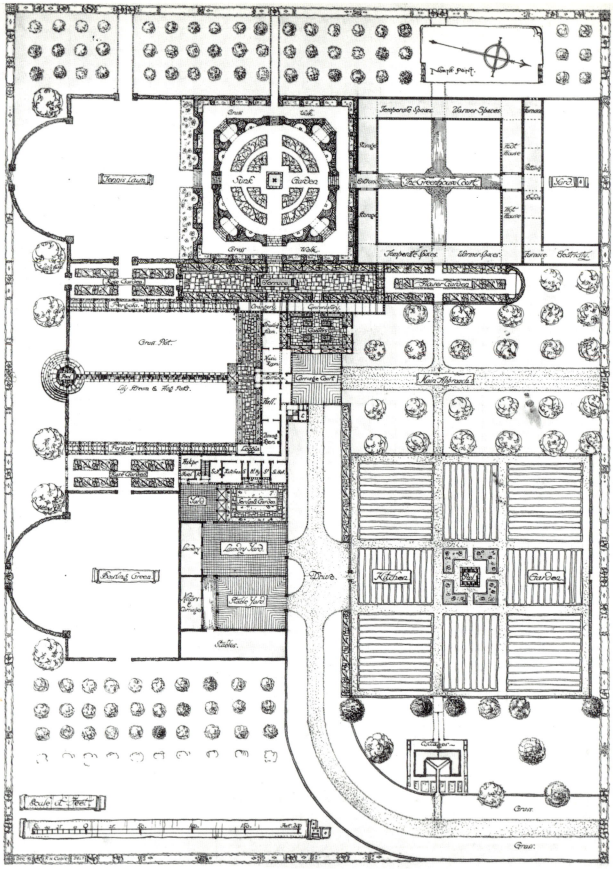

122] CHARLES EDWARD MALLOWS 1864–1915

Design for a house and garden

Unidentified, 1909
Pen and wash on board
480×365 mm. /$18\frac{7}{8} \times 14\frac{3}{8}$ in.

A final example of Mallows' theoretical design layouts for his articles in *The Studio* (XLVII, 1909) which sadly reveals how a love of graphic design can go too far. This garden becomes a series of claustrophobic, maze-like patterns on a sheet of paper, and has little connection with flowers and fresh air. It is a design for a garden-enthusiast, perhaps with particular horticultural interests, who requires as much as possible squeezed into the rigid rectangular plot. The house is L-shaped, one room wide, and almost lost in the complexity of the garden. It faces south to a formal garden, flanked by a bowling green and tennis lawn. The western half of the plot contains an elaborate sunk garden, a greenhouse court with hot, warm and temperate growing areas, an orchard, a long paved terrace with separate rose and flower walks, a conservatory and an orangery. The eastern half of the plot is devoted to function – staff-quarters and a servants' garden, more orchard, a large kitchen garden with attendant gardeners' cottages. As an exercise in self-containment and variety of activities it lacks only a swimming pool and private ice-rink.

UNIDENTIFIED DRAWINGS

123] CHARLES EDWARD MALLOWS 1864–1915

Design for a house and garden

Unidentified, *c.*1901
Pen on board
475×370 mm. /$18\frac{3}{4} \times 14\frac{1}{2}$ in.

This is another of Mallows' theoretical designs for his article in *The Studio* on 'Architectural Gardening' (see no. 114). The 'butterfly' plan, so called because the shape resembles a butterfly pinned out on a collector's board, was taken up as a challenge by many Arts and Crafts designers; a notable solution at Edward Maufe's Kelling Hall, is illustrated (no. 136). Here Mallows has simply demonstrated how the required garden spaces are accommodated on the ground. The butterfly plan was rather too stylized to be effective in garden terms, and no really good garden survives from this fashion.

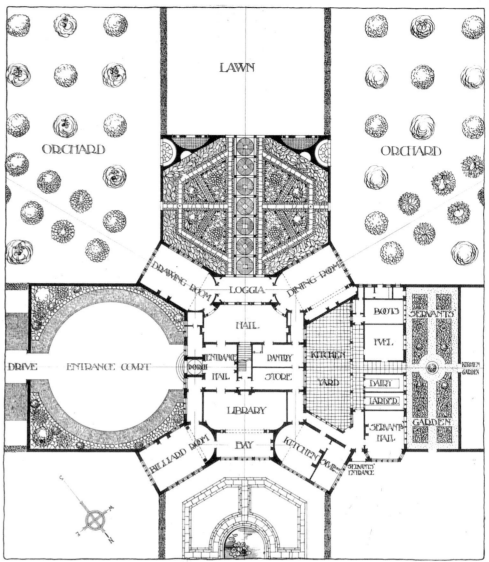

123

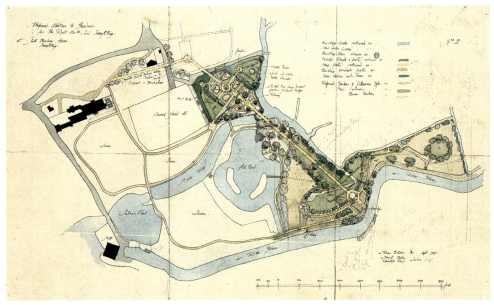

124

SOUTH STONEHAM HOUSE, SOUTHAMPTON

124] L. ROME GUTHRIE 1880–1958

Site plan for gardens

South Stoneham House, Swaythling, Southampton, 1907
Pen, pencil and coloured wash
350 × 580 mm. /13¾ × 22⅞ in.

The site plan for ambitious gardens planned on Lord Swaythling's estate beside the River Itchen, outside Southampton. The house is seen on the left i.e. west of the site, with lawns surrounded by streams, the Salmon Pool and Monk's River. Clearly the only ground dry enough for garden making is to the east, where L. Rome Guthrie proposed an enclosed formal flower garden and rosary with a long walk leading to a summerhouse overlooking the river. From his key it is clear he was proposing an interesting progression from formal enclosures and direct paths to the lawn, kept mown, which melted into 'wilderness' along the river banks.

The land proposed for the formal garden, east of the church yard, was the church Glebe, traditionally part of the clergyman's benefit. This must be an early example of the glebe being 'developed' – which has happened in so many villages this century.

125] L. ROME GUTHRIE 1880–1958

The Glebe Garden

South Stoneham House, Swaythling, Southampton, 1908
Pen and wash
711 × 755 mm. /28 × 29¾ in.

A detailed layout for the Glebe Garden, on former church land east of the church on the site plan, no. 124. This is in a much more competent hand and signed and dated by Guthrie himself.

The enclosed garden has become much more complex. There are now three main planting areas: the flower garden, the September garden and the spring garden, with a long east-west terraced grass-walk overlooking the rose garden – a triangle, edged on two sides by branches of the Monk's River. It is tempting to imagine that Guthrie may have discussed his ideas with Gertrude Jekyll, and he had certainly looked closely at *Colour Schemes for the Flower Garden* which had just been published. In this book she describes and illustrates her garden spaces at Munstead Wood: her spring garden has a circular grove with rocks set in the borders just as here. She felt that spring flowers were so delicate that they looked better in masses and the rocks gave them height; the spring garden was filled with drifts of arabis, primroses, small daffodils, tulips, wallflowers, *Tiarella cordifolia*, silver plants and gracious crown imperials.

The September garden, another Jekyll feature, was chiefly for Michaelmas daisies in shades of blue, mauve and white with artemesias, cinerarias and Jerusalem sage as a foil. At the eastern end of the terrace-walk a squarish enclosure is marked *Yellow garden*; its inspiration is Miss Jekyll's gold garden, which she advocated and sketched in *Colour Schemes*, to be planted with golden hollies, eleagnus, euonymus, brooms, helianthemums and snapdragons, all of sunny shades.

These schemes for South Stoneham were not carried out because of the death of Lord Swaythling.

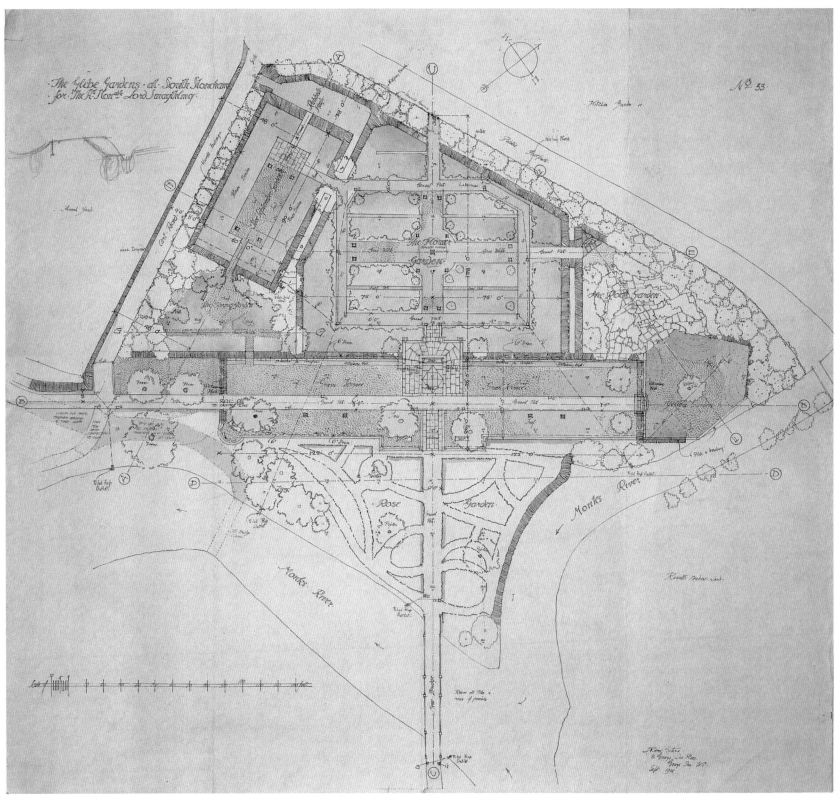

125

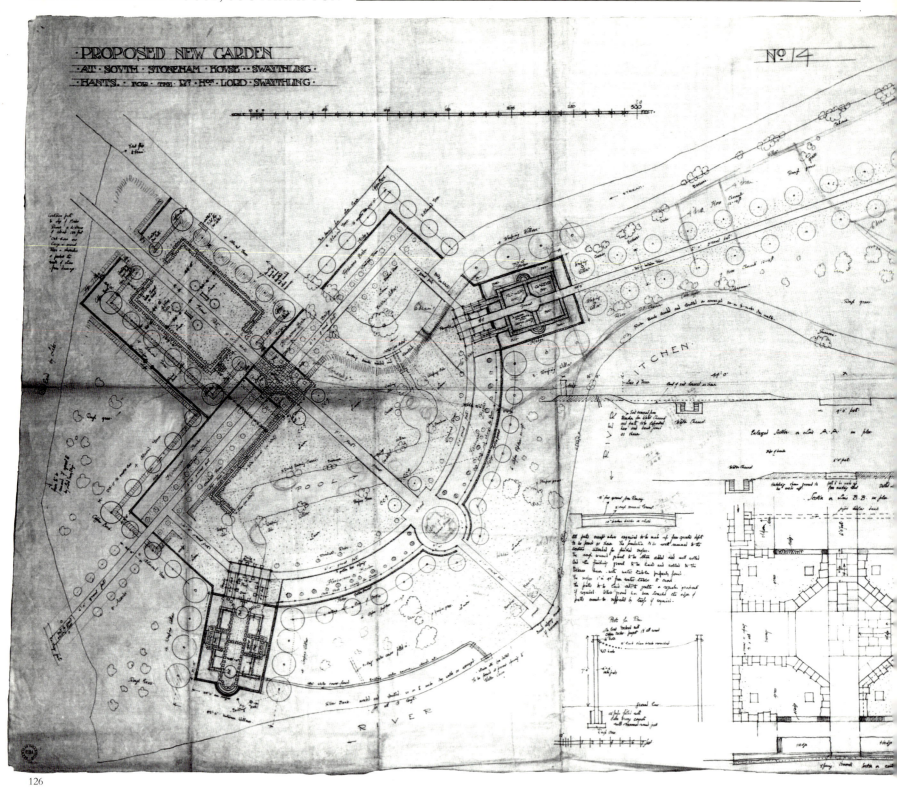

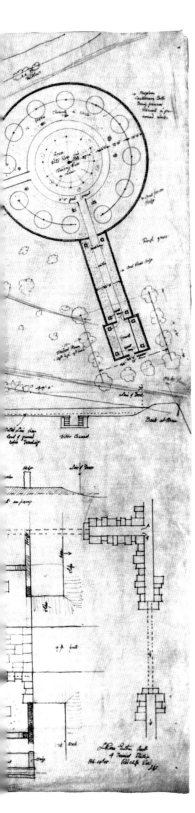

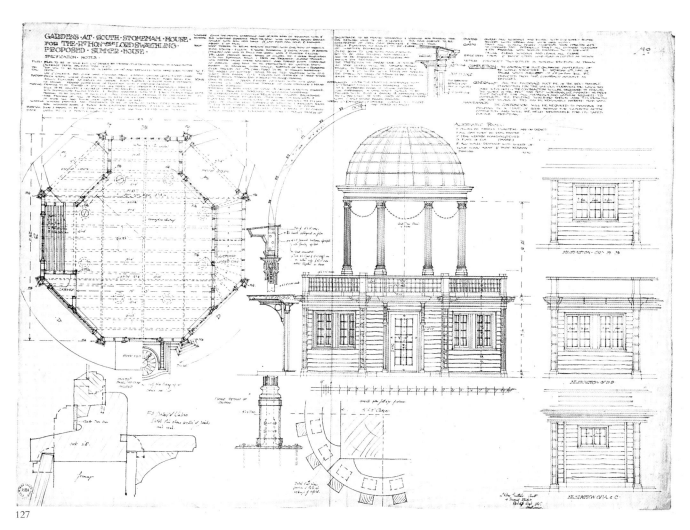

127

126] L. ROME GUTHRIE 1880–1958

A proposed new garden

South Stoneham House, Swaythling, Southampton, 1908
Pen and pencil
771×501 mm. /$30\frac{3}{8} \times 19\frac{3}{4}$ in.

A detailed layout plan for the garden at the end of the long walk on the site plan (no. 124), overlooking the River Itchen. This is a rather pedestrian and rigid plan forced onto the natural land and river form. The curved walk on the site plan has evolved into a semi-circular path flanked by herbaceous borders and standard roses, which links small enclosed garden rooms with the site for the summerhouse. A further axial walk crosses the spur of land via an avenue of weeping willows to a circular planting of horse chestnuts, with foxgloves, evening primrose and canterbury bells planted beneath them. Note the date of the drawing, *Feb. 14 '08*, i.e. too early for Guthrie to have seen Miss Jekyll's *Colour Schemes* which had such a beneficial influence on no. 125.

127] L. ROME GUTHRIE 1880–1958

Proposed summerhouse

South Stoneham House, Swaythling, Southampton, 1908
Pen on linen
510×700 mm. /$20 \times 27\frac{5}{8}$ in.

The riverside site was extremely wet and construction notes allow for elm piles to be driven to an average depth of three feet, and a base of eighteen inches of hardcore for the six-inch deep concrete platform. The summerhouse is wooden, clad in elm weather-boarding with a flat wooden roof and trellised balustrade. The dome is of trellis on oak supports.

This drawing appears to be a design, specification and contract. It has a final clause which demands completion of the building by Saturday 6th June 1908, and the signature would appear to be the contractor's signifying his agreement.

FERNHURST, SUSSEX

128] CHARLES FRANCIS ANNESLEY
VOYSEY 1857–1941

A house and garden design

Oakhurst, Ropes Lane, Fernhurst, Sussex, 1901
Watercolour on card
255 × 375 mm. / 10 × 14¾ in.

This is the architect's own watercolour of a house he designed for Mrs E.F.Chester at Oakhurst and now called Ropes and Bollards: it illustrates his rather stylized, designer's view of a garden, with flowers around the walls of the house rather like flowers on the border of a plate. It is a dream garden, painted for April, with scillas strewn across the grass and roses, hollyhocks and daisies all in bloom. This was very much the image of a garden as the necessary setting for a truly Arts and Crafts life which Gertrude Jekyll instilled into her contemporaries. Voysey's intense love of nature, transferred to his many designs for wallpapers and fabrics, was occasionally expressed in detailed garden designs for his houses, notably New Place, Haslemere.

128

TOOTING, LONDON

129] CHARLES FRANCIS ANNESLEY
VOYSEY 1857–1941

A house and garden plan

Dixcot, North Drive, Tooting Common, London, *c*.1899
Pen and coloured washes on linen
555 × 440 mm. /21 × 17⅜ in.

Voysey prepared two schemes for Mr and Mrs R.W. Essex
for Dixcot but neither were accepted, so he resigned. His
place was taken by Walter F. Cave (1863–1939) who, as
Gavin Stamp points out, built a very Voysey-like house.[27]
The simplicity of the garden design (a) is, however, peculiar
to Voysey's fine designer's mind, a serene garden, lightly
ornamented with the heart-shaped flower beds, the outdoor
expression of Voysey's trade-mark motif that he used
throughout his houses. The plan and elevation of the unbuilt
house (b) complete Voysey's perception of his whole design.

There are no garden drawings by W.F. Cave in the
Collection, though his garden at Ewelme Down is featured
by Gertrude Jekyll and Laurence Weaver in *Gardens for Small
Country Houses.*

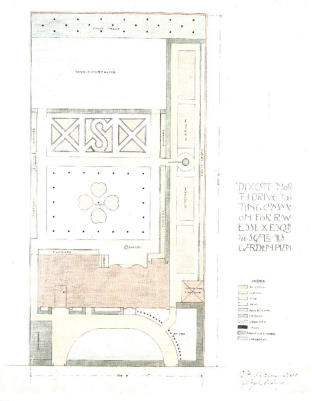

129a

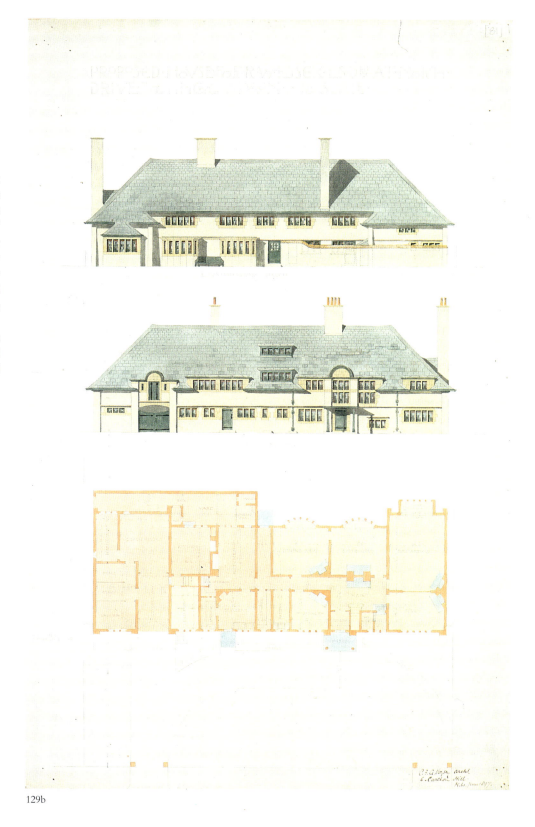

129b

TOWNHILL PARK, SOUTHAMPTON

130] L. ROME GUTHRIE 1880–1958

The garden house

Townhill Park, Southampton, 1912
Pencil and coloured washes
280×388 mm. /$11 \times 15\frac{1}{4}$ in.

A presentation sketch of the summerhouse designed to sit between the pergola cloister and the herb garden at Townhill, as marked on the layout plan of the garden, no. 131.

The drawing is signed *F.W.M 1922* which indicates that the scheme was revived after the war. Both summerhouse, pergola and garden still survive. In many ways this drawing represents the last of the Arts and Crafts simplicity; it shows the softness that well-filled beds, with small box or yew corner sentinels, and flowers that grow in paving cracks, bring to an architectural garden.

131] L. ROME GUTHRIE 1880–1958

Proposed new garden

Townhill Park, Southampton, 1912
Pen and pencil
510×700 mm. /$20 \times 27\frac{5}{8}$ in.

A compact enclosed formal garden of finest Arts and Crafts derivations, framed by a pergola walk or cloister with a central pool surrounded by flower beds and brick herringbone and tile inset paths. Lord Swaythling's house, Townhill Park, is at the top of the plan, where the path leads from the terrace, across a bowling alley walled in yew, to the formal garden. The elevations and the section on the sheet show the pergola to be simply of wood, with the uprights bedded in concrete, a structure which allows enough light for grass to grow along the walk. The grass path is supported with a paved edging.[34]

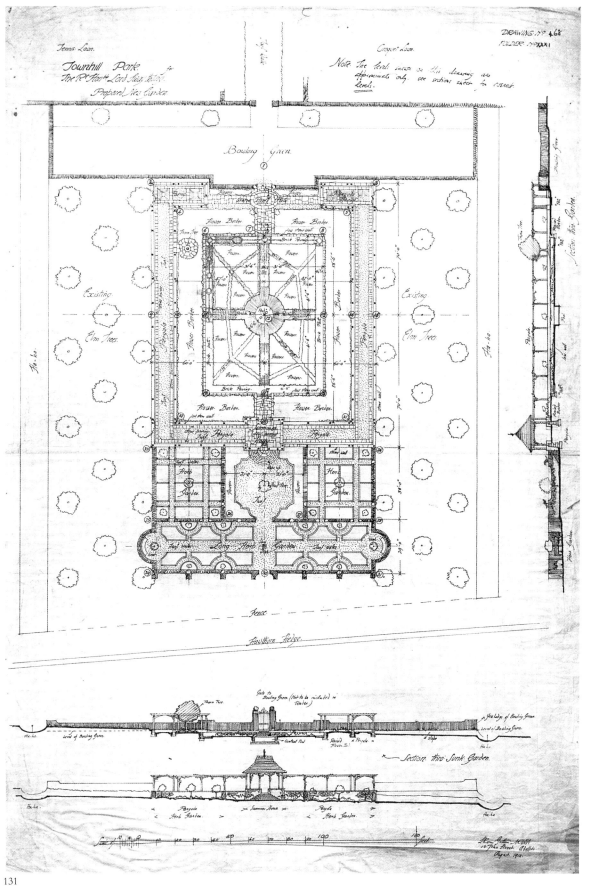

161

BUCKLER'S HARD, HAMPSHIRE

132]   MACKAY HUGH BAILLIE SCOTT 1865–1945

Clobb Copse

Buckler's Hard, Beaulieu, Hampshire, 1937
Watercolour
330 × 510 mm. / 13 × 20⅛ in.

Baillie Scott was an accomplished artist and he illustrated his work and philosophy in his book *Houses & Gardens*. This is the only watercolour of his in the Collection, and it echoes his most romantic taste for half-timbering and cottage garden flowers. He had a genuine love of flowers, especially in wilder settings and felt gardens should reflect their natural surroundings – he suggested that a house by the sea–cliffs where the wild thrift grows should have thrift edging the paths. But he designed essentially ordered and enclosed surroundings, holding true to his Arts and Crafts beliefs, both in the architect's duty to control every interior and exterior detail of his house and to the concept of enclosure as the basic idea of a garden.

His work at Seal Hollow, Sevenoaks, Kent is illustrated in *Gardens for Small Country Houses*;[38] his garden for Hon. Richard Strutt at St Catherine's Court, near Bath is in *The Studio: Modern Gardens 1926–7*,[39] and his garden for Burton House, Longburton in Dorset is in *Houses and Gardens*, 1906.[40]

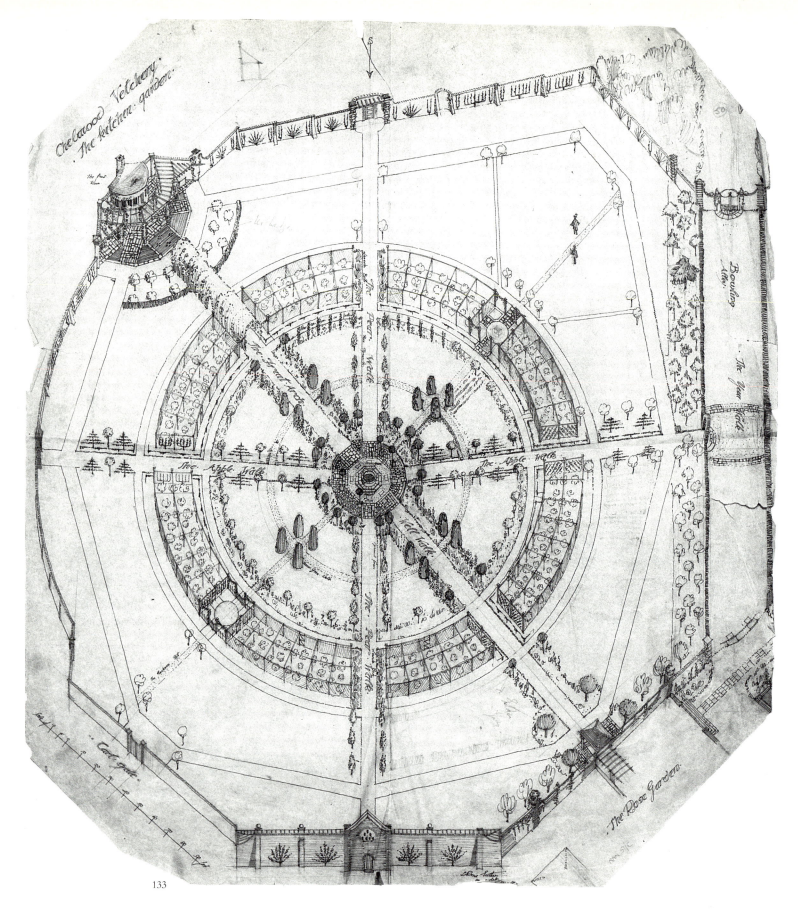

Chelwood Vetchery.
The kitchen garden.

164   133

CHELWOOD VETCHERY, SUSSEX

133] L. ROME GUTHRIE 1880–1958

The kitchen garden

Chelwood Vetchery, Sussex, 1908
Pencil and pen on tracing paper
700 × 616 mm. /27⅝ × 24¼ in.

L. Rome Guthrie designed the gardens, garden furniture and
buildings for Sir Stuart Samuel Bt between 1906–9. A kitchen
garden design of this detail is a rarity and this is the outstanding
drawing for Chelwood Vetchery, full of delightful and
amusing touches. The garden enclosure is entered from the
rose garden in the south-east corner; the whole kitchen garden
is walled, with fruit espaliered on all south facing walls. From
the pavilion at the rose garden gate the main diagonal walk
leads to the central dipping well, and continues diagonally to
the fruit arch and a small semi-circular fruit room built into the
far wall. The other main walk is the north–south pear walk,
with subsidiary apple walk and a gardeners' path, all viewed
isometrically, giving the impression of spokes in a crooked
wheel. The circle of fruit cages is neatly filled and every type of
cordon, pyramid, pillar and espalier has been illustrated.

134] L. ROME GUTHRIE 1880–1958

A fruit garden

Chelwood Vetchery, Sussex, 1908
List of fruit trees with plan key
700 × 616 mm. /27⅝ × 24¼ in.

The list of fruit trees (as planted) is a unique document in the
Drawings Collection. The varieties of gooseberries, rasp-
berries, currants and strawberries named are of particular
interest – who of us now can know the taste of a *Howard's
Lancer* gooseberry or a striped red-and-white currant, *Gloire de
Sablons*?

    Guthrie's garden for Chelwood Vetchery, which included
paved and grass terraces, pools and wrought ironwork, as well
as this kitchen garden was much praised and illustrated in
Jekyll & Weaver's *Gardens for Small Country Houses* in 1912.
The fruit room with its surrounding pergola, and the neatly-
planted and blossoming fruit arch are both illustrated there.

CHELWOOD · VETCHERY · No 83 ·
LIST · OF · FRUIT · TREES · AS · PLANTED · (CONT.)
FRUIT · BUSHES · ETC · IN · CAGES · NUMBERED · 1—8
SKETCH · PLAN · OF · KITCHEN · GARDEN · SHEWING · NUMBERS · OF · CAGES ·

FRUITS	1	2	3	4	5	6	7	8		
GOOSEBERRIES ·										
HOWARDS · LANCER · (WHITE)	16	-	-	-	-	-	-	-	16	
ALMA · (WHITE)	16	-	-	-	-	-	-	-	16	
KEEPSAKE · (YELLOW)	14	-	-	-	-	-	-	-	14	
LANGLEY · GAGE · (WHITE)	-	10	-	-	-	-	-	-	10	—
KEENS · SEEDLING · (RED)	-	10	-	-	-	-	-	-	10	
LANKASHIRE · LASS ·	-	10	-	-	-	-	-	-	10	
HEDGEHOG · (GREEN)	-	-	12	-	-	-	-	-	12	
RED · CHAMPAGNE · (RED)	-	-	12	-	-	-	-	-	12	10
X CHESHIRE · LASS · (WHITE)	-	-	-	-	-	-	-	-	12	
TOTALS · (PER · CAGE)	46	30	-	-	-	-	-	-	112	112
CURRANTS ·										
X BOSKOOP · GIANT · (BLACK)	-	-	-	36	-	-	-	-	36	6
RABY · CASTLE · (RED)	-	-	-	-	12	-	-	-	12	
RED · DUTCH · (RED)	-	-	-	-	12	-	-	-	12	
RED · SCOTCH · (RED)	-	-	-	-	12	-	-	-	12	
GLOIRE · DE · SABLONS · (STRIPED RED & WHITE)	-	-	-	-	-	13	-	-	13	
WHITE · DUTCH · (WHITE)	-	-	-	-	-	8	-	-	8	
TOTALS · (PER · CAGE)	-	-	-	36	36	21	-	-	93	93
RASPBERRIES ·										
X PERPETUAL · DE · BILARD (RED · AUTUMNAL)	-	-	-	-	-	-	29		29	
X GOLDEN · DROP · (YELLOW)	-	-	-	-	-	-	50		50	
X PROFUSION · (RED)	-	-	-	-	-	-	50		50	
X SUPERLATIVE · (RED)	-	-	-	-	-	-	-	139	139	40
TOTALS · (PER · CAGE)	-	-	-	-	-	-	129	139	268	268
x LOGAN · BERRIES ·	7	4	5	5	5	-	-	-	26	26
STRAWBERRIES ·										
X ROYAL · SOVEREIGN ·	170	128	-	-	-	-	-	-	298	
X GIVONS · LATE · PROLIFIC	-	-	126	-	-	-	-	-	126	
X VICOMTESSE · H · DE · THURY	-	-	-	151	-	-	-	-	151	
LATE · PINE ·	-	-	-	-	118	-	-	-	118	
X BRITISH · QUEEN	-	-	-	-	-	123	-	-	123	
X Dr · HOGG ·	-	-	-	-	-	-	115	-	115	
X St · ANTOINE · DE · PADUE · (PERPETUAL)	-	-	-	-	-	-	-	65	65	
X St · JOSEPH · (PERPETUAL)	-	-	-	-	-	-	-	58	58	
TOTALS · (PER · CAGE)	170	128	126	151	118	123	115	123	1054	1054

TOTALS . BUSHES & CANES = 499 . STRAWBERRY · RUNNERS = 1054.

*L. Rome Guthrie
3 Grays · Inn · Place · July · 7 · '08*

134

KELLING HALL, NORFOLK

135

135]   EDWARD BRANTWOOD MAUFE 1883–1974

The forecourt garden

Kelling Hall, Norfolk, c.1914
Sepia photograph

Sometimes the drawings in the Collection are accompanied by original photographs from the architect's office, as in this instance. The picture of Kelling Hall complete, with the forecourt garden planted, was probably for exhibition purposes, and it is a fine sepia image in its own right.

136]   EDWARD BRANTWOOD MAUFE 1883–1974

A bird's-eye view

Kelling Hall, Norfolk, 1912
Pen, drawn by J.B.Scott
340×540 mm. $/13\frac{3}{8} \times 21\frac{1}{4}$ in.

Edward Maufe is largely known as a church architect and most famous for Guildford Cathedral, which he designed in 1932. Kelling Hall was his first country house, built for H.W.A.Deterding, director-general of the Royal Dutch Petroleum Company, in the then highly fashionable 'butterfly' plan.

The 'butterfly' idea was suggested by Richard Norman Shaw at Chesters in Northumberland in 1891. The plan was formed by projecting wings at forty-five degree angles from the corners of a central hall, thus suggesting a butterfly impaled upon a collector's board with wings outstretched. Chesters was a place of pilgrimage for many young Arts and Crafts architects, and the butterfly plan was tried by E.S.Prior, Detmar Blow, M.H.Baillie Scott, Lutyens and Mallows.

136

Kelling Hall, Norfolk.
for H.W.A. Deterding Esquire.
C. Brantwood Maufe. Architect.

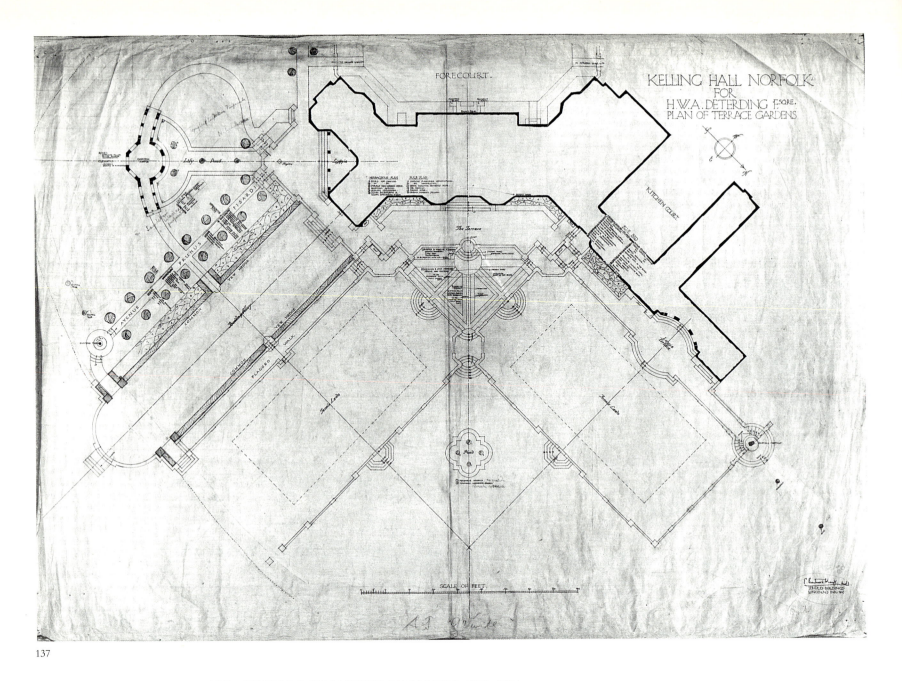

137

137] EDWARD BRANTWOOD MAUFE 1883–1974

Plan of terrace gardens

Kelling Hall, Norfolk, 1912
Pen on linen
550×760 mm. /$21\frac{1}{2} \times 30$ in.

Once adopted, the butterfly plan exacts allegiance throughout the garden, with every major feature carefully placed on the axes of the cross as set out here. The garden front faces the sea, but as Kelling is on the north Norfolk coast, this gives the house a bracing orientation to the north-east. Garden activi-

ties, tennis and bowling, would benefit from the sea air, but this terrace was probably of little use in all but the balmiest weather.

The plants for various beds have been neatly listed on the plan (above) and two areas of interest are reproduced as enlarged details (right).

The walls around the tennis lawns are low flint and brick retaining walls. The dotted line around the eastern edge of the garden, which makes the semi-circular end of the bowling alley and is then continued around the south of the garden, is a flint wall of heights varying between three and six feet, which was completely planted with roses and wall plants. There is a further drawing in the Collection marking every plant. The roses, in groups of three or four, include Dundee Rambler, *Rosa rugosa alba*, and the Penzance briers, *Lady Penzance* (yellow with a copper flush), *Amy Robsart* (deep rose pink) and *Julia Mannering* (pearly white). Aubretia, candytuft, cerastium, santolina and sedums were planted in wall crevices, with ferns, primroses, dwarf lavender and *Iris unguicularis*, the Algerian winter iris, at the wall foot.

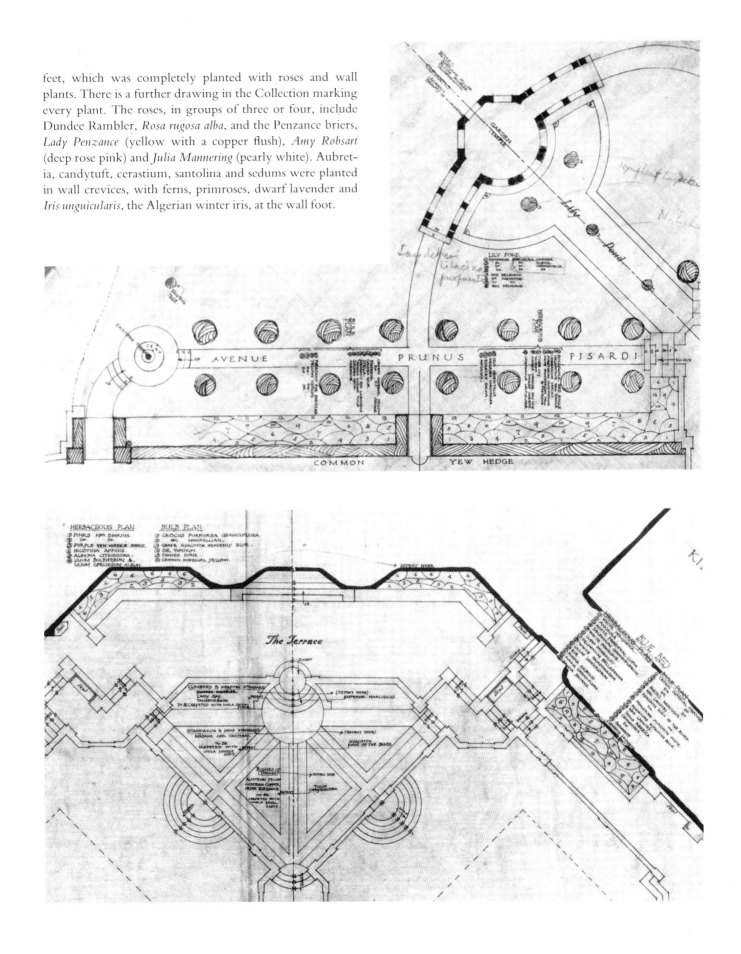

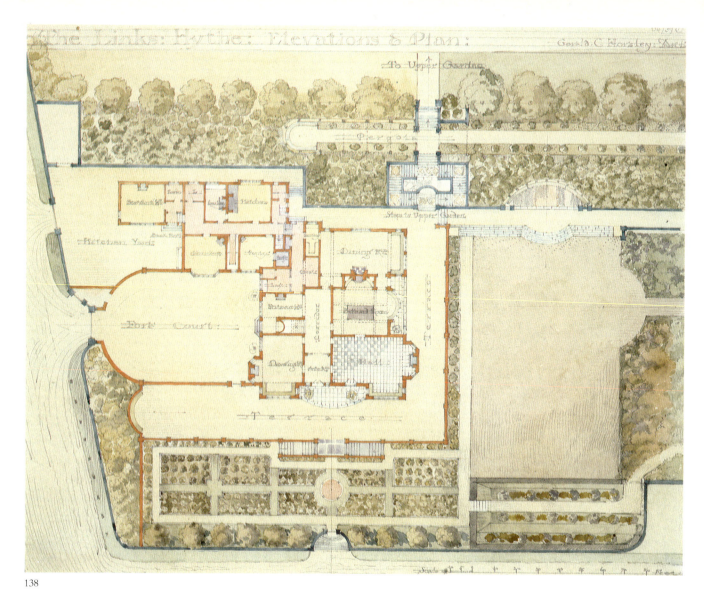

138

HYTHE, KENT

138]   GERALD CALLCOTT HORSLEY 1862–1917

Design for a house and garden

The Links, Hythe, Kent, 1914
Pen and watercolour
400 × 485 mm. /$15\frac{3}{4} \times 19\frac{1}{8}$ in.

Gerald Callcott Horsley was the son of the Victorian painter, J.C.Horsley, and he was a pupil and assistant in the Norman Shaw office and active in art and architectural politics of the 1890s. Many of his drawings are of finely decorated interiors for churches and country houses; he is not known as an architect with an interest in gardens, but The Links shows great accomplishment in Arts and Crafts house and garden style.

139]   GERALD CALLCOTT HORSLEY 1862–1917

The east elevation

The Links, Hythe, Kent, 1914
Pen and watercolour
230 × 485 mm. /$9 \times 19\frac{1}{8}$ in.

The Links demonstrates so well the pleasurable serenity of the 'Edwardian' garden. Each aspect of the garden has its differing character, yet there is a harmony in the whole which invites exploration. This garden allows for a range of uses – entertaining, sports, and children's games – yet limitations on the uses are accepted in order to retain the feeling of a *garden*, as opposed to a 'jigsaw-puzzle' of spaces.

139

140

140]   GERALD CALLCOTT HORSLEY 1862–1917

The south elevation

The Links, Hythe, Kent, 1914
Pen and watercolour
230 × 485 mm. /9 × 19⅛ in.

The south terrace overlooks a formal garden set out below a double flight of steps. This is the most decorative part of the garden, overlooked by the windows of the principal rooms, with the terrace providing the setting for cocktails, or the after-dinner cigarettes on a fine evening.

141

DEVONSHIRE LODGE, LONDON

142] OLIVER HILL 1887–1968

Plan of the garden

Devonshire Lodge, London W1, 1914
Pen on tracing paper
615 × 430 mm. /$24\frac{1}{4}$ × $16\frac{7}{8}$ in.

The radiant star paving in tiles on edge, set in Portland stone, is the dominant theme designed by Hill for Baron Oppenheim. His Modern Movement house and garden, Joldwynds at Holmbury St Mary, is illustrated, no. 149, in the next chapter. Hill, more than any other, seems to be the architect of his time; his chameleon-like talents and ability to choose any style might be termed a personal search for some stability after the war. During the twenties and thirties he was to design houses for socialites and lords, schools, housing estates, a hotel and much prestigious exhibition work, but his interest in gardens seemed largely left behind in an Arts and Crafts haven of the pre-War years.

141] GERALD CALLCOTT HORSLEY 1862–1917

The north and west garden terraces

The Links, Hythe, Kent, 1914
Pen and watercolour
450 × 535 mm. /$17\frac{3}{4}$ × 21 in.

The steeply rising land at the rear of the house is shored up with substantial terraces of clunch (hard chalk) or pale rough stone, partly supporting the grassed or planted banks. The high pergola enjoyed a view of the English Channel. Beyond the pergola was a 'wild garden', a natural area for growing spring bulbs and native woodland flowers as inspired by William Robinson. In ordinary gardens of the Edwardian era this desire for a patch of 'Nature' seemed to presage the rise of ecological consciences, which were to be shattered by the First World War. This is a small but significant reason, one of a myriad, for the regret that the whole Arts and Crafts Movement was killed by the war, and our ecological consciences took another fifty years to be re-born.

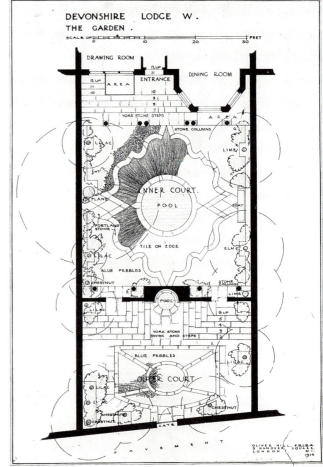

142

143

MOOR CLOSE, BERKSHIRE

143] OLIVER HILL 1887–1968

Perspective of proposed garden

Moor Close, Binfield, Berkshire, 1913
Pencil and crayon on grey paper
345 × 580 mm. /$13\frac{1}{2}$ × 22 in.

Oliver Hill was a 'chameleon' of an architect, brilliant in any number of styles, partly because of the timing of his career. He was William Flockhart's pupil, but studied Beaux-Arts mannerisms at the Architectural Association at the same time. On Lutyens' advice he had worked in a builder's yard for eighteen months when he left school, and this gave him his deep feeling for materials which becomes so evident here at Moor Close. He qualified in 1910, and showed every evidence of working in the intense Arts and Crafts manner which this garden, for C.Birch Crisp, shows, and which is the best of his work from the short time he had before the war. At the outbreak of war he volunteered for the London Scottish Regiment and subsequently won the Military Cross.

He returned to practice after 1918, inevitably unsettled himself, but also aware that the post-war world demanded a new kind of building, though what that was to be was unclear. So he became adept at almost any style, changing from the vernacular to Georgian to International Modern at will; his personality enabled him to do this well – 'he was the kind of architect who drove a Chrysler at 50 mph in the thirties, but made his own envelopes' is the way Margaret Richardson describes him.[35] Moor Close garden survives but it is in poor repair, and as the last of its kind deserves careful restoration.

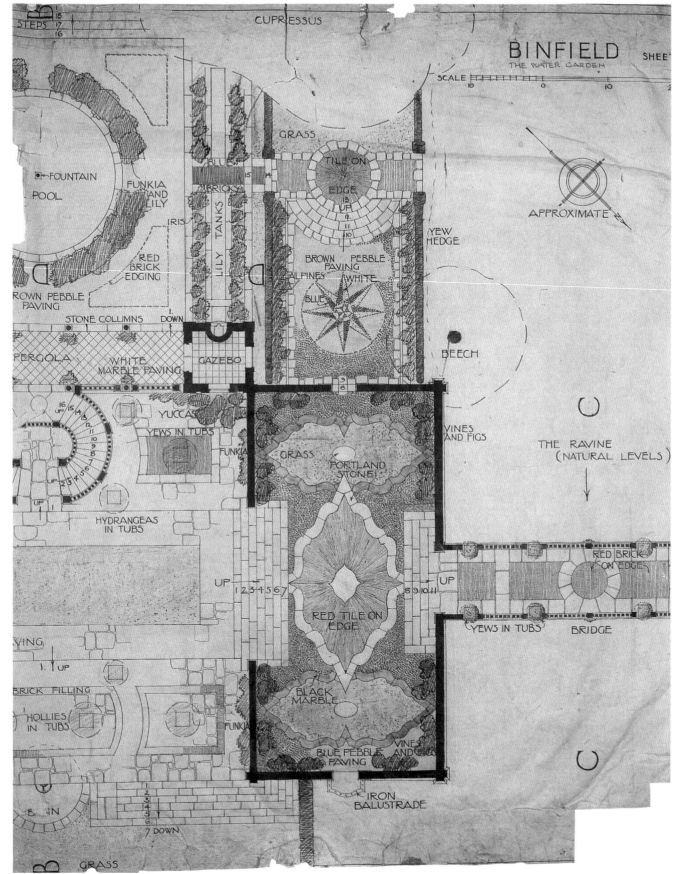

SECTION A·A

145

144] OLIVER HILL 1887–1968

Plan of the water garden pavings

Moor Close, Binfield, Berkshire, 1913
Pen and crayon
Detail taken from sheet
685 × 1430 mm. /27 × 56¼ in.
Scale ¼″ to 1′

Part of Hill's working plan to show the amazing combin-
ation of materials crowded into an intensively designed
space. He has used coloured pebbles and chippings, Portland
stone, black marble and white marble, small two-inch bricks,
tiles on edge and water, grass and herbaceous plants in a
riotous mix of patterns and textures. Oliver Hill knew
Gertrude Jekyll and had some knowledge of her kind of
planting. The radiant star for the sundial terrace at Moor
Close, made of tiles laid on edge, originally loose-set with a
dry mortar brushed in, was his special invention.

145] OLIVER HILL 1887–1968

Pavilions, pergolas, steps and pool

Moor Close, Binfield, Berkshire, 1913
Pen and crayon
Detail taken from sheet
810 × 1440 mm. /31⅞ × 56¾ in.

The flamboyance of this garden is captured in this section
through the main garden terrace with double curving
staircase, pavilions and a pergola all overlooking the pool in
its paved surround. No garden architecture like this had
appeared in an English garden since Sir Charles Barry's
Italianate confections, but it is important to emphasize that
the best Arts and Crafts architects, and Hill in this guise was
one of the best, returned to a comforting human scale in their
designs, so making them delightful.

MARLBOROUGH COLLEGE.
MEMORIAL GARDEN.
ERNEST NEWTON. R.A. AND SONS.
ARCHITECTS.

146

MARLBOROUGH COLLEGE, WILTSHIRE

146]   WILLIAM GODFREY NEWTON 1885–1949

Design for a memorial garden

Marlborough College, Wiltshire, 1923
Pen on board
405 × 550 mm. /16 × 21$\frac{5}{8}$ in.

William G. Newton was the youngest son of Ernest Newton. He served in the First World War and was awarded the Military Cross, and in 1920, while editor of the *Architectural Review*, he won the competition for a Memorial Hall and garden for his old school, Marlborough. This was the prelude to a distinguished academic and architectural career.

The Memorial Garden is related to the Speech Hall and to Butterfield's Chapel, which is approached by a dramatic flight of steps. The sunken court is paved in diamond patterns of two-inch bricks alternating with standard bricks. The surrounding walls are brick with Portland stone edgings; the central hexagonal pool is tiled with blue mosaic and has a bubble fountain. Horse chestnut trees line the road. The memorial garden, as drawn here, was clearly intended for gatherings after Chapel or in concert intervals from the Speech Hall – in days when the road beyond the trees was quiet. Sadly congregations and concert goers tend to retreat into the College gardens beside the Chapel and the Memorial Garden is little used.

WALPOLE HOUSE, LONDON

147] GEORGE HERBERT KITCHIN 1870–1951
Plan of the garden

Walpole House, Chiswick Mall, London, 1927
Pen
From sketchbook no. 30
140 × 235 mm. /$5\frac{1}{2}$ × $9\frac{1}{4}$ in.

G.H.Kitchin was a Winchester architect and antiquarian; he had a wide interest in old buildings and their decoration, and restored a Cromwellian cottage at Compton, just outside Winchester, for his own home. He wrote about the restoration and the making of his garden for *Country Life* in 1919.[36]

The Collection has thirty-two of Kitchin's sketchbooks, but they would seem mostly to be records of his travels in England and Europe rather than evidence of design commissions. Few of his working drawings have been located and it is therefore difficult to know just how many gardens he may have designed. He notes that these sketches were made for Mrs Robert Benson in April and October 1927. The present owner of Walpole House, Jeremy Benson, confirms that his grandmother did not carry out the design shown here and in the following drawing. They were probably the outcome of an enthusiastic conversation with Mrs Benson, who laid out this fine garden in her own way.

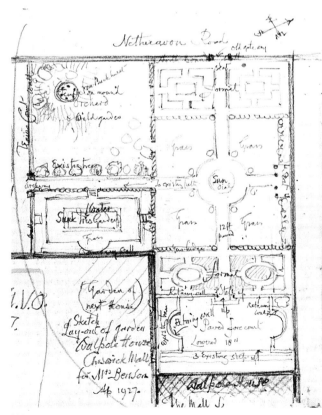

147

148

148] GEORGE HERBERT KITCHIN 1870–1951
Perspective of the garden

Walpole House, Chiswick Mall, London, 1927
Pen
Sketchbook No. 30
140 × 235 mm. /$5\frac{1}{2}$ × $9\frac{1}{4}$ in.

This is Kitchin's idea of how he thought the Walpole House garden should look, sketched in the garden during a visit in 1927. Mrs Robert Benson was in the process of designing her garden; she paved the house terrace but made no beds because of the shade of an old mulberry, she built retaining walls rather as here, and designed her own lily pool in a rectangular shape with rounded ends.

Kitchin is known to have done rather more at Lyegrove, Badminton, in Gloucestershire, for Lady Westmorland. In *The Englishwoman's Garden* she wrote of how he was 'highly recommended' and came and made a sunken lily pool 'where cabbages and brussels sprouts had grown'. She continued, 'the pool was a pretty shape, surrounded by paving and retaining walls of Cotswold stone, reached on each of the four sides by shallow steps'.[37] Kitchin also introduced yew hedges at Lyegrove, and had a definite talent for topiary, as his own carefully conserved garden at Compton shows.

The sketchbooks include two other notable gardens, Mathern Court at Chepstow, the garden of H.Avray Tipping, architectural editor of *Country Life*, and Gertrude Jekyll's Munstead Wood. Kitchin seems to have been very much a figure of his time, a gentlemanly, cultivated, and talented architect and gardener, happily searching out the essence of old England and things English.

Fig. 23] Bentley Wood, Halland, Sussex, designed by Serge Chermayeff for himself, 1936, and the garden by Christopher Tunnard: the garden front from the south west.

5

THE MODERN MOVEMENT GARDEN

1925–1939

The brief, bright story of the Modern Movement's influence on gardens in England can be plotted in its entirety from the drawings in the Collection. That there are so few drawings, and even fewer gardens, indicates how fragile this influence was, sandwiched between two World Wars and shattered by the second of them. Gardens may seem to be a trivial matter for the filling of such a sandwich, but that is somehow just the point; what happened to gardens only reflected what was happening in the wider world, and – as when a man's fingers close upon a moth's wing – such excessive violence seems all the more pitiable. This is the story of twentieth-century gardens in England, as they might have been.

When ordinary life stood up and dusted itself off in the early 1920s, the Arts and Crafts gardens were out of place. They were the creations of old and disillusioned men, and as they were so perfectly Edwardian in mood and character, they too were disgraced and dead. A fragment of their philosophy, a left-over love of nature, was rapidly transforming itself into a love of the great outdoors, and hiking expeditions, camping, sunbathing and 'goff' were all the rage, with a little gardening thrown in. The seed companies, Sutton's of Reading and Carter's of Holborn were quick to revive and flourish, and heaven was modestly priced in packets of annuals – mignonette, pot marigold, godetias and Virginian stock, that were sprinkled on spring earth and enjoyed on summer afternoons. The flowers and the sunshine mattered far more than the kind of gardens they grew in, though the cottagey and crazily-paved variety of garden seemed an easy favourite. Oliver Hill came back from the War and designed two amusing examples, for Fox Steep at Crazies Hill, Wargrave in Berkshire (1924) 'for Hansel and Gretel' (this was Nikolaus Pevsner's attribution), and Woodhouse Copse at Holmbury St Mary in Surrey (1925) which would have suited Snow White equally well. In both cases he asked the eighty-five-year-old Gertrude Jekyll to plant cottage gardens.

Fig. 24| The formal garden for Bentley Wood, designed by Christopher Tunnard, looking south. The plinth to the right of the steps was intended for Henry Moore's *Recumbent Figure*, which Chermayeff asked the sculptor to take back in 1938.

Clearly a new spirit of adventure was needed, and it appeared to be blowing across on the Channel breezes, but as yet had no name. The brightest garden designers in France were the brothers Vera, André and Paul; having been dammed by Le Corbusier as 'witnesses to a dead spirit' their work in the twenties was coming very much alive. Their own garden, on a small triangular plot in a suburban setting in St Germain-en-Laye, was made up of sharply cut triangles of brilliant green grass outlined in white gravel; a low wall of white concrete zig-zagged across a lawn to the accompaniment of a band of *Stachys lanata*, and their neat box edgings cocked a snook at tradition by being twice as wide as they were high. In 1926 they made a garden at Hyères for the Vicomte de Noailles – another triangle, this time enclosed by a mirrored wall which reflected the splintered wedges of paving and planting that fanned across the garden in an unnervingly asymmetrical way. Their whole idea was to mock and joke at the old order, to put Cubism on the ground. It was a game, and the playful Vicomte soon changed it for another, by a brilliant young architect Gabriel Guevrekian, whose triangle of brick-built flower boxes, chequerboarded with squares of paving, made what was to become the smallest of the great gardens of the world.[1]

In Belgium, a garden architect named Jean Cancel-Claes was making small, svelte gardens with smooth white concrete paviours set amongst grass and flowers, and in Stockholm a band of architects were forming a movement to design gardens of the severest architectural shapes softened with what they called 'free and luxuriant vegetation'. A Swiss, M. Correvon, had dubbed certain plants *formes architecturales* and acanthus, fatsia, New Zealand flax, *Viburnum davidii*, periwinkles and ivies were decreed the smartest contrasts to concrete. In England, in the mid-twenties, no one would dare dream of putting concrete into a garden.

The most powerful forces in architecture and design were of course coming from Germany and France, but in 1925 they were still only rumblings; Frederick Etchells' translation of Le Corbusier's *Vers une Architecture* was not to be published for two years, and only a very few people knew the names of Walter Gropius or Mies van der Rohe. It was therefore all the more surprising that a man who made model trains in Northampton should ask one of the greatest names in German design to build him a house. Peter Behrens (1868–1940) had been the most prominent architect in Germany before the war, Walter Gropius was his pupil, and through him Behrens had become the *eminence grise* of the Werkbund and Bauhaus movements. Behrens had started as a painter, then adopted architecture and the applied arts and thoroughly rejected Art Nouveau. As designer to the German electrical conglomerate AEG he had built 'the most beautiful industrial building ever erected up to that time', a turbine factory in Berlin in 1909, but he also applied his belief in 'purity of form' to electric kettles and street lamps.[2] Mr Bassett-Lowke, the model engineer, was attracted to Behrens' early houses of plain oblong forms, walls without windows but just a hint of decoration, flat roofs and plain doorways ('Honesty and saneness' says Pevsner 'that replaced the sultry dreams of Art Nouveau aesthetics'.[3] So this is why the drawings for New

Ways, No. 508 Wellingborough Road, Northampton, of 1925 (nos 151–2) are such a treasure. This amazing house, with its 'jazzy' German Expressionist staircase window which cuts the front in half, the freestanding light piers straight from Secessionist Vienna, a room (moved from a previous Bassett-Lowke home, 78 Derngate, Northampton)[4] decorated by Charles Rennie Mackintosh, with black walls and furniture and orange, grey, blue and yellow stencilling, was the beginning of the Modern Movement in England. And, outside the house, what did these jazzy, new age people find in their garden? It seems unbelievable, but there it is, drawn by Professor Behrens' *atelier* in Vienna, an old fashioned English crazy-paved garden, probably crawling with lobelia and pansies. There never has been a more vivid demonstration of the sentimentality that tethers us to bad taste in gardens.

So it was going to take some cool and perceptive young minds to drag English gardens into the modern age. All of them, with the exception of Oliver Hill, would have to come from elsewhere, but colonial sleepiness and Hitler's Germany would see to that. What we did not know, could not have known, was that so many of the designers of the future would be only passing through.

In 1930, there was a young Canadian designer in London, trained as a landscape architect and horticulturalist, named Christopher Tunnard (1910–79). He had seen the new gardens on the continent; he had encountered the talk and work of the new voices in art, Henry Moore and Barbara Hepworth, and he had learned of Japanese 'occult' symmetry and the Zen reverence for minimalist art, a single stone or a branch against the sky, from the potter Bernard Leach. Tunnard was possessed of enough energy, enthusiasm, and anger, to declare himself a Modernist. Modern was a very exciting word in 1930, implying a militant rejection of moral, emotional and financial ties to the familiar ways of doing things and expressed in 'shocking' hair-cuts, clothes and love affairs. Young designers screamed for 'relevance' and 'serving the purposes of the people', but, as David Dean has noted in his book of drawings of the thirties, though the needs ('homes fit for heroes had been promised') and the new materials were there, the young architect found 'the instruction manuals dog-eared and almost comically out of date'.[5] As a young landscape architect, Christopher Tunnard could only theorize, as he did in a series of pieces in the *Architectural Review*, but he could do little about gardens or landscapes until someone built the right kind of building to go with them.

The touchstone figure was to be the refugee architect, Erich Mendelsohn (1887–1953).[6] He came to London in 1933 and formed a partnership with Serge Chermayeff (b.1900), a Russian who was educated in England and married to the heiress of the furniture company, Waring and Gillow. Mendelsohn and Chermayeff created a sensation with their designs for the De La Warr Cure Resort at Bexhill-on-Sea, a complex of shops, cinema, hotel and the pavilion with extensive gardens, designed with all the flowing forms and lucid geometry that typified Mendelsohn's department stores and villas in Germany. For reasons of cost, only the now famous De La Warr Pavilion was built. However, it was quite clear that Mendelsohn, who had been to talk of 'organic architecture' with Frank Lloyd Wright in Taliesin in Wisconsin, understood how his low-slung, rectangular buildings should relate to their landscapes and to restrained and equally geometric settings.

By 1935 Mendelsohn was working in Jerusalem (though he finally emigrated to the United States in 1941), but his brief time in London had inspired both Chermayeff and Tunnard, and a young Australian architect, Raymond McGrath. The Chermayeffs decided to settle in Sussex, in a house of Chermayeff's own design at Bentley Wood, near Halland; this was to be the *cause célèbre* of the thirties, because Uckfield Rural District Council refused planning permission for this modern glass and steel box to be built in their countryside. Chermayeff persevered and built his house, and consulted Christopher Tunnard from the start about the garden. The Collection does hold a few sketches for Bentley Wood, but none with a significant garden connection. Accompanying *Country Life* photographs are more informative. Figure 23 illustrates the house from the south-west; the approach is from the opposite, east, side to what appears to be a walled enclosure. Once inside the house, from the glass-walled rooms downstairs and from the bedroom balconies, the view southwards over the downs is revealed. Tunnard carefully thinned the existing copse to make the miniature park-like surroundings, with paths through the wood, which expressed the right concoction of masses (greenery) and voids (glades), the leanest distillations of eighteenth-century landscape theories which he felt were right for modern gardens. Once again, living elements were being moulded to fit a new art.

The formal garden (fig. 24) is an extension of the house, as barely functional as the rooms indoors. The paving extends from the glass doors of the dining room to make a spacious terrace, with an inviting cat-walk extending to the viewpoint. In thirties minds the eighteenth-century Picturesque view was newly framed in white wood or steel, and this coincided neatly with the structural framework of rolled steel joists which made a viewing frame into a motif to be used here, at Hill's Joldwynds (no. 149), and at Highpoint (no. 160) and High and Over (fig. 27).

The empty plinth at Bentley Wood tells its own story. Chermayeff asked the young Henry Moore for a figure for the plinth, for which £300 was the agreed price and the architect paid £50 deposit. Moore, who was very close to these sculptural architects of the thirties, felt his work should be in sympathy with the predominant horizontals of the site and its landscape, and decided to carve a reclining figure in Hornton stone, intending it to be 'a kind of focal point'. While working on this figure, he later recalled that he realized 'the necessity of giving outdoor sculpture a far-seeing gaze . . . my figure looked out across a great sweep of the Downs, and her gaze gathered in the horizon. The sculpture . . . had its own identity and did not *need* to be on Chermayeff's terrace, but it so to speak *enjoyed* being there, and I think it introduced a humanizing element. It became a mediator between modern house and ageless land'.[7]

Moore's *Recumbent Figure*, fifty-five inches long, was delivered to the garden in September 1938. The following year the Chermayeffs decided to leave for America, they did not pay the balance but requested a return of the deposit of £50 and asked Moore to take his figure back. Kenneth Clark had just entered Moore's life at that time and he arranged for the Tate Gallery to buy the figure; however, it was promptly lent to the New York World's Fair of 1939, and so it too spent the duration of the War in America, eventually coming safely home in 1945. Mendelsohn and Chermayeff did not return.

But there was still the Australian, Raymond McGrath (1903–77) to build houses for Tunnard's gardens. The Collection has a few of McGrath's drawings for their most well-known project, St Ann's Hill at Chertsey in Surrey, which was set into a fine mature park, which Tunnard exploited with great skill.[8] The shining white 'picture frames' on the house balcony and around its outdoor rooms captured the forms of 150-year old Cedars of Lebanon, he girdled a massive clump of rhododendrons with a paved pool garden, and juxtaposed mellow Georgian walls with modern sculpture by Carl Milles. This is Tunnard's most effective demonstration, with a characteristic

Fig. 25] Methley School, Yorkshire, designed by Oliver Hill, 1938–9, perspective drawn by J. D. M. Harvey. The mix of curving outlines for drives and paths and strictly geometrical forms for flower beds epitomizes the Modern Movement's garden style.

wit, of how the best of the past could be made to serve the modern lifestyle.

But the most exciting find in the Collection is Land's End, Garby, Leicester (no. 157) for which Tunnard designed a garden, in the best Modern manner, in *Gardens in the Modern Landscape* (fig 26). Land's End not only makes the most of its view, but has a garden that is eminently practical and manageable in twentieth-

century conditions. Instead of bemoaning broken backs and bank balances over the costs of a garden, if only we had seen the sense in this kind of design. The terrace is plain, uncluttered, set flush with the grass for easy mowing, the most intensively gardened area is enclosed with a thick hedge (not of unreachable heights) and laid out in squares of alternating paving and grass or plants. Thus the areas prone to invasion from ground elder or convolvulus are contained and treatable, they can be planted according to desire or ability in any given year, and put down to extra grass, again flush with the paving, when less garden is required. Outside this 'garden' the rest of the plot has a closer relationship with nature that means less maintenance, makes for good contrast, and allows 'meadow' and 'wildlife' gardening that were – surprisingly – just as much the rage of the thirties as they are now. Indeed, the thirties had a strong 'ecological' conscience that we just conveniently brushed aside and forgot for almost fifty years.

Further aspects of Modern Movement gardens are shown in the drawings for Oliver Hill's Joldwynds (no. 149), the roof garden for Highpoint (no. 160) and in the illustration of Amyas Connell's High and Over on Amersham Hill (fig. 27), for which the Collection has some drawings, but no garden material. Concrete-edged beds of truncated triangles or rhomboidal form were very suitable for long or angled buildings, as at High and Over and at a school at Methley in Yorkshire by Oliver Hill, for which the Collection has a perspective by J.D.M.Harvey (fig. 25); Hill made the building look like a biplane parked upon the tarmac apron, which must have been tremendously amusing for the schoolchildren. It was at Joldwynds, Holmbury St Mary in Surrey, built for the barrister Wilfred Greene in the late twenties, that Hill demonstrated his characteristically instantaneous grasp of the mix of eighteenth-century theory and Modern streamlining that the Modern Movement garden required. The no-nonsense approach drive, balanced with dark

Fig. 26] Garden design for Land's End, Garby, Leicester, 1938 drawn by Gordon Cullen for Christopher Tunnard's *Gardens in the Modern Landscape*. This is Tunnard's more detailed design for the house by Raymond McGrath. (See nos 157 and 158.)

masses of foliage (this house was also built in an existing garden) is beautifully illustrated in the perspective, no. 149, again by J.D.M.Harvey. The house was surrounded with plain paved terraces, sculptural steps with white concrete retaining walls and a plain rectangular pool viewed through the white framework of the loggia wall. It is all in the past, for Joldwynds was subsequently demolished (a justifiable act, said the anti-Modernists, since a house by Philip Webb had been demolished to make way for it).

The two blocks of flats in Highgate, Highpoint 1 and 2, built by the Tecton Partnership in the mid-thirties are, on the other hand, now highly prized and carefully preserved. Thirties designers saw buildings in the sky as the modern technological answer to chic living for young professional couples who did not want to be bothered with children, dogs or gardens. If necessary, the garden could be also elevated, as this one is, and still serve its purposes. The flats have balconies for sunbathing, the garden provides tennis courts, and the third desirable asset, a view of a green landscape, requiring no lawn mowing, from which dreams of the English countryside could be fuelled, for these new urban dwellers. This is exactly why the eighteenth-century landscape features, gentle green moundings and curvings, with clumps of greenery, an ornament or two and a glimpse of water (a Capability Brown park in the miniature of the mind's eye) fulfilled the requirements of such avant-garde architects as

Fig. 27] High and Over, Amersham Hill, Buckinghamshire, designed by Amyas Connell (Connell, Ward & Lucas) 1934. This entrance front was given flower beds in shuttered concrete edgings, though required a more harmonious planting than these rose bushes.

Berthold Lubetkin's young partners in Tecton.

But what Christopher Tunnard advocated, and these examples give glimpses of, was not easy to achieve. The English may have been happy enough to adopt new styles of dress, jazz, Morris motorcars and air circuses, but they were deeply conservative about their gardens. There was even a great middle-ground of sentimentality that firmly resisted the cries of the brave new world. For every one High and Over or Bentley Wood there were thousands of mock-Tudor three-bedroomed semis with mock Tudor-cottage gardens, not to mention the honestly thirties houses with Crittall metal-windows and sunray front doors, that strode alongside arterial roads where gardens bloomed with crazy paving, rose bushes and gnomes fishing in the rockery pool. The rising tide of the popular gardening press was adamant that this nation of garden owners was each one his own master, free to buy and try everything that the seedsmen, nurserymen and sundries-men advertised. Restraint was hardly in the air. Besides, gardens were no longer just for looking at or strolling in; by some strange paradox the society that had accepted mobility, by bicycle, motor car, charabanc and train, as never before, now demanded that the home plot give better and better value for space and money. What was the good of a subtle organic relationship between a clump of ferns and the trunk of a rather fine tree, if the children's swing had to hang from the tree's branch and the scuff patch covered everything with dust? Those desirable 'formes architecturales', the devilishly prickly acanthus only brought juvenile screams, and the aesthetically fashionable Fatsia japonica was hardly a riot of colour; the smooth transference from paved terrace to grass to beds of flowers did not keep tricycles and footballs at bay. No, the Modern gardens, creations of idealistic intellectuals who thought the garden could be a kind of modern art, simply did not fit with the modern consumer lifestyle any more. The first crack of what was to become the yawning abyss had opened, and the English garden owner parted company with his garden as a setting for good design.

But the nation of gardeners was not entirely to blame. As Sylvia Crowe recognized in a chapter she dubbed 'The Contemporary Garden' in her book, Garden Design in 1958 – 'The process of relating first the classic pattern to the organic world, and then re-imposing a formalized pattern, is in tune with the eternal struggle of the artist to relate the physical world to the conceptions of men's minds'.[9] For one glorious moment, precisely determined when Henry Moore felt his Recumbent Figure

'enjoyed' being in the Chermayeff's garden at Bentley Wood, garden design had regained the pedestal to share with – not only architecture – but sculpture, painting and the other arts finding a new means of expression in the thirties. The coming war was to end all that, and any concerted movement of Modern art was to be shattered. The artists who could bring garden design to these dizzy heights, could see no future, and when Christopher Tunnard left for America in early 1939, the fate of the Modern garden was sealed. He had left the job half-done, and it was to be finished elsewhere; not by him,[10] but by Lawrence Halprin and Thomas Church in California and Roberto Burle Marx in Brazil. They did what Sylvia Crowe had identified as the creative rather than merely the analytical process – imposed their own 'dynamic and individual form . . . which can only issue from the spirit of an artist'.[11] Thus Modern gardens, like Modern art, demand a kind of osmotic process, in that their physical expression can only come via the mind and spirit of the artist.

The Festival of Britain in 1951 was a great opportunity for young landscape designers, under the wing of the architect Hugh Casson, to show how garden spaces could enhance even that ephemeral Utopia, and might do the same for new housing schemes or new towns. The Collection has all Peter Shepheard's designs for his portion of the South Bank site, (for the Moat Garden and Bandstand Garden see nos 162–3). They are models of professionalism and good design, and fulfilled their purpose; both the landscape design profession and their paymasters were convinced that their future role was in the design of new towns and large industrial and commercial developments. That was as it should be, but not good for my story; Peter (now Sir Peter,) Shepheard even admits that he had too few opportunities to design gardens in his distinguished career since that time (fortunately he is doing more now in semi-retirement). His elegant and eloquent book Modern Gardens, published in 1953, gathered in Tunnard and the thirties gardens, the Americans Richard Neutra, Thomas Church and Lawrence Halprin, and Roberto Burle Marx, and all the Festival of Britain designers, but it has not needed revision or rewriting since.

Modern Gardens had seemed an epitaph, but the discovery of James Lever's drawings in the Collection, at least comes as a hopeful footnote. James Lever (1900–1971) was not an architect; he trained at Ontario Agricultural College and returned to England as a garden designer with a good knowledge of plants. He clearly had a great talent for absorbing architectural styles, he was capable of sensitive design and then adding rich and interesting planting. His garden for Sir George Harvey at West Kingston in Sussex of 1937 (no. 150) with a plain and elegant pool is exactly in keeping with the plain white Modern house, for whom the architect is not known. His drawings for the garden of the comfortable mock-Tudor villa, Ashridge (for which no location is known) show him maintaining a good standard of design in the face of considerable demands from the client, even though Ashridge's garden is clearly on the downhill run towards what I am forced to call 'jigsaw-puzzle gardens' (see Chapter 6). James Lever's drawing of the club at Angmering Court catches so superbly the thirties style, that it makes an irresistible farewell to the decade.

James Lever practised well and successfully at garden design for the rest of his career. If there had been more like him I feel we would have had a much greater legacy of awareness of Modern Movement gardens, workable and attractive gardens, like the one at West Kingston, which would have complemented their houses. He had brought the art down from the dizzy heights of the great artists, but he had made it understandable – and therefore acceptable – to more ordinary people. But really, as far as Modern Movement gardens go, England has only a pitiable few; most sadly, the same way that we have no national sensitivity to Modern Art, we have no national willingness to even consider that there might be any use or beauty in that kind of garden anyway. At the deepest level, one is forced to conclude, there was something in Modernism that our national character plainly did not like.

I can think of only one substantial post-war contribution that still carries the banner of good design that was set up by Chermayeff, Tunnard and Moore consistently through the last thirty years, and that is the Span housing projects conceived and designed by the late Eric Lyons (1912–80) and his partner Ivor Cunningham. The Collection is in the process of acquiring more drawings by the partnership so for this book there is just one, Eric Lyons concept sketch from the very beginning of his idea, in 1956, for what has come to be a typical Span house and garden plot. The Span estates have won every housing award on offer, they have been praised to the limit by every critic and architectural guru, and they have *worked*: by following the Modern Movement concepts of respect for the existing landscape, especially mature trees, in the garden sites that were being redeveloped, by giving each house its small private space out of doors, and by setting groups of houses in well-organized and beautifully planted park-like settings, they have worked happy miracles in giving people the kind of surroundings that they love to live in and willingly maintain. From the begining of the projects, from Parkleys at Ham, Surrey in 1956, through Templemere, Weybridge 1964, Spangate, Blackheath 1963, Westfield, Ashstead, 1969, and after Eric Lyons' death to Mallard Place at Kingston upon Thames in the early 1980s, in the hands of Ivor Cunningham, they have continued to demonstrate just how effectively the tenets of the Modern Movement can be the key to successful design for late twentieth-century lives. They are almost – among the windy acres of litter-strewn grass and broken trees, and the impractical flowerings of civic pride in the new towns, the only really worthwhile examples.

Regarding Modern art, Marina Vaizey wrote in the *Sunday Times* of 8 January 1989, 'Britain is in a piquant situation'; for the first time in living memory it has become 'socially acceptable', great private collections are being made here, but the new public appreciation comes at a time when prices are high and funds are low. Hence, the National Art Collection Fund for buying in some important modern works for the nation. But paintings remain in existence, gardens do not, and just as the recognition of the Modern Movement garden came late in the day, so their social acceptance is yet to come. By then, will there be any gardens left to collect?

HOLMBURY ST MARY, SURREY

149] OLIVER HILL 1887–1962

An entrance front

Joldwynds, Holmbury St Mary, Surrey, 1930
Pencil, crayon and chalk,
drawn by J.D.M.Harvey, 1932
502 × 749 mm. /19¾ × 19½ in.

In the mid-1920s Hill had designed a thatched and timbered house, Woodhouse Copse, in Holmbury, and Gertrude Jekyll had made the garden with layers of rough stone terraces and borders of pinks and aubretias. Almost instantly, the brilliant Hill converted to the white concrete curves of Modernism and, unlike Professor Behrens, he realized that the garden had to change also. Joldwynds was set into the slope of its mature garden site to make best use of the backdrop of dark trees, and it was approached by this unadorned but beautifully correct turning circle of gravel. The view from the south-facing slope of Holmbury Hill across Surrey and Sussex to the sea (on a clear day), was concealed until one reached the garden side of the house, with its large plate glass windows, viewing balconies and framework of white concrete-clad steel. The outdoor spaces – the paved sitting terraces reached by a white concrete circular stair, and the severely rectangular pool with a paved surround – were essentially a part of the concept of the house, which was a complete set of indoor and outdoor spaces for worshipping the sun and the landscape.

At Joldwynds, Oliver Hill made the most important opening statement in the history of Modern Movement garden design: he realized the ideal of indoor/outdoor living, providing functional outdoor spaces and varying picturesque views of the landscape. The Modern Movement house in England was to be as much a viewing platform as the Palladian mansion; the Modern Movement garden in England would understand and adapt the ideas that suited the English landscape best, those of the eighteenth-century landscape park, to suit twentieth-century lives.

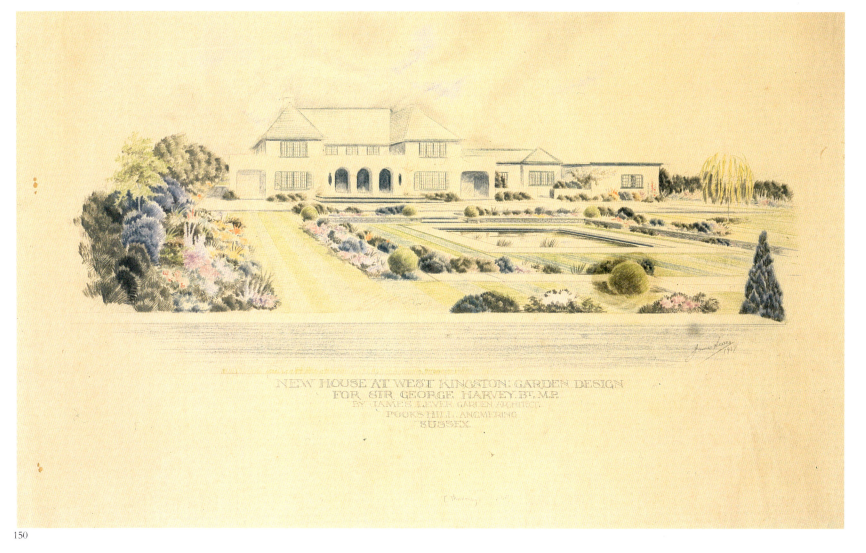

NEW HOUSE AT WEST KINGSTON: GARDEN DESIGN
FOR SIR GEORGE HARVEY. Bᵗ. M.P.
BY JAMES LEVER GARDEN ARCHITECT.
POOKS HILL. ANGMERING
SUSSEX

150

WEST KINGSTON, SUSSEX

150] JAMES LEVER 1900–71

Design for a garden

West Kingston, Sussex, 1937
Pencil and crayon
560 × 760 mm. /22 × 30 in.

The drawing is inscribed: *New House at West Kingston: Garden Design for Sir George Harvey, Bt., MP., by James Lever, Garden Architect, Pook's Hill, Angmering, Sussex*. James Lever was not trained as an architect but had the ability, all too rare in garden designers, to absorb the essential elements of the design of the house. He has caught perfectly the dictums of the Modern Movement for clean design and white forms, but modified the harshness to make a believable and pleasurable garden. The pale plain pavings, the elegant square pool, the low steps, as well as the mowing lines on the lawn and the ground cover planting, all illustrate the thirties ideal of a modern garden for modern lives. The planting, for which he carefully worked out the plans, is very much in keeping with its time; he has used the 'architecturally' contrasting forms of spikes, mounds and carpets and intends a firm base planting of 'low maintenance' shrubs, especially miniature conifers, with added patches of colour from bedding flowers. The maintenance of the whole leisure area, plus a kitchen garden, was well within the capabilities of the by now universal, single gardener, with 'a little family help'.

NEW WAYS, NORTHAMPTON

151]   PETER BEHRENS 1868–1940

Perspective

New Ways, No. 508, Wellingborough Road,
Northampton, 1925
Print of pen and pencil drawing
368 × 425 mm. /$14\frac{1}{2}$ × $16\frac{3}{4}$ in.

This was the first Modern Movement house in England, designed for W.J.Bassett Lowke, owner of a firm of model engineers. Professor Peter Behrens was a notabe pioneer of modern architecture in Germany in the early 1900s; he rejected Art Nouveau and designed revolutionary factories. He was architect and designer for the giant German electrical company, AEG, for whom he designed an early electric kettle in 1910. After the war he lived and taught in Vienna, and this design came from his office there.

152]   PETER BEHRENS 1868–1940

Garden layout plan and section

New Ways, No. 508, Wellingborough Road,
Northampton, 1925
Print of pen and pencil drawing
660 × 826 mm. /26 × $32\frac{1}{2}$ in.

The most remarkable thing about this drawing is that this revolutionary modern house, designed by the great Dr Behrens, should have a garden that resorts to cosy, old-fashioned English crazy-paving. It illustrates vividly the fact of history that garden design lags behind the other arts; it was to take almost ten years for an English landscape architect, Christopher Tunnard, to express a theory of modern gardens for modern houses.

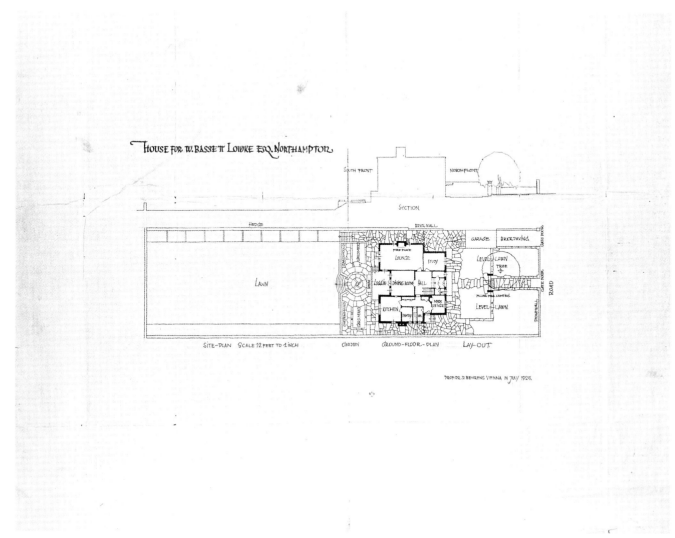

153

154

HOUSE CALLED 'ASHRIDGE'

153] JAMES LEVER 1890–1971

A garden design

Ashridge for Mr C. Tournoff, *c.* 1935
Pen, pencil and crayon on tracing paper
235 × 350 mm. /$9\frac{1}{4}$ × $13\frac{3}{4}$ in.

James Lever presented these designs for a garden called *Ashridge* in a hand-made folder of tracing and drawing paper measuring 450 × 375 mm. The house and garden cannot be traced and do not appear in a list of fifty completed commissions, but the representation of this typical 1930s garden is an excellent example of its period, both from stylistic and professional points of view.

This plan shows the medium-sized garden of what will be revealed as a Tudor-style suburban detached house. The requirements are those of an ideal couple with two children: a kitchen garden, greenhouse, herbs and fruit, a play area and summerhouse, plenty of lawn and colourful borders which both screen the neighbouring plots and provide all-the-year-round interest.

154] JAMES LEVER 1890–1971

Garden details

Ashridge for M.C. Tournoff, *c.* 1935
Pencil and crayon on tracing paper
450 × 375 mm. /$17\frac{3}{4}$ × $14\frac{3}{4}$ in.

The mock Tudor style of Ashridge, a house like a million others in suburban Surrey or Sussex, made the ideal family home of the 1930s. The phrase 'hedgeless forecourt' indicates a Modern Movement idea that banished the clutter of fences and walls from new estate building to give a greater flow to the landscape settings as they were seen from the road. This was adapted from the American 'automobile suburbs' of the twenties; James Lever trained at Ontario Agricultural College so may well have come to England with an awareness of those North American ideas.

155

156

155] JAMES LEVER 1890–1971

Garden with retaining walls

For Ashridge, *c.* 1935
Pencil and crayon
140 × 210 mm. / $5\frac{1}{2} \times 8\frac{1}{4}$ in.

Here the former sandpit has been turned into a simple sunken garden. The purpose of the sketch is to show an alternative treatment for the rock garden east of the house on the garden layout plan (no. 153). Instead of casually laid rocks the garden is now formally terraced in an Arts and Crafts manner, with brick retaining-walls and a paved path leading to a seat. This was an expensive operation for a family garden, even in the 1930s, so the wise garden designer allowed his client the choice. James Lever has bowed to tradition with clipped rounded clumps of box on his walls, but the general planting is of the modern, labour-saving, landscape type, with the popular weeping willow – the only tree many clients wanted, usually in highly unsuitable places.

156] JAMES LEVER 1890–1971

A landscaped garden

Ashridge, *c.* 1935
Pencil and crayon on tracing paper
100 × 200 mm. / $3\frac{7}{8} \times 7\frac{7}{8}$ in.

The view north of the whole length of the garden from the summerhouse shows the landscape planting of shrubs and trees and the island beds that are outlined on the garden plan. This modest sketch is remarkable, for it shows a 1930s use of the screen planting and serpentine borders which had been banished from gardens since the 1870s. Edwin Lutyens and his fellows of the Arts and Crafts Movement did not believe in the serpentine line – there was in Nature, 'no such thing as a free curve' Lutyens had said, and they had all designed accordingly. A feeling for organic design returned with the younger generation's backlash against those who were responsible for the War; garden design in the thirties reasserted the links with the English landscape style of the eighteenth century, in miniature, and this was to be the guiding motif of gardening in the later twentieth century.

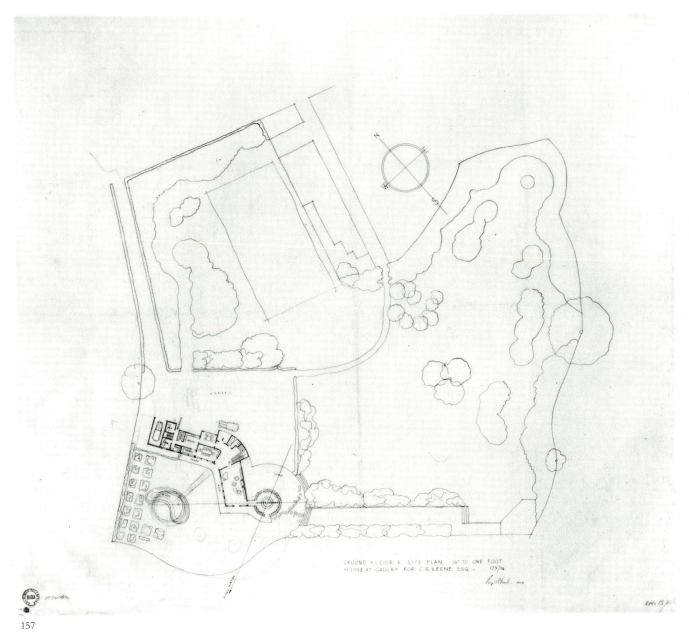

157

GARBY, LEICESTER

157] RAYMOND McGRATH 1903–77

A house and garden

Land's End, Garby, Leicester, 1937
Pen and crayon on tracing paper
760 × 830 mm. /30 × 32⅝ in.

This drawing and that following are from a number of Raymond McGrath's drawings in the Collection, and are of particular interest as Land's End's garden was designed by Christopher Tunnard and illustrated in *Gardens in the Modern Landscape*.[12] Either McGrath or Tunnard have begun to sketch the garden on this tracing. As the subsequent sketch (reproduced on page 183) shows, the main feature of the garden was an enclosed rectangle which led off from the terrace, which was divided into squares, alternately grass or paving, with small shrubs and alpines in planted squares.

158] RAYMOND McGRATH 1903–77
Principal front

Land's End, Garby, Leicester, 1937
Pen and crayon on tracing paper
510 × 640 mm. /20⅛ × 25¼ in.

Land's End was one of the few Modern houses designed by this brilliant young Australian architect in the thirties; his most famous house is St Ann's Hill at Chertsey in Surrey, for which the Collection has drawings, but none of the garden. This elevation of the house shows the circular plunge pool which was in the foreground of the view from the principal rooms; the view extended, via a ha-ha, across 'thirty miles of typical shire landscape'.[13]

158

159

'SPAN' ESTATES

159] ERIC LYONS 1912–80
Design sketch

Span house and garden, 1956
Crayon on card
381 × 610 mm. /15 × 24 in.

Eric Lyons helped initiate the 'Span' housing projects in the mid-fifties, so this is one of his earliest design sketches. It illustrates part of his concept that contributed much to their outstanding success, namely the care taken to retain mature trees and shrubs from the old garden sites that were being re-developed, provide a small private space for each house, and plant both private and public spaces with durable and attractive new shrubs and trees. This initial concern for the surroundings encouraged the continuing care of the landscape settings, which was established and much copied by other housing developers at a much later date. Over fifty 'Span' estates were planned by the Eric Lyons Cunningham Partnership between the mid fifties and early eighties, mostly in suburban Surrey and Kent. Almost every estate won at least one housing award; they continue to be highly desirable places to live and the maturing garden settings, maintained by the community, are a major factor in their undoubted success.

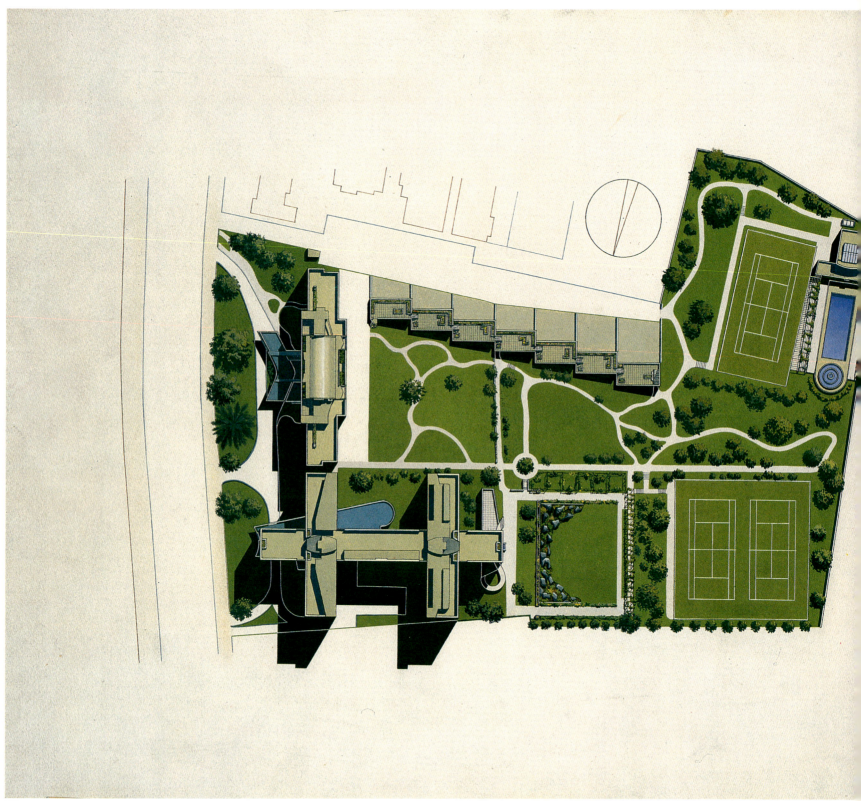

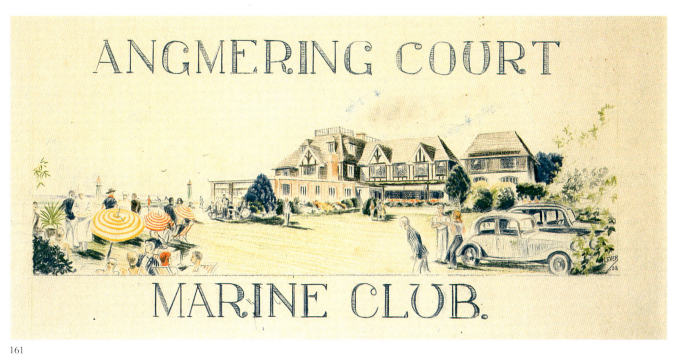

161

HIGHGATE, LONDON

160] TECTON
BERTHOLD LUBETKIN b. 1901

A roof garden for Highpoint 1 and 2

Highgate, London, 1938
Print with pen and gouache
390 × 550 mm. /$15\frac{3}{8} × 21\frac{5}{8}$ in.

Lubetkin came to London from Paris in 1930 to work with a group of young Architectural Association students, who formed a partnership, Tecton. Highpoint 1, built in 1935, was their first large housing scheme, and Highpoint 2 followed two years later, after considerable local opposition had been overcome. This plan shows both the blocks of flats completed, with the garden designed at first floor level to be viewed and enjoyed by as many residents as possible. The major part of the space is given over to a green wilderness, a miniature park-like landscape of meandering paths, which assumes the surreal touch of the thirties when it is realized that it is not on the ground, and is not really for experience (though every resident has access), but rather for use as a garden in the mind's eye. It is however, a most interesting proof of Christopher Tunnard's theory that the forms of the English landscape movement, were just what modern architecture required as a suitable green foil.

ANGMERING COURT, SUSSEX

161] JAMES LEVER 1900–70

Marine Club

Angmering Court, Sussex, 1938
Pencil and crayon
500 × 760 mm. /$19\frac{3}{4} × 30$ in.

Though not particularly interesting in garden design terms, this presentation drawing depicting the lawn of a south coast sailing club says much about 1930s taste and design. James Lever was a successful garden designer whose work aptly illustrates the ability to charm his clients. How could the Marine Club house committee resist his proposals to set their new terrace bar on a lush lawn with a rich planting of evergreens and colourful shrubs and flowers? He has caught the delights of a sunny morning at the club perfectly – with the cars, clothes, the sun-umbrellas and the splendidly attired chef offering Pimm's No. 1 Cup and canapés, the sense of well-being is complete. It reminds us so well that the late thirties too had golden days, at least for these cherished mortals, before they had to hang up their blazers and slacks and change into khaki and navy blue.

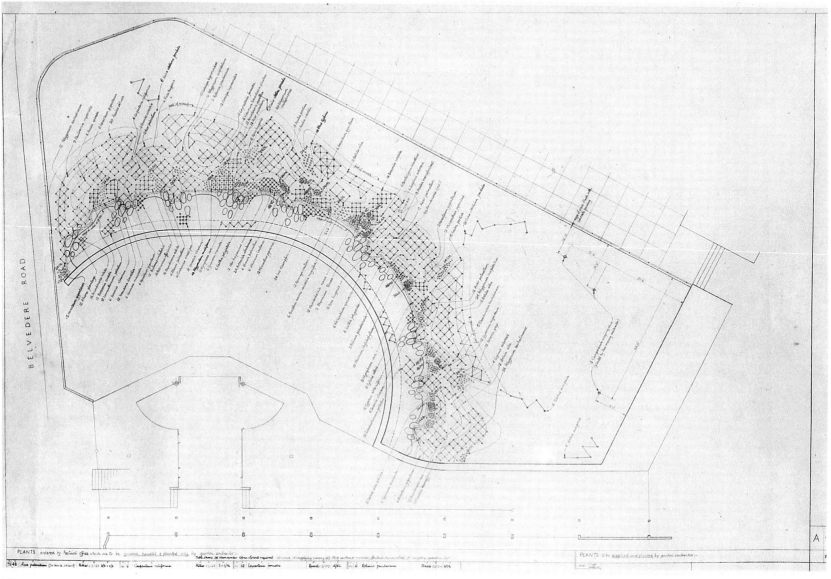

162

FESTIVAL OF BRITAIN

162]   PETER SHEPHEARD b. 1913

A planting plan for the moat garden

Festival of Britain, London, 1951
Pen on tracing
700 × 1000 mm. /$27\frac{5}{8} \times 39\frac{3}{8}$ in.

Peter Shepheard was the landscape architect for the Festival site between Waterloo Bridge and the railway bridge, that is

to say, around the Festival Hall. He has described the project as essentially the creation of a designed townscape; the site was mainly paved to cope with the large numbers of visitors to the various exhibitions, and the planting was used for ornament and for screening sitting areas. The Moat Garden was the most definite planted feature of this part of the site, and conceived as a water and planting barrier to shelter the sitting terrace of a tented tea-restaurant (bounded by a curved wall on the plan).

The planting plan is a model of clarity and good detail. As can be seen, the moat was planted with water lilies (*Nymphaea vars*) and other aquatics, and bordered by a 'picturesque shore' of carefully placed rocks. The richest planting was banked behind these rocks – large and carefully balanced clumps of Gunneras, *Rheum palmatum, Heracleums, Crambe orientale*, Bamboos, Meadowsweets, *Phormium tenax* and other grasses, with the flowers of tree lupins, romneyas, roses and azaleas. The trees on the outer rim and on the grass were birches, willows, rhus, *Catalpa bignonoides* and elms. It must be remembered that this was an 'instant' garden, planted in a few months with pot-grown specimens and twenty-five-foot high trees so that it was ready for the Festival's opening in May and bloomed throughout the summer. In the stock-starved situation of nurseries in post-war Britain it was a considerably greater achievement than are the instant plantings of garden festivals in the 80s.

Another significant point is that the Festival brought the people of post-war Britain, and on the whole urban people, in close touch with such dramatic looking plants as *Phormium tenax*, the great sword leaves of New Zealand flax, and Gunneras (giant rhubarb) for the first time. These were among the 'architectural' plants which designers of the 30s had deemed suitable for urban and modern settings, but they had only been used in a few select housing schemes and private gardens until they bloomed on the South Bank.

163] PETER SHEPHEARD b. 1913

A bandstand garden

Festival of Britain, London, 1951
Pen on tracing
550×920 mm. /$21\frac{1}{2} \times 36\frac{1}{4}$ in. part of sheet

There were a number of mature trees on the Festival site that were carefully saved, and several of these were incorporated into the bandstand garden. An essential philosophy of the design team, led by Sir Hugh Casson, was that wherever people sat down they must be in close proximity to handsome plants and flowers. Thus there were frequent groupings of both squared planters and round concrete and plaster pots filled with tulips, petunias or chrysanthemums according to season.

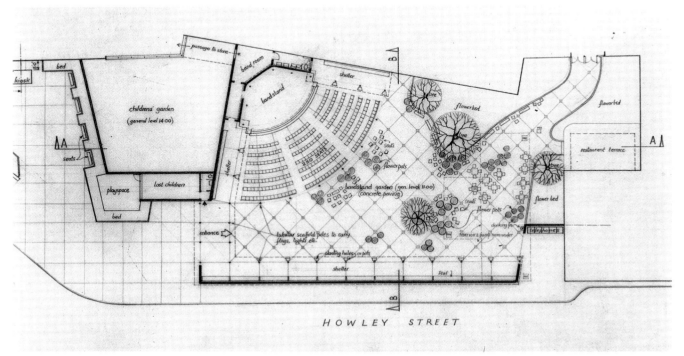

163

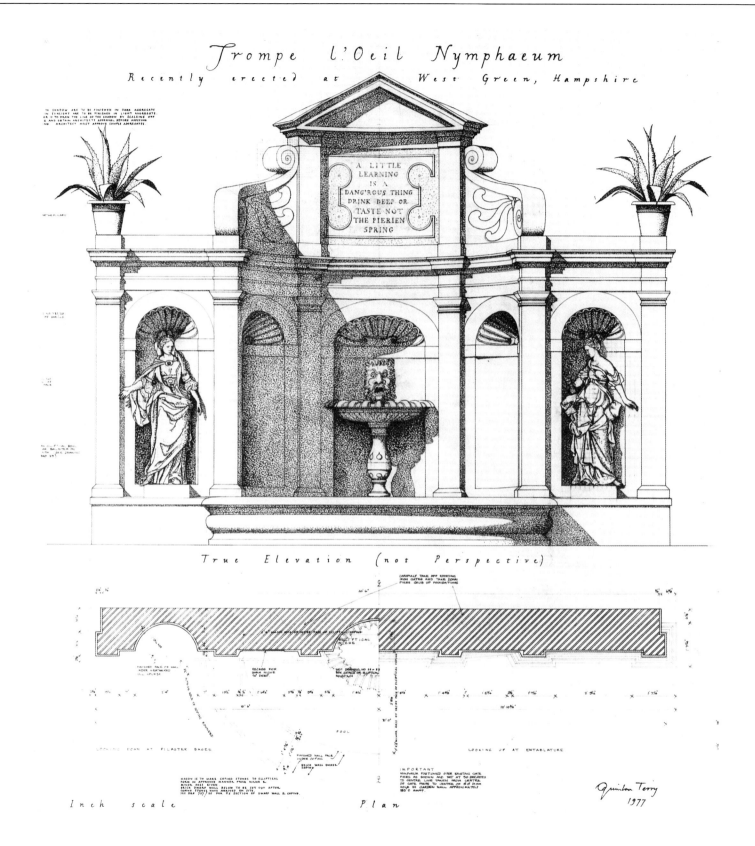

Trompe l'Oeil Nymphaeum
Recently erected at West Green, Hampshire

A LITTLE
LEARNING
IS A
DANG'ROUS THING
DRINK DEEP OR
TASTE NOT
THE PIERIEN
SPRING

True Elevation (not Perspective)

Inch scale *Plan*

Quinlan Terry
1977

Fig. 28] The Nymphaeum, West Green Manor, Hartley Wintney, Hampshire; designed by Quinlan Terry for Lord McAlpine.

6
CONTINUING CLASSICISM
1920 to the present day

Modernism was not the only direction for a young architect of the 1920s to take; he had a choice. With his usual vision, David Dean puts it thus: '. . . as an educated man might enjoy both Swinburne and Eliot, or Bach and Cole Porter, so . . . the world was all before him where to choose, and an admiration for Lutyens did not disqualify him from a very different admiration for Lubetkin . . .'[1] It was a good time to be around, but – as David Dean's comparisons make clear, the choice was really between the philosophies of the old men and those of the young. Sir Edwin Lutyens might have been England's and the Empire's most famous architectural name, for Queen Mary's Dolls' House and New Delhi, but he was never very fond of the RIBA. Much more symbolic of the professional old guard was Sir Reginald Blomfield, then nearly seventy, who had written *The Formal Garden in England* (1892) almost thirty years before, had been President of the Institute, as well as winner of its prestigious Gold Medal, immediately before the War, and was determinedly opposed to Modernism. He waged a long campaign against the new ideas, staunchly supporting the 'grand manner'. That there may have been few people left after the war to pay for the grand manner was perhaps an old man's oversight, but he was still a powerful voice in the Institute and had much support. There was some irony in that he, who had come from a time when architects had so deeply believed themselves to be artists and craftsmen, now found himself allied to those whose chief anti-Modernist jibe was that architecture was now a profession which needed to please its clients and few clients, they said, would want to pay for such artistic fantasies as white concrete boxes with concrete and periwinkled gardens. (They were, of course, so sadly right.)

The mainstream of the Institute was determined that the Centenary, due to be celebrated in 1934, should be marked by the absolute certainty that the profession was soundly and sensibly organized to put on a brave face to its clients' future. And of course it was, and it did, through the changing tastes of the next fifty years, until HRH The Prince of Wales spotted that notorious carbuncle on the same brave, perhaps now brazen, face.[2] But in that same period the Institute also fostered an undercurrent of architecture of which Prince Charles could only approve; quietly, almost underground, a discreet and self-effacing continuation of the grand manner has gone on pleasing clients for houses and gardens and some of these drawings are illustrated in this chapter.

The artistic yearnings of young architects could not be instantly washed away in the twenties, and these feelings tended to be allied to an interest in gardens. Oliver Hill, ever enthusiastic, and the young Geoffrey Jellicoe (b.1900) were the first architects to join the recently founded Institute of Landscape Architects. This new element in the design scheme of things was set up in 1929 by a group of garden designers and horticulturalists to amend what they felt was a poor standard of garden design. Its first President was the planner and landscape architect, Thomas Mawson, but architects were encouraged and welcomed. And so were women, and two of the earliest members were to be Brenda Colvin and Sylvia Crowe, fresh from horticultural college; these three, Colvin, Crowe and Jellicoe, were to create the art of landscape design in England during the next fifty years. Theirs is not largely a story of gardens, for this young profession had a vocation in the larger landscape, nor is it a story that can be told here, for landscape architects' drawings have rarely found their way into the Collection, unless they were also architects. Geoffrey Jellicoe was both, and it is a matter for mutual pride that the Collection holds his first major project and what he, now in his eighty-ninth year, regards as his last. The latter, his designs for the Moody Botanic Garden at Galveston in Texas, at present being put on to the ground, make the post-script to this book, for reasons which will become very clear. His first achievement, the drawings he made with J.C.Shepherd (1896–1970) for their book, *Italian Gardens of the Renaissance* is my present starting point, and perhaps requires some explanation.

When Sylvia Crowe wrote in *Garden Design* of the process for designing a modern garden, she was identifying a point in time as well as in artistry: it was 'a process of relating first the classic pattern to the organic world, and then re-imposing a formalized pattern. This was 'in tune with the eternal struggle of the artist to relate the physical world to the conceptions of mens' minds'.[3] Geoffrey Jellicoe had a strong intuitive belief in this 'eternal struggle', as being a landscape architect's no less than a painter's or sculptor's, right from the beginning of his career amidst the rumblings of Modernism at the Architectural Association School where he taught in the mid-twenties. When he and J.C. 'Jock' Shepherd decided to use their Rome Scholarship to spend the spring measuring and drawing the Italian villa gardens, it was an interesting and a remarkable decision that was to rule the course of Jellicoe's whole career, and, I suggest, the course of a mainstream of garden design in this century. In deciding to return to the 'classical patterns' of the past, he consciously chose the time when he felt that the art of garden design was both in tune and on a par with the other arts. He realized that a building alone was not enough, that its surroundings were very important, and he rejected the French, Scandinavian and Japanese sources of Modernism that others accepted. Was it a longing for some sunshine or an intuition of genius that motivated the trip to Italy; it is now too long ago for even Sir Geoffrey to be sure, but for whatever reason they went, the drawings that they made are both beautiful and influential.

Of course, architects have been on sketching trips to Italy at every opportunity, and some have drawn the gardens. Charles Tyrell's watercolour plan of Villa d'Este at Tivoli of 1821 is reproduced here, no. 58; the Collection has also the Villa d'Este and the fountain at Villa Albani in Rome drawn by David Mocatta (1806–89), a pupil of Sir John Soane; Thomas Hardwick's plan of Villa Madama – a garden that Jellicoe also found inspiring – and some Italian gardens in a volume of drawings by Henry Parke (d. 1835). The late nineteenth and early twentieth centuries had seen a spate of books on the villa gardens, as a new wave of enthusiasts (largely American) discovered them; these included Edith Wharton's *Italian Villas and their Gardens* with watercolours by Maxfield Parrish, of 1904; Sir George Sitwell's *On the Making of Gardens*, 1909, as well as lavishly photographed volumes from the *Country Life* stable. But Jellicoe and Shepherd were the first and only to work hard enough to scale and proportion the gardens with technical accuracy; Mrs Wharton and Sir George were perceptive and eloquent in analysis of the philosophy and its effect, but the gardens' age-old secrets were locked away in their measurements, as in a book of spells, which these two young architects sought to translate.

Italian Gardens of the Renaissance made its first appearance in the autumn of 1925. It was a small book, with a short introductory essay printed in English and Italian by Jellicoe, but largely filled with the drawings and a lot of charmingly amateurish black-and-white photographs. They are amateurish in photographic terms only, for what was important were their points of view, which were part of the survey and drawing process and therefore elaborated on the theories being observed. The Collection holds the complete set of original drawings for the book; they are of two kinds – the plans in pen and grey washes by J.C. Shepherd and the pen and ink perspectives drawn by Geoffrey Jellicoe. The washed drawings have been reproduced here in colour for the first time, so as to appreciate that in reality they are subtly and beautifully shaded, as well as having acquired a fine patina of age.

The drawings were meant to carry their own, three-dimensional, message effectively; Geoffrey Jellicoe's brief introduction pinpointed the aspects of design they embodied. He began with the Villa Madama in Rome, the work of Raphael (1483–1520) and Antonio San Gallo (1485–1546) which he thought 'the greatest conception of a country pleasure house of the Renaissance' and the strongest influence on garden design; he describes the villa as a suite of garden reception rooms spreading from a centre court to theatres and loggias and 'to terrace upon terrace of garden'.[4] Within fifty years of Villa Madama's creation, i.e. by about 1570, the Italian gardens had reached their zenith. They were made by noble minds looking for a lost Eden, minds that were capable of harmonizing formality with informality, of fitting the gardens into the scale of their landscape and by imbuing them with a sparkle of warmth and colour. To these sensual pleasures was added the psychological purpose of bringing contentment to their owners; they thus have differing characters, some had dignified rooms to please highly developed minds, others – and he cites Villa Gamberaia – were full of surprises, wonders and 'frivolity of temperament'. The line between frivolity and chaos could be difficult to find; at Gamberaia the strong axis of the bowling alley – stretching from one end to the other of its plan, with a cross-axis – made it possible to fit in such a variety of spaces (no. 166). The Boboli in

Florence, on the other hand, were gardens for great entertainments; the empty gardens held a latent power 'that could embrace whole masses' and their vitality depended upon people flooding the terraces (see nos. 167–8). Jellicoe acknowledged the need for shade and cooling waters; Villa d'Este presented a refreshing spectacle, 'a vast rumbling organ', and the cascade at Villa Garzoni was cleverly divided to fit the scale of the landscape (nos. 164–5). The Italian light was so dazzling that bright colours were not missed; the subtle shadings from dark cypress-green, through box, yew, ilex and to the lighter lemon trees, was cooling and soothing.

These insights were very much his personal visions from the jottings on his pad, expressive of the life of the gardens. He wrote briefly of 'framed views' and perspectives, but really such things are all explained visually in the drawings. Jellicoe found these Italian gardens to be essentially humanist creations; he felt they were the best reference point from the past for the creation of landscapes and gardens for the brave new world; the softer face of Modernism. Undoubtedly the book *Italian Gardens of the Renaissance* was seen by all young architects of the late twenties and early thirties; it remains a classic and has not been surpassed in its effective expression of the multi-dimensional and real world upon a flat page. But as it took skill and intuition to capture the gardens, so it would take skill and determination to put the precepts into practice in a very different world from the sixteenth century of the Medicis and Cardinal d'Este. How Geoffrey Jellicoe tackled that is the story of his career which he has eloquently explained in lectures and books.[5] Here, I want to examine other drawings from the 1920s to the present-day in the light of this classical inspiration.

The Collection has over 250 projects by Harry Stuart Goodhart-Rendel (1887–1959) and I have included six of his garden drawings here. He was a distinguished and scholarly figure of the twenties and thirties in both architecture and the musical world. He was President of the Architectural Association 1924–5, Slade Professor of Fine Art at Oxford 1933–6 and President of the RIBA 1937–9; music had been his first love, but he chose architecture as a career, having no real need to work at all because of an inheritance from his grandfather Lord Rendel, which included Hatchlands at Clandon (a fine eighteenth-century house with a Robert Adam interior and now the property of the National Trust). He was clever and adaptable as a designer, went through a brilliant flash of Modernism (which bore no gardens) and settled into mainly safe, classically inspired houses for rich clients. He did not do a great deal of garden work, though he was as capable of designing gardens as any other aspect of design, for example a memorial chapel for King Edward VII at Bagshot Park in Surrey, cottages in his home village or a school music room. That said, his drawing for the East Garden of Langham Old Hall (no. 176) in Rutland is a delight and stands comparison well with the Shepherd and Jellicoe villa garden drawings. Goodhart-Rendel altered and extended Langham Old Hall in 1927–8, and it would have been in character for him to have attempted the Renaissance virtues of enclosure and scale, harmony and rhythm, all of which are achieved well in this shadowed perspective. The plan of the terrace and sunk garden (no. 177) is clever in the way the normal squares and rectangles have been pushed into rhomboids in order to fit the site, but it is veering towards the over-clever. His London garden for 39 Charles Street, off Berkeley Square (no. 180) is coolly smart and suitable for where an outdoor room rather than a garden is required, but the design for Roehampton Court (no. 179) where every requirement of a prosperous suburban family has been fitted in 'jigsaw puzzle' fashion, is verging on a garden designer's bad dream. At Roehampton Court, designed in 1923, the new motorcar dictates the curving drive and the turning circle; the family require a large terrace for parties, a swimming pool and lawns, and lawn tennis court as well as one of the new all-weather ones by *En-Tout-Cas*, and a paddock for the children's pony. The flower gardens are the acceptable remnants of the Arts and Crafts tastes, a double border for mixed shrubs, herbaceous perennials and annuals, and an enclosed rose garden for the new Hybrid Tea varieties to be grown in solitary state, well covered with the pony manure. The kitchen garden is reduced to thoroughly modern proportions; no more the vast Victorian spaces for hundredweights of asparagus and strawberries or even the Arts and Crafts belief in a self-sufficiency of peaches and nectarines (such things were too expensive to grow and could be bought from the stores) and here, one man and a boy could manage the salads, beans and peas and winter vegetables. This competent arrangement of garden functions, it hardly seems a *design*, for Roehampton Court is really a very important drawing for it foretells one of the fates of the twentieth-century garden, which was to be all spaces for all activities for every member of the family. It has the detachment of a project, and was clearly not designed for anyone with the remotest interest in gardening.

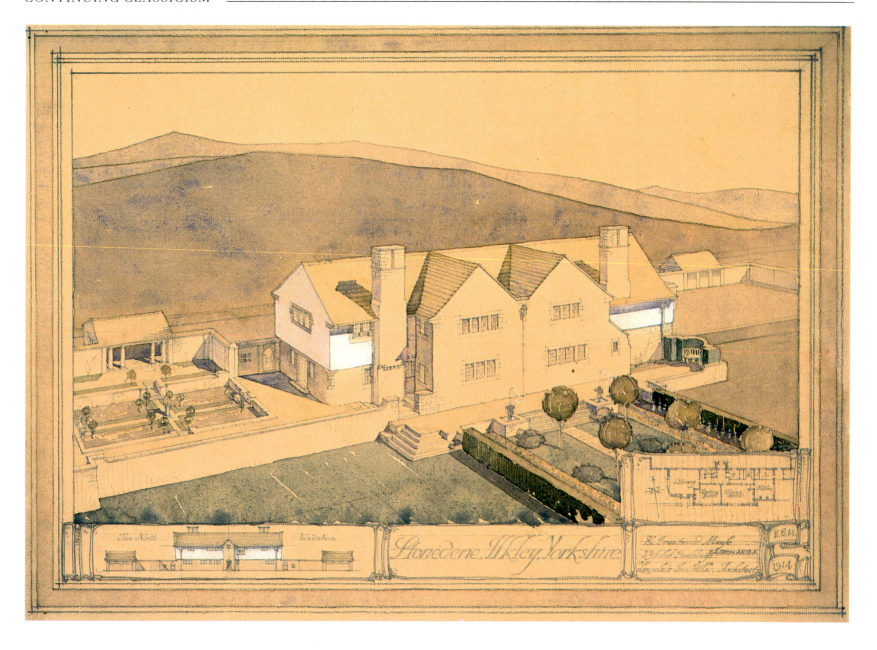

Fig. 29] Stonedene, Ilkley, Yorkshire by Edward Maufe, 1914.
This perspective for a house and garden from before the First World
War seems to suggest that the Arts and Crafts ideals would have
been perpetuated by younger architects, had not the War intervened.

There is one other clever garden design by H.S.Goodhart-Rendel in the Collection, a fan-shaped layout for the front of a house called Arthingworth Manor in Northamptonshire, which he drew in the late 1930s, but the commission was never executed. The impression left by the Goodhart-Rendel drawings is one of scholarly, well-mannered competence. The same impression is given by the drawing of Weston Corbett Place in Hampshire, designed for Conrad Heseltine in 1936 by Darcy

Braddell and Humphry Deane, who had a flourishing between-the-wars practice in serene country houses. Edward Maufe, whose flamboyantly Arts and Crafts Kelling Hall is illustrated (nos 135–7) also adopted well-mannered restraint in Stonedene at Ilkley (see fig. 29) and in his later houses, including Shepherd's Hill and Yaffle Hill in Dorset. Scholarly good manners seem to be suggesting gardens as polite enclosures or neat vistas and leaving them there.

In architectural circles of the 1920s there were a number of 'fads' besides Modernism; H.S.Goodhart-Rendel was keen on Victorian churches, long before their charms were due for re-appraisal by John Betjeman. Old manor houses such as Cold Ashton near Bath and Avebury Manor in Wiltshire were being rescued and restored by the *Country Life* set, but the people that wanted new houses seemed to be keen on Georgian things. These Georgian tastes in architecture and that poetry so popular at the time seem to collide in the unhappy union of Gerald and Dorothy Wellesley, architect and poet respectively, and later Duke and Duchess of Wellington. In 1925 they bought an exquisite Georgian house, Penns in the Rocks at Groombridge in East Sussex, and effectively started the craze. Gerald Wellesley and his partner Trenwith Wills were well mannered classicists only too capable of restoring old Georgian or building new Georgian houses as their clients required. As John Martin Robinson so nicely puts it at the beginning of *The Latest Country Houses* – 'In the 20s, it was thought that an enthusiasm for Georgian things was just one of the many passing fads, it was not foreseen that it would become permanent'.[6] Good manners tipped over into neo-Georgianism in the work of a succession of architects direct from Wellesley and Wills, through Phillimore and Jenkins, to Raymond Erith and Quinlan Terry and so to the present-day. The Collection has many of the drawings of Claud Phillimore (b.1911) and Aubrey Jenkins (b.1911) but nothing of great garden interest. The drawings of Raymond Erith (1904–73) are still mainly in private ownership, but Lucy Archer's thorough study of her fathers work tells of only two significant garden achievements, a splendid terrace, balustraded stair and fountain for Culham Court near Henley (1956) and a garden for The Pediment, Aynho, Northamptonshire made with his client, Miss Watt, as a very special commission over twenty years and up until his death.[7] Quinlan Terry's work, (he joined Erith in 1962 aged twenty-five and became a partner seven years later) has included notable garden buildings for West Green

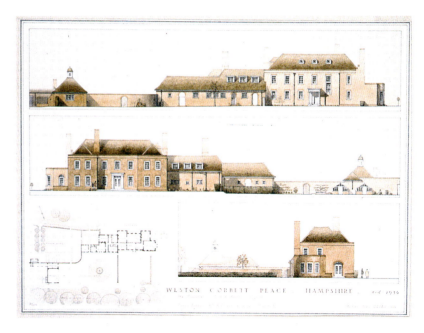

Fig. 30] Weston Corbett Place, near Basingstoke, Hampshire, by Darcy Braddell and Humphrey Deane, 1936, epitomizes the cooly classical approach to gardens of successful architects between the wars.

Manor, Hartley Wintney, West Wycombe Park, Little Roydon in Kent and Michael Heseltine's Orangery at Thenford in Northamptonshire. He has not designed, at least to date, gardens *per se*; he has tended to add his work to fine gardens that already existed.[8]

So, in this vigorous neo-Georgian architectural style that has lasted from the 1930s to the present-day, where are the gardens? The answer is a sobering thought, and requires a fairly complex explanation. Firstly, to go back to the twenties and take a look at gardening from a design-conscious perspective outside of the architectural world. *The Studio* magazine offered a wide coverage of the arts and an annual special volume devoted to gardens. The 1926–7 Special Winter Number *Modern Gardens British and Foreign* with a text by Percy Cane, featured the work of mainly architects, who have already been mentioned here, M.H.Baillie Scott, Edmund Wratten and Walter Godfrey, E.Guy Dawber[9] and Oliver Hill, as well as several by Cane himself, who was very successful. As the thirties progressed the names of the designers of the 'best' gardens change; they are no longer architects, but landscape architects, (Brenda Colvin, Milner White & Partners, George Dillistone), landscape contracting firms, (Vernon Brothers, George Whitelegg and Thomas

Mawson's Lakeland Nurseries), and freelance designers, one delightfully named Harley Merry FRHS.[10] *The Studio* garden numbers, always lavish productions, ceased in 1940; they were revived after the War, in a reduced format, edited by Frank Mercer and Roy Hay, and totally devoted to labour-saving ideas and plants. As the subject of garden design disappeared from *The Studio* garden volumes, so it would be true to say that it had a low priority in general amongst gardeners after the War. Theirs was a massive struggle to rescue gardens from wartime neglect and carry them on in the face of rising costs; labour-saving ideas and low maintenance planting were the only aims, producing a design *malaise* that lasted until the early 1960s. There was, quite simply, no longer any money for high professional fees; the reverse was that no architect or landscape architect could contemplate trying to earn a living from gardens, and the subject fell out of these professional milieux almost altogether. It fell into the hands of garden consultants who had a variety of qualifications, usually horticultural, and to the landscape contracting firms.

When English gardens did revive in the sixties, they did so under these varying influences. And the revival was to be predominantly neo-Georgian in every way, so the architects, despite their lack of physical involvement in design, can still have the satisfaction of being the trend-setters. For three house designs by Claud Phillimore and Aubrey Jenkins, the Dower House, Arundel and Buckhurst Park and Ribblesdale Park near Ascot, the gardens were done by Lanning Roper. This eminent garden consultant, who had both exquisite design taste and a thorough knowledge of plants, began working in the early sixties, building up contacts through William Woods of Taplow, who were the finest landscape contractors of the day, and personal connections. He provided exactly the kind of serene, flower-filled and livable settings for neo-Georgian and real eighteenth-century houses, and though he was capable of a great range of work, most of his commissions were for these kind of houses and gardens.[11] Lanning Roper did at least one garden for a Raymond Erith house, Wellingham at Ringmer in Sussex, and several for John Griffin of Newbury; he also linked gardens with an influential name from the world of interior design, John Fowler, who was instrumental in forming the post-war Georgian taste with his restorations of National Trust houses and revivals of delicious designs for chintzes and wallpapers. John Fowler was also a very talented gardener, and introduced – or reminded us of – the

delights of pleached hornbeams, Versailles tubs and trellis pavilions by using them in his own garden at the Hunting Lodge in Hampshire (now owned by the National Trust).

These newly classical gardens have an eclecticism that can be brave and charming but so easily borders on confusion. John Fowler's sources were French; there is also a taste for sundials, obelisks, and ball finials and topiaried box and barrelled yew which has come from seventeenth-century gardens via the Cotswolds and houses like Stanway and Snowshill Manor. Two other gardens, Ralph Dutton's Hinton Ampner in Hampshire and the Cokes' Jenkyn Place just over the Surrey border at Bentley, where Trenwith Wills advised, illustrate the English gentleman's preference for cool Palladianism in garden buildings and orderly atmosphere. This has usually been inspired by a meeting of minds between the architect and owner which becomes a very personal expression in the individual garden and no longer a simple matter of attribution to an architect. So many of the beautiful gardens of the present-day are the result of the devotion over the last twenty years or so, of distinguished and cultured amateurs, quite capable of exerting good English compromise and melding distant sources into personal harmony; many, like David Verey at Barnsley House in Gloucestershire, were scholars capable of designing their own Palladian garden temple. In this richness of talent, attribution becomes blurred, and though it should never be overlooked, (a failing of gardeners) allowances must be made for its complex nature and the passage of time. Percy Cane's[12] design at the Barnes' Hungerdown House in Wiltshire and Russell Page's[13] at The Dower House, Badminton, in Gloucestershire both contributed greatly to these lovely gardens. Over all the influences already mentioned a 'Lutyensesque' aura has been laid within the last ten years and his rediscovered talents have been celebrated; his use of Chinese Chippendale patterns has encouraged this revival in seats, fences and bridges, his all-too-ubiquitous wave-backed garden seat (for which there is no formal design drawing) implies his blessing on too many of the wrong kind of gardens, but mostly his influence has been purely beneficial, in that it comes hand in hand with that of his great partner, Gertrude Jekyll. Her influence is denied in vain by any present-day gardener; it has been inescapable, and in the example and writings of Rosemary Verey at Barnsley House, Christopher Lloyd at Great Dixter and Penelope Hobhouse at Tintinhull,[14] it has become, as Edwin Lutyens believed, the true adornment of present-day gardens.

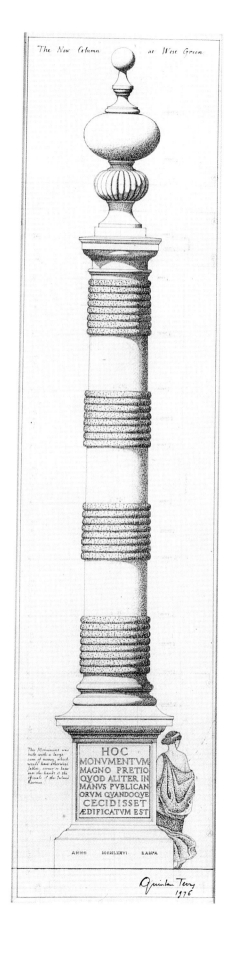

The New Column at West Green

This Monument was built with a large sum of money, which would have otherwise fallen, sooner or later, into the hands of the officials of the Inland Revenue

HOC
MONVMENTVM
MAGNO PRETIO
QVOD ALITER IN
MANVS PVBLICAN
ORVM QVANDOQVE
CECIDISSET
ÆDIFICATVM EST

ANNO   MCHLXXVI   LAMDA

Quinlan Terry
1976

And this would certainly not have happened if the architects had been left in charge.

This chapter is called 'Continuing Classicism' because it is an unfinished story. I do not know whether architects will go back to designing gardens, but on the basis of the latest examples, I hope not. Classicism in an architect's hand may produce a well-mannered competence but there is also a coolness, a dullness even, that lies heavy on the true nature of a garden's delight. I suspect that this is inherent in the professionalism that architects have adopted, and though the tenets of Palladio and even Lutyens may stand up to technology-aided and structured design processes, the sensual and psychological processes of designing a good garden will not.

All is not lost, for a much wider world has learned the basis of garden design; the necessary preliminaries of harmony with the setting, the balancing of masses and voids and of static and moving spaces, adherence to a proper scale and the provision of pattern and flowers are all now well taught in books and design courses. The lessons implied by the Jellicoe and Shepherd drawings of the Italian villa gardens have been learned. But what of the surprises, wonders, 'frivolity of Temperament' and the serenity and delight that those gardens gave their owners and to everyone who has seen them down the years? Have we become such a solemn society that no one can make us laugh in a garden any more? I fear we do take gardening too seriously and need another court jester in the Osbert Lancaster mould. The one architect who did work in gardens, loved his own garden and had the right personality to cast a certain wizardry and delight over everything he did was Clough Williams-Ellis (1883–1978) whose drawings appear here, nos 182–4. Clough, as he was universally known, practised architecture for an incredible seventy-five years; he began as an Arts and Crafts man and had time to see all he believed in slip into disrepute and rise again. He settled into the fashionable classicism, but he was always very much his own man, the indefatigable and fiercely patriotic Welshman, willing to fight environmental battles in America or build a house in Shanghai. His love of gardens was expressed at

Fig. 31] West Green Manor, Hartley Wintney, Hampshire, by Quinlan Terry, 1976 for Lord McAlpine, indicates the welcome return of wit into the garden; the inscription here suggests that the monument was built with money that would otherwise have fallen into the hands of the Inland Revenue.

his own house, Plas Brondanw, and most famously in his fantasy Italian village in a garden, Portmeirion. His drawings for Nantclwd Hall and his further designs for fountains, a seat and gates, which have been chosen from the large collection of his drawings, are the best evidence of his sure eye, and his wit and humour. He was just the kind of architect a garden needs. But, all is not lost; with the right client meeting the right architect, England can still manage an almost Renaissance frivolity. I have often heard Lord McAlpine's garden at West Green Manor, Hartley Wintney (which is the property of the National Trust) called 'the best post-war garden in England'. It is certainly my favourite, for the tingling atmosphere of its *potager*, the mix of smells and shapes and the scent of impermanence, as if the whole garden might blow away and not be there next year, which is uncannily magic. West Green is a mixture of fairly neat formality in parterres, wilderness and witty buildings, the last designed by Quinlan Terry in an on-going partnership with Lord McAlpine since 1973.[15] More ideas 'have been thown up into the air' writes Clive Aslet in his book on Quinlan Terry's work, than it has been practical or possible to build. These include a triumphal arch for the first lady Prime Minister, a Chinese orangery and a pagoda boathouse. On the ground in the garden at West Green there are cleverly elliptical urns, of which Clive Aslet's description is irresistible: 'They illustrate the seriousness of garden architecture. The urns are oval and gadrooned (bulging in shape), and also fluted in spirals. To keep the flutes parallel around the ellipsoid was a deep mathematical puzzle. The design took Terry a whole month to detail and the mason three months to make'.[16] There is also a Nymphaeum or 'Prospettiva' of dazzling trompe-l'oeil (fig. 28) which masks the cowshed, and the most provocative folly (fig. no. 31), a tall column, next to the road, inscribed in Latin but telling the passer-by: 'This monument was built with a large sum of money, which would otherwise have, sooner or later, fallen into the hands of the tax-gatherers'.[17] Such a timeless sentiment, that would perhaps even make a Medici or the 'Crab' Cardinal Gambara of Lante smile, brings modern classical gardens back to an almost Renaissance relevance. It is, after all, merely a matter of knowing the difference between being serious, and taking things too seriously, for gardens cannot live under the latter regime.

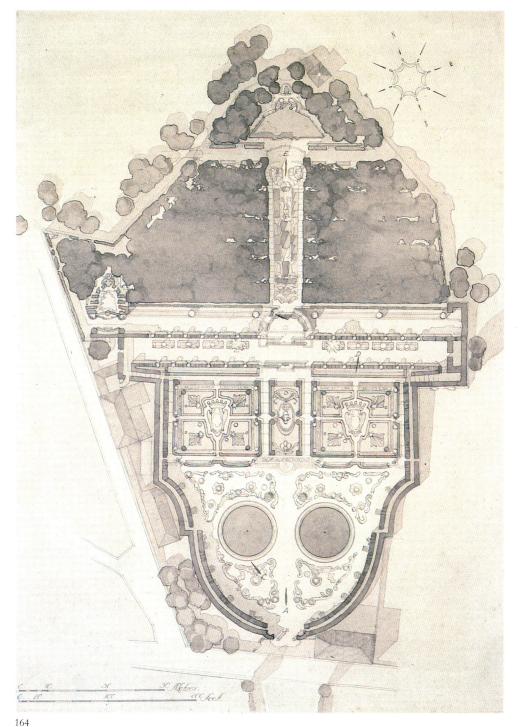

164

VILLA GARZONI, COLLODI

164] JOHN CHIENE SHEPHERD b. 1896 and
GEOFFREY ALAN JELLICOE b. 1900

A plan

Villa Garzoni, Collodi for
'Italian Gardens of the Renaissance' 1925
Pencil, pen and sepia wash
640 × 492 mm. /24¼ × 19⅜ in.

There is an element of isolation about this great garden which is actually cut off from its villa by a public road, seen on the west side of this plan. Geoffrey Jellicoe describes the garden as follows: 'The lower parterre is furnished with twin circular pools and family heraldry in box and is outlined into curve and counter-curve with double scalloped hedges. From this level, three promenade terraces rise spectacularly against a background of trees, the uppermost terminating in a charming garden theatre. Axially, in the centre, steps and stairways ascend to a great cascade that parts the woods and disappears against a statue of Fame deep in the *bosco* at the summit . . . Technically the gardens . . . are a box of baroque optical tricks: the cascade, for instance, widens as it ascends, making it look more abrupt when seen from below and longer when seen from above'.[18]

165] JOHN CHIENE SHEPHERD b. 1896 and
GEOFFREY ALAN JELLICOE b. 1900

A bird's-eye perspective

Villa Garzoni, Collodi for
'Italian Gardens of the Renaissance', 1925
Pen
352×642 mm. $/13\frac{7}{8} \times 25\frac{1}{4}$ in.

I remember being told by Sir Geoffrey Jellicoe that both he
and 'Jock' Shepherd toiled over the measuring and noting of
the gardens as a joint exercise, but the watercolours were
really Shepherd's work and the bird's-eye sketches were his
own. Having established that point, the works will still be
attributed in tandem. However, this pen bird's-eye view of
Villa Garzoni and its garden will have a familiar look to those
who know Sir Geoffrey's subsequent work. Its particular
purpose was to reveal the importance of the hilly Italian
landscape in the creation of these gardens. This sketch shows
how the Villa, built from 1652 onwards, was angled towards
the view of its garden parterre.

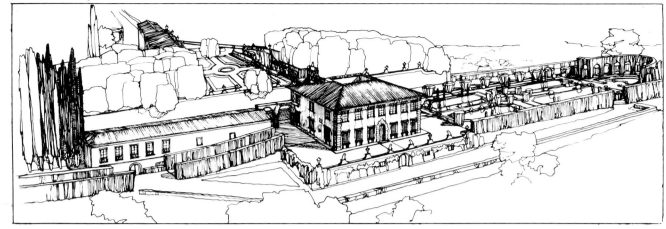

166

VILLA GAMBERAIA, SETTIGNANO

166] JOHN CHIENE SHEPHERD b. 1896 and
GEOFFREY ALAN JELLICOE b. 1900

A bird's-eye perspective

Villa Gamberaia, Settignano, Tuscany for
'Italian Gardens of the Renaissance', 1925
Pen
211×620 mm. /$8\frac{1}{4} \times 24\frac{3}{8}$ in.

This, for Geoffrey Jellicoe, is the ultimate *giardino segreto*, in that nothing is known about the designer of this wonderful garden or how it came to be made. Villa Gamberaia, and the making of this drawing at the outset of his career, has been a constant inspiration in his work, and he makes several references to it in his writings. The most obvious garden influence was in his design for the parterre with a semi-circular water-curtain at the far end, on the south front, at Ditchley Park in Oxfordshire for Ronald and Nancy Tree, immediately before the Second World War.

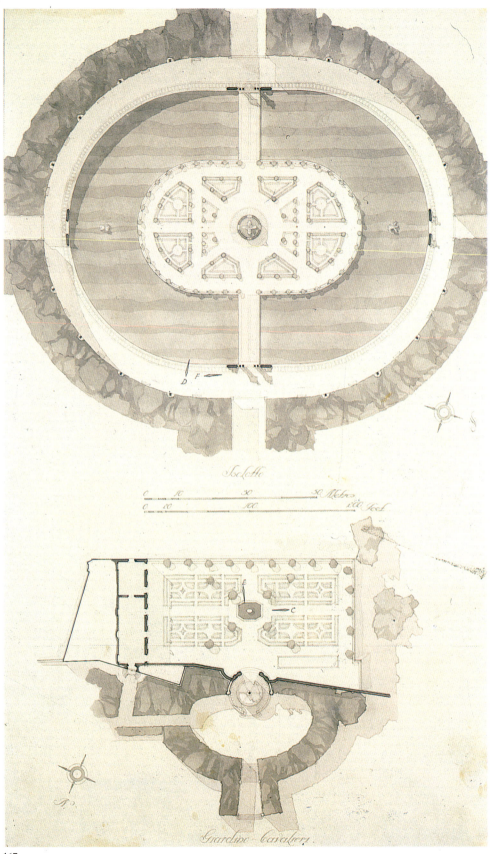

BOBOLI GARDENS, FLORENCE

167] JOHN CHIENE SHEPHERD b. 1896 and
GEOFFREY ALAN JELLICOE b. 1900

Plans of the 'Isolotto' and the 'giardino segreto'

Boboli Gardens, Florence, for
'Italian Gardens of the Renaissance', 1925
Pencil, pen and sepia wash
421 × 654 mm. /16$\frac{5}{8}$ × 25$\frac{3}{4}$ in.

J.C. 'Jock' Shepherd and Geoffrey Jellicoe went to Italy on a scholarship in the summer of 1925 for an intensive study trip to measure and sketch the great villa gardens. Their work was printed mostly in black-and-white, but some of the original drawings in the Collection have been re-photographed in colour for illustration here to reveal their subtle shading and beauty. These drawings had a profound effect on both Shepherd and Jellicoe, and on almost every young designer of the 1920s and 30s who was interested in gardens. For the first time the fascination of these gardens, to some extent the secret of their longevity and greatness, was dissected, analyzed and enumerated. These were not merely romantic or artistic visions, nor even the wise wordy descriptions of such perceptive viewers as Edith Wharton or Sir George Sitwell, these were the hard factual evidence of the creation of beautiful spaces.

This first drawing of the Boboli is in two parts. The top plan, marked *Isolotto* is the the Piazzella dell'Isolotto, the ocean fountain in its garden setting surrounded by water. The setting for the fountain was designed by Alfonso Parigi in 1618 and was supposedly based on the Maritime Theatre at Hadrian's Villa at Tivoli.

The lower plan is of the *giardino segreto* at Boboli, the Giardino del Cavaliere which was made for Cosimo III in the seventeenth century.

168] JOHN CHIENE SHEPHERD b. 1896 and
GEOFFREY ALAN JELLICOE b. 1900

Plan and section of the Pitti Palace

Boboli Gardens, Florence, for
'Italian Gardens of the Renaissance', 1925
Pencil, pen and sepia wash
439 × 620 mm. / $17\frac{1}{4}$ × $24\frac{3}{8}$ in.

This is the plan and section of the Pitti Palace and the
amphitheatre – the central section of the Boboli gardens. The
central axis from the *cortile* of the Palace and extending up the
hill was set out in 1549 by Nicolo Tribolo for Cosimo I

de'Medici. The amphitheatre was made in 1637 for an
Equestrian Ballet to celebrate the marriage of the Princess of
Urbino and Ferdinando de'Medici II.

The chief premise of *Italian Gardens of the Renaissance* was
that the chosen villas and their gardens represented the
highest achievement of humanism in artistic terms, especially
in the way in which the landscape of Italy was sensitively used
to express man's noblest intentions. Geoffrey Jellicoe felt that
these gardens somehow represented man reaching close to
the realms of God; the technical achievement, the symbolism
and allegorical connections inspired by these gardens were to
be the constant thread in his long career.

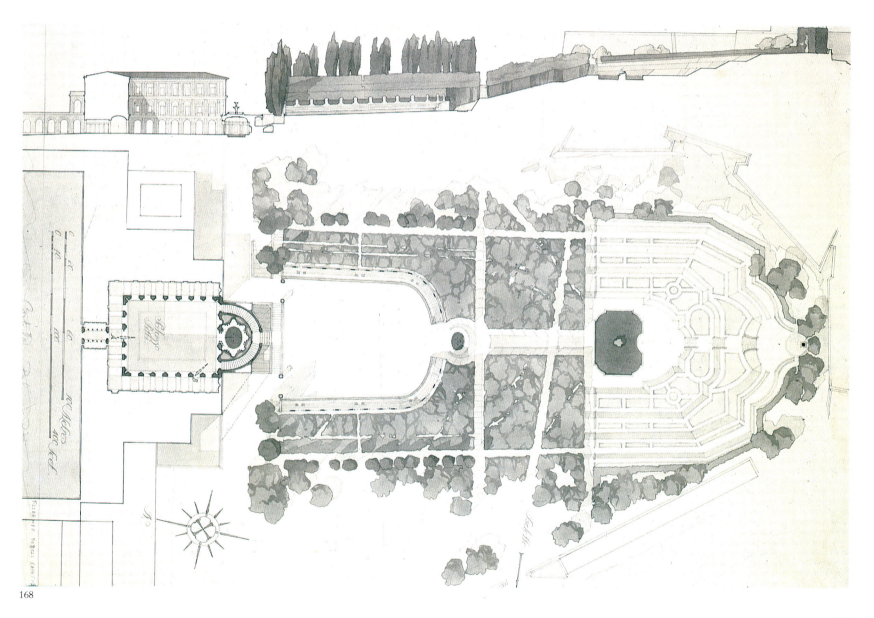

168

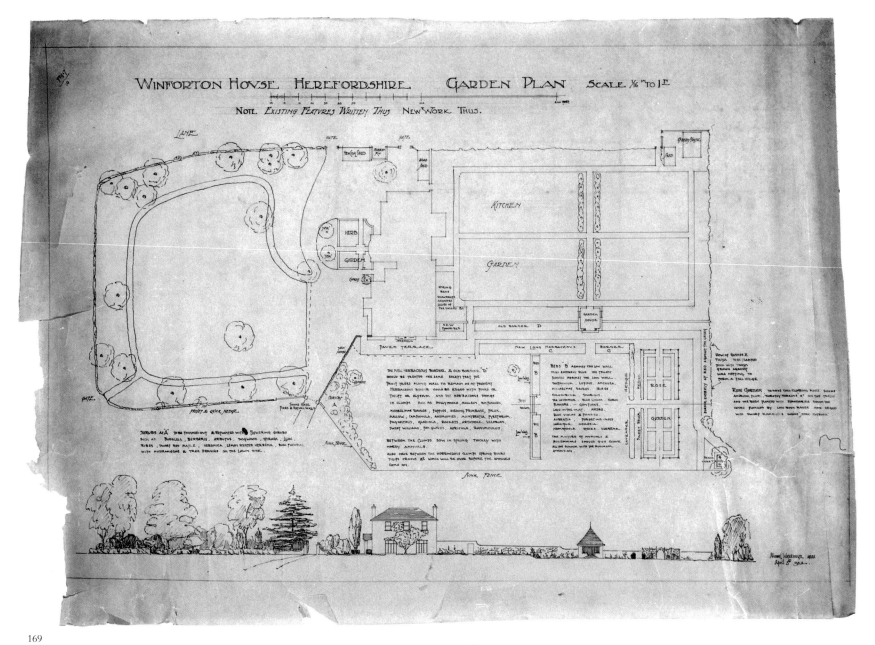

169

WINFORTON HOUSE, HEREFORD

169] MICHAEL WATERHOUSE 1888–1968

Designs for a garden

Winforton House, Hereford, 1922
Pen on tracing paper
700×980 mm. $/27\frac{5}{8} \times 38\frac{5}{8}$ in.

The Collection holds fifty-eight drawings detailing the remodelling of an existing house and garden for T.R.Merton by Michael Waterhouse, the grandson of the Victorian architect, Alfred Waterhouse. The garden drawings reproduced here are a good example of conventional design for a medium sized garden of the 1920s.

The garden plan, $\frac{1}{16}$th″ to 1′ scale, shows the house in the centre of a roughly rectangular plot. The existing 'front' garden is grass with mature trees and shrubs surrounded by a privet and thorn hedge. The new feature on this side of the house is a herb garden, (see no. 170). Much of the 'back' garden is occupied by a kitchen garden in four plots. The new work proposed is to build a garden house, a new paved terrace, new long borders and a formal rose garden. The architect has, unusually, given concise and clear planting instructions on the plan.

170] MICHAEL WATERHOUSE 1888–1968

A herb garden

Winforton House, Hereford, 1923
Pen on tracing paper
550 × 775 mm. / $21\frac{5}{8} \times 30\frac{1}{2}$ in.

A simple and instructive layout plan for a small paved herb garden outside the new dining room of Winforton House. The architect gives no planting details for this garden so it may have been already planted by the client. Small, formal herb gardens were revived by the Arts and Crafts Movement as decorative as well as tasteful features; during the nineteenth century herbs had been relegated to the corners of kitchen gardens and only prominent in cottagers' plots. William Robinson allowed rosemary as deserving a place in gardens but thought little of rue or thymes: Miss Jekyll used many scented plants and designed some herb gardens, but the greatest revivalist was Eleanor Sinclair Rohde, whose books and articles on old English herbals and herb gardens were first appearing at this time.

171] MICHAEL WATERHOUSE 1888–1968

A garden seat

The herb garden, Winforton House,
Hereford, 1923
Pencil and wash
435 × 540 mm. / $17\frac{1}{8} \times 21\frac{1}{4}$ in.

A neat, small seat with solid wooden ends to fit at the end of the paved terrace walk in the herb garden (no. 170). Both the smallness, four-feet wide, and the position of the seat indicate that in the modern life of the twenties, a perch near the house for taking a cup of coffee or glass of sherry offered a break in the housewife's day.

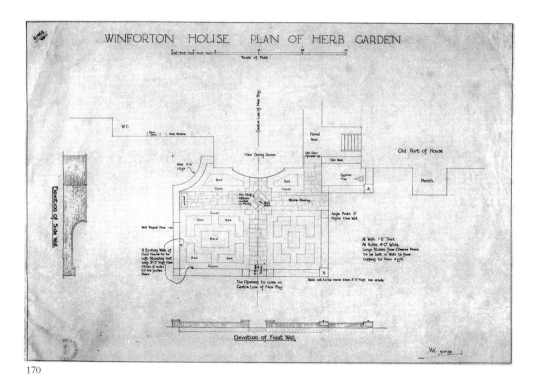

170

171

VILLA MEDICI, FIESOLE

172] JOHN CHIENE SHEPHERD b.1896 and
GEOFFREY ALAN JELLICOE b.1900

Section through the garden

Villa Medici, Fiesole for
'Italian Gardens of the Renaissance', 1925
Pencil, pen and sepia wash
304 × 445 mm. /12 × 17½ in.

It was Geoffrey Jellicoe who wrote the text for *Italian Gardens of the Renaissance* and he praised the Villa Medici for its wonderful situation, set into the hillside in such a way that the two major terraces had a clear view of a panoramic countryside. It is a comparatively modest villa, designed *c.*1460 by Michelozzo Michelozzi for Cosimo the Elder's son Giovanni. The upper terrace garden, on the same level as the villa, is used as an outdoor salon; the garden terrace below is reached by a steep stair, and may have been originally intended for fruits and vegetables. In 1925 when Shepherd and Jellicoe visited Villa Medici it was the home of Lady Sybil Scott and the architectural historian, author of *The Architecture of Humanism*, Geoffrey Scott; He and Cecil Pinsent had recently restored the garden.

172

VILLA D'ESTE, TIVOLI

173] JOHN CHIENE SHEPHERD b 1896 and
GEOFFREY ALAN JELLICOE b. 1900

Plan of the garden

Villa d'Este, Tivoli for
'Italian Gardens of the Renaissance', 1925
Pencil, pen and sepia wash
655 × 481 mm. /25¾ × 19 in.

Cardinal Ippolito II d'Este made his great garden between 1560–75, reputedly in times of frustration and boredom with ecclesiastical politics. This elevation shows how the villa is sited at the top of a flight of terraces, so accurately but sensitively shaped that they might have been created by divine hand rather than that of a mere Cardinal. The plan of the gardens reveals the logical geometry that is the basis of pleasure in a garden full of constant surprises and delights. At Villa d'Este there are water delights, the Pathway of One Hundred Fountains, the Bollori staircase, the Fountain of the Owl which once made the sounds of birdsong, the Fountain of the Organ which once made music, and pools, grottoes, statuary, groves and mazes, all combined into a playground for the child in every man and woman.

173

DALHAM HALL, SUFFOLK

174] HARRY STUART GOODHART-RENDEL
1887 – 1959

A rose garden

Dalham Hall, Suffolk, 1929
Pen on tracing paper
410 × 470 mm. /16⅛ × 18½ in.

As with some of Charles Mallows' drawings this plan shows how too much detail and accuracy can effectively destroy the delight of a living garden. Paviours drawn relentlessly are desolate, and the 'dotted' indication of grass poses some very real problems in mowing and maintenance.

185] HARRY STUART GOODHART-RENDEL
1887 – 1959

A pavilion for the rose garden

Dalham Hall, Suffolk, 1929
Pen on tracing paper
640 × 755 mm. /25¼ × 29¾ in.

A long loggia of classical inspiration to face into the rose garden. It was to be built of brick against an old wall, with stone footings and two stone Doric columns supporting a stone frieze and arch. The two low, outside seats at each end are a nice touch. These two drawings, the rose garden plan and the pavilion, are the only ones for Dalham and there is no evidence as to whether the work was ever carried out.

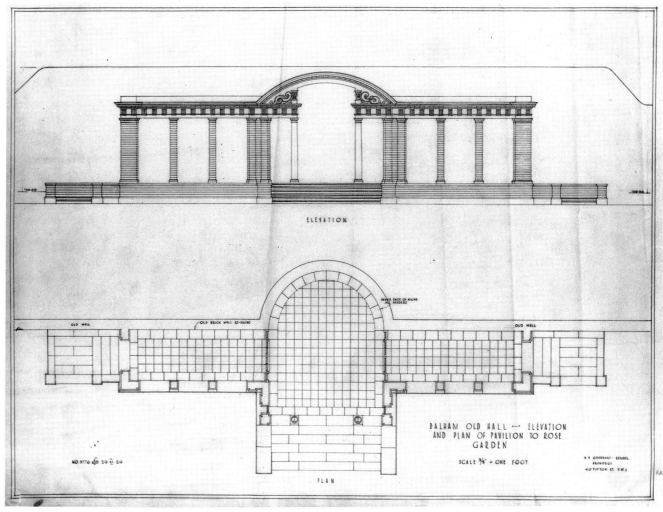

ELEVATION

DALHAM OLD HALL — ELEVATION
AND PLAN OF PAVILION TO ROSE
GARDEN

SCALE ⅜" = ONE FOOT

PLAN

175

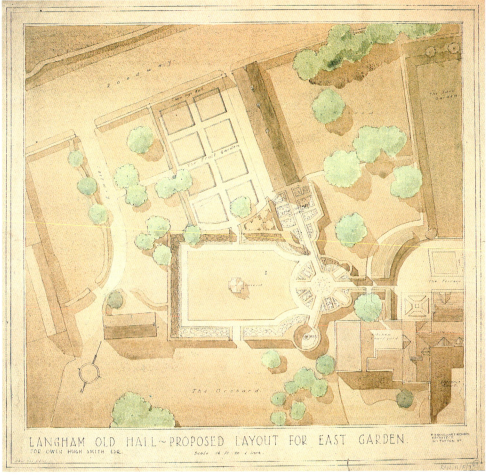

LANGHAM OLD HALL ~ PROPOSED LAYOUT FOR EAST GARDEN.
FOR OWEN HUGH SMITH ESQ.   Scale 16 ft to 1 inch.

176

LANGHAM OLD HALL, RUTLAND

176] HARRY STUART GOODHART-RENDEL
1887 – 1959

Proposed layout for the East Garden

Langham Old Hall, Rutland, 1927–8
Print with coloured washes
515×540 mm. $/20\frac{1}{4} \times 21\frac{1}{4}$ in.

Goodhart-Rendel was a prominent architectural scholar, writer and public figure, President of the RIBA immediately before the Second World War and owner of Hatchlands in Clandon, Surrey (now owned by the National Trust), where Gertrude Jekyll had designed a formal garden for his grandfather, Lord Rendel. His garden plans are scholarly and soundly architectural. In this plan he has fitted symmetry and

balance into an awkward site with great skill, using the rounded flower parterre (seemingly inspired by a nineteenth-century rosary garden), to link a number of diverse elements – the well, the dovecote lawn enclosure, the orchard, fruit garden and meadow, and sunken gardens—to the house and its terrace. The shadowed perspective presents a garden one would love to wander in; the presence of a 'meadow' at the end of the 1920s is interesting and it would have been for spring flowers in grass, with the grass cut late to allow seeding, just as we imagine the invention of 'ecological' gardening of the 1980s.

177] HARRY STUART GOODHART-RENDEL
1887 – 1959

A plan of the terrace and sunken garden

Langham Old Hall, Rutland, 1927
Pen on tracing paper
600×895 mm. $/23\frac{5}{8} \times 35\frac{1}{4}$ in.

Goodhart-Rendel was interested in nineteenth-century architecture, and this plan indicates a veering back to a highly stylized garden plan after the straightforward geometry of the Arts and Crafts Movement. In this and the shaded perspective he is clearly dealing with an awkwardly shaped site, into which a formal garden has to be fitted. It was in answer to the pressures imposed by small sites and less garden labour that a modern, contorted formalism had to grow, unless owner and designer were prepared to give way to informal treatments, of which there is an interesting hint in the screen planting along the road boundary on the west. But it is a clever answer, with an angled, flowerless parterre terrace enclosed by yew hedges and leading to a sunken level lawn for croquet, and a summerhouse built into the garden wall which offers views back over the whole garden.

178] HARRY STUART GOODHART-RENDEL
1887 – 1959

A balustrade to the terrace

Langham Old Hall, Rutland, 1928
Pen on tracing paper
510×905 mm. $/20\frac{1}{8} \times 35\frac{5}{8}$ in.

Sections, elevations and plans detailing the balustrade and walling in a classically-inspired design for the house terrace as shown on the previous plan. The open balustrade divided the terrace from the flower parterre; the solid walls were used at the end where the grass bank occurred.

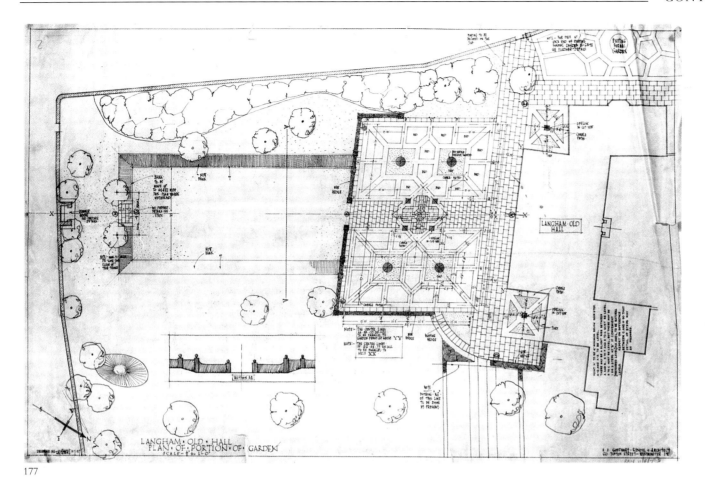

177

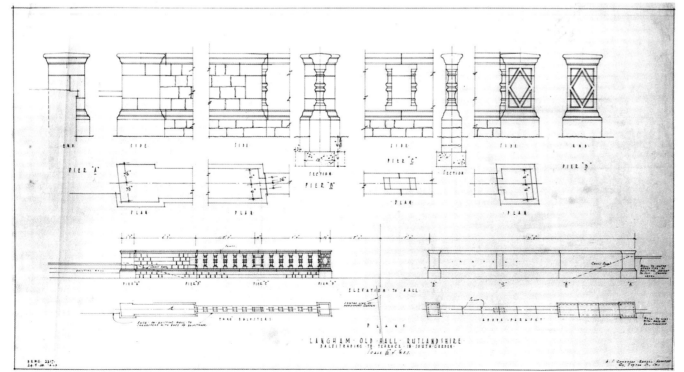

178

ROEHAMPTON, LONDON

179] HARRY STUART GOODHART-RENDEL
1887–1959

A proposed garden

Roehampton Court, London, 1923
Print on linen
460 × 370 mm. /18⅛ × 14½ in.

The idiom of twenties-living is captured in this plan for a garden in the smartest of London surburbs. Roehampton Court introduces the 'jigsaw puzzle' style of garden design, with a sophisticated solution to fitting the ever increasing demands of modern life into an ever smaller space. The

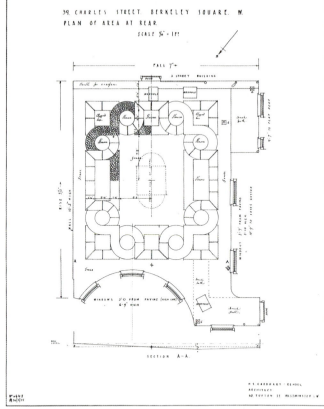

180

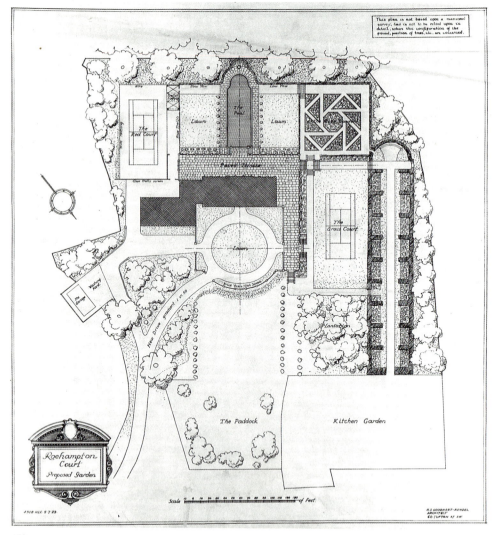

179

advent of the motorcar dictated the gentle curve of the drive, the turning circle and the retreat for the chauffeur and his vehicle to the service yard and garage area. Many Edwardian designers allowed for the convenience of both horses and motors but this is the beginning of the age of the car as the only necessary form of transport.

The family at Roehampton Court required a large terrace for parties, a swimming pool and lawns to lounge on; a grass court was still preferred for tennis, but the new hard court was a must for keen players. The children would have been deprived without a pony, so there had to be a paddock, as far from the house as possible and where the pony would not object to the increasing roar from the road. Neither would the gardeners in the kitchen garden. The only interesting areas for flowers are the long walk, with yew buttresses dividing them into fashionable single-colour bays, and the rose garden, a room for the new hybrid tea varieties which bloom from June till Christmas and are good for cutting, but are leggy plants, ugly and best grown on their own, so only worth visiting in their prime.

39 CHARLES STREET, LONDON

180] HARRY STUART GOODHART-RENDEL
1887 – 1959

A garden

39 Charles Street, Berkeley Square, London W1, 1925
Pen on tracing
460 × 370 mm. /18⅛ × 14⅝ in.

A balanced plan for a confined, deeply shaded and very dry London garden area which provides an interesting pattern to be viewed from windows above. The materials are to be paving with cobbles set to emphasize the pattern of circles turning into squares, and making small beds for summer flowers. This design compares interestingly with Oliver Hill's design for Devonshire Lodge of 1914 (no. 142). Even for gardens in the smartest parts of London, a sober and functional feel replaced Edwardian flamboyance immediately after the War.

IDEAL HOUSE

181] D. H. McMORRAN 1904–65

An elevation and garden plan

Daily Mail Ideal Home and Garden, 1927
Pen and pencil
Detail from sheet:
510 × 685 mm. /20⅛ × 27 in.

An elevation and garden plan from a sheet of designs chosen by the *Daily Mail* as the Ideal Home of 1927, and featured in the exhibition of that year. The garden seems sadly unimaginative; a bland front plot, a 'sun trap' at the side of the house for secluded sunbathing, and the main garden devoted to tennis and some vegetables. There is also a garage and garage entrance, to fit an Austin 7. This makes an interesting comparison with Goodhart-Rendel's Roehampton Court (no. 179) – a contemporary house with a far more elaborate garden, but the desire for sun, outdoor activity and a motorcar are shared.

·VIEW·FROM·ROAD·

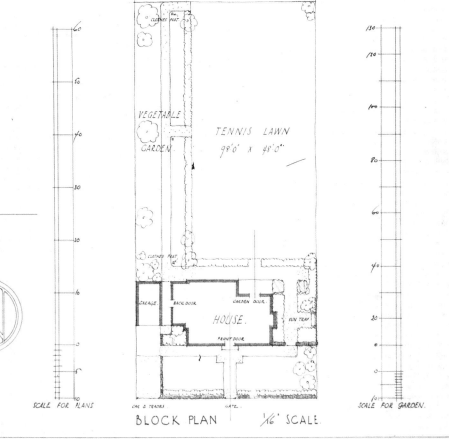

BLOCK PLAN 1/16' SCALE

181

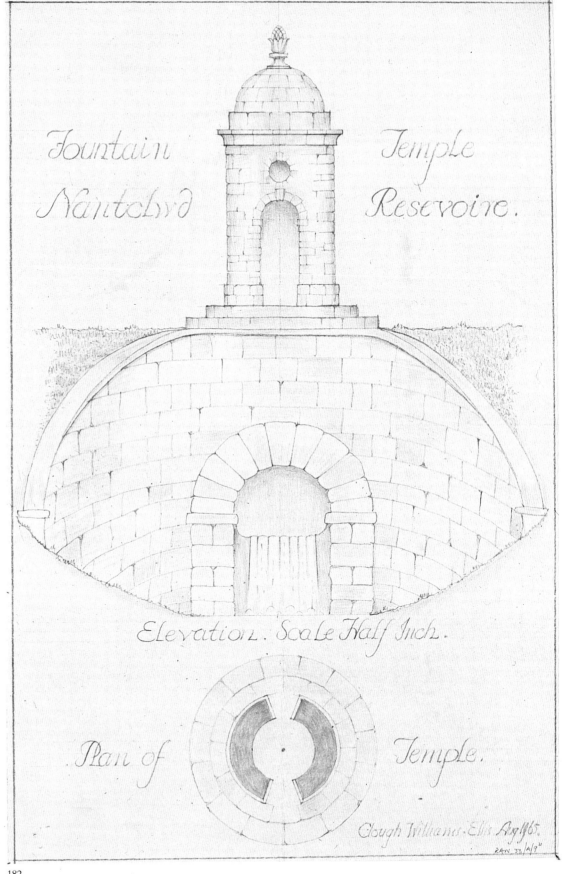

Fountain Temple

Nantclwd Resevoire.

Elevation. Scale Half Inch.

Plan of Temple.

Clough Williams-Ellis Aug 1965.

NANTCLWYD HALL, CLWYD

182] CLOUGH WILLIAMS-ELLIS 1883–1978

A fountain temple

Nantclwyd Hall, Clwyd, Wales, 1965
Pencil and crayon
510 × 330 mm. /20$\frac{1}{8}$ × 13 in.

Clough Williams-Ellis's stream of designs for Nantclwyd included features and ornaments for the park landscape. He built bridges to carry the new drive, erected a domed and pillared rotunda on a grassy knoll in purely eighteenth-century style, and added further theatrical touches with statues of strange animals. This partly functional, partly ornamental design was for the reservoir outfall, confined to a kind of grotto built of rough stone. The little temple with sophisticated detail and pineapple ornament, from which one views water in one direction and land in another, somehow mimics those impressive monuments of nineteenth-century water engineers, *English* engineers, that mark the dams of Bala, Vrynwy and the Elan valley. It must be remembered that Clough's long, lively, active and often controversial life and career spanned not only delightful buildings of Arts and Crafts and Italianate theatrical origins but also a passionate patriotism, which fought to protect the Welsh landscape from exploitation.

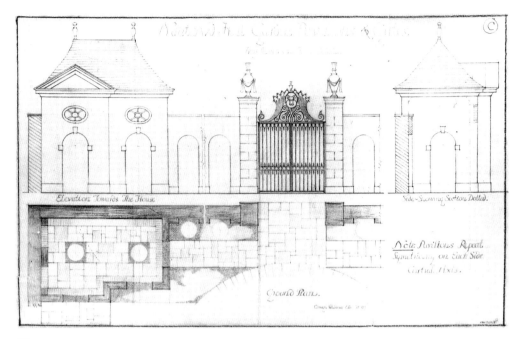

183

183] CLOUGH WILLIAMS-ELLIS 1883–1978

Garden pavilions and gates

Nantclwyd Hall, Clwyd, Wales, 1959
Pencil and crayon
465 × 740 mm. /18$\frac{1}{4}$ × 29$\frac{1}{8}$ in.

Nantclwyd was Clough Williams-Ellis's most important post-war commission. He re-modelled and re-orientated the house for Sir Vivyan Naylor-Leyland between 1956 and the early seventies. The original house faced north, and in making it face south he turned the former service yards into lawns and terraces, which were enclosed and decorated with these pavilions and gates, built in what John Martin Robinson describes as a 'cross between Cape Dutch and the sort of theatrical Italianate usually encountered only in sets for operas'.[29]

The pavilions and gates, built almost exactly as designed, face down a long lawn ornamented with blocks of clipped yew, antique vases and a small open gazebos. The paving, detailed on the drawing, using stone and inset cobbles, extends to link both gazebos to the wide terrace at the side of the house.

184] CLOUGH WILLIAMS-ELLIS 1883–1978

Fountain detail

Possibly for Nantclwyd Hall, Clwyd, Wales, *c.* 1960
Pencil and crayon
510 × 330 mm. /20$\frac{1}{8}$ × 13 in.

Clough Williams-Ellis designed endless alternative projects for Sir Vivyan Naylor-Leyland, whom he called his 'insatiable collaborator and client' during his years working at Nantclwyd Hall. 'Whenever my client visits the place', Clough recalled, 'there will always be a crop of new ideas'.[20] There were Palladian dog kennels, a duck fort (a castellated shooting platform), and many temples and follies; client and architect did not always agree and nowhere near all the designs were built, nor are all the drawings in the Collection. This fountain detail, not marked for Nantclwyd, just may be the contentious tall jet which John Martin Robinson says Sir Vivyan 'would never' agree to in his garden.[21]

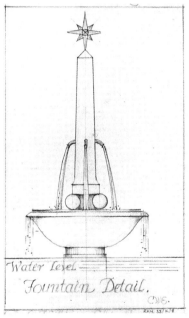

184

7

GARDEN BUILDINGS

The Drawings Collection has an abundance of garden buildings, simply because architects have always enjoyed designing them. They are a part of many of the gardens already illustrated in this book, and twenty-eight more are added here as examples in their own right. Besides the pleasure in building small buildings, architects have often used them for experimental purposes. In 1968 Alistair Rowan wrote an essay around some of the drawings for garden buildings in the Collection, and highlighted the impressive number of 'firsts' in architectural history that these seeming trifles can claim: the *first* accurate re-use of the Greek Doric Order is Athenian Stuart's Doric Temple for Hagley Park of 1758, the *first* pure neo-Palladian designs are the temples built at Lord Burlington's Chiswick House between 1717 and 1721; the *first* Gothic revival is the loggia for Shotover Park in Oxfordshire, and the *first* sham castles are at Castle Howard, Yorkshire. And, as he continues, the importance of these 'novelties' was just that they often led to important conclusions – 'The Hagley temple foreshadows the whole Greek, revival, . . . Lord Burlington's innovations dominated the architectural [and landscape garden] thought of two generations . . . and the full consequences of the ideals expressed at Shotover and in Castle Howard's castles can be reckoned only in terms of all High Victorian art.'[1]

So, these 'irresponsible little buildings'[2] must not be too easily discounted, especially nowadays. As with the Quinlan Terry buildings for West Green (see figs. 28 and 31) it is a matter of taking them seriously, but not being too serious about them. For they are essentially delightful, and none more so than the shingle-roofed summerhouse that Robert Smythson, or possibly his son John, found in Chelsea in the early seventeenth century (no. 185). It was most likely built of painted wood and would not have lasted for long; but the shape of its roof is echoed in some of the earliest garden pavilions or gazebos that we still have, those that adorn the courtyard at Montacute House in Somerset (see no. 95). Also, the same roofs have survived in the lodges of

Campden House at Chipping Campden; the house was destroyed in the Civil War and the small pavilions were rescued and restored as part of the Arts and Crafts revival of seventeenth-century taste by Frederick Landseer Griggs and the Campden Trust in the late 1920s.

The ephemeral nature of garden buildings – they were usually built for pleasure rather than posterity – means that few from the seventeenth century survive: the same must apply to the drawings for them, which were probably never highly valued. The exceptions as regards materials are where they were built in stone as part of the garden walls, as at Montacute, or in the Scottish gardens of Edzell and Barncluith, which are illustrated in the drawings by J.J.Joass nos 96–101. Again, it was the Arts and Crafts architects' enthusiasm for these old pavilions that caused them to be recorded for inspiration, and also for restoration, at the height of the influence of William Morris's Society for the Protection of Ancient Buildings. The sketches G.H.Kitchen made at Trentham and Lilleshall, and his drawing of Pope's Seat in Cirencester Park (no. 22) were the products of the same enthusiasm.

But that is to run on ahead through the centuries. The idea of introducing classical buildings into the garden came at the beginning of the eighteenth century from Lord Burlington's appreciation of the paintings of Claude and the Poussin brothers, and, as Alistair Rowan pointed out, he directed the whole Palladian revival from Chiswick House and his earliest garden buildings there. His pavilion by the lake is illustrated here (no. 192) and the remarkable story of the survival of the Kent and Burlington drawings, one of the sagas of the Collection, is sketched in my Introduction. Almost equally influential, and from the same period, are the three drawings by James 'Athenian' Stuart (1713–88), the archetypal Grand Tourist and aesthete, trained as a painter of fans, whose study of Grecian remains ensured him a successful career as a classical expert. His drawings are extremely rare, and the designs identified and acquired by John Harris for the Collection from a London dealer in 1977 are a great treasure.[3] Stuart puts us in touch with Kent and Rousham with his sketch of the arched building called a Praeneste; this Praeneste, his Ionic loggia and garden building with Aphrodite, all have this exquisite classical connection in its purist form, which is refreshing in the light of so many restorations and rebuildings.

The introduction of the classical temple brings a new use for a garden building, as a rendezvous or at least half-way point in a perambulation or barouche-ride around the garden or park. I have, rather casually, used what seem to be four interchangeable terms so far – garden house, gazebo, pavilion and temple. A garden house implies modesty; Pliny the Younger enjoyed his small vine-shaded house where he could lie on the couch and imagine himself in the wood. 'Garden house' is the most suitable term for the small garden buildings of the Arts and Crafts revival, with the right implications of convenience, modest comfort and momentary escape. A 'gazebo', a corruption of gaze-about, is – like the Smythson gazebo – an open building for looking out from, often raised on a second story – the Montacute buildings are truly gazebos. A 'pavilion' implies real escape – a miniature and often rather grand house – which allowed life to be lived for a while in freedom from the rules and rigours of the main establishment: it is an idea that spans the centuries – the Trianon for Hampton Court (no. 9) was just this kind of escape house, so was the Prince Regent's Royal Pavilion at Brighton, and so was Gertrude Jekyll's 'Hut', at Munstead Wood, which she used when she felt the need to economize.

Thus the pavilion implies a distance from the house, and so does the temple. The architectural innovation and perfection that Lord Burlington and 'Athenian' Stuart introduced with their temples were necessary to their role in transforming the natural landscape into something sublime. The temple, for its Olympian connotations, especially if it was to commemorate a friend (as was James Paine's design for Gopsall Park, no. 17) and for its use as a distant trysting-place (they were sometimes called 'Temple d'Amour') had to be worthy and worth visiting. I am reminded of Peter Hunt's awful warning: 'It might be unwise to suggest isolated temples to visit, involving a long drive and then a long walk in the park to find a small building which circumstances of temper, heat or bad lunch could easily render negligible.'[4]

But it would be impossible to dwell on the subject of garden buildings without recognition of the architect who despaired of such classical finesse and the dullness of the Brownian landscapes that provided settings for such temples. This jollifier of garden buildings was Sir William Chambers (1723–96) who travelled to India and China and worked in Italy before settling down in England in 1755. Between 1757 and 1763 he designed and built twenty-five buildings for Princess Augusta of Wales's garden at Kew; she was an imaginative and enthusiastic client and Chambers entertained Her Royal Highness with Chinese temples, an aviary, menagerie, a Roman triumphal arch in ruin, a Turkish mosque, the Alhambra (in Moorish style) as well as sufficient classical temples. Most mystical of all was the famous Chinese Pagoda, nine storeys above the ground, tapering slightly, adorned with eighty enamelled and gilded dragons and red lacquer balconies (no. 193). Only five of the twenty-five buildings survive but happily one is Chambers' Pagoda, sadly shorn of dragons and red lacquer, but at least presiding over a continuing tradition in the equally flamboyant presence of the new Princess of Wales Conservatory by Gordon Wilson (1987).

Garden houses, gazebos, pavilions, temples and pagodas are for people to look at, meet in or use as a refuge from a sudden squall (which surely has much to do with their popularity in English gardens), but architects have also loved to design buildings for plants. They have also had rather more competition in this sphere, from gardeners and horticulturalists who understood better the complex heating and humidifying systems that various plants required; the most famous greenhouse designer of all, Sir Joseph Paxton, began as the Duke of Devonshire's Head Gardener, and his first great triumph was the special house he built for the giant water-lily, *Victoria regia amazonica* – the structure inspired by the ribs of its leaves – which coaxed it into flower for the first time in England. That was in 1849, but Paxton was a long way along the road to the most splendid Victorian conservatories; the idea of the garden house which would protect and conserve greenery through the winter was first used about a century earlier. The word 'greenhouse' is attributed to John Evelyn, and he recorded the first one known at Ham House, sometime before 1677, built for the Duke and Duchess of Lauderdale. These early greenhouses or conservatories were light-weight structures; there was a faint aesthetic notion that houses for plants should be made of tree branches or thin trunks and with a comparatively small area of glass, which was made in small panes by blowing and spinning out. The purpose of the early greenhouses was purely to protect the precious imported

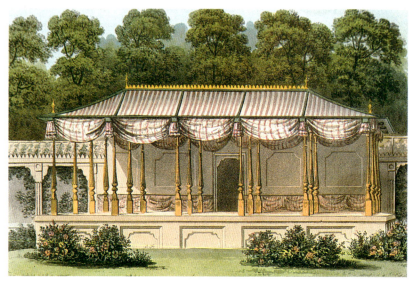

Fig. 32| *Humphry Repton's design for an* orangerie *for the Royal Pavilion, Brighton, 1805, in winter guise. The glass roof and window panes were all removable so that the orange trees could be brought out in the summer.*

Fig. 33| *Right: The* orangerie *in summer guise, with striped awnings transforming it into a* chiosk.

evergreens, oleanders, bays, myrtles, the variegated hollies and some treasured orange and lemon bushes, from winter frosts. So many of these houses and their cargoes must have been burnt to a cinder by the stoves and braziers which were used to heat them in mid-winter.

The sketch by William Newton (1735–90), no. 187, which probably dates from around 1760, is for a modest country gentleman's garden; Newton considers, as he crosses out and alters his page notes, the appropriate gaiety and lightness for a greenhouse, and suitably chooses bright colours, fire colours, or *all the Seven Colors of the Sun*. Newton is a little-known architect, but his efforts have immediacy and charm, and perhaps he illuminates what the more ordinary mid-eighteenth-century gardener was doing. His peers were, at the same time, feasting upon exotic fruits, pineapples, bananas, grapes and peaches which could be grown in heated glasshouses. Good quality iron for framed construction was easily available by the 1780s, and there was an increasingly scientific approach to the building of houses of very specialized kinds for the desired fruits, and the scented acacias and rhododendrons and colourful geraniums and

ericas which the plant hunters brought home. As these buildings became more specialized they acquired a galaxy of differing names – hothouses, stove houses, peacheries, vineries – and became increasingly ugly. They were banished to the walled garden or domestic purlieus of the house, and largely leave the realm of the architect. For very special show places, such as the Royal Botanic Garden at Kew, which became one of England's most subtly acquired national assets after the death of the gardening Princess Augusta of Wales in 1771, the architect was allowed a say, though it is interesting to note that Jeffry Wyatville's drawing for the Exotic House (no. 200) is chiefly devoted to the Perkins heating-system rather than design!

Some architects accepted the scientific take-over, some did not. The whole Wyatt dynasty left a trail of elegant conservatories and greenhouses over English gardens;[5] Robert Adam, on the other hand, gave up plant houses shortly after his exquisite classical greenhouses for Kedleston (1759 and never built) and Croome Court – garden temples of stone with pediments and porticoes, which made little concession to their green occupants.

But one special building, the orangery – essentially close to the house or part of the pleasure garden – retained a warm place in the architectural heart. Oranges, and lemons, the elegant bushes and trees with their jewel-like fruits and evocative scent, were prized by English gardeners from the middle of the sixteenth century. The word 'orangery', from the French *orangerie*, was actually adopted for the grove-like garden made by setting out the fruit trees in their tubs for the summer, as at Versailles and Chiswick House. In her book *Glass Houses*, May Woods searches for the first use of the word to describe a building, and comes up with Humphry Repton's *Design for an Orangerie* (figs 32–3) for the Royal Pavilion at Brighton in 1805. She illustrates his delicious invention – an iron-framed building on a stone platform, with large fixed and swivelling windows to shelter the orange trees in winter; in summer both windows and roof were to be removed from the now empty house, which was then decked with striped awnings and swags to transform it into what he calls a *chiosk*.[6] Perhaps because this royal orangery was not, sadly, built, the name for the building was not substantiated, for mid-nineteenth-century dictionaries still used it for the garden and not the building.

The naming of houses for plants is a game of endless diversions and contradictions; names were undoubtedly changed as new fashions took over and the plants that, at first seemed to need such special requirements, so often adjusted to the characteristic spirit of compromise in their adopted English homes. Fern houses became popular with the fern craze of the mid-nineteenth century, and there is a special aesthetic appeal in the contrasts between the giant exotic ferns and the arching lattice of a fine building, but with the revival of the taste for hardy ferns, grown in the home woods and by the waterside by William Robinson, the fernery went out of use too. The First World War brought an effective end to the vast gardening establishments that tended the orange trees, the vines and peach houses, and it is only in botanic gardens that the particular house for a particular species of plant has been perpetuated.

In England, in general the first fifty years of this century saw only the decline and dilapidation of all kinds of garden buildings, and so many of them have been lost. For the more ephemeral fashions there were never even design drawings; the craze for rusticity is represented by two rare drawings of extremes, the George Repton sketch that is apparently a cow byre (no. 197), and the last word in rustic retreats, the Duke of Bedford's log cottage on his estate at Endsleigh in Devon (no. 198). But, not many hermitages, grottoes or even aviaries seemed to attract the services of an architect.

Fortunately, garden buildings of all kinds have now come back into popular esteem. The fernery at Ashridge, designed by Matthew Digby Wyatt in 1864 (no. 203) has recently been restored. Within the last twenty years the buildings' conservation movement has taken good care of these small buildings of every kind, and many have been rescued and restored at the instigation of the Georgian Group, SAVE Britain's Heritage, the National Trust, English Heritage and the Landmark Trust. They well repay our care, for any wander around a park or garden observing the habits of fellow visitors will soon reveal how people enjoy discovering a small temple or old greenhouse. And if we are more likely to be having cream tea in the orangery and inspecting old photographs in the vine house, with not an orange or grape in view, then at least we still have these precious little buildings. Best of all, present-day architects, Quinlan Terry, Charles Morris and the Terry Farrell Partnership, are still finding it possible to design amusing and interesting garden buildings. Even if this is the architect's only future role in the garden it is well worth having. Let us hope it will always be so.

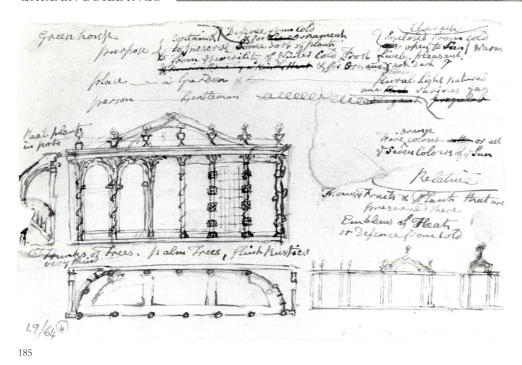

185

WILLIAM NEWTON 1735–90

A greenhouse appropriate for a gentleman

c. 1760
Sepia pen
110 × 170 mm. /$4\frac{3}{8}$ × $6\frac{3}{4}$ in.

William Newton is really working out his ideas as he goes along on this sheet of sketches relating to an early greenhouse *to preserve some sorts of plants from [the] severity of winter cold, frost.* He is trying out different forms of roof supports – *Trunks of trees and very thin, palm trees, flint Rustics* and has noted the top of the building decorated with *Real plants in pots* – presumably for summer only. The glazing for one section is sketched in, but the overall impression is that he is not really clear about the building at all; these may have been his first thoughts for a subsequent design produced for Mr Dalbiac, for whom he worked at Durdans in Surrey and Hungerford Park in Berkshire.

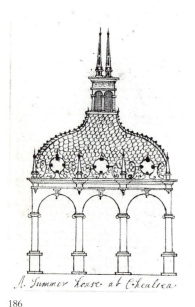

186

ROBERT SMYTHSON c.1535–1614 or
JOHN SMYTHSON d.1634

A summerhouse

Chelsea, London, 1609 or 1619
Sepia pen
108 × 64 mm. /$4\frac{1}{4}$ × $2\frac{1}{2}$ in.

This little drawing from the Smythson Collection makes it clear that from the beginning of the seventeenth century garden buildings were essentially delightful and ornamental. They were also, invariably, insubstantial, made of painted wood, as this one probably was, and leaving not a trace behind. It is not known whether this drawing was made during Robert Smythson's visit to London in 1609 or John's trip in 1619 and there is no clue as to which Chelsea garden was adorned with this pavilion. But imagine it, with painted blue or green arches, gilded finials, perhaps red shingled roof and a white and gold dolls' colonnade on top. The good thing about insubstantiality is that it gives us the opportunity to rebuild such delights.

GEORGE HERBERT KITCHIN 1870–1951

A garden house

Lilleshall, Shropshire, c.1910
Pencil
Page from 1909 sketchbook
145 × 230 mm. /$5\frac{3}{4}$ × 9 in.

This appears to be a design by Kitchin rather than merely a sketch. He notes that the garden house is *to fit existing steps in New formal garden, Lilleshall.* There is an alternative facade for the pavilion and a rough ground plan. Few of Kitchin's professional drawings survive and little is known of his architectural work; it seems most likely that this was a 'discussion' design and not a firm commission.[7]

GEORGE HERBERT KITCHIN 1870–1951

A garden pavilion

Trentham, Staffordshire, 1909
Pencil
Page from 1909 sketchbook
145 × 230 mm. /$5\frac{3}{4}$ × 9 in.

This is one of Sir Charles Barry's domed pavilions at Trentham, sketched by G.H.Kitchin, who spent a great deal of time travelling around England and Europe recording notable architectural details. The Collection holds thirty-two of his sketchbooks.

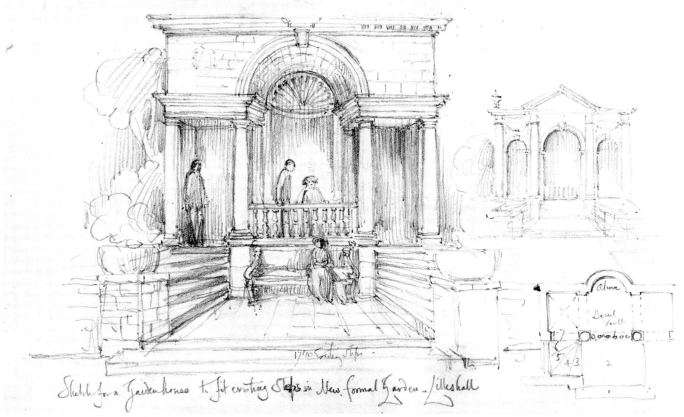

Sketch for a Garden house to fit existing Steps in New Formal Garden - Lilleshall

187

A garden pavilion Trentham Staffs.
Aug 31 '09

188

189

189] JAMES STUART 1713–88

A garden loggia

15 St James's Square, London, *c.*1764
Pen, pencil and grey and yellow washes
310 × 250 mm. /12¼ × 9⅞ in.

James 'Athenian' Stuart became a celebrated and successful authority on Grecian art and architecture after a study and sketching trip to Greece in the early 1750s. Drawings by him are of the greatest rarity, and this loggia, and the following two garden buildings, come from a volume of designs by Stuart and Sir Edward Lovett Pearce (d.1733) which came up for sale in 1977 and were bought for the Collection.

The walls adjoining this loggia seem to suggest an urban setting, and with the ascription of the statue as a Crouching Venus or Aphrodite accompanied by Eros (by Dr B.F. Cook of the British Museum) and owned by Thomas Anson, the drawing may well be for the garden of 15 St James's Square, Anson's house, which was built by Stuart in 1764–6.[8]

190] JAMES STUART 1713–88

A neo-classical version of the Praeneste

Rousham, Oxfordshire, *c.*1760
Pen and wash
200 × 195 mm. /7⅞ × 7⅝ in.

This is much the most exciting of the 'Athenian' Stuart drawings from the gardener's point of view, and is a version of William Kent's arched Praeneste in the Venus Vale at Rousham, which he designed in 1738. Stuart has drawn a plan and elevation with Kent's dimensions.[9]

191] JAMES STUART 1713–88

A garden loggia with Ionic supports to a balustrade

*c.*1760
Pen and brown wash
185 × 250 mm. /7¼ × 9⅞ in.

This is the third of the Stuart drawings with a garden connection, but little is known of the use or situation of this building. He has drawn a delightful loggia, with Doric columns supporting three pediments and taller Ionic supports to a frieze and balustrade, ornamented with four vases. There is the hint of a wall on the left, which like no.189 perhaps indicates an urban setting.

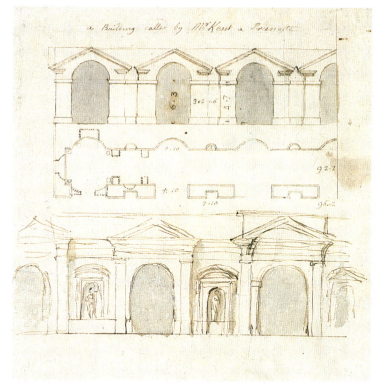

190

191

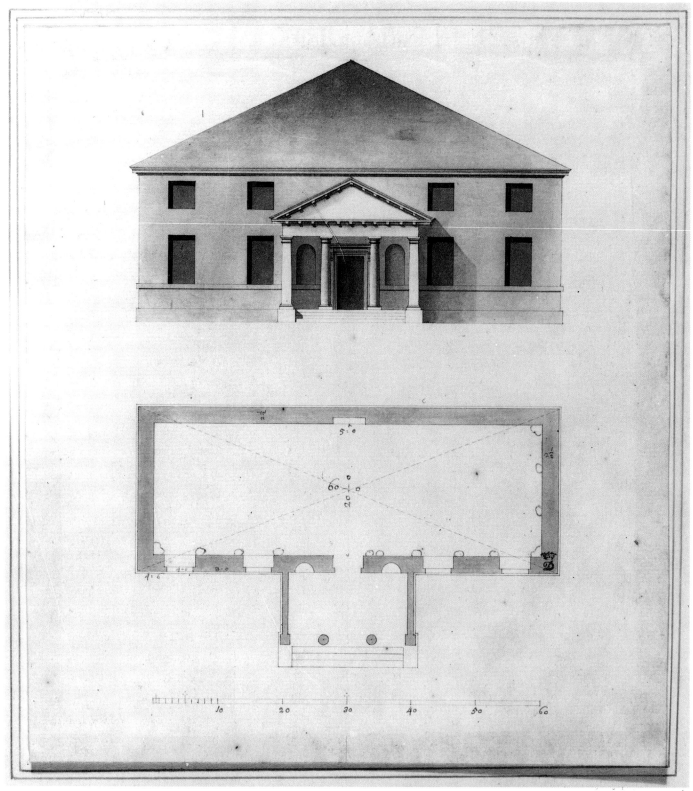

192

192] RICHARD BOYLE, 3rd EARL OF BURLINGTON 1694–1753

A pavilion

Chiswick House, London, *c.*1717
Pen and wash
222 × 197 mm. /8¾ × 7¾ in.

This elevation and plan, drawn by Henry Flitcroft, is one of two designs for the garden at Chiswick by Lord Burlington. The pavilion was built near the River Thames, on the east side of the basin of water between the amphitheatre and the bridge. The other drawing in the Collection is for an orangery. Both were designed by a very young Lord Burlington, who was twenty-three in 1717, the date given, and built within a few years. This was before Burlington met William Kent, whom he famously encouraged to leap the fence and see all Nature as a garden, thus instigating the English landscape movement.

As well as being a symbolic drawing in terms of garden history, this modest design must also represent one of the greatest treasures of the RIBA, the Burlington-Devonshire Collection, which contains works by Palladio, Inigo Jones, and John Webb as well as Lord Burlington. The story of these drawings is told briefly in the Introduction, for it was the possession of the Palladio drawings which inspired and enabled Burlington to begin a Palladian revival.

193] SIR WILLIAM CHAMBERS 1723–96

A pagoda

Kew Gardens, London, 1761
Pen and watercolour
610 × 430 mm. /24 × 17 in.

This famous drawing is the second or revised design for the pagoda, 163 feet high, which exists in Kew Gardens, one of five survivors of the twenty-five buildings Chambers designed for Augusta, Dowager Princess of Wales between 1757 and 1763. The inspiration for this, 'the most ambitious and splendid chinoiserie garden structure in Europe' came from two engraved representations of the Porcelain Tower of Nanking and the Chinese Tea Pagoda of 1669 and 1756 respectively. Chambers' pagoda has nine stories above the ground floor, tapering slightly, all the viewing balconies protected with Chinese rails in red lacquer, and the canopies glittering with glazed tiles. The eighty dragons, whose positions and expressions can be seen clearly in this high-contrast print from the now fading watercolour, were also coloured and glazed.

194

194] JOHN ADEY REPTON 1775–1860

A conservatory

Spring Park (Woodchester Park) Gloucestershire, c. 1820
Pen and wash
200 × 270 mm. /$7\frac{7}{8}$ × $10\frac{5}{8}$ in.

An alternative or second design to the following one, this is described as being of rectangular shape with a low pitched glass roof. Both drawings indicate that the buildings were to be the chief ornament to a garden of exotic plants, set in basket-edged beds.

After Humphry Repton's death in 1818, it was John Adey Repton who carried out sophisticated commissions in Holland and Germany, perpetuating his father's design ideas. In 1822 he worked for German princes, notably Prince Hardenburg at his estate near Potsdam, for whom he designed the Hardenburg basket, made of outwardly curving, jointed wooden slats with a pretty zig-zag edging. This kind of basket edging, around beds of exotic, American plants or even English favourites of the clove pink, marigold and columbine varieties, were John Adey's most personal style.

It is interesting that he also thought gardens to be most worth his time; in 1826 he quoted twenty guineas as his daily charge for landscape fees, but only ten guineas with a percentage on the work for architectural fees.

195] JOHN ADEY REPTON 1775–1860

A conservatory

Spring Park (Woodchester Park) Gloucestershire, c. 1820
Pen and wash
255 × 365 mm. /10 × $14\frac{3}{8}$ in.

This drawing is for a conservatory of trellis work, octagonal in plan with a dome. This design and the previous one were made by John Adey Repton for Lord Ducie at Spring Park, where he worked on his own after his father's death in 1818.

John Adey was Humphry Repton's eldest son and he was born almost totally deaf. He was a pupil of William Wilkins of Norwich, then worked for John Nash and finally joined his father; his life was totally devoted to work and his antiquarian interests.

196] THOMAS ALLASON 1790–1852

A greenhouse

Alton Towers, Staffordshire, c. 1820
Pencil, pen and watercolour
220 × 625 mm. /$8\frac{5}{8}$ × $24\frac{5}{8}$ in.

Thomas Allason assisted the 15th Earl of Shrewsbury in the laying out of the gardens at Alton Towers between 1814 and 1827. Most of the buildings in that romantic valley garden were designed by a little known architect, Robert Abraham, including the famous domed conservatory. Whether this is an Abraham building sketched by Allason is not clear, but it has a great elegance. It would seem to be attached to a stone wall behind, and may have been part of the house.

195

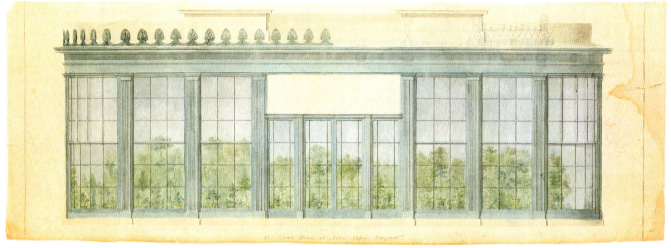

196

197]   GEORGE STANLEY REPTON 1786–1858

A Picturesque cow-byre

*c.*1805
Pencil, pen and wash
f.21v and f. 22 from sketchbook
100 × 160 mm. /4 × 6$\frac{3}{8}$ in.

George Stanley Repton was Humphry Repton's youngest son, and he went to work in John Nash's office at the age of sixteen. The Collection holds two sketchbooks from the earliest years in the office; this drawing is from the comprehensive volume, of ninety-four pages, which is full of little drawings, but not many have a garden connection. The interest in this drawing, which appears to be for an ornamental cow-byre (to shelter the cows for an ornamental dairy) is in its construction of tree trunks, with a thatched roof and removable hurdles. The building is thought to have been for Lord Robert Spencer's Woolbeding House in Sussex, but is reminiscent of the Nash designs for Blaise Hamlet, many of which were drawn by John Adey or George Stanley Repton. If this is a subsidiary building for an ornamental dairy, four cows seem to be enough for an afternoon of rural escape.

198]   SIR JEFFRY WYATVILLE 1766–1840

The Swiss Cottage

Endsleigh, Devon, *c.*1815
Pen and watercolour
205 × 250 mm. /8$\frac{1}{8}$ × 9$\frac{7}{8}$ in.

The Duke of Bedford's rural retreat in Devon, where the main house was only ever referred to as a cottage, was designed by Repton, with buildings by Wyatville, in 1810–11. The so-called Swiss Cottage was an alternative retreat, a '*bijou* rustic pavilion' in the garden. This building still exists and was restored by the Landmark Trust in the 1970s.

197

THE SWISS COTTAGE

AT THE *Duke of Bedford's* RUSTIC VILLA *at Endsleigh.*

198

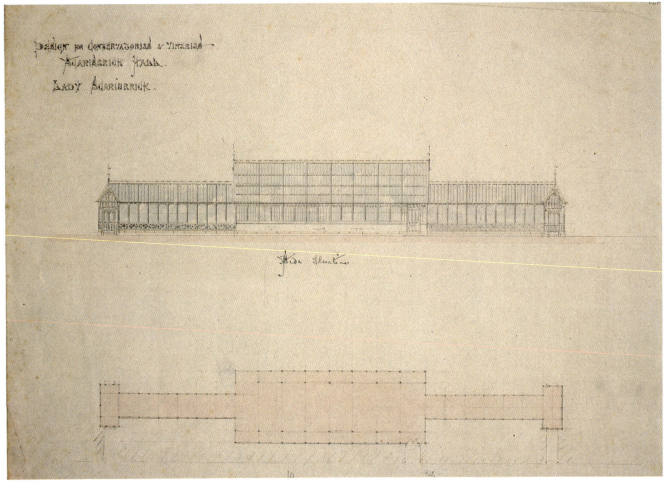

199

199] EDWARD WELBY PUGIN 1834–75

A conservatory

Scarisbrick Hall, Lancashire, c. 1862
Pen and blue and pink washes
545 × 760 mm. /21½ × 30 in.

The drawing is titled: *Design for Conservatorias and Vinarias Plan and side elevation*. It was drawn for Lady Scarisbrick by the son of the great romantic Gothicist, Augustus Welby Northmore Pugin: Pugin senior had enlarged and elaborated Scarisbrick Hall between 1837 and 1845, but died in 1852. Edward Welby Pugin took over the practice and this is one of his additional designs for Scarisbrick. It shows a highly sophisticated building, in technological and visual terms, and bears an interesting resemblance to the conservatory in the unidentified garden drawing from the Pugin Collection (no. 75).

200] SIR JEFFRY WYATVILLE 1766–1840

A plan and section of an exotic house

Kew Gardens, 1800
Pencil, pen and watercolour
575 × 435 mm. /22⅝ × 17⅛ in.

The purpose of this drawing is to explain the heating system for an iron-framed hothouse, and the note *The Hot Water Apparatus arranged and fixed by A. M. Perkins* suggests an advertisement or exhibition brochure. The instructional value of the drawing, whoever it was intended for, is of great interest now and illustrates the boiler system clearly and explains its workings.

Britwell Court: Proposed Clock-tower & Pigeon-house.

Scale Halfinch = One foot.

201] ALFRED WATERHOUSE 1830–1905
& PAUL WATERHOUSE 1861–1924

The clock tower and pigeon-house

Britwell Court, Burnham, Buckinghamshire, *c*.1855
Pen and pencil

There are 125 drawings for Waterhouse & Sons 'general aggrandizement' of Britwell Court for W.Christie-Miller between 1875 and 1896. Alfred Waterhouse, a prolific and reliable architect of great charm and distinction, begetter of the Natural History Museum in South Kensington, London, the Prudential Assurance building in Holborn and Girton College, Cambridge, was not noted for his interest in gardens. But these buildings, which are essentially estate buildings, demonstrate the typically Victorian paternalistic concern for the gardener's world. At Britwell Court, the cooing of the doves has only to be silenced by the tollings of the bell that marked the hours of the working-day for the growers of salads and strawberries. Here is just that aura of discipline and hard work tempered by kindness to feathered-friends and to the pensioner with his basket for vegetables, that was the essence of the Victorian gardening establishment.

202] JOHN JAMES JOASS 1868–1952

Details from a garden

Barncluith, Lanarkshire
(Strathclyde Region) 1893
Pen and pencil
355 × 510 mm. /14 × 20⅛ in.

This drawing by Joass of the garden at Barncluith shows details of the thatched dovecote, the ice-house and the fountain. The dovecote is attractive and very much to 1890s taste, but out of keeping in this early seventeenth-century garden. It would have been a rare gentleman of that period who had such a small and ornamental item in his garden; dovecotes and pigeon-houses of earlier times were large, free-standing structures, more for the farmyard than the garden, for the filling of many pigeon pies and for the supply of valuable manure. Surviving dovecotes such as that at Athelhampton in Dorset and Rousham in Oxfordshire have hundreds of pigeon-holes; Athelhampton's is supposed to have a thousand. Dovecotes of the small and garden variety, such as this one, were beloved of the nature lovers of the Arts and Crafts period much as bird feeders are by gardeners of today.

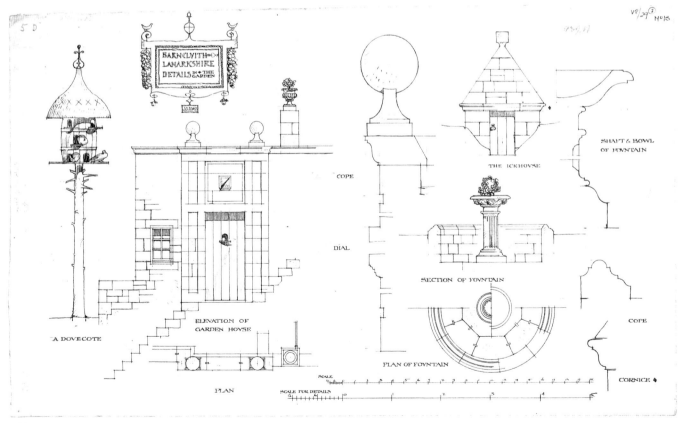

202

THE RIGHT HON^{BLE}

THE EARL OF BROWNLOW.

THE FERN HOUSE AT ASHRIDGE.

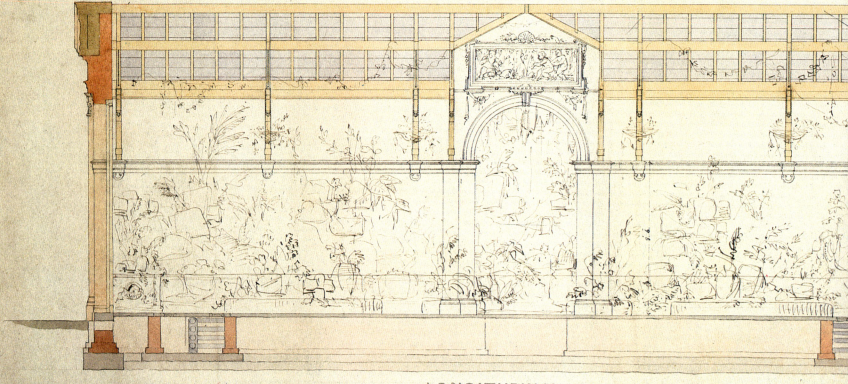

LONGITUDINAL SECTION.

SCALE OF | | | | | | | | | | | | | | | | | FEET

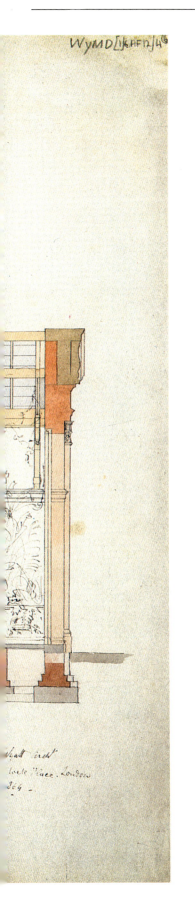

203] SIR MATTHEW DIGBY WYATT 1820–77

Elevations of a fern house

Ashridge, Hertfordshire, 1864
Pencil, pen and watercolour
495 × 650 mm. /19½ × 25⅝ in.

Ferns had become popular about ten years before the date of
this design through the publication of a handbook on fern
collecting by Thomas Moore. Clearly the assistant who
sketched the contents of this fern house did not know what
ferns were! Ashridge, the magnificent early nineteenth-
century house and garden, largely created by the Earl and
Countess of Bridgewater with Repton and Wyatville (see
nos. 50–57), belonged to Lord Brownlow at this time.

204] SIR MATTHEW DIGBY WYATT 1820–77

Plan of a fern house

Ashridge, Hertfordshire, 1864
Pencil, pen and watercolour
495 × 650 mm. /19½ × 25⅝ in.

The plan for the fern house reveals a grotto and a *dripping well*
in the arched bay at the rear. There is a fanciful layout for the
fern beds and a note *The pavement may of course be tessalated if
desired.*

The fern craze lasted until the end of the nineteenth
century, when gardeners returned to growing native
varieties out of doors.

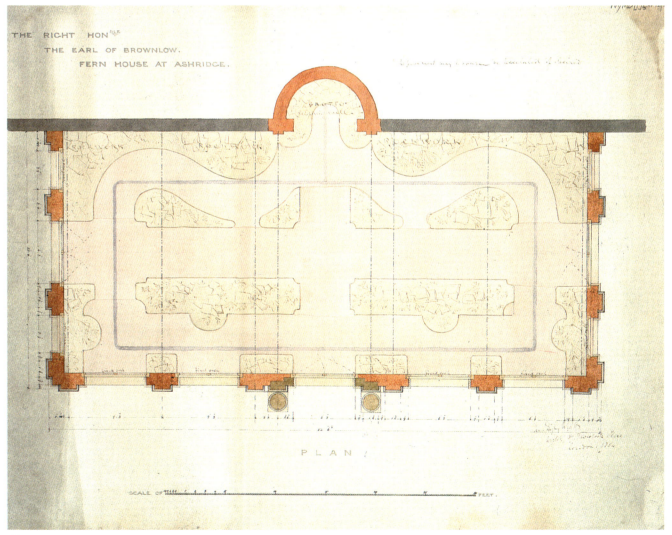

204

205] R. SHEKLETON BALFOR *d.* 1915

A garden pavilion

Submitted for Tite Prize Competition, 1894
Pen
(a) Perspective 1067 × 749 mm. /42 × 29½ in.
(b) Plan 660 × 991 mm. /26 × 39 in.

R. S. Balfour entered four drawings of this project, a section, elevation and this perspective and plan of a Baroque building which needs to grace a park rather than a garden. It is clearly an academic exercise and effectively illustrates his ability to rise to a grand classical challenge in his mind's eye. In addition to Balfour's sketches of the garden at Montacute nos. 93–5; the Collection also holds an Architectural Association Evening Class project by him for a house, 1887–8, but no further architectural work, only topographical drawings.

TITE·PRIZE·COMPETITION
DESIGN·FOR
A·GARDEN·PAVILION
OVERLOOKING·A·LAKE.1894.

205a

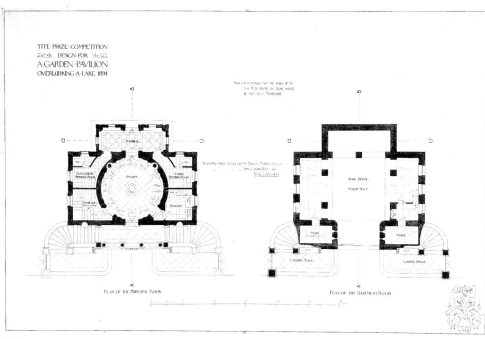

205b

206] FRANK L. PEARSON 1864–1947

Loggia at the end of a lake

Hever Castle, Kent, 1908
Sepia pen
495×975 mm. $/19\frac{1}{2} \times 38\frac{3}{8}$ in.

Frank Pearson, the son of the great Victorian church architect, John Loughborough Pearson, took over his father's practice and his richest client, William Waldorf Astor, at his father's death in 1897. He made many additions and adornments to Hever Castle and designed all Astor's architectural garden features in the Italian Renaissance style. This exhibition drawing for one of the last and most elaborate Italianate features at Hever represents the last fling of Italianate as opposed to true Renaissance inspiration. The creation of the garden at Hever enriches the (unwritten) story of the Italian garden in England, but in no way represents truly its date of 1908, in the midst of the Arts and Crafts Movement in gardening. This drawing belongs stylistically with Trentham and Drumlanrig, and another eighteen years were to pass before the essence of Italian gardens was revived by Shepherd and Jellicoe.

206

207

207]   ARTHUR BERESFORD PITE 1861–1934

An orangery and garden

Burton Manor, Wirral, Cheshire, 1910
Pen and watercolour
Detail from sheet 690 × 990 mm. /27⅛ × 39 in.

The section from north to south through the garden shows the orangery in the background, and the elaborate walls, gates, gazebos and pool which Pite designed. The damp stains, clearly noticeable on this drawing, emphasize the fragility of these working drawings, which in so many cases have been subjected to appalling storage conditions before they came to the Collection. The walls and gates for Burton Manor are illustrated as nos. 50–7.

208]   ARTHER BERESFORD PITE 1861–1934

An orangery

Burton Manor, Wirral, Cheshire, 1910
Pen and watercolour
Detail from sheet 685 × 1020 mm. /27 × 40⅛ in.

Arthur Beresford Pite was a distinguished architectural figure of the 1890s and 1900s but his output was relatively small and Burton Manor appears to be his only significant garden design work. His client was H.N.Gladstone, the son of the Prime Minister, and Pite designed the architectural details while Thomas Mawson and his firm, Lakeland Nurseries, did the planting-design and planting. This is the south elevation of a neo-classical orangery to be built in pink Cheshire stone.

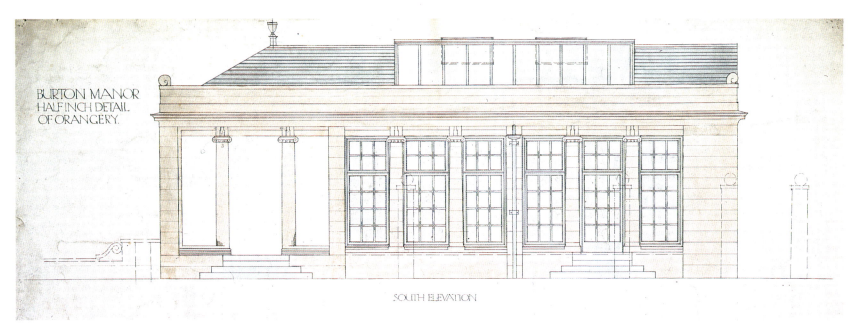

BURTON MANOR
HALF INCH DETAIL
OF ORANGERY.

SOUTH ELEVATION

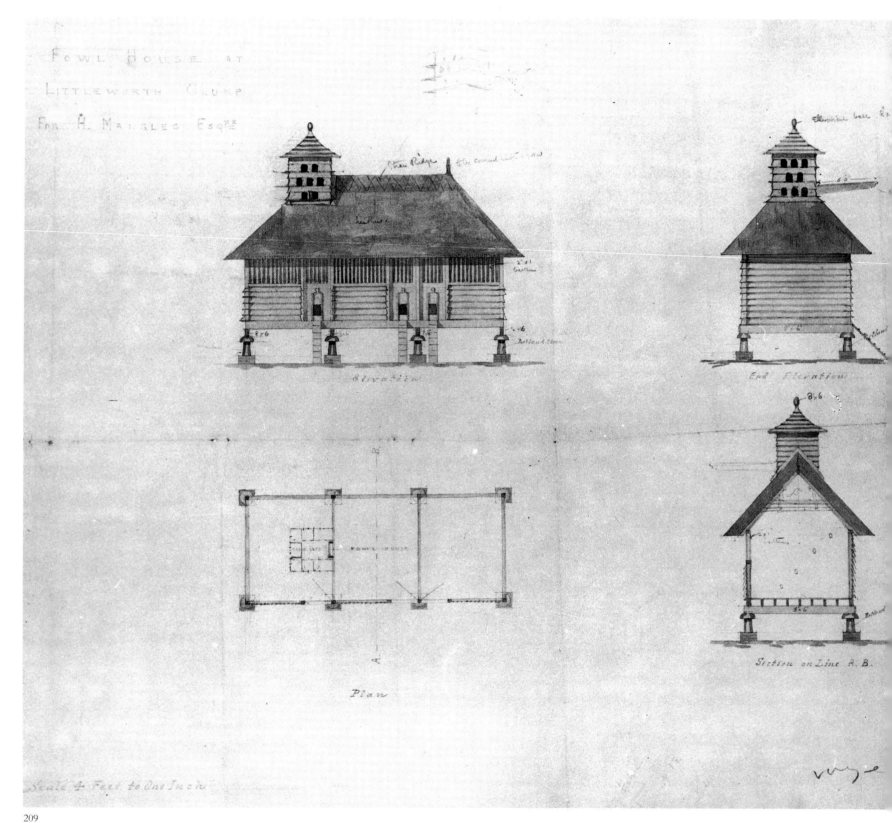

FOWL HOUSE AT
LITTLEWORTH CLUMP.
FOR H. MANGLES ESQRE

Elevation

End Elevation

Plan

Section on Line A. B.

Scale 4 Feet to One Inch

209] EDWIN L. LUTYENS 1869–1944

A fowl house

Littleworth Cross, near Farnham, Surrey, 1889
Pencil and coloured washes
560 × 760 mm. /22 × 29⅞ in.

A small wooden building standing on staddle stones, with ramps and hatches for the hens, partly open slatted sides and a thatched roof with a straw ridge and a pigeoncote. This is one of Edwin Lutyens' very earliest designs for a commission from a family friend and patron, Harry Mangles, for whom he also designed a gardener's cottage and other garden buildings. The building still exists, though it has changed over the years; it has a tiled roof and has come down from its staddle stones and no longer provides a home for hens.

210] EDWIN L. LUTYENS 1896–1944

A garden house

Littleworth Cross, near Farnham, Surrey, c. 1890
Pen, pencil and coloured washes
545 × 780 mm. /21½ × 30¾ in.

The inscription *earliest Lutyens original* is by A. G. Butler who annotated the Lutyens drawings while he was preparing the *Memorial Volumes*, published by Country Life in 1950. This little building is almost certainly a design for Harry Mangles, the rhododendron expert who lived at Littleworth Cross, near Farnham, and for whom Lutyens also designed the fowl house (no. 209) and a gardener's cottage. A similar garden house, half supported on the wall of the former kitchen garden, still exists. Mr Mangles must join the list of Lutyens' most important patrons, for he not only indulged his youthful ideas for amusing buildings, but also, of course, introduced him to Gertrude Jekyll.

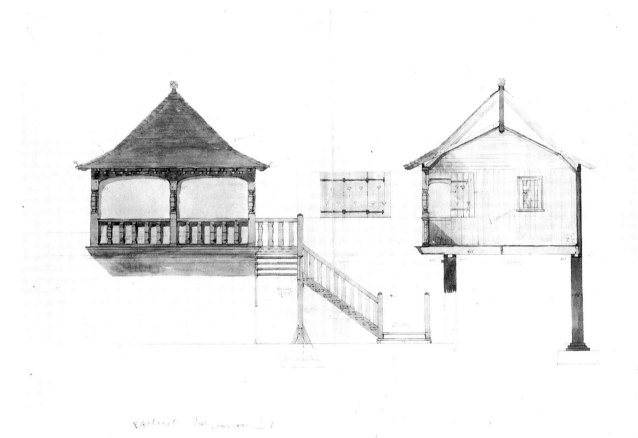

210

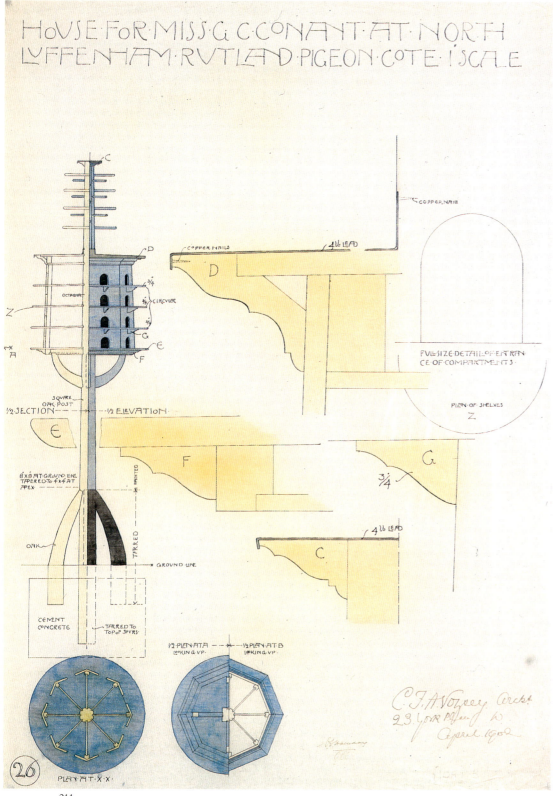

HOUSE·FOR·MISS·G·C·CONANT·AT·NORTH
LUFFENHAM·RUTLAND·PIGEON·COTE·¹⁄SCALE

**211] CHARLES FRANCIS ANNESLEY
VOYSEY 1857–1941**

Elevation and plan of a pigeoncote

The Pastures, North Luffenham, Leicestershire, 1902
Pencil and coloured washes on linen
780 × 560 mm./30¾ × 22 in.

This commission was carried out for Miss G. Conant at The Pastures, for whom Voysey altered and added to the house. The pigeoncote was built but no longer exists. This drawing compares interestingly with the dovecote at Barncluith drawn by J. J. Joass (no. 202); these are buildings for bird lovers, ornamental and benevolent garden features that are a long way removed from their larger forerunners, built in the days when they were a live game larder and a trip into the yard or garden supplied the fillings for pigeon pie.

212] CLOUGH WILLIAMS-ELLIS 1883–1978

An apple and garden house

Oare House, Wiltshire, 1924
Pencil, pen and coloured washes
370 × 350 mm. /14⅝ × 13¾ in.

This drawing and that for a garden seat (no. 246) are from an important commission for Geoffrey Fry. Clough Williams-Ellis was most interested in the commissions that allowed him to build in different styles and sizes of building, which he has most colourfully illustrated at Portmeirion in Wales. He enjoyed the Oare House buildings for the same reason; he built a large, free-Classical house, and then returned to a romantic vernacular tradition – with every care and the same attention to detail – for this most covetable of small buildings. The drawing is a fine tribute to Clough's latter-day Arts and Crafts integrity, inspired by M. H. Baillie-Scott. The idea of an apple house was one of the Arts and Crafts favourites, a twentieth-century substitute for the model dairy enshrining a decorative earthiness: but they had the practical purpose of storing fruit at the required temperature, now no longer so easy in centrally heated houses.

211

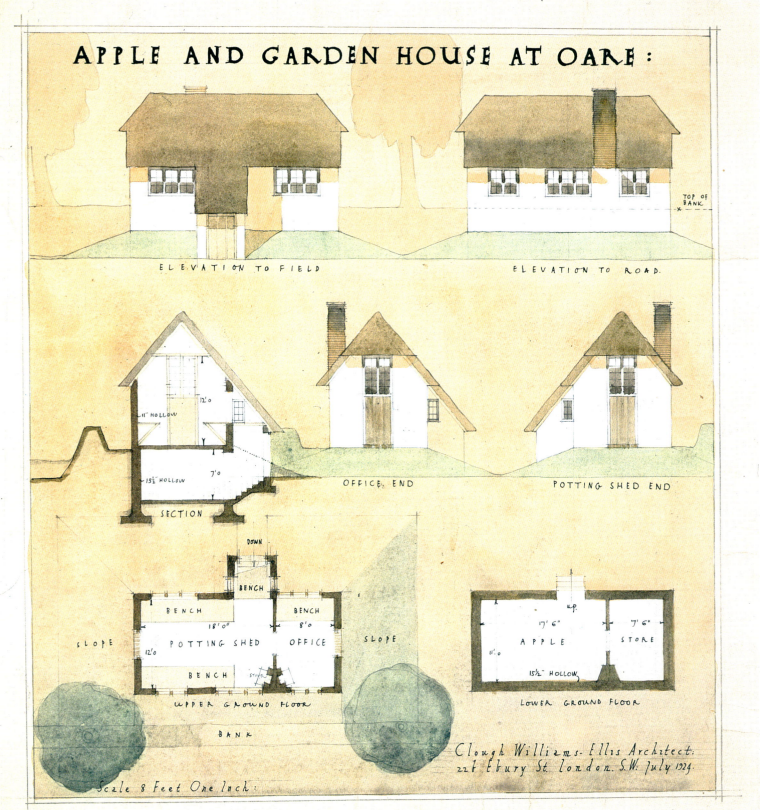

APPLE AND GARDEN HOUSE AT OARE:

ELEVATION TO FIELD

ELEVATION TO ROAD.

11" HOLLOW

12'0

15½" HOLLOW   7'0

SECTION

OFFICE END

POTTING SHED END

TOP OF BANK

DOWN

BENCH

SLOPE

BENCH   BENCH

18'0"   8'0

12'0   POTTING SHED   OFFICE

BENCH

SLOPE

UPPER GROUND FLOOR

BANK

UP.

17' 6"   7' 6"

APPLE   STORE

11'0

15½" HOLLOW

LOWER GROUND FLOOR

Clough Williams-Ellis Architect.
22b Ebury St. London. S.W. July 1924.

Scale 8 Feet One Inch:

Fig. 34] Design for a gateway to the vineyard for Oatlands Palace, Surrey, *c.* 1635 by Inigo Jones.

8

GARDEN ORNAMENT

These final forty-four drawings chosen from the Collection and featuring ornamental miscellanea, are presented with a mixture of nostalgia and optimism. I found them all to be irresistible, for varying reasons, but – after relating ornaments to their gardens in the body of the book (i.e. the orange tub for Ashridge no. 55 and the sundial for Ascott no. 79) these were all that were left. Architects may have been endlessly intrigued by the design of garden buildings, but it is my sad conclusion that they have never really contributed much to garden ornament. This is almost certainly because of our enduring passion for anything classical – vases, urns, seats, sundials and wrought iron gates – and either the plundered originals or exact replicas were used to ornament gardens. In such cases – as with Philip Hardwick's beautiful sepia washed drawing of the vase at Hampton Court, (no. 238) it was the architect's almost recreational pleasure to merely draw such objects. Their education taught them that there was little point in improving on perfection.

But this *laissez-faire* attitude can only last so long, and even the finely classical becomes debased by careless copying. For the last ten years has there has been a revived interest in garden ornaments and a growing market for all kinds of things from 'pet rocks' to wheelbarrow seats, that can conceivably be put into a garden. There have also been, in the aftermath of every Chelsea Flower Show, howls regarding the sheer awfulness and bad taste of many of these things. Is it too much to hope that present-day architects might take a new interest and rescue us?

There are, however, further difficulties. The essence of architectural design is that it is for a specific place. Every garden is a specific place, and in an ideal world, like that of Edwardian Arts and Crafts England, every garden would have a particular crop of its own designs for walls, gates, seats, sundials etc. dispensed at the architect's judgement. Clearly that now cannot be, but equally clear are the pitfalls of endless reproductions falling like snow in summer over every garden of the western, and Japanese, world. We are now prepared to pay one-thousand pounds for a

garden seat, a reproduction by a great designer such as Thomas Chippendale or Edwin Lutyens, each of whom might merit a few pence in design royalties. The cost is almost entirely taken up in production and marketing; to produce these historic designs is expensive, because it is out of date. Reproduction is rightly for purposes of conservation, to restore an object to its garden after the original has rotted, or been spirited, away. But surely for the rest of us it would be better to spend a fair proportion of our money on good design, and rather less on antiquated craftsmanship? These drawings then are not to encourage a veritable crop of Voysey gates or even Walter Godfrey seats, but for gentle visual infection of the modern gardener's mind.

Most of my nostalgia is for the lost art of garden enclosure, and almost half of these drawings are for gates and walls. These enclosing elements are the very history and meaning of gardens: the walls of a Persian paradise garden and of a medieval bower were both strongly and beautifully built, and the earliest gardens in this book, those that Robert Smythson knew at the opening of the seventeenth century, were surrounded with crenellations, balustrades and rusticated arches and doorways. It was our eighteenth-century love affair with nature that made us forget about walls as essential to garden design, and it was the mid-nineteenth-century Victorians who revived wall building as an architectural art. Drawings for walls are such lovely things, these for Alfred Waterhouse's Eaton Hall (no. 231), A.B. Pite's Burton Manor (no. 228), and Phillimore and Jenkins' Knowsley Hall (no. 234) lie in elegant layers on the page.

In reviving medievalism and Jacobean design the Arts and Crafts architects revived enclosure, but largely in appreciation of old walled gardens and spaces and their restoration, and in the use of hedges as living walls.

We have really been restoring old walls and planting hedges, both admirable activities, ever since. But, with our ambivalence towards the wild and our return to garden-rooms which keep both beleagured nature and vandal man at bay, perhaps it is time

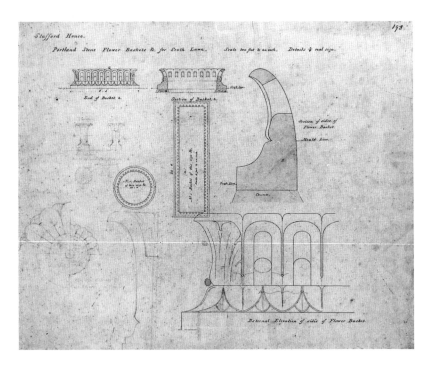

Fig. 35] Flower baskets in Portland stone by Sir Charles Barry for Stafford House, London, *c.* 1845. The flower basket is perhaps the most desirable garden ornament that still awaits revival.

for the re-instatement of beautiful walls?

Arthur Beresford Pite's drawing for Burton Manor in Cheshire (no. 221) shows just how effective walls are to create a garden; some of his gate designs are also here, and it is interesting to note the variety of designs for different parts of the garden, each of which expressed changes of mood and function according to the way he used the materials and the structure. If walls defend the garden, then the gate is the most significant symbol of glorious expectation, that passport to paradise, most evocatively the shuttered door in the wall that leads to our secret garden. Gateways have always implied this magical symbolism and thus have attracted the most important architects, who could find no time for border layouts. Even Inigo Jones (1573–1652) can be drawn into the garden with his gate designs. The gateway to the vineyard for Oatlands Palace (fig. 34), designed for the vanished garden that King Charles I knew, is the inspiration for so many rusticated and pedimented eighteenth-century gateways.

Traditionally, gates are for two purposes, keeping animals out and letting people in. The animals come first because of these curiously early detailed designs for a five-bar field-gate which

allows me to recruit the famous gardener, Philip Miller (1691–1771) in to my book. The freehand drawing with carefully noted measurements (no. 215), and the draughtsman's worked up version (no. 216) have travelled together down the years and across England to find their way into the Collection. It is thought that Sir William Chambers found them at The Hoo in Hertfordshire, where they had been left by Capability Brown, who had brought them from Trentham, which was one of the great estates that Philip Miller knew well. Romancing perhaps, but the stalwart Miller, Curator of the Chelsea Physic Garden for fifty years, author of a *Gardener's Dictionary* and *Kalendar*, 'bibles' of the mid-eighteenth century, had a sound and quiet knowledge of such things. These two old drawings make interesting comparison with Charles Voysey's field-gates, decorated with hearts and seductive handles (and one wittily with a lamp) which he designed as road entrances for his houses. This use for gates has truly disappeared, killed by our universal reluctance to get out of the motorcar and open them.

With our late twentieth-century taste for gardens that are outdoor rooms, or a series of them, it is time for the foot-gate, a 'people-gate' to be revived. One of the most endearing, and valuable, aspects of the Arts and Crafts philosophy was the strict adherence to a human scale. Pergolas and arbours fitted two people exactly, steps were made for leisurely tread, the lawn *allée* between flower-filled borders – 'delicious to one's sentient boot-sole' in Henry James's irresistible tribute to English grass[1] – offered an attractive vista, but not too long a walk to the seat in the garden house at the end. But most emphatically, the comforting human scale was celebrated in foot-gates. Gertrude Jekyll did not believe a garden should have any other kind of gate; her 'front' entrance to Munstead Wood, illustrated from the Lutyens sketchbook (no. 90–92) was an oak-boarded latch gate, simply because the peace of her garden was not to be shattered by anyone's pony and trap and certainly no motorcar, and she felt that the first gift of any garden should be its sense of a refuge from the hurly-burly of the outside world. The principal entrances to some of Lutyens' finest houses, Deanery Garden at Sonning and Folly Farm at Sulhamstead among them, were slatted or latticed oak or green painted gates in the garden wall.

Fig. 36] *Opposite:* Sir Jeffry Wyatville's sketch of the sundial and steps from the terrace at the Duke of Bedford's cottage at Endsleigh, Devon.

Many of the Arts and Crafts architects designed lovely foot-gates; it is fascinating to observe Charles Voysey adapting his basic detailed design for special places and people, and his wicket gate for Spade House at Sandgate in Kent (no. 217) has the piquancy of being for his famous client, H. G. Wells. Most desirable of all, certainly as a drawing, is Clough Williams-Ellis's green gate hung on pink piers with characteristically humorous 'Clough-style' ornament (no. 224).

The most exciting of our modern revivals is for trelliswork and treillage. 'Trellis' is the basically simple construction of light-weight wooden slats; 'treillage' is the architectural form of the craft. Trellis has been used for centuries to support plants, either against walls, on free-standing pyramids or arches, and as a framework for hedges; Elizabethan gardens sported thorn, briars and eglantine wound through lattices topped with birds, galleons and crowns. Architects were most likely deterred by the ephemerality of trellis until the Dutch and the French invented treillage. Even in the seventeenth century its construction was immensely expensive and time-consuming, and it was only done for the richest garden owners, usually Kings and Cardinals. Chantilly, Versailles and Villandry are still the best places to see the art perpetuated, but the modern revival is really possible from the gardening books of the period, notably J. van der Groen's *Le Jardinier du Pays-Bas* (1681), D'Argenville's *Theory and Practice of Gardening* (translated into English by John James, 1712) and the drawings of Pierre Le Nôtre. It can thus be appreciated what a compliment Henry Holland was paying to the Prince Regent's taste with his suggestion of treillage for Carlton House (no. 239). Repton and Loudon also used it, but their efforts pale beside the truly French genius for this art. The predominance of the French must account for the set of five unidentified French drawings found with the Pugin Collection, which are all reproduced here, nos 236–7 and 240–42. The mystery of their provenance invites speculation, but we can well imagine how Augustus Welby Pugin or his son Edward, both ardent Catholics, might have come across them on a trip in France and would have found them attractive for the construction details of a treillage 'cabinet' and the corbeille, or flower basket, that they contain. There is a novelette to be woven around this anonymous young artist finding this delightful garden with its flower basket in the Rue de Richelieu (as recorded on the drawing), but for the present purposes these five small drawings offer a late treat, for I feel they are among the most charming watercolours in this book.

The later Victorians, undaunted, mastered treillage in spectacular ways (e.g. at Ascott for the Rothschilds) and Thomas Mawson moved it into the twentieth century (Thornton Manor, Cheshire for Lord Leverhulme), and most recently Russell Page revived it for the garden of the Dower House at Badminton. Its use in France was often allied to trompe l'oeil painting, for latticed perspectives can deceive the eye and focus on the painted illusion; in this way treillage is coming back into fashion, along with a talented new wave of mural painters, and promises delightful decorations both inside the house and in garden buildings and the garden.

Water is such an important feature in the garden that it is surprising that architects do not seem to have designed many pools. The two examples shown here, Detmar Blow's waterfall pools for Charles Hill Court in Surrey (no. 243) and Edward Maufe's semi-circular and fluted pool for a garden at Buxted in Sussex (no. 244) are both superbly restrained examples of water features for a formal garden. They are particularly interesting for their constructional details, especially as the Maufe drawing shows the use of concrete, but I think the strongest point they make is that if a pool is to be anything but the purest geometrical shape, it requires a very well trained eye to judge just how far decoration can be used before it crosses the boundary of good taste.

The mention of concrete, and the Peter Shepheard flower pots for Time and Life Building (no. 252) allow a last regretful glance back to the Modern Movement, and the missed opportunities in not just garden design, but in good design for modern features and ornaments, and the acceptance of concrete in the garden. In the modern gardens of the thirties, and especially at the Festival of Britain after the war, there was a tremendous optimism that well-designed pavings, plant containers, pools and seats in concrete would be affordable by so many gardeners. Peter Shepheard's *Modern Gardens* of 1953 and Sylvia Crowe's *Garden Design* of 1958, both showed and extolled the virtues of shuttered walling, moulded edgings for flower beds and pools, plain and textured paviours and cone-shaped flower pots: the original cone 'planter' was designed for the Festival by Maria Shephard and Frank Clark. The cement industry responded intelligently – commissioning the best designers to produce objects, which were displayed in the Cement and Concrete Association's garden at Wexham Springs, Slough in Buckinghamshire. But concrete was spurned and rejected by the English gardening public, and for a variety of reasons: in part it was the failure of the Modern Movement to substantiate a new mood in garden design, it was also that landscape architects took to effectively employing concrete paviours and furniture in public landscapes (making them automatic anathema to gardeners) and that parts of the concrete industry could not resist using concrete to produce cheap imitations – fakes – of classical balustrades and vases, which became the epitome of bad taste. The failure of concrete has played a signficant part in both the success of re-constituted natural stones as an acceptable way of making new classical ornaments and features, and in the consequent revival of our taste for classical gardens. It is a sad story. Concrete, however, had and still does have, its moments in the hands of individual gardeners and for very specific situations can turn the impossibly expensive into the art of the possible; Harland Hand's wonderful garden in Berkeley, California, is made entirely of concrete 'rocks', which he is very proud of, and as they nestle amongst the most exquisite flowers and play host to purple aloes, silvery sedums, echiums, hemerocallis and the daintiest pink roses, they are totally successful.

The last drawings are for garden favourites, seats and sundials. Once again, William Newton (1735–90) is at work, sketching and crossing out as he contemplates seats to suit the various later eighteenth-century fashions for classical, Gothick and chinoiserie. Classical benches have also inspired the John Hungerford Pollen watercolour (no. 247) and Clough Williams-Ellis's 'couch' (to be cast in concrete) (no. 246). The finely-drawn design for the Gothic revival seat at Tregothnan House, in Cornwall by Lewis Vulliamy, which looks more like a niche for a cathedral, shows the extremes of stylistic detail that were required to produce the authentic gloominess of a High Victorian garden. The sheet of drawings by Edwin Lutyens for a seat to go around a tree for William Robinson at Gravetye Manor (no. 248) is almost certainly the only design of any detail he did for a garden seat; the now ubiquitous wave-backed design was re-measured and drawn up from a surviving original seat. This Lutyens drawing almost certainly dates from the late 1890s, when he was still a young and struggling architect. Gertrude Jekyll had introduced him to William Robinson, who was a very rich man, with an estate of a thousand acres and the lovely

Gravetye Manor in Sussex, who would hopefully give him some lucrative commissions. Lutyens spent a weekend at Gravetye in the spring of 1897; he thought the daffodils were breathtakingly beautiful and was fascinated by a little white owl nesting outside his window, but Robinson gave him no large job, and the only tangible result seems to be this seat, which was built for the garden but no longer survives.[2]

The rough pencil sketch for a seat around a tree in his own garden, by Charles Holden (1875–1960), probably made as a reminder to himself of the following weekend's task, allows me to draw this distinguished architect into my garden book. Holden had a busy career building large hospitals in partnership with H. Percy Adams, underground stations for London Transport and the Senate House for London University. His relaxation was his own garden at Harmer Green, Welwyn in Hertfordshire, to which he was passionately devoted; this sketch and a few other rough plans for his own garden are with his drawings, showing the moments of escape he allowed himself from long office hours spent on grand and prestigious commissions, for which he is now greatly admired.

To end with sundials, seems appropriate, for they introduce the element of time into the garden. From biblical times sundials were used for practical and decorative purposes; in England, since the mid-nineteenth century they have been treasured rather more for the contemplative thoughts they inspire from their inscribed mottoes. Lutyens' sundial for Woodside (no. 254) is to be carefully carved with *Che sarà sarà* (What will be, will be); others much used were *Sic vita transit* (So passes life) and *Sic vita dum fugit stare vedetur* (So life while it flies seems to stand still). Perhaps this last is especially appropriate for it suggests the *raison d'etre* for the architect in the garden. As Sylvia Crowe pointed out in *Garden Design*, the part played by time makes garden design different from the other arts: 'There is no garden which can spring to life as a fully finished work of art', and time is needed for every design to come into its own.[2] From that point it is vulnerable to neglect and misunderstanding, and a loss of the original intention. The best hope for our seemingly never-changing, but actually ever-changing gardens is in the harmony and good proportions of their sound design, and in the architectural strength that keeps the garden's spirit alive.

Walls and Gates

213] SIDNEY E. CASTLE 1883–1955

Drive gates

Giggs Court, Marlow, Buckinghamshire, 1920
Pencil and watercolour
460 × 740 mm. /18$\frac{1}{8}$ × 29$\frac{1}{8}$ in.

Sydney Ernest Castle is not a well-known architect, but he was a fine and talented artist; he studied drawing under Sydney Newcombe and Ernest Godman and became especially adept at illustrating medieval and Tudor architecture. He was not known for his interest in gardens but this delightful watercolour of well-crafted gates for Giggs Court at Marlow deserves to be included in this book. The RIBA have a fine collection of his pen drawings, mostly for domestic Tudor style buildings of the 20s in which he was an expert; he wrote and illustrated *Domestic Gothic of the Tudor Period* in 1928.

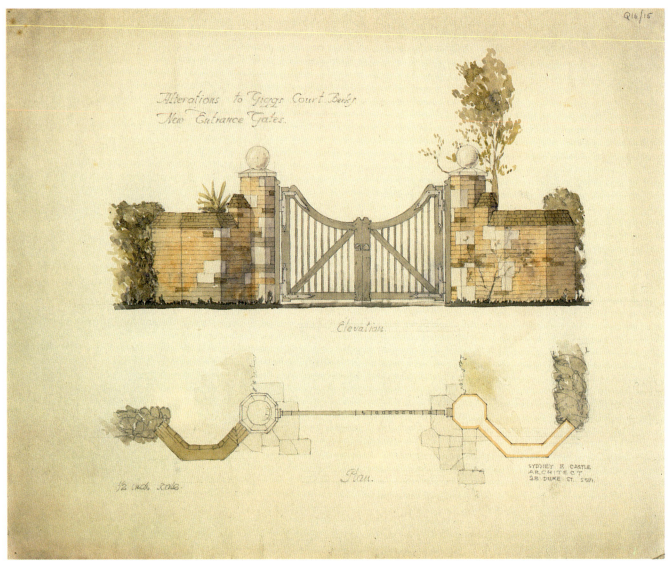

213

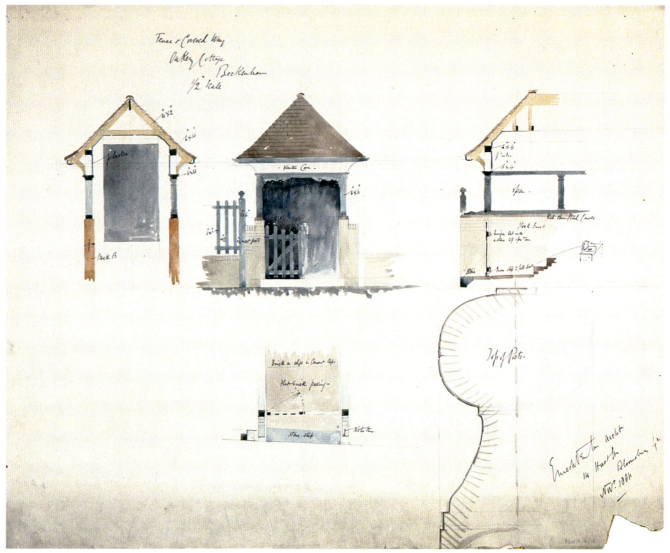

214

214] ERNEST NEWTON 1856–1922

A fence and covered way

Oakey Cottage, Beckenham, Bromley, Kent, 1881
Pencil, sepia pen and wash
535 × 660 mm./ 21 × 26 in.

An early drawing in Newton's own hand, made within two years of setting up his own practice at 14 Hart Street, Bloomsbury, London, after leaving the Norman Shaw office. This is the only drawing for Oakey Cottage, and it seems to be one of those favoured commissions from a family friend which are given to help a young architect along. The covered way is a delightful garden device, notably used by Philip Webb at Great Tangley Manor in Surrey, an idea which the young Newton would have carefully noted.

Newton's connections in this part of Kent were well forged for he was to do many more commissions in the area, notably Buller's Wood at Bickley, one of his most famous houses.

215]   PHILIP MILLER 1691–1771

Field-gate

Trentham Hall, Staffordshire, *c.*1760
Pen on cartridge
170 × 210 mm. /6¾ × 8¼ in.

This attribution is uncertain but irresistible, inspired by the annotation *Miller the Gardener's drawing*. Philip Miller was the Curator of Chelsea Physic Garden for fifty years; he was well-known for *The Gardener's and Florist's Dictionary* which first appeared in 1724 and went through many editions, and for the *Gardener's Kalendar*. He was also a figure of repute in all the great gardens of England, and it would have been in character for him to have provided this gate drawing in response to a request while he was visiting Trentham.

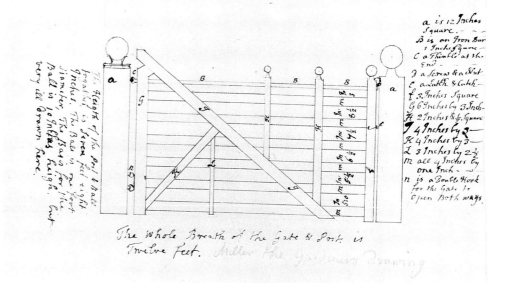

215

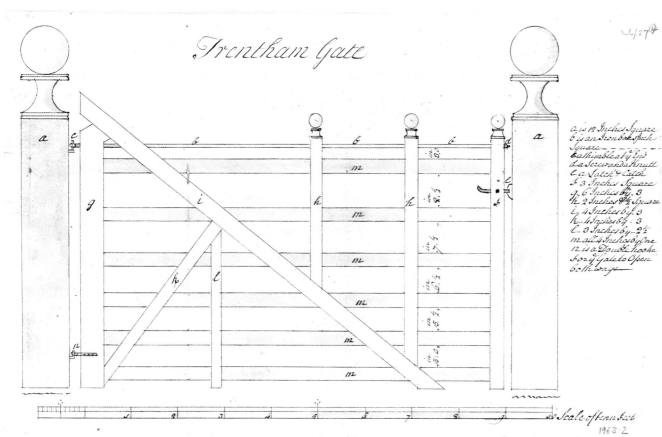

216

216] ANONYMOUS ARTIST

Field-gate

Trentham Hall, Staffordshire, *c.*1760
Pen
220 × 367 mm. /$8\frac{3}{4}$ × $14\frac{1}{4}$ in.

The finished working drawing made from the previous measured sketch with full and careful construction details. These two modest drawings have a colourful past; they came to the Collection in a volume of drawings by Sir William Chambers for Thomas Brand's The Hoo in Hertfordshire, dated 1765. Chambers was at The Hoo after Capability Brown and Brown is the only connection with Trentham, where he began working in the early 1760s and his first fees are recorded in 1764. Dorothy Stroud says Brown began his 'Fresh Account' for Trentham in 1762 and was paid £200 in 1764 and further payments afterwards.[3] Did Brown or his surveyor find this very useful gate drawing at Trentham and remove it to The Hoo for further use?

217] CHARLES FRANCIS ANNESLEY VOYSEY
1857–1941

An entrance gate

Spade House, Sandgate, Kent, 1901
Pen, pencil and coloured washes
565 × 385 mm. /$22\frac{1}{4}$ × $15\frac{1}{8}$ in.

A sheet of half-scale details and a drawing of the complete gate and hanging with dimensions from a commission from the writer, H.G.Wells, for his garden at Sandgate. Voysey's specification at the corner of the sheet reads: 'Deal gate to be painted white and hung on wrought iron strap hinges to match kitchen doors of house and wrought hooks built in to brick or stone piers. Provide the p.c. sum of 17/- for gate catch to be provided by Messrs T.Elsley & Co. Spandril walls to be in local rough stone. Prove and fit one 6″ × 6″ post with gate catch fitted to same to hold gate open.'

217

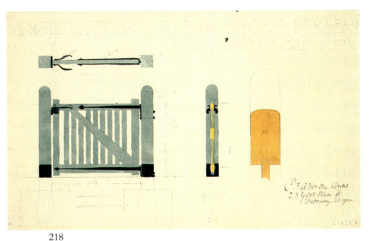

218

219

218] CHARLES FRANCIS ANNESLEY VOYSEY
    1857–1941

A foot gate

Prior's Garth (now Priorsfield), Godalming, Surrey, 1900
Pen and coloured washes
340×565 mm. $/13\frac{3}{8} \times 22\frac{1}{4}$ in.

A sheet of details for a gate in English oak for a house by
Voysey for F.H.Chambers, where Gertrude Jekyll helped
with the garden. The sheet provides all the necessary details
for the making and hanging of this gate. The iron hinges end
in Voysey's heart motif which he used as a detail on all his
commissions. The Collection has designs for a bookplate for
Mr Chambers but no designs for the house or garden.

219] CHARLES FRANCIS ANNESLEY VOYSEY
    1857–1941

A gate and sundial

The Pastures, North Luffenham, Rutland, 1902
Pen, pencil and coloured washes
545×715 mm. $/21\frac{1}{2} \times 28\frac{1}{8}$ in.

A sheet of details with typical Voysey economy of style; he
habitually crammed full size and small scale drawings, plans
and elevations on to a single sheet, though he was too much
the consummate designer to arrange it badly. He used the
wash to highlight important details; here they are the
moulding details for the gateposts, a gatepost's lead capping
and the gate itself, with its unique, attached lamp.

The pencil details are for the sundial, on a pretty base on
top of an hexagonal plinth, with a plain angle-cut stem.

220] CHARLES FRANCIS ANNESLEY VOYSEY
1857–1941

A gate, newel cap and handrail

for R.W.Essex, for Dixcot, Tooting, London, 1897
Pencil and watercolour
780 × 560 mm. / $30\frac{3}{4}$ × 22 in.

Voysey, the supreme graphic designer, made his sheets of working details with the same skill as he designed his wallpapers. These gate details are labelled as for R.W.Essex, the client for Dixcot at Tooting, for which the house and garden layout is illustrated, no. 129. Even with revisions, Mrs Essex did not like Voysey's designs for the house and he resigned as architect.[4]

Voysey used standard gate details over and over again, as part of his economy of labour and paperwork when designing a house and its fittings. Here are the iron hinges with heart-shaped ends and the curving handle which would delight the palm of one's hand, in his characteristic style. Such details, drawn with an almost puritanical restraint, but with just a hint of romanticism, catch the essence of Voysey's style and personality.

220

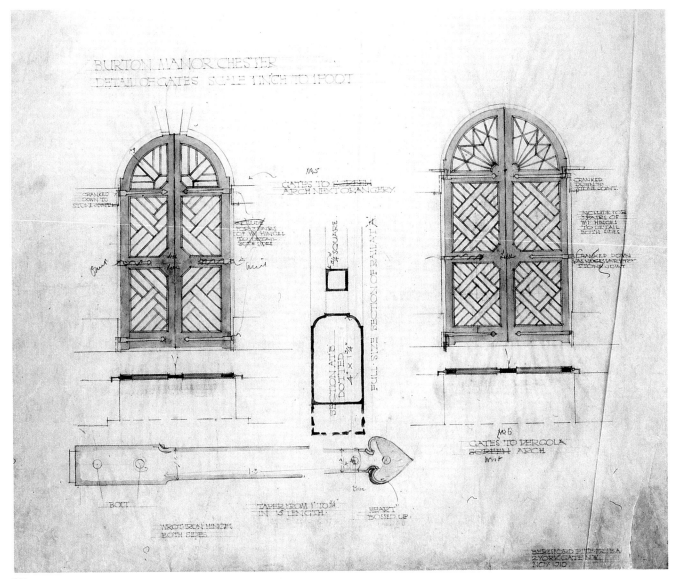

221

221] ARTHUR BERESFORD PITE 1861–1934

Wall-gates

Burton Manor, Wirral, Cheshire, 1910
Pencil with sepia and grey washes on tracing paper
520 × 575 mm. /$20\frac{1}{2}$ × $22\frac{5}{8}$ in.

Most of the twenty-one drawings in the Collection for
Burton Manor are for gate and wall details, which formed
the chief substance of the work carried out there by A.B.Pite.
These are two of the latticed wooden gates, which were all
slightly different in design, made for the garden, with a
working detail of the heart-shaped hinge.

222] H.S.GOODHART-RENDEL 1887–1959

Walls and gates

Broad Oak End, Bramfield, Hertfordshire, 1922
Pen on tracing paper
625 × 560 mm. /$24\frac{5}{8}$ × 22 in.

The walls to be built of brick with Portland stone cappings to
the piers. Three thousand bricks already on the site were to be
used and more obtained from Collier's at Reading if
required. Gate A is of the classically plain variety, in the
manner of a service gate, and gateway B has an ornamental,
Spanish touch.

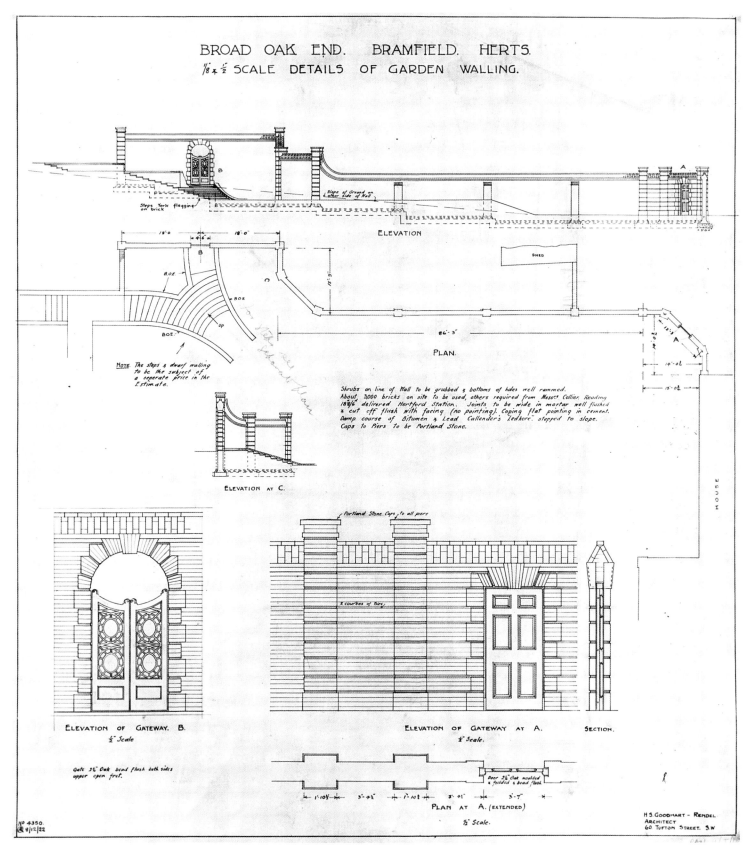

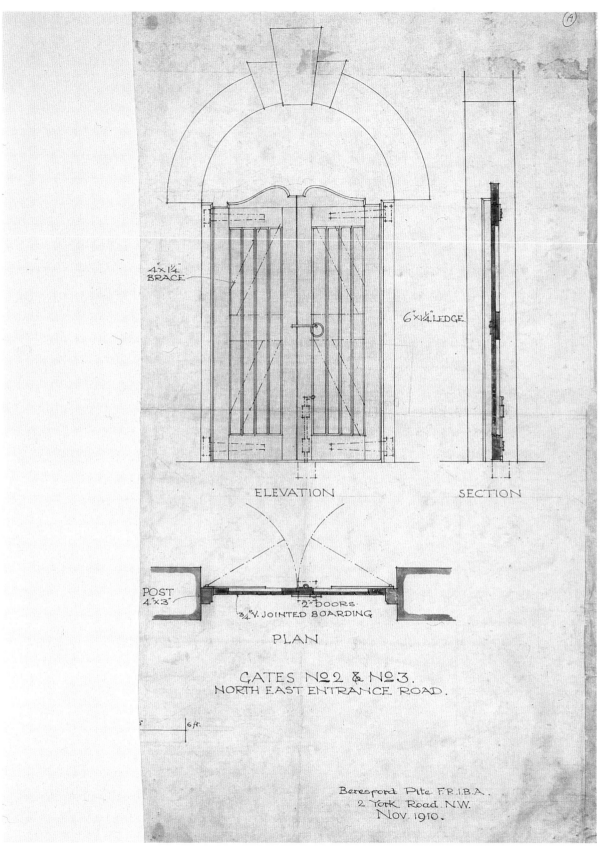

4"x 1¼"
BRACE

6"x 1¼" LEDGE.

ELEVATION

SECTION

POST
4"x 3"

2" DOORS.

¾" V. JOINTED BOARDING

PLAN

GATES Nº 2 & Nº 3.
NORTH EAST ENTRANCE ROAD.

6 ft.

Beresford Pite F.R.I.B.A.
2 York Road. N.W.
Nov. 1910.

266

223] ARTHUR BERESFORD PITE 1861–1934

A screen gate

Burton Manor, Wirral, Cheshire, 1910
Pen with coloured washes on linen
Part of a sheet, left side cut
420 × 230 mm. /16½ × 9 in.

A wooden screen gate (design no. 3) to be set in a walled arch in the boundary of Burton Manor. As can be seen from the cut left-hand side of this sheet, it was part of a larger drawing showing design no. 2 aswell. When the Pite drawings came into the Collection they had been cut to fit the hanging sheets of a storage cabinet; this was probably done in the office, where details such as this would be used over and over again, and adapted to other commissions.

224] CLOUGH WILLIAMS-ELLIS 1883–1978

Gate-piers and gates

Unidentified
Pencil and watercolour
610 × 325 mm. /24 × 12¾ in.

This is a miscellaneous drawing in the Clough Williams-Ellis papers and the whereabouts of the design is unknown. It is however a lively and colourful detail for a green wooden gate between brick piers. The piers are topped with typical Williams-Ellis flamboyant vases of Baroque pedigree. The design comes from his South Eaton Place office so may be for a London garden.

225] CLOUGH WILLIAMS-ELLIS 1883–1978

Yard gates

Possibly for Dalton Hall, Westmorland, 1975
Pencil and crayon
330 × 510 mm. /13 × 20⅛ in.

Clough Williams-Ellis began working to alter Dalton Hall for Mr and Mrs Anthony Mason-Hornby in 1968. He made a semi-circular formal garden in front of the house to link it with its surrounding parkland. The garden was enclosed with a hornbeam hedge, with a pair of gates on the axis of the house portico, leading into the park. The stone used in this drawing leads to the supposition that it was for Dalton, possibly for a pair of extra gates at the end of the scheme. Dalton Hall was Clough Williams-Ellis's last commission, the date of this drawing shows that he did it when he was ninety-two years old, without any diminution of his flair.

224

225

Price with and without the arch for 3 door

Craig y Parc
Gate to Kitchen
Garden at S.E.
Angle.

226] CHARLES EDWARD MALLOWS 1864–1915

A moon gate

Craig y Parc, Pentrych, Cardiff, Gwent, 1913–4
Pencil sketch
265 × 180 mm. /$10\frac{3}{8} \times 7\frac{1}{8}$ in.

One of Mallows' less polished sketches, a detail produced on the spur of the moment for a particular need. Though not an accurate drawing this *Gate to Kitchen Garden at S.E. Angle* is one of his cleverest designs. The drooping curve was beloved of Arts and Crafts designers, and for this heavy, panelled oak gate Mallows has made the curve a semi-circle, and then completed the circle by the oak frame set into the stone arch. The circle thus becomes a clair-voyée, offering vistas in and out of the walled kitchen garden.

Note the drawing inscription: *Price with and without the arch for 3 doors*; the walled kitchen garden, even in 1913, was fast becoming a rarity, an expensive luxury, and a high wall and even higher gateways would be dispensable in favour of the lower wall and gateway of the implied alternatives. The Collection has only six drawings for Craig y Parc and no further garden details. For the complete house and garden design layout by Mallows see no. 121.

227] EDWIN L. LUTYENS 1869–1944

Designs for an iron gate

Orchards, Godalming, Surrey, 1899
Pencil and pen
Three pieces from larger sheets

Two rough preliminaries and a more finished detail for the wrought iron gate to the Dutch Garden at Orchards designed for William and Julia Chance. The more finished sketch is annotated: *Note – The architect is to be consulted as to lock, handle and hinges*. Lutyens was very interested in such details as a result of his study of traditional ironwork in south-west Surrey with Gertrude Jekyll, and the inspirations of many of his designs can be seen in her collection of vernacular artefacts which is in Guildford Museum.

The gate was subsequently built but to a much simpler design than any of these, with a similar central top finial, rather like a small urn, which became a mark of Lutyens' ironwork designs.

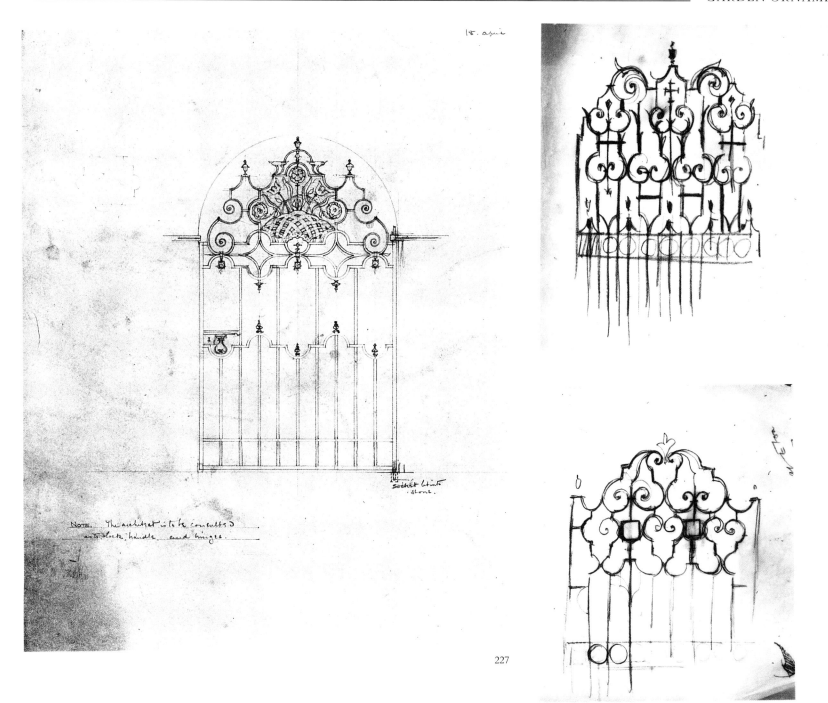

18. april

NOTE. The architect is to be consulted as to locks, handle, and hinges.

socket into stone.

227

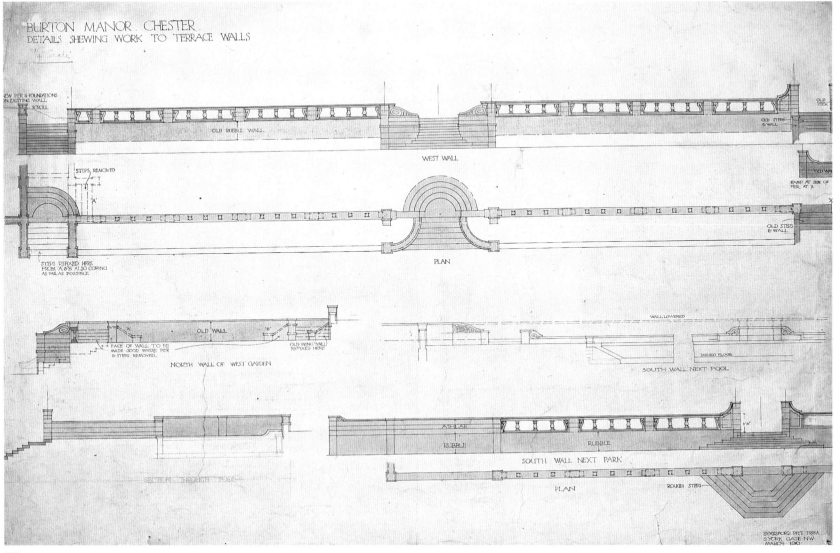

BURTON MANOR. CHESTER.
DETAILS SHEWING WORK TO TERRACE WALLS

228

228] ARTHUR BERESFORD PITE 1861–1934

Terrace walls

Burton Manor, Wirral, Cheshire, 1909
Pen on linen
1010 × 630 mm. /$39\frac{3}{4} × 24\frac{3}{4}$ in.

A fine example of how elegant a detailed drawing for walls and balustrades can be; the walls are to be built in the pink stone quarried in Cheshire. The orange-washed areas are for new work and the grey is already existing. This drawing is one of twenty-three which were part of a fragmented commission, for garden architecture at Burton Manor, extensively altered by Nicholson & Corlette in 1904.

229] ALEXANDER ROOS born *c.*1810

A garden balustrade with dolphins and seahorses

Unidentified, *c.*1835
Sepia pen
152 × 250 mm. /6 × $9\frac{7}{8}$ in.

This drawing by Roos for a garden detail is from a bound volume drawings dated from the 1830s. The volume hints at many mysteries; some of the drawings are especially fine, as this one, and inspired by Roman and Pompeiian decoration, as this balustrade may well be. There are also dainty garlanded ceiling designs in the Adam style; some drawings are annotated in Italian, as would be expected from the artist's Italian background, but some words appear in French, and some of the topographical sketches, including one of a Pompeiian garden are less sophisticated.

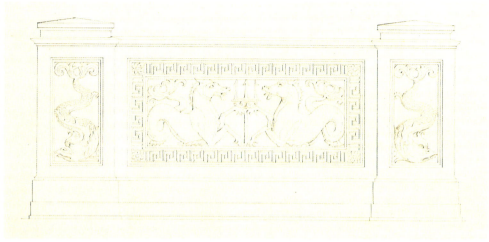

229

230] SIR CHARLES BARRY 1795–1860

Details of a balcony and balustrade

Kingston Lacy, Dorset, 1836
Pen and coloured washes
552 × 400 mm. /$21\frac{3}{4}$ × $15\frac{3}{4}$ in.

One of fifteen drawings relating to the remodelling of Kingston Lacy which Barry carried out for W.J.Bankes MP between 1835–9. This sheet of details for a classical balustrade is signed and dated by Barry, 9 February 1836, though the drawing is of course by an assistant.

The collection holds most of the drawings for Barry's grandest projects, including the Travellers' and Reform clubs and the Houses of Parliament; he applied himself to garden details with the same thoroughness as for the Royal Gallery ceiling or the Reform's serving hatch pulleys. This Kingston Lacy balustrade is an especially nice touch from the great architect as it enhances the garden surroundings of this splendid seventeenth-century house, now owned by the National Trust.

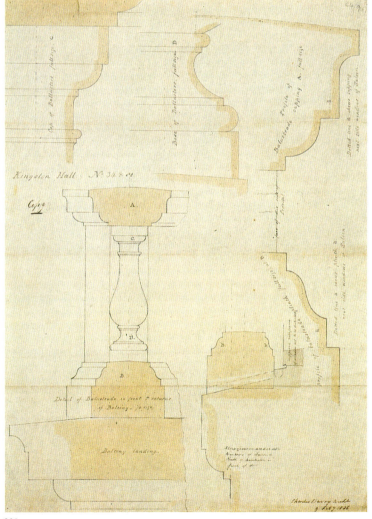

230

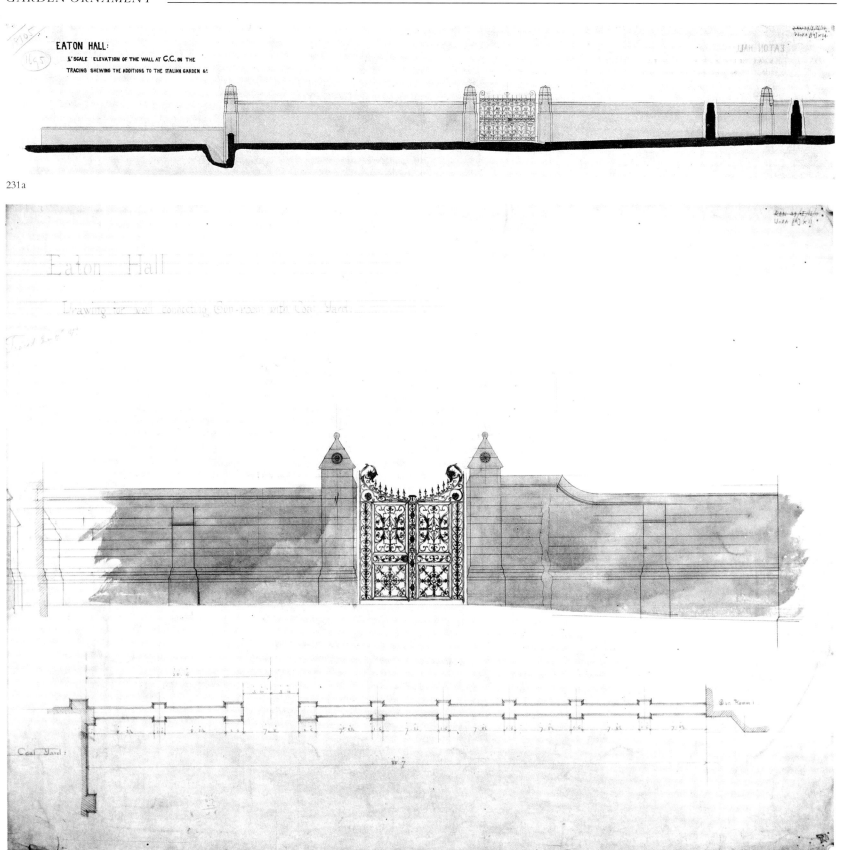

EATON HALL:
¼" SCALE ELEVATION OF THE WALL AT C.C. ON THE
TRACING SHEWING THE ADDITIONS TO THE ITALIAN GARDEN &c

231a

231b

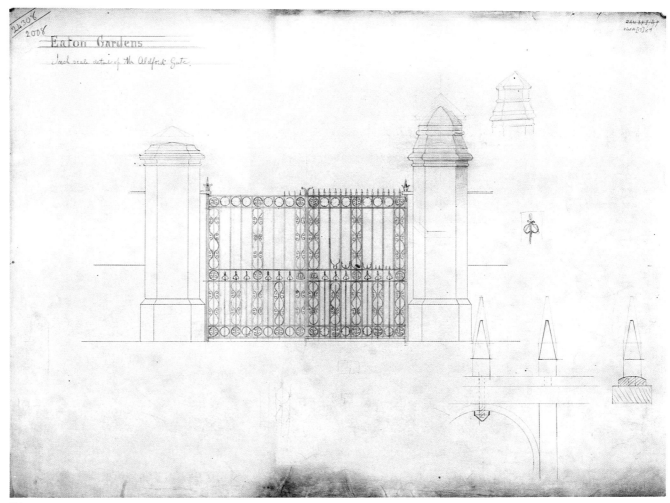

Eaton Gardens

Inch scale details of the Aldford Gate.

231c

231] ALFRED WATERHOUSE 1830–1905
Walls and iron filigree gates

Eaton Hall, Cheshire, *c*.1885
Pen

Even for the architect of the most impressive Victorian Town Halls, of Oxford and Cambridge colleges and the Natural History Museum in London, the re-modelling of Eaton Hall for the Duke of Westminster 1870–83 was one of Waterhouse's most lavish commissions. Almost all he did, with the exception of the chapel, has been subsequently demolished; Waterhouse was not interested in gardens but he did know how to enclose them in the most substantial and inventive ways, when money was no object. These three drawings are from a considerable collection of Eaton Hall details, and they are fine examples of the Victorian Gothic tradition in gates and walls. It was unusual for walls to be 'designed'; the English countryside is adorned with miles of park wallings that have been built and repaired in estate tradition by the estate craftsmen over the centuries. It was only in late Victorian times that the wall became a conscious symbol of the wealth of the newly-rich.

232

232] ALEXANDER ROOS b. *c.*1810

A garden niche to hold a statue

Unidentified *c.*1835
Pencil, pen and watercolour
104 × 167 mm. /$4\frac{1}{8}$ × $6\frac{5}{8}$ in.

Roos had an Italian background and it is thought that he came to London after finishing his studies in Rome in the early 1830s. The scale on this drawing is marked in French and the quality of the detail has something in common with the unidentified French drawings illustrated nos. 240–1. However, so little is known of his life and work that it is impossible to make any positive French connection. This drawing is another, along with nos. 229 and 233 from the bound volume of his designs which was presented to the Collection in 1909.

233] ALEXANDER ROOS b. *c.*1810

A garden balustrade with urns

Unidentified, *c.*1835
Pen, pencil and watercolour
120 × 155 mm. /$4\frac{3}{4}$ × $6\frac{1}{8}$ in.

This balustrade of tile-work of Pompeiian inspiration, and the previous garden niche drawing, are the most discretely garden-like of the Roos drawings, and yet they seem decorative, and more likely ideas for wall paintings. As he was chiefly known for interior decorations during his period of working in England between 1830 and 1858, both these drawings and the evidence of the bound volume of 163 designs, would imply his interest was in painted gardens rather than planted ones.

233

234]   CLAUD PHILLIMORE 1900–86 and
       AUBREY JENKINS 1902–77

Walls with roundels

Knowsley Hall, Lancashire, 1954
Pen and pencil on tracing paper
510 × 760 mm. /20⅛ × 29 in.

Phillimore and Jenkins continued building classical country
houses in England from after the 1939–45 war and into an age
when it was thought such things were no longer being done;
their architecture has been well described in John Martin
Robinson's *The Latest Country Houses*[5] but the gardens were
usually done by someone else (Lanning Roper at the Dower
House, Arundel and Buckhurst, Ascot) or were taken care of
by a good gardening owner.

   However, the partnership had to be included here, and
these impressive walls, for a refurbishment of Knowsley Hall
for Lord Derby in the 1950s, show the competent and
classical kind of design which ensured their success. Most
people would have thought that walls such as these were a
forgotten art in 1954.

235]   ALFRED WATERHOUSE 1830–1905
       PAUL WATERHOUSE 1861–1924

Walls

Britwell Court, Burnham, Buckinghamshire, c.1885
Pen

The second drawing from the 125 by Waterhouse & Son for
Britwell Court to be reproduced here (see no. 201) illustrates
the love of elaborate and decorative walls which was so much
part of Victorian paternalistic ownership. In the late
nineteenth century the wall, which was what the masses in
the outside world saw, became an expression of solid
respectability and wealth as never before.

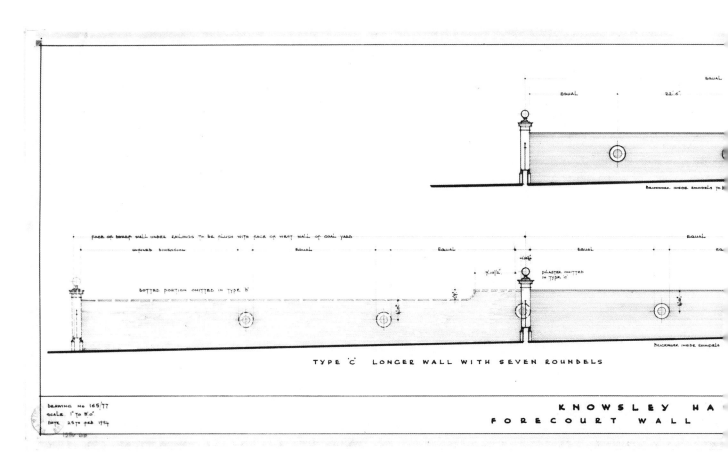

234

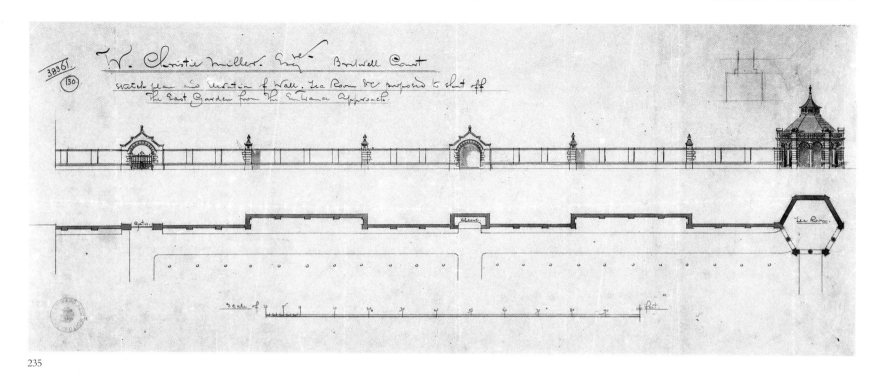

235

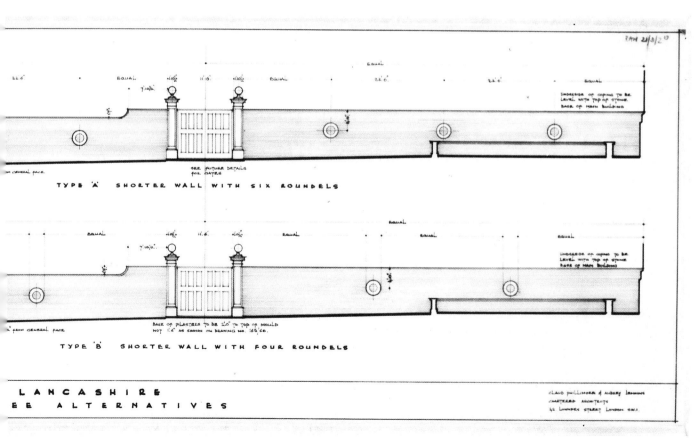

TYPE 'A'   SHORTER WALL WITH SIX ROUNDELS

TYPE 'B'   SHORTER WALL WITH FOUR ROUNDELS

LANCASHIRE
EE ALTERNATIVES

A Hofseds d'flann

Note
Ce jardin contient Petition
un demi arpent.

Jardin du Cercle des Etrangers,
rue de Richelieu, à Paris.

Terrasse.

Coupe sur la longueur du jardin.

Treillage

236] ANONYMOUS FRENCH

Plan of 'Jardin du Cercle des Etrangers'

Rue Richelieu, Paris
Pen and coloured wash
451 × 279 mm. /17¾ × 11 in.

This is the garden where the artist found the flower basket on the right which is illustrated as the circle in the centre of neatly drawn flower beds and walks. It is the most charming Paris garden, overlooked by the house terrace, and protected from its neighbours by high walls. There is a small 'wilderness' at the end, on a higher level, above the formal round pool.

237] ANONYMOUS FRENCH

Design for a corbeille, or trellis flower basket

Unidentified, c. 1750
Pen and coloured wash
330 × 216 mm. /13 × 8½ in.

The drawing is inscribed: *Dessin du Treillages de la Corbeille de fleurs qui je trouve placé dans le jardin de la maison ditte de Cercle . . . Etrangers, rue de Richelieu a Paris*

The plinth of the basket is made of ebony, and the rim is of oak; the 'triangles' of trellis are of chestnut, with an oak strut every six feet to strengthen the basket.

This flower basket is particularly interesting: Repton first illustrated a corbeille or wicker edging for a flower bed in his plan for Mrs Wake at Courteenhall in 1791, and then sprinkled them all over the lawn of the Royal Pavilion at Brighton in 1805. Another version, by Repton, appears at Sheringham, in Mrs Upcher's flower garden (no. 40).

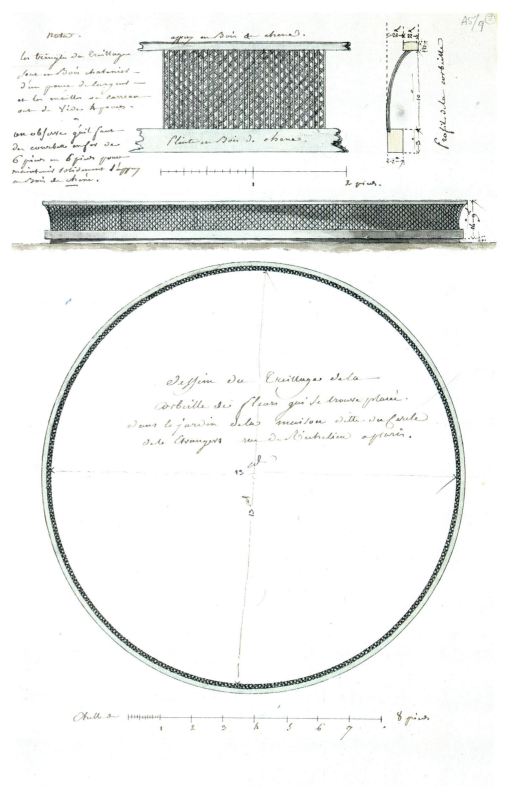

237

238

238] PHILIP HARDWICK 1792–1870

A vase

Hampton Court Palace, *c.* 1810
Pencil and sepia wash
335 × 240 mm. /21 × 9½ in.

Hardwick was a successful architect and surveyor who worked mostly on churches but he also had a great interest in Italian buildings. The Collection has a number of measured drawings from the years he spent in Italy from 1776–9. His drawing skill was evidently put to good use from time to time, as in this detail probably made while he was Clerk of Works at Hampton Court in 1810. He has marked the drawing *removed to Windsor*.

239] HENRY HOLLAND 1745–1806

Treillage design

Carlton House, London, 1787
Sepia pen
f.23 from the Carlton House sketchbook
120 × 190 mm. /4¾ × 7½ in.

Henry Holland was the son of a Fulham builder, who became an architect, married the daughter of Lancelot 'Capability' Brown and then built Carlton House and the Royal Pavilion for the Prince of Wales. This, the only vaguely garden related drawing in the Carlton House sketchbook, is inscribed by Holland: *Carlton House June 1787 Design for the Trelliage next the garden*.

240] UNIDENTIFIED FRENCH

'Façade Principale du Cabinet de Treillage'

Jardin de Tivoly, *c.* 1780
Pen and coloured washes
356 × 238 mm./ 14 × 9½ in.

The pavilion is of an elaborate, typically French design, which makes Henry Holland's sketch for Carlton House (no. 239) look very unsophisticated. The trellis is to be of chestnut, as in the construction of a corbeille (no. 237), and it would seem that the entire pavilion is of wood, rather than partly iron.

Carleton House June 1787
Design for the Trilliage next the garden

239

Façade Principale de la Cabine de
Trillages de Tively.

240

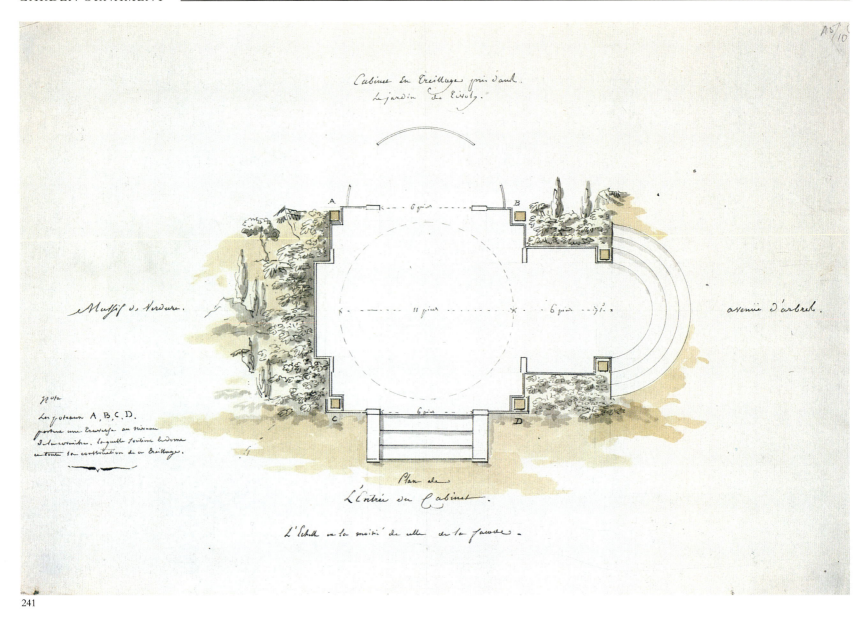

241

241] UNIDENTIFIED FRENCH

A plan for a 'Cabinet de Treillage'

Jardin de Tivoly, *c.* 1780
Pen and coloured washes
238 × 356 mm. /9½ × 14 in.

This plan describes the platform for the trellis pavilion, of
the preceding design. The pavilion is to be surrounded by
planting, which has been partly drawn in elevation. The
pavilion on this platform appears to be set within a woodland
garden or *jardin anglais*, which is shown further in no. 242.

242

242] UNIDENTIFIED FRENCH
A plan and elevation 'pour L'Escalier'

Jardin de Tivoly, *c.*1780
Pen and coloured washes
238 × 356 mm. /9½ × 14 in.

This is the final drawing in a set of five of French origin that are together in the Collection, and appear to be in the same hand. The plan for '*Le Jardin du Cercle des Etrangers*' and the flower basket in the centre of it are illustrated nos. 236 and 237. This drawing shows the view from the Cabinet de Treillage (Jardin de Tivoly) towards the woodland of a *jardin anglais*, the term which the French adopted in the later eighteenth century for a small wild garden which was attached to a formal layout.

These five drawings are of a delightful quality, which seems to add more to their mystery. Might they have come as the portfolio of some young artist or garden designer looking for a job? Or perhaps they were picked up by a travelling architect who liked the designs? The designs are inspiring, especially for the flower basket which was a desirable garden ornament.

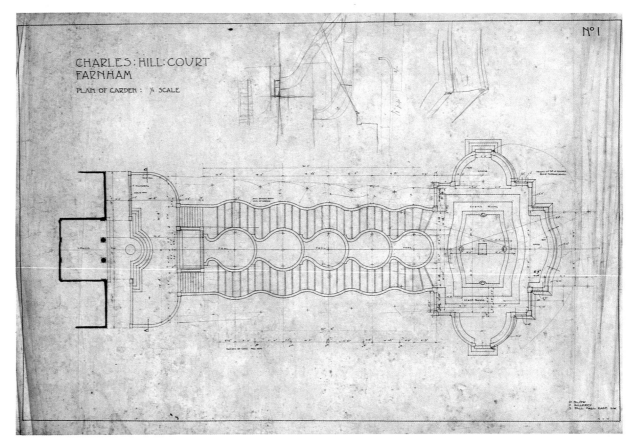

243a

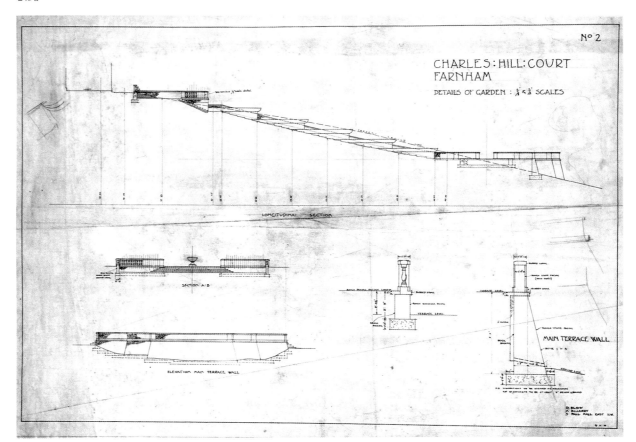

243b

Water

243] DETMAR BLOW 1867–1939

Waterfall pools

Charles Hill Court, Elstead, Surrey, 1900
(a) Plan
(b) Elevation
Pen and pencil on tracing paper

Blow was a devoted Arts and Crafts man, who began his career by accompanying the intermittently mad Ruskin on a journey across France, and ended it in a tumultuous relationship with the 2nd Duke of Westminster, the fabulous 'Bendor'. In between he built his own lovely house and garden, Hilles, Harescombe in Gloucestershire and worked in three houses in the Woodford valley in Wiltshire (Wilsford, Lake and Heale) which all have stunning gardens. His ingenuity and skill is clearly evident from this waterfall pool; this is part of a small amount of his material which has recently come into the Collection. He is not a well-known architect and seemed always rather too much in need of money to be able to spend much time on garden design. The best account of his personality and career is given by Clive Aslet in *The Last Country Houses*.[6]

244] EDWARD BRANTWOOD MAUFE 1883–1974

A garden pool

Shepherd's Hill, near Buxted, East Sussex, 1927
Pen on tracing paper

This is an exceptional design for a pool, showing the assurance with which Maufe, chiefly a church architect and most notably the architect of Guildford Cathedral, can adapt paving pattern to a garden pool. He has also adapted the traditions of design with stone or marble to concrete, coloured with Blue Cementone and cut with 'full $\frac{1}{2}''$ white joints' for the base of the pool, which has York stone edging, The pool was built at the edge of a paved terrace and jutted out into a long lawn flanked by parallel paved paths.

Edward Maufe's first country house and garden, for Kelling Hall in Norfolk, is illustrated nos. 135–7. Shepherd's Hill was one of his few later houses, from between the wars, when he did not usually do detailed designs for the garden, as at Kelling. He built his own house and garden at Yaffle Hill, Broadstone, Dorset in 1929.

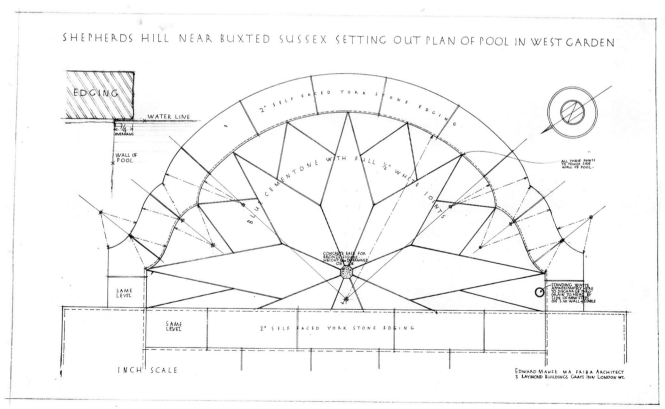

Tregothnan.

Design for Garden Seat at end of Walk,
between Screen Wall and Conservatory.

286

245

Garden Seats

245] LEWIS VULLIAMY 1791–1871

A Gothic seat

Tregothnan, Cornwall, 1850
Pencil and wash
560 × 380 mm. /22 × 15 in.

The exquisite drawing for a Victorian Gothic garden seat is marked: *Design for Garden Seat at end of Walk between Screen wall and Conservatory*. It is a new addition to ten drawings for this Gothic lodge in the Collection. Vulliamy was not known for garden work, but he did have one significant gardening client; he built Dorchester House on Park Lane (subsequently demolished to make way for the hotel) for Robert Staynor Holford, who began Westonbirt Arboretum in Gloucestershire in 1829. Vulliamy also designed some garden buildings for Westonbirt in Gloucestershire.

246] CLOUGH WILLIAMS-ELLIS 1883–1978

A fluted seat

Oare House, Pewsey, Wiltshire, c.1930
Pencil and coloured washes
410 × 510 mm. /16$\frac{1}{8}$ × 20$\frac{1}{8}$ in.

This wonderfully comfortable-looking seat, almost a couch, semi-circular and set in a yew-hedged bay, was part of the commission for Oare House for Geoffrey Fry. The seat, to be cast in concrete, has a four-foot high curved back and short seat, and it stands on a semi-circular plinth paved in a fanlike pattern. There appears to be no other design quite like it, even from Clough Williams-Ellis's inventive mind.

247] JOHN HUNGERFORD POLLEN 1820–1902

A classical bench

Reigate Priory, Surrey, 1898
Pencil and coloured washes
180 × 330 mm. /7$\frac{1}{8}$ × 13 in.

John Hungerford Pollen has pencilled on this drawing *Proposed seat end of Long Alley, Priory*. He designed armorials, stained glass, fireplaces and other interior details for Lady Henry Somerset at Reigate Priory in the 1890s. This seat was built in a rather simplified design in brick and stone, and two other seats were built in the sunken garden.

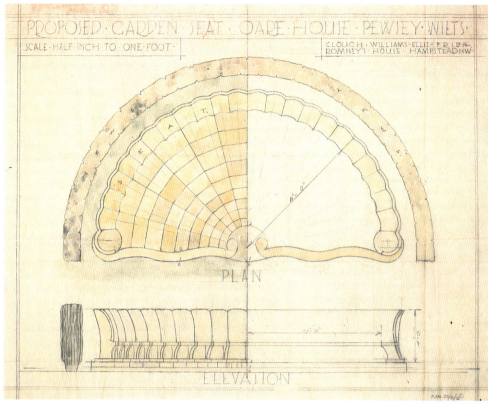

246

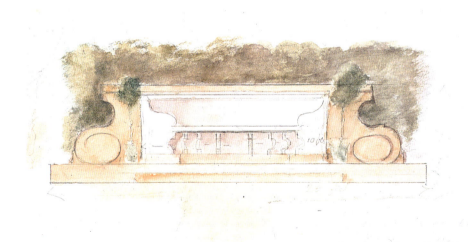

247

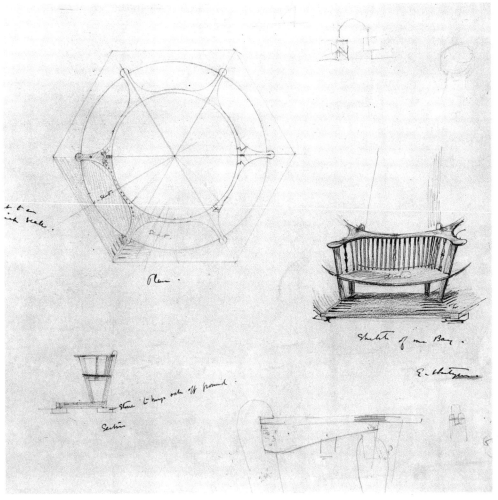

248

248]   EDWIN L. LUTYENS 1869–1944

A garden seat around a tree

Gravetye Manor, near East Grinstead, Sussex, 1898
Pencil and pen on tracing paper
380 × 580 mm. /15 × $22\frac{7}{8}$ in.

Sketch and measured plan for a seat to go around a tree for
William Robinson's garden at Gravetye. This drawing is
marked *Tracing sent 19/3/98 to Mr Robinson*. Gertrude Jekyll
introduced Lutyens to William Robinson, who was rich and
at the height of his gardening fame, in the hope that Lutyens
would be given work in connection with Gravetye, the
Tudor house and 1,000 acre estate which Robinson had
bought in 1885. Lutyens had stayed at Gravetye in April of
the previous year, 1897, and wrote to Mrs Gerard Streatfield,
for whom he was building Fulbrook at Elstead in Surrey, that
Gravetye was magnificent, carpeted with daffodils, and that
he was especially enchanted with owls that used a nesting box
near his bedroom window. The garden seat was the only
direct commission from Robinson, almost a year after this
visit.

249]   CHARLES HOLDEN 1875–1960

A garden bench around a tree

Harmer Green, Welwyn, Hertfordshire, c. 1910
Pencil
127 × 200 mm. /5 × $7\frac{7}{8}$ in.

Charles Holden was the distinguished architect of great
hospitals (e.g. Bristol Royal Infirmary), First World War
Memorials, London University in Bloomsbury and London
Underground Stations (including London Transport's head-
quarters at 55 Broadway in Westminster). His career started a
decade later than most of the Arts and Crafts architects and he
never had a country house practice. However, he still shared
the love of gardens and using his hands which his fellows
expressed in their work, but the only garden he is known to
have designed was his own, in a familiar axial and well
ordered style, and only faint sketches of this survive. This
little sketch, from a loose scrap of paper, represents a
momentary idea put on paper, perhaps to remind him to
build the seat when he next had an afternoon in the garden.

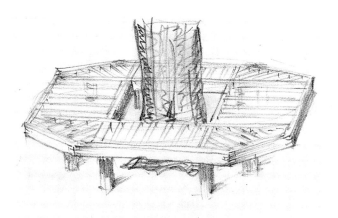

249

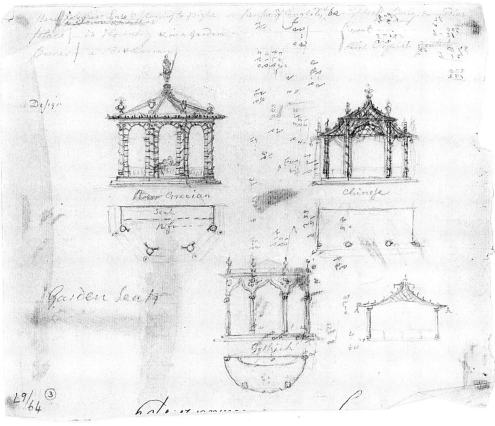

250

251

250] WILLIAM NEWTON 1735–90

Grecian, Gothick and Chinese seats for a nobleman, c. 1765

Pencil
160 × 190 mm. /6¼ × 7½ in.

The Collection acquired a considerable number of drawings by this little known late eighteenth-century architect in 1891. This is one of six designs for garden buildings, which were thus a very minor interest of Newton's. These seat sketches have an instant appeal across the years, with the calculations and alterations fresh from the moment they were made.

The drawing is inscribed by Newton: 'Use – Pleasure & ease & pleasing of sight ... therefore of Quality must be Lightness, Lively, Commodius [sic] Place – in the Country, in a Garden ... (therefore) Rural Owner – a Nobleman ... (therefore) rich, Elegant, Gentile.' (Rich and Gentile, the old spelling for genteel, have been crossed out.)

251] WALTER H. GODFREY 1881–1961

A trellis seat

Ascott, Wing, Buckinghamshire, c. 1914
Pen

Walter Godfrey absorbed the Picturesque Tudor tradition from Devey's work (e.g. his additions to Old Surrey Hall in south-east Surrey), but was extremely interested in garden designs. He wrote a book, *Gardens in the Making*, published in 1914, essentially re-stating Reginald Blomfield's taste in formal gardens of traditional inspiration, from *The Formal Garden in England*, which had appeared over twenty years earlier. Both this seat and Godfrey's parterres for Ascott (see no. 181) were illustrated in his book. The gardens at Old Surrey Hall and at Herstmonceux Castle may also owe something to him, but at the time of writing, his garden plans are still in family ownership and no detailed study of his work has been made.

Flower Baskets and Sundials

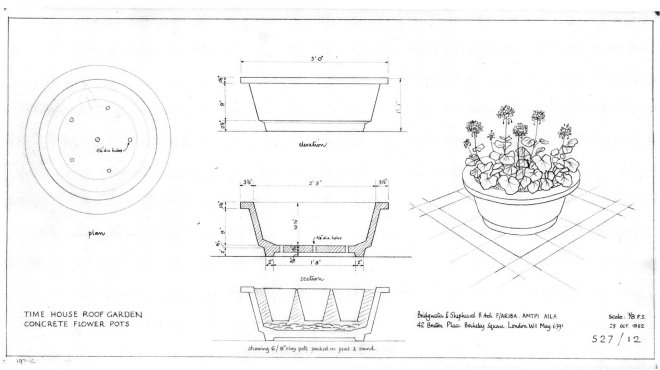

252

252] PETER SHEPHEARD *b.*1913

Flower pots

Time and Life Building, New Bond Street, London, 1952
Pencil on tracing paper
290 × 530 mm. /$11\frac{3}{8}$ × $20\frac{7}{8}$ in.

A practical concrete container for flower pots for the roof
garden of Time and Life Building. The drawing is a model of
a constructional drawing for garden details, giving all the
necessary information and instuctions for use, and incor-
porating the small perspective that conveys the idea to the
layman i.e. the board member who is likely to be authorizing
the expenditure.

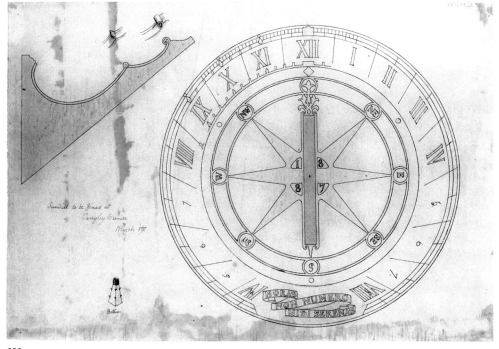

253

253] PHILIP WEBB 1831–1915

Face for a sundial

Great Tangley Manor, Wonersh, Surrey, 1887
Pen and coloured washes on linen
430 × 630 mm. / $16\frac{7}{8}$ × $24\frac{3}{4}$ in.

Webb made additions and alterations to Great Tangley, one of Surrey's most impressive half-timbered houses dating from 1584. His work here is now recognized as one of the first attempts to faithfully reproduce the spirit of the old building and the details of its craftsmanship, thus lighting the spark of the Arts and Crafts Movement. His most notable addition to the house was a covered entrance way for which the drawing is in the Collection, and which was imitated by Ernest Newton. The young Edwin Lutyens was also greatly influenced by Webb's work here.

The sundial, together with Webb's study of tulip heads (no. 86) is a bow to the importance that gardens and flowers were to have for the Movement, from the consummate craftsmen, William Morris's own architect, who was its prime mover.

254] EDWIN L. LUTYENS 1869–1944

Sheet of sketches for a sundial

Woodside, Chenies, Buckinghamshire, 1893
Pen, pencil and green wash
2125 × 560 mm. / 71 × 22 in.

Woodside was the first garden formally designed in partnership with Gertrude Jekyll. The main feature is a descending terrace walk, flanked by flower borders and yew hedges, from the house down to the River Chess. Lutyens made modest alterations to the house for Adeline, Duchess of Bedford, to fit in the garden design. The sundial survives in good condition on one of the platforms of the walk.

This sheet contains a full-size section of the moulding profile at the top of the column, a $\frac{1}{2}''$ to a foot scale plan and a sketch of the sundial. Lutyens' handwritten NB reads: 'To be in Portland stone standing on 2 steps. The upper step shaped on plan. Turned column. On the cap is carved the motto *Che sara sara*. On the *east side* centrally the word *che*. On the south side *sara*, on the West side *sara*. On the north side the cap will be left plain. On the north side in place of Dial will be carved the legend *I tell of none but Sunny Hours*.'

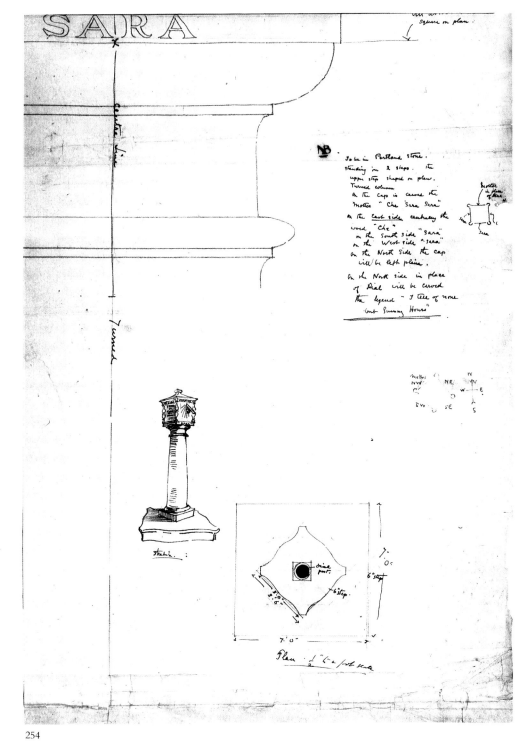

254

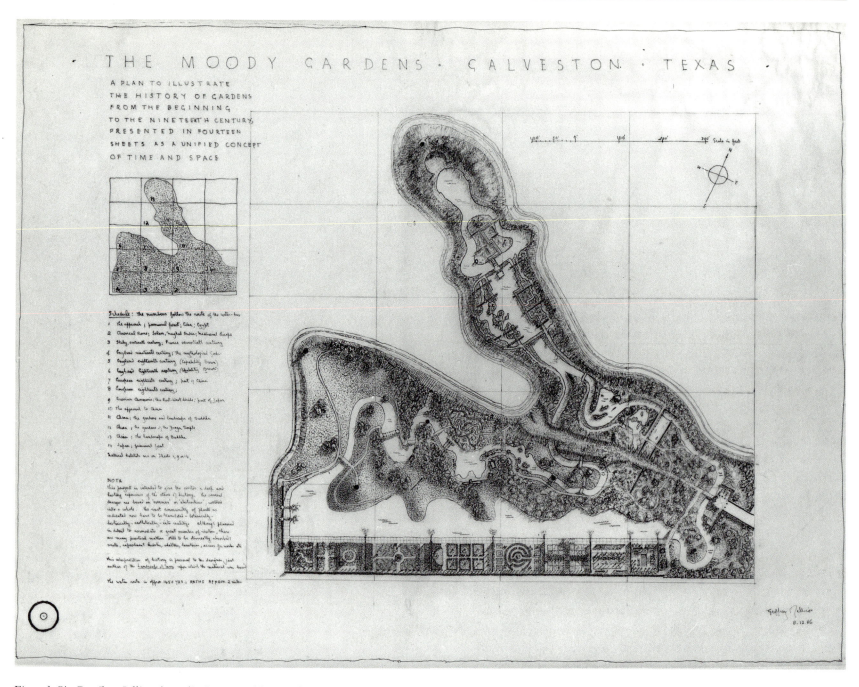

Fig. 37] Sir Geoffrey Jellicoe's preliminary grid layout for the Moody Gardens, Galveston, Texas.

9

TOWARDS THE TWENTY-FIRST CENTURY
Geoffrey Jellicoe's Moody Gardens

The measured drawings and perspectives of the Italian villa gardens which Geoffrey Jellicoe made with J.C. 'Jock' Shepherd in 1925, were the starting point of his career.[1] He remembers how he enjoyed the feel of those gardens, how measuring and pacing them taught him about scale and proportion, and he acknowledges that their beautiful shapes emerging on the paper as he drew them, have stayed with him for the rest of his life. Some of the drawings for *Italian Gardens of the Renaissance* have been illustrated in Chapter 6, and all of the originals are in the Drawings Collection. In many ways these drawings for the Moody Gardens at Galveston, Texas, are the corollary to that wonderful company of Boboli, Medici, Gamberaia, d'Este and the rest; in these drawings Sir Geoffrey offers his personal interpretation of the history of the gardens and landscapes of our world, which have been his abiding passion for most of this century. He wanted his first drawings and these, for what, in his eighty-ninth year he regards as his last large commission, to be housed together in the Collection. This wonderful acquisition allows me an inspirational ending to this book.

The preliminary grid layout of the Moody Gardens (fig. 37) is inscribed by Sir Geoffrey as follows: *A Plan to illustrate the history of gardens from the Beginning to the Nineteenth Century, presented in fourteen sheets as a unified concept of time and space*. This complete set of originals in black pen on tracing paper, all measuring 720×955 mm. ($28\frac{3}{8} \times 37\frac{5}{8}$ in.) were drawn throughout 1986. An additional drawing of the entire site showing the relationship of the gardens to the west landscape, dated June 1985 is also in the Collection.

The site for this project is among the sands and marshes of the coast of the Gulf of Mexico; it is a water park, with the waterways contained and protected by a system of dykes and locks, and the water-bus is the intended mode of visitor-transport. The water-bus route travels anti-clockwise and is just over three-quarters of a mile; the land path is two miles long. Sir Geoffrey has arranged his detailed drawings in the sequence followed by the water-bus, which relate to the grid plan as follows:

1 The approach; primaeval forest: Eden; Egypt
2 Classical Rome; Islam: Mughal India and Medieval Europe
3 Italy, sixteenth century; France, seventeenth century
4 England, nineteenth century; The mythological gods
5 England, eighteenth century; Capability Brown
6 England, eighteenth century; Capability Brown
7 European eighteenth century; part of China
8 European eighteenth century
9 Russian Chinoiserie; the East-West divide; part of Japan
10 The Approach to China
11 China; the gardens and landscapes of Buddha
12 China; the gardens of the Dragon Temple
13 China; the landscape of Buddha
14 Japan; primaeval forest

Sir Geoffrey has made final additional notes:

This project is intended to give the visitor a deep and lasting experience of the ethos of history. The several designs are based on 'essences' or 'abstractions', welded into a whole. The vast community of plants as indicated now have to be translated – botanically – historically – aesthetically – into reality. Although planned in detail to accommodate a great number of visitors there are many practical matters still to be discreetly absorbed: seats, refreshment kiosks, shelters, lavatories, access for works etc.

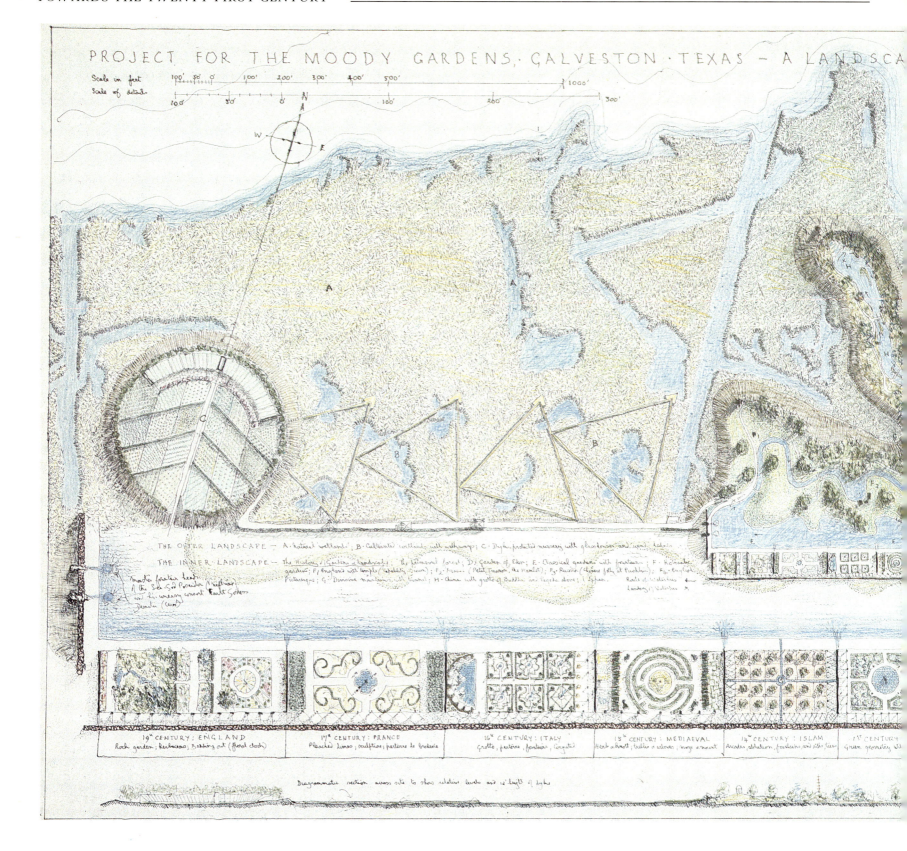

PROJECT FOR THE MOODY GARDENS, GALVESTON · TEXAS — A LANDSCA

Scale in feet
Scale of detail

THE OUTER LANDSCAPE — A. natural wetlands; B. Cultivated woodlands with walkways; C. Dyke-protected nursery with glasshouses and semi-tropics

THE INNER LANDSCAPE — the History; (Gardens & landscapes); the primaeval forest; D. Garden of Eden; E. Classical gardens with fountains; F. Reticulate garden; F¹ England with temple (reputedly Green); F². Manor (Petit Trianon, the hamlet); F³ Russia (chinese folly at Pushkin); F⁴ English Picturesque; G· Dinosaur mountains with tunnel; H. China with grotto of Buddha and Pagoda above; I. Japan.

19ᵗʰ CENTURY : ENGLAND
Rock garden; herbaceous; Bedding out (floral clock)

17ᵗʰ CENTURY : FRANCE
Pleached limes; sculptures; parterre de broderie

16ᵗʰ CENTURY : ITALY
Grotto, parterre, fountain, longata

15ᵗʰ CENTURY : MEDIAEVAL
Herb a mott; trellis & arbours; mays a mount

14ᵗʰ CENTURY : ISLAM
Arcades, ablution, fountains and silks; trees

13ᵗʰ CENTURY
Green geometry

Diagrammatic section across site to show relative levels and 12' length of dyke

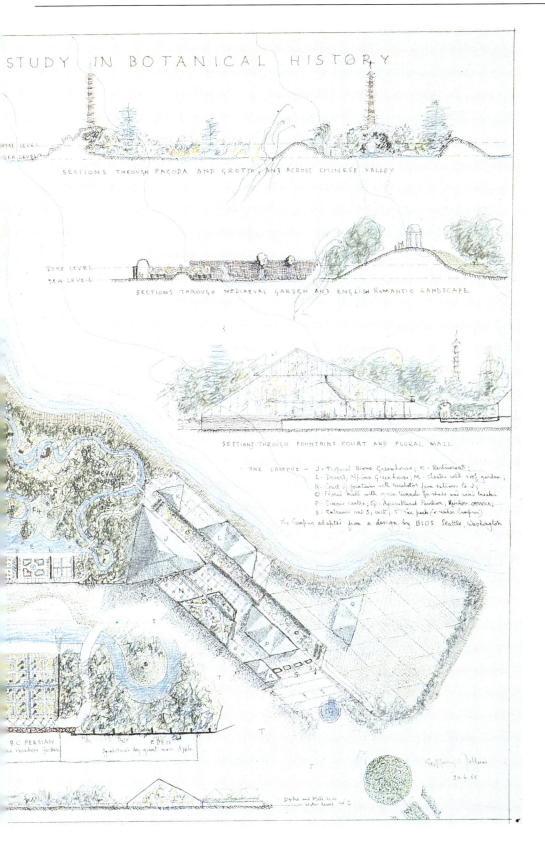

STUDY IN BOTANICAL HISTORY

DYKE LEVEL
SEA LEVEL

SECTIONS THROUGH PAGODA AND GROTTO AND ACROSS CHINESE VALLEY

DYKE LEVEL
SEA LEVEL

SECTIONS THROUGH MEDIAEVAL GARDEN AND ENGLISH ROMANTIC LANDSCAPE

SECTIONS THROUGH FOUNTAINS COURT AND FLORAL MALL

THE CAMPUS — J. Tropical Biome Greenhouse; K. Restaurant;
L. Desert, Alpine Greenhouse; M. Theatre with roof garden;
N. Court of fountains with escalator from entrance to J;
O. Floral mall with ..... for shade and .....;
P. Science centre; Q. Agricultural Pavilion; ..... service;
S. Cafeteria and 3 .....; T. Sea park (or water campus)
the campus adapted from a design by BIOS Seattle, Washington

B.C. PERSIAN
12 Paradise Gardens

E. DEN
..... key giant moss Apple

Dyke and Mall level
Water level 12'0

255]

The Moody Gardens:
Project for the West Landscape, June 1985

This preliminary drawing for the whole shoreland site is reproduced here in colour, though the original is in pen on tracing paper and the same format as the other drawings. Sir Geoffrey believes that attractive and 'user-friendly' drawings are an important link between the designer and the visitors to his gardens; this is an example of the prints that he has hand-coloured for public display at the Gardens.

The designed-sequence of gardens are to be seen at the right-hand (eastern) end of this plan, with the Great Glasshouse which is the visitor centre, and the Great Dyke, marked N, hatched as the protection to the gardens.[2] This drawing further shows that much of the site is to be conserved as wetland. Extending westwards from the Gardens Sequence is a series of elevated walkways of triangular pattern which create an alternative route (the direct route is along the southern boundary) to the protected nurseries, glasshouses and propagation beds, which are the 'workshop' of the gardens.

This mammoth and imaginative project is intended to be linked with the book that Geoffrey and Susan Jellicoe published in 1975, *The Landscape of Man*. This was a wide-ranging study of the mythological landscapes and the gardens we have loved since the world began; but to those who knew Geoffrey and Susan Jellicoe it was also a record of their travels and perceptions. Susan Jellicoe had a profound knowledge of Persian gardens and was part-author of a book on Mughul gardens, and she was a brilliant photographer of all her husband's works; they had been behind the Iron Curtain, to the Middle East and Far East, as prime movers of the International Federation of Landscape Architects, Geoffrey had worked on schools and hospitals in Zambia after the war and in the West Indies in the 1960s. He knew and admired Ben Nicholson, Henry Moore, Joan Miró and Roberto Burle Marx; he had tracked the inspirations of Einstein, Edmund Burke, Jung and Grant Allen's *Physiological Aesthetics* (1877); he had designed landscapes to respond to power-generation, particle-physics at Harwell Research Station, cement winning in Derbyshire and new town development at Hemel Hempstead. He had made gardens for King George VI and Queen Elizabeth and the Memorial Landscape to President John F. Kennedy at Runnymede in Surrey. A fragment of all these aspects was somewhere in *The Landscape of Man*, and finds an echo in these design drawings.

The detailed designs for the Moody Gardens are reproduced in sequence on the following pages.

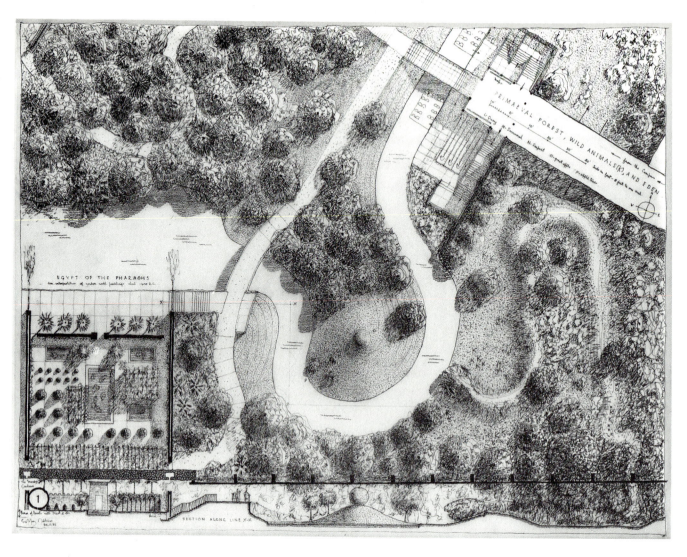

256]

1. Primaeval forest, wild animals and Eden

This is the first, easternmost, section of the garden; the wide promenade approach leading from the Greenhouse Visitor Centre and campus is shown in the top right hand corner. It leads to the landing-stage, where the water-buses are drawn up; the path continues via the Garden of Eden, across a bridge to the Egyptian garden, so that visitors on foot also see the gardens in the correct sequence.

The curving tongue of land recalls the serpent's head, here with a giant apple form for an eye; Geoffrey Jellicoe explored this theme with a proposal for a serpentine mound in Hyde Park, which would be a companion shape for the Serpentine itself and use spoil from the Park Lane underground car parks.[3] He also created this primitive form for the lake at Sutton Place in Surrey, which was to be presided over by a Henry Moore sculpture.

The water-bus passes through Eden, to the landing promenade at *Egypt of the Pharaohs – An interpretation of garden wall paintings about 1400 BC*. The garden is square – 'the symbol of reason ... the pure creation of man alone'[4] – which seems to appear on earth first as the base for the pyramids.

296

257]

2. *Classical Rome; Islam: Mughal India; Medieval Europe*

The water-bus approaches from the left; the garden of Classical Rome is *An abstract from the House of the Yettii at Pompeii*. The elevation drawn at the bottom of the sheet shows the covered peristyle (A) surrounding the small garden of square pools and fountains (B).

The next garden occupies a rectangular space: *The 17th century gardens of India and Kashmir, echoing the Persian garden carpet, are the majestic culmination of the symbolism of the Persian Paradise Garden*; here are the crossing waters of the rivers of heaven and earth and square beds of rich colour and pattern.

There is a central pavilion with a couch symbolizing the leisured enjoyment of these gardens; Geoffrey Jellicoe wrote that 'like one of the magic carpets of the Arabian nights' the forms and delights of these gardens flew west to Granada and the Alhambra, and to cast their sympathetic influence over all the gardens of our western world'.

In contrast, the medieval garden is introspective and defensive; a maze baulks the way to heaven, the pleasure gardens are fenced, piety is implicit in the herbal beds and the 'moist turf seat' must be the garden's hair shirt.

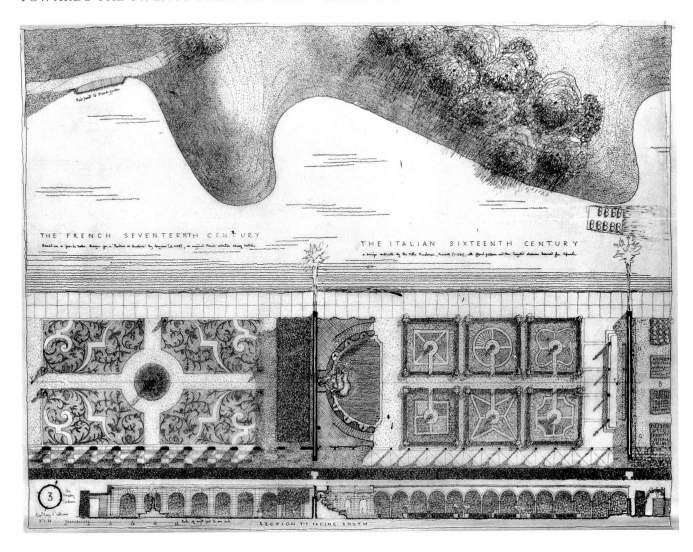

258]

3. *The Italian sixteenth century; the French seventeenth century*

The water-bus appears to be accelerating away from the medieval gloom into the light of the Renaissance. The Italian sixteenth-century garden design is motivated by the Villa Piccolomini at Frascati of *c.*1560 with flower-patterns of symbolic shapes, and the water feature is guarded by caryatids inspired by those in the garden of the Farnese Palace, Caprarola. The caryatids are of human scale and celebrate the essential humanism of the Italian Renaissance garden triumph.

The French seventeenth-century garden is a box *broderie* based on a pre-Le Nôtre design by Jacques Boyceau, whose *Traité du Jardinage* was published in 1638, a few years after his death; he was a gentleman gardener, a courtier, who worked on the Luxembourg Gardens for Marie de Medici.

298

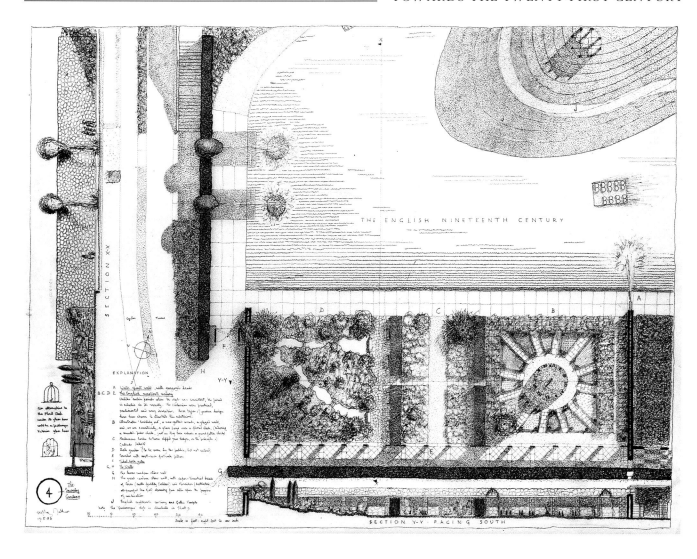

259]

4. The English nineteenth century

The last of the formal gardens reflects the eclectism of the Victorian garden in England. Three kinds of design are used here: (B) has segmental beds for 'bedding-out' around a central floral clock covered with a glass dome 'as an eccentricity'. (*This parodies a mantle clock just as Big Ben echoes a grandfather clock.*) Garden (C) is the double herbaceous border between yew hedges planted in the style of Gertrude Jekyll, and (D) is the Rock Garden, to be seen but not entered by the visitors.

The bottom left-hand corner of the sheet shows the tidal lock-gate (F) which controls the water within the gardens sequence area. (H) is the Great Random Stone Wall, also shown in section x-x, which guards this western end of the gardens; it is adorned with giant heads of Ceres and Poseidon who survey our progress through the centuries.

The water-bus is nearing the farther bank, where the gothic Temple of eighteenth-century England looks over the water from its hill.

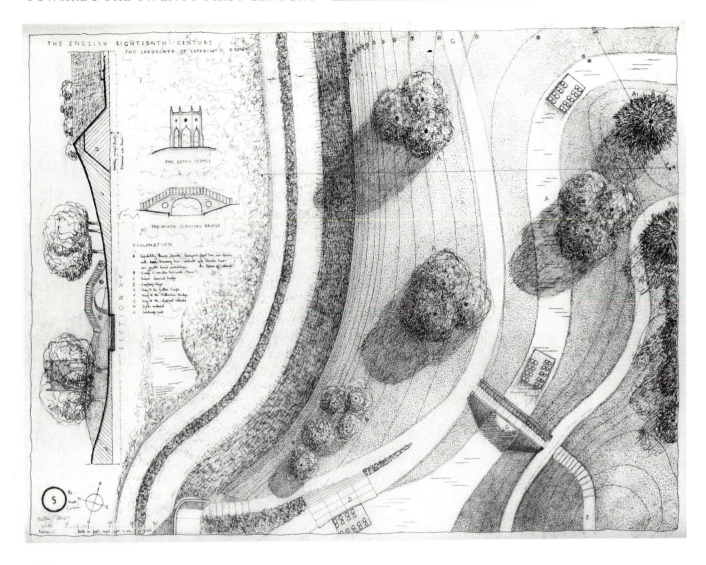

260]

5. *The English eighteenth century: the landscape of Capability Brown*

The waterway sweeps northwards through a Brownian landscape of gentle undulations, shaven lawns and clumps of hardwood trees with clipped 'browsing lines'. The water-bus passes beneath the minor classical bridge (C) which is illustrated in elevation; the Gothic temple is also shown in elevation – it is inspired by the recently-restored Gothick tent at Painshill in Surrey, one of the most evocative ornaments of

Charles Hamilton's Picturesque garden.

The sweeping contours of this drawing and the next, the shadowed clumps of trees and the details of buildings here, and on the following two sheets, show Sir Geoffrey's mastery of his native English landscape style. All this has been as much a part of his designer's *equipage* as the Italian villa gardens, though of course the scale is quite different.

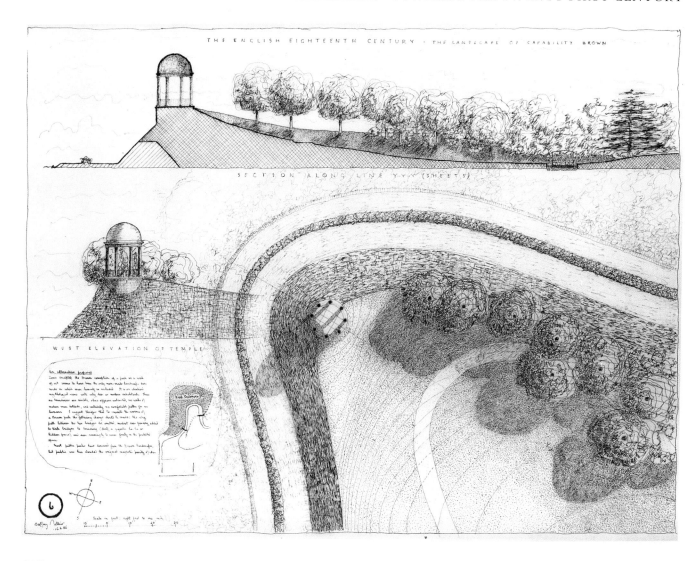

261]

6. *The English eighteenth century: the landscape of Capability Brown*

The water-bus does not enter this extreme western corner of the garden, which is dominated by a domed temple, or rotunda, on an exaggerated site above the garden perimeter.

At the bottom left-hand corner of the drawing is a note for a suggested alteration: *An attractive proposal*, to remove the walkway that is shown and devote this corner of the landscape park to a herd of deer. Sir Geoffrey points out that the 'original majesty purity' of the English landscape idea was man's creation of a sweeping panorama in which he himself played no part, and animals were the only living ornaments. It is suggested that this part of the landscape garden should be reserved for the deer, that appear to roam freely, but would be constrained by the garden boundaries and discreet fencing.

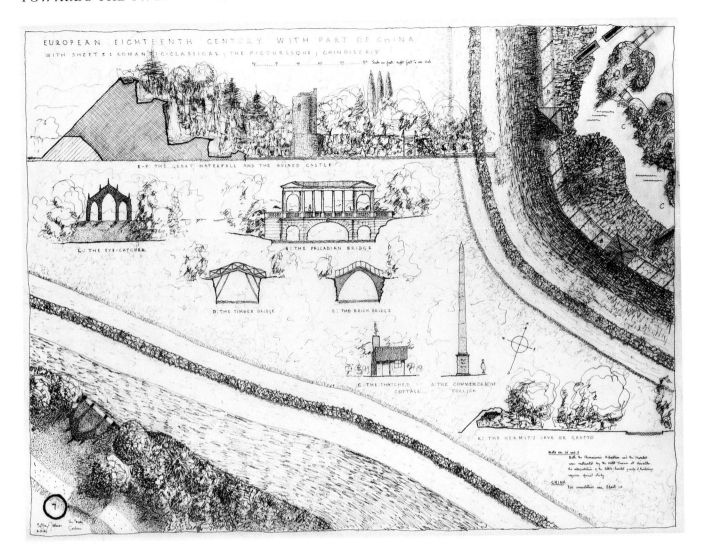

262]

7. *European eighteenth century with part of China*

This sheet sounds confusing and requires careful explanation: this is deep into the 'alligator's jaw' between the two areas of the garden. The bottom of the sheet shows the northern boundary of the Brownian landscape, which is now becoming the Picturesque, with its sham-castle eye-catcher against the sky at (L). At the opposite corner of the sheet is the edge of the 'upper jaw' of the gardens, devoted to the Oriental. But this part of China is fortuitously in view, for it acknowledges

the influence of Chinoiserie in English eighteenth-century taste.

The central part of the drawing, the area of water, is used for detailed drawings of the buildings that both romantically and classically minded designers brought into their landscapes. The sites for most of these are identified on the next sheet, which enters the heartland of man's garden making.

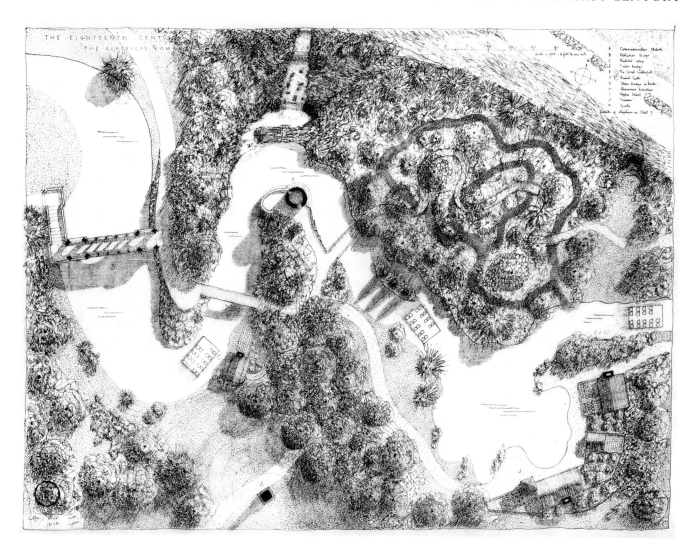

263]

8. *The eighteenth century: the Classical – Romantic*

Here the water-buses travel slowly around the meanders for there is much to see. The water approach from the left of the sheet, the west, is under the splendid Palladian bridge (derived from Wilton House, Wiltshire) and around a tight bend passing the Thatched Cottage on the right bank. The landform of the south bank is now more extreme, with deeper dells and thickly planted hillocks; the waterway is closely planted and becomes shaded, shadowy and (hopefully) faintly terrifying, in preparation for the Ruined Castle

(F) on the promontory. This is a journey which begins in the smooth open waters of the classical calm, and ends amidst the dark pools and inlets of the Romantic imagination, at its extreme in the craze for Chinese pagodas and pavilions and furniture at the end of the eighteenth century.

Much of the north bank land here is occupied by the Chinoiserie Arboretum, to be filled with the first rhododendrons, bamboos, kalmias, wisterias, honeysuckles and jasmines that were brought out to the west.

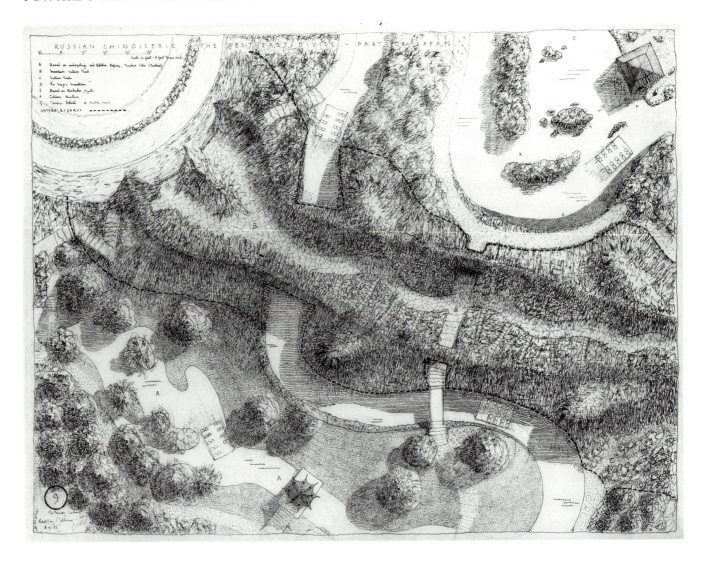

264]

9. *Russian Chinoiserie; the east-west divide; part of Japan*

This is also a complex area, at the very core of the garden. The area (A) represents the island dotted lake of Tsarskoye Selo near Leningrad; then the water-bus follows around a tight hairpin meander into the shadow of the east-west divide, which is in fact a Nature Trail along the spine of the garden, which leads directly back eastwards to the entrance. For the water-bus there is a dark tunnel under this 'divide' which emerges into the land of the rising sun, Japan. The top right hand corner of the drawing shows the features of the garden of Kinkaku-ji, Kyoto, the paradise garden for Buddha to walk in; the name means Golden Pavilion, which is in the corner, marked (F) half standing in the water. The Tortoise Island (G) was also part of the Heian symbolism introduced into the original water garden, as here.

304

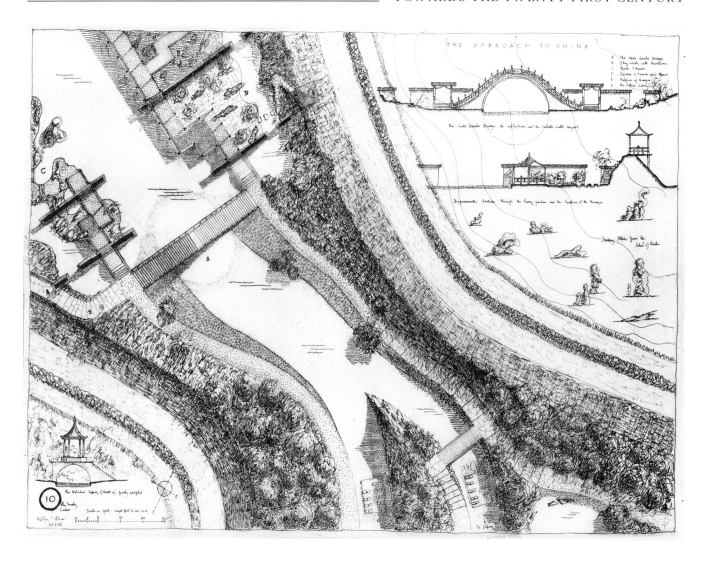

265]

10. *The approach to China*

This is the central section of the northward pointing peninsula of land which leads to the climactic landscape of Buddha. Here, the water-bus has passed through the fringes of the Japanese garden that will eventually be seen on the return journey, and passes beneath the Jade Girdle Bridge, with its full moon reflection in the water. North of the bridge, in the top left hand corner of the sheet, the character of the Chinese garden asserts itself: a common phrase for

garden-making quoted by Maggie Keswick in her book *Chinese Gardens*, translates literally from the Chinese as 'piling rocks and digging ponds',[5] and these rock-islands are just that process. On the right is the Peony garden; this flower, now beloved of western gardeners, originated in China and is a symbol of wealth and elegance. From the Peony Garden stepping stones lead to the Pavilion of the Breezes.

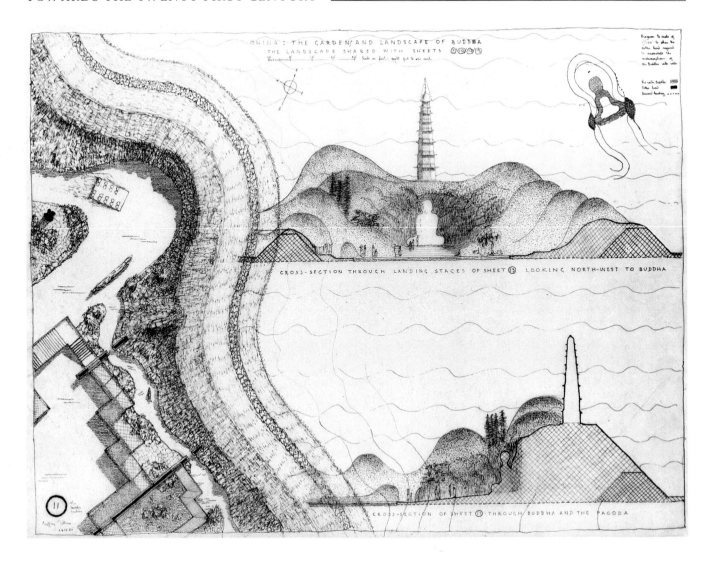

266]

11. *China; the gardens and landscape of Buddha*

Sir Geoffrey has suggested that the whole peninsula of land north from this point is enlarged, as shown in the sketch in the top right hand corner of this plan, to allow for the shadow of Buddha to be echoed in the water form.

The waterway shown on the left hand side of this drawing is really still only the approach to the gardens of the Dragon Temple, which are shown on the following sheet. The space on this sheet has been utilized for a cross-section through the landing-stages shown on sheet 13 (no. 268), looking north-west, to the final great view of the garden, the Buddha carved on rock, with the Pagoda above him.

306

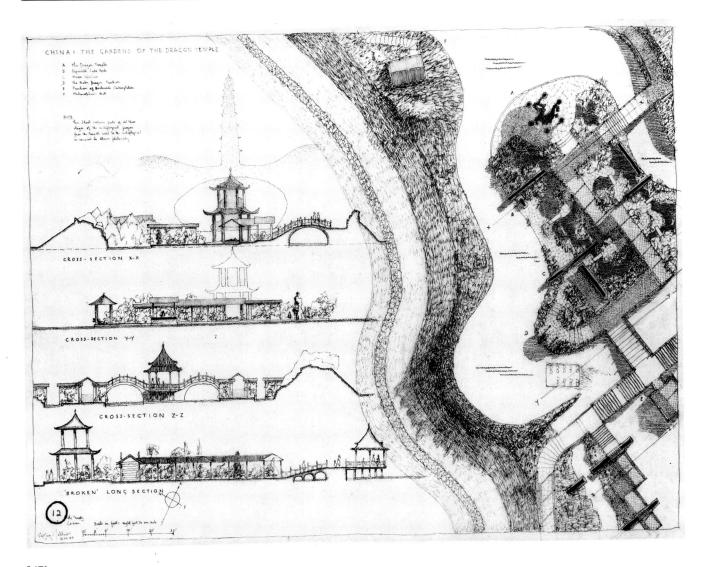

267]

12. *China; the gardens of the Dragon Temple*

This sheet shows the island contained within the form of the water Buddha. This island is devoted to the familiar themes of the willow-pattern plate garden, which are seen against the towering Pagoda in the distance. At this fantasy level it will be enjoyed by the many Americans of Chinese origin, and their appreciation will exceed that of the Europeans. But the gardens also offer deeper philosophies to those that search for them; Geoffrey Jellicoe has noted: *This sheet contains parts of all three stages of the metaphysical progress from the tangible world to the metaphysical as conceived in Chinese philosophy.* The goal of the Dragon Temple is reached via the Philosopher's Hut, the pavilion of Backward Contemplation, the Baby Dragon Pavilion, the Moon Window and the Exquisite Jade Rock.

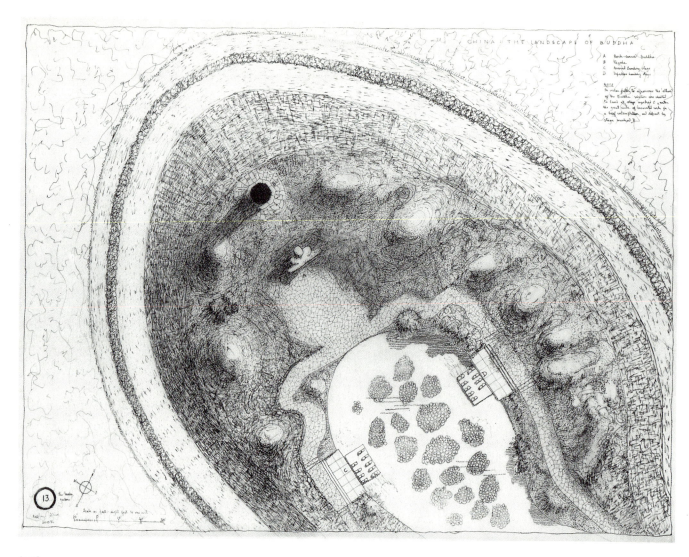

268]

13. *China; the landscape of Buddha*

The Buddha carved of rock, presiding over the circular rock-floored arena, is the climax of the gardens. The landing stages are for arrival at (C) and departure on the opposite side. The note reads: *In order fully to experience the 'ethos' of the Buddha, visitors are invited to land at stage marked C, enter the great circle of excavated rock for a brief contemplation, and depart by stage marked D.*

308

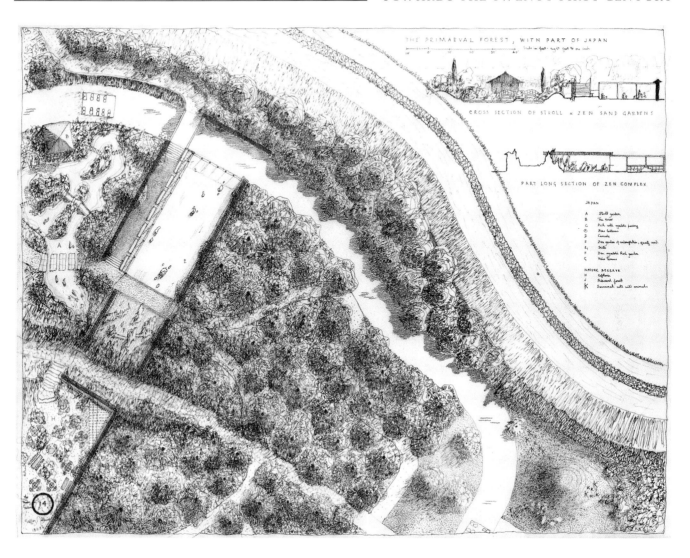

14. *The primaeval forest with part of Japan*

The Japanese garden of the Zen Buddhist tradition has been a familiar form and inspiration to western gardeners since the early years of the twentieth century. Here are the most familiar features – the Tea House beside the water, the Stroll Garden ornamented with lanterns and the raked sand garden with symbolic rocks; this last, most usually inspired by the most profound and austere of the Zen gardens at Ryoan-Ji, Kyoto, has been the most intriguing inspiration of all.

From here the water-bus returns through the Nature Reserve to journey's end and the landing-stage. Long before he knew of this commission for the Moody Gardens at Galveston, which are being implemented now, but will not be completed until well into the twenty-first century,

Geoffrey Jellicoe had endorsed humanism in our surroundings; now we have taken this journey in the water-bus of the imagination around the Moody Gardens, his words make an appropriate ending to my book: 'If we liken our present civilisation to a ship voyaging in uncharted, dangerous seas, with no knowledge of where we are going and indeed why – then its structure is critical. Our present ship is built of the tested materials of classicism, and these we should be unwise to discard until we are certain that those of a new structure are stronger and more appropriate. But this does not apply to the contents of the ship, and as furnishings we can dredge things out of the deep that we had never even dreamed existed.'[6]

Notes

INTRODUCTION:
Architects in the Garden

1. 'The Italian garden does not exist for its flowers: its flowers exist for it: they are a late and infrequent adjunct to its beauties, a parenthetical grace'. Edith Wharton, *Italian Villas and their Gardens*, 1904.
2. David Watkin, in *The Rise of Architectural History* Arch. Press, 1983 ed. p. 163, comments: 'The victory of the Modern Movement in the 1940s meant that English architects now deliberately rejected all traditions, so that the historical collection of drawings assembled by the Royal Institute of British Architects came to be seen rather as an archive for … historians than a source of inspiration for architects.'
3. See Harris, Lever, Richardson, *Great Drawings from the Collection of the Royal Institute of British Architects* Trefoil, London 1986.
4. David Watkin, *op. cit.*, p. 164.
5. Dr Christopher Thacker was Gardens Inspector in the Historic Buildings & Monuments Commission of the Department of the Environment for the first 5 year term in compilation of the Gardens Register, 1982–7. He has now been succeeded by David Jacques.
6. Jill Lever and Margaret Richardson's *The Art of the Architect*, Trefoil, London 1984, has a comprehensive introduction and long captions to the drawings concentrating upon techniques and interpretation.
7. Lever & Richardson, *ibid.*, p. 19.
8. Lever & Richardson, *ibid.*, p. 18.
9. See *Robert Adam and Kedleston*, Leslie Harris, 1987.
10. The fullest story of the Burlington-Devonshire Collection is contained in an unpublished typewritten catalogue of the RIBA drawings by John Harris and Prunella Fraser; most of the material has been subsequently reprinted in the B volume of the published catalogue, under Burlington, ed. Margaret Richardson and others, 1972.
11. J. Dixon Hunt, *William Kent … An Assessment and Catalogue of his designs*, 1987.
12. Benjamin Disraeli's *Lothair* thinly disguises Trentham as Brentham. It was first published in 1869/70.
13. Lord Powerscourt, *Description and history of Powerscourt*, 1903, p. 77; also H. Colvin, *Dictionary of British Architects*, London 1965, pp. 697–8.

THE SEVENTEENTH CENTURY
Masons, Gardeners and Gentlemen 1609–1714

1. See *Architectural History*, vol. 5, 1962, 'The Smythson Collection', ed. Mark Girouard, p. 23.
2. Details from *Smythson Collection* catalogue entry, S vol. RIBA catalogue, p. 92.
3. Girouard, first published as *Robert Smythson and the architecture of the Elizabethan era*, 1967; revised and reissued as *Robert Smythson and the Elizabethan Country House*, Yale, 1983.
4. See Girouard, *ibid.*, p. 38.
5. Girouard, *idem*.
6. See Roy Strong, *The Renaissance Garden in England*, London 1979, pp. 120–2, including a reference to on 1602–14 with similar Mannerist circles.
7. Robert Smythson's obituary is quoted on p. 92 of the S volume of the catalogue and Girouard, pp. 82–3.
8. Girouard, *ibid.*, p. 97.
9. Strong, *op. cit.*, pp. 60–2.
10. Strong, *ibid.*, p. 62.
11. Strong, *ibid.*, p. 63.
12. Strong, *ibid.*, pp. 88–9.
13. *Ham House*, Victoria and Albert Museum guide, London 1976, 4th edn.
14. *Ibid.*, p. 61.
15. In the Library of Christ Church, Oxford.
16. ibid., p. 47 … William Talman's 'unconventional and innovative use of the bird's-eye view for architectural design was an important step in the development of architectural draughtsmanship, though one not fully taken up until the nineteenth century'.
17. See Sir George Clark, ed., *The Later Stuarts 1660–1714* OUP Oxford 1963, p. 186; also Gertrude A. Jacobsen, *Life of William Blathwayt*, London 1932.
18. S. Switzer, *Ichonographia Rustica*, 1718, vol. 3, pp. 113–27, quoted by J. D. Hunt, Journal of Garden History vol. 8, p. 260, and *Style and Idea in Anglo-Dutch Gardens*, Antiques, N.Y. Dec. 1988.
19. John Harris, *William Talman, Maverick Architect*, London 1982.
20. Girouard, *op. cit.*, pp. 182–3, 251–7, re. Smythson's working at Welbeck.
21. Girouard, *op. cit.*, pp. 279–83 for Huntingdon Smithson's work and monument at Bolsover.
22. Girouard, *op. cit.*, Appendix 11, pp. 297–302, for the chronology of Bolsover and destruction by

Parliamentary forces, which included the Fountain Garden. It is tempting to think that John the Younger's sojourn at Bolsover until his death in 1717, allowed him to repair some of the damage to the work of his forebears.
23. Girouard, *op. cit.*, p. 46, 'Hardwick remains the supreme triumph of Elizabethan architecture'.
24. Rosalys Coope, *Jacques Gentilhâtre*, Gregg International, London, RIBA Catalogue, 1972.
25. Girouard, *op. cit.*, *Architectural History*, 1962.
26. Strong, *The Renaissance Garden in England*, pp. 56–9.
27. Girouard, *Robert Smythson and the Architecture of the Elizabethan Era*, 1966, later republished as *Robert Smythson and the Elizabethan Country House*, 1983.
28. Strong, *op. cit.*, p. 60.
29. Strong, *ibid.*, pp. 87–8.
30. Strong, *ibid.*, p. 89.
31. David Green, *Gardener to Queen Anne*, Plate 1 is the plan. The Indenture of December 1714 for letting the nursery to Carpenter and Smith is printed as Appendix iv.

THE EIGHTEENTH CENTURY
Art and Nature

1. Joseph Addison, writing in 1712, uses the Dutch 'landskip' from which our word landscape was derived.
2. Professor W. J. Hoskins, *The Making of the English Landscape*, London 1970 ed., p. 138.
3. The Hiorn drawings, catalogued with additional research by Dr T. F. Friedman, in the G–K volume of the RIBA Drawings catalogue, 1973.
4. Woolfe & Gandon, *Vitruvius Britannicus*, London 1767, quoted by Friedman, *ibid*.
5. For a complete catalogue of Kent's surviving drawings and their locations see John Dixon Hunt, *William Kent, Landscape Garden Designer*, Zwemmer, London, 1987.
6. Quoted from Gill Hedley ed., *Capability Brown and the Northern Landscape*, exhib. cat., Tyne & Wear County Museums, 1983.
7. Dorothy Stroud, *Capability Brown*, Faber & Faber, London, 1975 ed., Christopher Hussey quoted from preface to 1950 ed.
8. Hussey, *op. cit.*, p. 31.
9. Hussey, *ibid*.
10. *Correspondence of Thomas Gray*, ed. Paget Toynbee and Leonard Whibley, 1935, III p. 1107.

11. Keith Goodway, letters to the author, Sept/Oct 1986.
12. John Betjeman, *Summoned by Bells*, Murray, London 1960, p. 99.
13. Repton, *Designs for the Pavilion at Brighton*, see David Peake, Guide to Sezincote, p. 8.
14. Humphry Repton, *Observations on the Theory and Practice of Landscape Gardening*, 1803, facsimile ed., Phaidon, Oxford 1980.
15. The Red Book for Brandsbury is at Dumbarton Oaks Library, Trustees of Harvard University, Washington DC.
16. A list of Red Books and their known locations is contained in the exhib. cat., *Humphry Repton, Landscape Gardener, 1752–1818*, University of East Anglia, Norwich 1982.
17. Edmund Burke's quotation is engraved as the frontispiece to the Red Book for the Royal Pavilion, Brighton, 1805, in the Royal Library, Windsor Castle.
18. Patrick Goode, 'The Picturesque Controversy', *Humphry Repton*, exhib. cat., *op. cit.*, p. 38.
19. Kedrun Laurie, *Humphry Repton*, exhib. cat., *ibid.*, p. 25.
20. *Ibid.*
21. J. H. Plumb, *The First Four Georges*, Batsford, London 1956, pp. 13–4.
22. David Watkin, *Thomas Hope and the Neo-Classical Idea*, Murray, London 1968, p. 158.
23. Patrick Goode, 'The Picturesque Controversy', *Humphry Repton*, exhib. cat., *op. cit.*, p.34.
24. Watkin, *op. cit.*, p. 174.
25. Nairn, Pevsner and Cherry, *The Buildings of England, Surrey*, Penguin, London 1971, p. 194 charts the 'disgraceful and depressing' decline of The Deepdene, which fell into disrepair in the ownership of British Rail and was sold for demolition in 1969. A new office block now occupies the site and the garden has virtually returned to the wild.
26. Watkin, *op. cit.*, p. 187.
27. Goode, *op. cit.*, p. 40.
28. Published in 1728.
29. *The Gentleman and Cabinet Maker's Director*, 1754.
30. Brown worked at Luton Hoo for the 3rd Earl of Bute in 1764. According to Dorothy Stroud, *Capability Brown*, p. 133, 1975 rev. ed., a fragment of the Luton Hoo plan by Brown was sold in London in 1950 and is now in the Metropolitan Museum, New York. Miss Stroud further records Arthur Young's enthusiasm for the park, including a dam and wooden bridge, in 1770 (p. 134) and it is tempting to suppose that this drawing might also relate to Luton Hoo.
31. Letter to the author, 16 October 1986.
32. Kedrun Laurie, *Humphry Repton Landscape Gardener 1752–1818*, eds. Carter, Goode and Laurie, p. 21., quoting J. C. Loudon 'Strictures on Mr Repton's Mode of using Slides and sketches', 1806 and William Mason to William Gilpin, letter

26 Dec 1794, Mavis Batey, *Garden History* Feb. 1973, p. 23.
33. Repton's deliberate concern for so much screen planting resulted from his annoyance that Sir Peter Burrell's mother had refused to sacrifice her familiar and comfortable house for the new one Repton wanted to build. Thus the cluttered duck pond and poultry yard around the existing house had to be screened as effectively as possible.
34. George Carter, *Humphry Repton, Landscape Gardener, 1752–1818* op. cit. p. 48.
35. The Collection holds three letters from Thomas Daniell to Sir Charles Cockerell dated 12 Dec. 1810, 30 Dec. 1810 and 14 January 1811. The first notes the request about the ivy as quoted, the second is an acknowledgement of the turkey etc., and the third, a longer letter, deals with Daniell's doubts about the siting of the Brahmin bulls.
36. Priscilla Boniface ed., *In Search of English Gardens: the travels of John Claudius Loudon and his wife Jane*, Lennard pub., London 1987, p. 43.
37. *Ibid*, p. 50.
38. *Ibid*, p. 49.
39. *Ibid*, p. 50.

THE NINETEENTH CENTURY
Victorian Formal Gardens

1. Note by John Betjeman pp. 9–10, Betjeman and Taylor eds., *English Love Poems*, Faber, London 1957.
2. Brent Elliott, *Victorian Gardens*, Batsford, London 1986, p. 10.
3. For the explanation of the Wyatt family, and why Jeffry Wyatville changed his name, see introduction to the RIBA catalogue volume, ed. Derek Linstrum, 1974.
4. Linstrum, *ibid*.
5. RIBA Drawings Collection catalogue *The Office of J. B. Papworth*, ed. George McHardy, London 1977.
6. The full title is *Rural Residences, consisting of a series of designs for cottages, decorated cottages, small villas and other ornamental buildings*, &c., 1818, 2nd ed. 1832.
7. *Hillier's Manual of Trees & Shrubs* offers further information on Loudon's plants: *Cotoneaster buxifolias* and *Calophaca wolgarica* are both prostrate varieties of small-leaved shrubs, and standards would indeed be curious specimens. *Araucaria imbricata*, now *A. araucana* is the Chilean pine we know as the Monkey Puzzle tree.
8. Brent Elliott, *op. cit., p. 13* on 'The Rise of the Head Gardener' *et passim*.
9. W. A. Nesfield, manuscript submission to HRH Prince Albert and the Commissioners for the Improvement of Buckingham Palace, in the RIBA Drawings Collection.
10. W. A. Nesfield, *ibid*.
11. Elliott, *op. cit.*, p. 74.
12. John Betjeman *Ghastly Good Taste*, National

Trust/Hutchinson, London, ed. 1986, p. 99.
13. See B volume of RIBA Drawings Collection catalogue, ed. Margaret Richardson, London 1972.
14. Elliott, *op. cit.*, p. 90.
15. Elliott, *op. cit.*, p. 78.
16. William Robinson, *The English Flower Garden*, Murray, London 1883, 3rd ed. 1893, pp. 2–4.
17. Coombe Abbey gardens are now part of Coventry City Council's Coombe Abbey Country Park and a large part of William Miller's garden survives in a fine condition. There is an excellent history of Coombe Abbey by Robin Moore, Jones-Sands Publishing, Coventry 1983, available at the Country Park.
18. Benjamin Disraeli's *Lothair*, a novel in three volumes, London 1869–70, features Trentham disguised as Brentham.
19. Jane Loudon 'A Short Account of the Life and Writings of John Claudius Loudon', Appendix ii in John Gloag, *Mr Loudon's England*, 1970.
20. William Robinson, *The English Flower Garden*, 3rd ed., 1893, pp. 2–3.

THE ARTS AND CRAFTS GARDEN
1890–1914

1. Margaret Richardson, *The Architects of the Arts and Crafts Movement*, RIBA Drawings Series, Trefoil, London 1983. The basic thesis of this book is that the office system of London encouraged both the buildings and drawing styles of the Movement. Because the Collection holds almost complete coverage of this period, Margaret Richardson's book is the most comprehensive source.
2. There is no material in the Collection relating to Rodmarton Manor. Clive Aslet, *The Last Country Houses*, Yale, London 1982, describes its building and furniture design; my chapter 3 in *The English Garden in Our Time*, London 1986, emphasizes the garden.
3. *Old West Surrey*, 1st ed. London 1904 illustrated a large collection of cottage artifacts which Miss Jekyll collected; they are now in Guildford Museum.
4. *Gardens of a Golden Afternoon; The Story of the partnership between Edwin Lutyens and Gertrude Jekyll*, Viking, London 1982. Penguin paperback 1984. *Miss Jekyll; portrait of a great gardener*, is the full title of Betty Massingham's biography, Country Life, London 1966.
5. Christopher Hussey, *Life of Lutyens*, Country Life, London 1951; attributed a great deal to garden-making: 'the lovely sequence from Miss Jekyll's at Munstead to the enamelled carpets of Delhi; gardens of which the geometry left nothing to chance yet the forms and colours of nature were given their freedom, and the shapes of trees seen to greater advantage for their humanized surroundings. These elements, and the light suffusing them, had ... been his first love since

boyhood . . . and remained a prime inspiration of his creative invention.'

6. Reginald Blomfield's assertion in *The Formal Garden in England*, that garden design was the proper business of architects, identified him as William Robinson's prime target, and their acrid controversy was carried on in the Author's prefaces to further editions of *The English Flower Garden* and *The Formal Garden in England*. Robinson also published a slim volume of his opinions on *Architects' Gardens*; his main criticism was that they should pay more attention to flowers.

7. Gertrude Jekyll's drawings, just over 200 folders of them, are in the library of the College of Environmental Design, University of California, Berkeley. There is a microfilm of much of her collection in the RIBA Library, 66 Portland Place, WI, and the National Monuments Record, Fortress House, Savile Row, London WI.

8. The Lutyens volume of the RIBA Drawings Collection catalogue, ed. Margaret Richardson, 1972, and in process of revision.

9. The Munstead Wood sketchbook illustrated was rescued from the rubbish being removed from Lutyens' 5 Eaton Gate office in 1939 by one of his assistants, R. A. Wood. It was presented by Mr Wood to Lutyens' daughter, Lady Ridley, and is on long term loan to the Collection in the names of the Misses J. S. and J. Ridley.

10. Charles Voysey's drawings are catalogued in a single volume, ed. Joanna Symonds, 1976.

11. Thomas Mawson (1861–1933) strongly influenced Charles Mallows' style, and the book with which Mallows assisted, *The Art & Craft of Garden Making* was immensely popular, running into five editions between 1900 and 1926. Mawson began garden designing via his family contracting and nursery business, and qualified as a town planner. He became very successful and eminent, President of the Town Planning Institute and a founder member of the Royal Fine Art Commission and first President of the Institute of Landscape Architects. His drawings are in Preston Public Library in his native Lancashire.

12. Christopher Hussey, *Country Life*, London, vol. LIII, 1923, p. 349.

13. David Dean, *The Thirties: Recalling the English Architectural Scene*, RIBA Drawings Series, Trefoil, London 1983, p. 42.

14. Alan Powers, *Oliver Hill Architect and Lover of Life 1887–1968*, London 1988.

15. David Watkin, Ch. 4, 'The History of the "English" Tradition 1900–45'.

16. The story of Edwin Lutyens and Herbert Baker and the buildings of New Delhi is told by Robert Grant Irving in *Indian Summer*, Yale, London 1981.

17. Sir Robert Lorimer's drawings are in the Scottish National Monuments Record, Edinburgh.

18. Eitan Karol *and* Finch Allibone, exhib. cat. *Charles Holden, Architect 1875–1960*, London 1988, quoting C. H. Reilly, p. 6. The Collection has one garden design by Adams, Holden & Pearson, for a house at Gerrard's Cross, Buckinghamshire, for Miss Blackwell; it is a tennis-lawn with flower borders to one side and a pergola at the end.

19. Karol *and* Allibone, *ibid.*, pp. 15–16 quoting *The British Architect*.

20. The Glynde School for Lady Gardeners was founded in 1902 by Frances Wolseley, later Viscountess Wolseley. Gertrude Jekyll, William Robinson and Ellen Willmott were among the patrons, and the 'college' (as it came to be called) trained young women to earn their own livings as growers, nurserymen and head gardeners. Undoubtedly both Frances Wolseley's and Gertrude Jekyll's military connections conspired towards them working together on the King Edward Sanatorium project; the students made and planted the garden, probably for little charge.

21. Blomfield, *The Formal Garden in England*, pp. 185–6.

22. *ibid.*, p. 31.

23. The Hut is an artist's vernacular cottage, with a large studio-cum-sitting room and two small bedrooms; Gertrude Jekyll used her small house in order to live in her garden and watch her large house being built. In later years she let it to friends or used it as a base for the Munstead Wood *pot-pourri* manufacture.

24. Gertrude Jekyll, *Home and Garden*, 1900, pp. 21–2.

25. *ibid.*, p. 22.

26. Jane Brown, *Gardens of a Golden Afternoon*, p. 96 *et passim* on the Lutyens/Jekyll theories of garden design.

27. Gavin Stamp and Andre Goulancourt, *The English House 1860–1914*, 1987, p. 134.

28. Margaret Richardson, *Architects of the Arts and Crafts Movement*, p. 87.

29. Jekyll and Weaver, *Gardens for Small Country Houses*, pp. 131–2.

30. Gavin Stamp, *The English House*, p. 144.

31. XLV 1908.

32. XVII 1910.

33. See n. 6, ch. 4.

34. The pergola 'cloister' was not to Miss Jekyll's taste and not used by Lutyens, but was a favourite device of Thomas Mawson, notably for Stoke Poges Memorial Gardens in Buckinghamshire and for both Thornton Manor, Wirral and The Hill, Hampstead for Lord Leverhulme, who hated to have to stand still in his gardens.

35. Margaret Richardson, *Architects of the Arts and Crafts Movement*, p. 137.

36. 'Compton End near Winchester, the residence of Mr G. H. Kitchen', *Country Life*, 23 Aug. 1919.

37. Alvilde Lees-Milne and Rosemary Verey, *The Englishwoman's Garden*, p. 149.

38. Jekyll and Weaver, *Gardens for Small Country Houses*, pp. 59–60.

39. *Modern Gardens, British and Foreign*, Special Winter Number of *The Studio* 1926–7, ed. C. G. Holme and Shirley Wainwright, p. 53.

40. Baillie Scott, *Houses and Gardens*, 1906; rev. ed. 1913 Baillie Scott & Beresford, and illustrating much of the partnership's work in houses and gardens.

THE MODERN MOVEMENT GARDEN
1925–39

1. This small garden by Guevrekian, illustrated by Christopher Tunnard, in *Gardens in the Modern Landscape* and Peter Shepheard in *Modern Gardens*, and in many articles on both modern gardens and Modern Movement buildings, has been remembered and imitated by students and designers down the years.

2. Nikolaus Pevsner, *Pioneers of Modern Design*, Penguin, London 1978 ed., p. 203.

3. Pevsner, *ibid.*, p. 202.

4. The RIBA Drawings Collection has a frieze for 78 Derngate, Northampton, the only Charles Rennie Mackintosh drawing in the Collection.

5. David Dean, *The Thirties: Recalling the English Architectural Scene*, p. 9.

6. See *Erich Mendelsohn, Architectural Drawings*, exhib. cat., Verlag Willmuth Arenhovel, Berlin 1988.

7. Roger Berthoud, *The Life of Henry Moore*, Faber, London 1987 pp. 155/6.

8. Christopher Tunnard, *Gardens in the Modern Landscape*, pp. 126–137.

9. Sylvia Crowe, *Garden Design*, pp. 73–5.

10. See my essay on Tunnard in *Eminent Gardeners* to be published by Viking, London 1989.

11. Crowe, *op. cit.*, p. 77.

12. Christopher Tunnard, *Gardens in the Modern Landscape*, house and garden in Leicestershire drawn by Gordon Cullen, p. 75.

13. *ibid.*, p. 75.

CONTINUING CLASSICISM
1920 to the Present day

1. David Dean, *The Thirties: Recalling the English Architectural Scene*, Trefoil 1983, RIBA Drawings Series, London 1983, p. 81.

2. Prince Charles' speech at a Royal Gala Evening to celebrate the 150th anniversary of the RIBA, Hampton Court, 30 May 1984.

3. Sylvia Crowe, *Garden Design*, Country Life, London 1958, 3rd imp. 1965, pp. 73–5.

4. Jellicoe and Shepherd, *Italian Gardens of the Renaissance*, London 1953 ed., p. 3.

5. The latest and most concise of Sir Geoffrey Jellicoe's lectures upon his career 'The Guelph Lectures in Landscape Design', University of Guelph, Ontario 1983. See also my *The English Garden in Our Time*, Antique Collectors Club, London 1986.

6. John Martin Robinson, *The Latest Country Houses*,

Bodley Head, London 1983, p. 11.

7. Lucy Archer, *Raymond Erith Architect*, Cygnet Press, London 1985.

8. Clive Aslet, *Quinlan Terry; The Revival of Architecture*, Viking, London 1986.

9. The Collection has only two drawings by E. Guy Dawber.

10. In those days the Fellowship of the Royal Horticultural Society was restricted by eminence or examination.

11. Jane Brown, *Lanning Roper and his Gardens*, Weidenfeld & Nicolson, London 1986, paperback 1988.

12. Percy Cane's autobiography *The Earth is My Camera*, London 1950, tells of his work.

13. Russell Page was an eminent landscape architect who worked mostly in France and America. At the time of writing, his drawings remain at risk at his last home in Belgium and it is to be profoundly hoped they find a safe haven.

14. Tintinhull Manor in Somerset, the property of the National Trust, has a garden originally made by Phyllis Reiss, a follower of Gertrude Jekyll. Under the care of Penelope Hobhouse the garden has blossomed with ravishing beauty and skill whilst remaining faithful to Mrs Reiss's ideas, but at the same time demonstrating a modern planter's restoration of Jekyllian theories.

15. Aslet, *op. cit.*, pp. 119–26 on West Green buildings.

16. Aslet, *ibid.*, p. 123.

17. Aslet, *ibid.*, p. 121.

18. Geoffrey Jellicoe, Villa Garzoni, *Oxford Companion to Gardens*, p. 217.

19. John Martin Robinson, *The Latest Country Houses*, p. 85.

20. John Martin Robinson, *ibid.*, p. 97, quoting from Clough Williams-Ellis *Architect Errant*, 1971.

21. Robinson, *ibid.*, p. 97.

GARDEN BUILDINGS

1. Alistair Rowan, *Garden Buildings*, Country Life Books, London 1968, p. 3.

2. Rowan, *ibid.*

3. See John Harris, 'Newly acquired Designs by James Stuart in the British Architectural Library, Drawings Collection', *Architectural History*, vol. 22, 1979.

4. Peter Hunt, *Shell Gardens Book*, London 1964, p. 180.

5. For further description of the Wyatt contribution to garden buildings see May Woods and Arete Warren, *Glass Houses*, Aurum Press, London 1988, p. 107.

6. Woods and Warren, *ibid.*, pp. 92–3.

7. In his 1909 sketchbook G. H. Kitchin notes a design for a sundial for Lilleshall, for 'Millie Duchess' of Sutherland, (sketchbook no. 20).

8. John Harris, *op. cit.* vol. 22, 1979. p. 74.

9. The word *Praeneste* comes from the ancient Roman site of the Temple of Fortuna Virilis at Lazio, where water tumbled down the hillside through arched terraces, allowing the water to be viewed from above. The place is now called Palestrina.

GARDEN ORNAMENT

1. *English Hours*, 'in Warwickshire', OUP 1982, p. 113.

2. Sylvia Crowe, *Garden Design*, p. 92.

3. Dorothy Stroud, *Capability Brown*, pp. 149.

4. Gavin Stamp, *The English House* 1860–1914, p. 134.

5. John Martin Robinson, *The Latest Country Houses* pp. 124–32 *et passim*.

6. Clive Aslet, *The Last Country Houses*, pp. 244–50.

TOWARDS THE TWENTY-FIRST CENTURY
Geoffrey Jellicoe's Moody Gardens

1. Geoffrey Jellicoe was born in London in 1900, and educated at Cheltenham College and the Architectural Association, gaining his Diploma in 1923. The Rome Scholarship offered him the chance to study the Italian gardens immediately afterwards, and he was convinced by the experience that 'architecture was part of the environment and therefore incomplete when considered in isolation'. He has frequently acknowledged that this 'timeless idea has always remained the basis of the thought, design and execution' of his work.

2. The complete site can be seen as resembling a yawning alligator, divided into two jaws; these two land areas differ in character and represent 'the duel emotions that have informed all human feelings and art' – the romantic, biological and irrational, and the classical, mathematical and rational.

3. The theoretical scheme for creating the mounds in Hyde Park, using the spoil which had to be disposed of from the Park Lane underground car parks, was described in *Studies in Landscape Design*, vol. 3, 1970, p. 79–83.

4. See Jellicoe, 'Square One' in *Studies in Landscape Design*, vol. 1, 1960, p. 115.

5. Maggie Keswick 'The making of a Chinese garden', p. 115, *Oxford Companion to Gardens*.

6. From the Forward, p. xii, *The Guelph Lectures on Landscape Design*, Sir Geoffrey Jellicoe, 1983.

Bibliography

THE FOLLOWING VOLUMES OF THE CATALOGUE OF THE RIBA
DRAWINGS COLLECTION WERE PUBLISHED BY GREGG
INTERNATIONAL, LONDON

A, 1968
B, ed. Margaret Richardson and others, 1972.
C–F, ed. Margaret Richardson, 1972.
G–K, ed. Jill Lever, 1973.
L–N, ed. Jill Lever, 1973.
O–R, ed. Jill Lever, 1976.
S, ed. Margaret Richardson, 1976.
T–Z, ed. Jill Lever, 1974.
Colen Campbell, ed. John Harris, 1976.
Jacques Gentilhâtre, ed. Rosalys Coope, 1972.
Inigo Jones/John Webb, ed. John Harris, 1972.
Edwin L. Lutyens, ed. Margaret Richardson, 1972.
The Office of J. B. Papworth, ed. George McHardy, 1977.
The Pugin Family, ed. Alexandra Wedgewood, 1977.
The Scott Family, ed. Joanna Heseltine, 1981.
Edward Stevens, ed. Susan Beattie, 1975.
Vivisenti, ed. John McAndrew, 1974.
C. F. A. Voysey, ed. Joanna Symonds, 1975.
The Wyatt Family, ed. Derek Linstrum, 1974.

GENERAL BIBLIOGRAPHY OF BOOKS CONSULTED AND FOR
FURTHER READING

Abdy, Jane and Gere, Charlotte, *The Souls*, Sidgwick & Jackson, London 1984.
Aslet, Clive, *The Last Country Houses*, Yale, London 1982.
Aslet, Clive, *Quinlan Terry: the Revival of Architecture*, Viking, London 1982.
Blomfield, Reginald, *The Formal Garden in England*, 1892, facsimile ed. Waterstone, London 1985.
Brooke, E. Adveno, *The Gardens of England*, London 1857.
Brown, Jane, *The English Garden in Our Time*, Antique Coll. Club, Woodbridge 1986.
Brown, Jane, *Gardens of a Golden Afternoon*, Allen Lane, 1982.
Carter, George: Goode, Patrick & Laurie, Kedrun, *Humphry Repton, Landscape Gardener 1752–1818*,
    Sainsbury Centre for the Visual Arts, Norwich & London 1982.
Crowe, Sylvia, *Garden Design*, Country Life, London 1958, 3rd imp. 1965.
Dean, David, *The Thirties: Recalling the English Architectural Scene*, Trefoil, London (RIBA Drawings Series), 1983.
Elliott, Brent, *Victorian Gardens*, Batsford, London 1986.
Georgian Arcadia, Architecture for the Park and Garden, for the Georgian Group Golden Jubilee, Colnaghi, London 1987.
Girouard, Mark, *Robert Smythson and the Elizabethan Country House*, Yale, London 1983 (originally published as *Robert Smythson and the Architecture of the Elizabethan Era*, 1969).
Gloag, John, *Mr Loudon's England*, Oriel Press, Newcastle upon Tyne 1970.
Godfrey, Walter H. *Gardens in the Making*, London 1914.
Gradidge, Roderick, *Dream Houses*, Constable, London 1982.
Green, David, *Gardener to Queen Anne: Henry Wise 1653–1738 and the Formal Garden*, Oxford University Press, London 1956.
Harris, John, ed., *The Garden: A Celebration of One Thousand Years of British Gardening*, Mitchell Beazley/New Perspectives, London 1979.
Harris, John, *The Design of the English Country House, 1620–1920*, Trefoil, London 1985.

Harris, John,; Lever, Jill and Richardson, Margaret, *Great Drawings from the Collection of the Royal Institute of British Architects*, Trefoil, London 1986.
Harris, Leslie, (G. Jackson-Stops ed.) *Robert Adam & Kedleston*, The National Trust, London 1987.
Hedley, Gill, ed., *Capability Brown and the Northern Landscape*, Tyne & Wear County Museums, Newcastle upon Tyne 1983.
Hunt, John Dixon, *William Kent, Landscape Garden Designer*, Zwemmer, London 1987.
Jaques, David, *Georgian Gardens – The Reign of Nature*, Batsford, London, 1983.
Jekyll, Gertrude, *Colour Schemes for the Flower Garden*, London 1908 (reprinted Penguin 1983 and Antique Coll. Club 1983).
Jekyll, Gertrude, and Weaver, Lawrence, *Gardens for Small Country Houses*, Country Life, London 1912. (Reprinted, Antique Coll. Club 1981.)
Jekyll, Gertrude, *Home & Garden*, London 1900 (Reprinted, Antique Coll. Club, 1982).
Jellicoe, Geoffrey and Susan; Goode, Patrick and Lancaster, Michael, eds., *The Oxford Companion to Gardens*, OUP, London 1986.
Jellicoe, Geoffrey , *The Guelph Lectures on Landscape Design*, University of Guelph, Ontario 1983.
Jellicoe, Geoffrey, *The Landscape of Civilisation created for the Moody Historical Gardens designed and described by Geoffrey Jellicoe*, Garden Art Press, Suffolk, forthcoming.
Jellicoe, Geoffrey and Susan, *The Landscape of Man*, London 1975.
Karol, Eitan and Allibone, Finch, *Charles Holden Architect 1875–1960*, RIBA Heinz Gallery, London 1988.
Lees-Milne; Verey, Alvilde and Rosemary, *The Englishwoman's Garden*, Chatto & Windus, London 1980.
Lever, Jill, and Richardson, Margaret, *The Art of the Architect. Treasures from the RIBA's Collection*, Trefoil, London 1984.
Massingham, Betty, *Miss Jekyll: Portrait of a Great Gardener*, Country Life, London 1966.
Mawson, Thomas, *The Art and Craft of Garden Making*, London 1900.
Plumptre, George, *The Latest Country Gardens*, Bodley Head, London 1988.
Powers, Alan, *Oliver Hill Architect and Lover of Life 1887–1968*, Moulton Pubs., London, 1989.
Richardson, Margaret, *The Architects of the Arts and Crafts Movement*, Trefoil, London (RIBA Drawings Series), 1983.
Robinson, John Martin, *The Latest Country House*, Bodley Head, London 1984.
Robinson, William, *The English Flower Garden*, London 1883.
Rohde, Eleanor Sinclair, *Herbs and Herb Gardening*, Medici Society, London 1936.
Rowan, Alistair, *Garden Buildings* (RIBA Drawings Series) Country Life, 1968 London.
Scott, Mackay Hugh Baillie, *Houses and Gardens*, London 1906.
Sedding, John Dando, *Garden Craft Old and New*, London 1891.
Shepheard, Peter, *Modern Gardens*, Architectural Press, London 1953, 3rd imp., 1958.
Stamp, Gavin and Goulancourt, Andre, *The English House 1860–1914*, London 1987.
Strong, Roy, *The Renaissance Garden in England*, Thames & Hudson, London 1979.
Stroud, Dorothy, *Capability Brown*, Faber, London 1950, rev. ed. 1975.
Taylor, Geoffrey, *The Victorian Flower Garden*, Skeffington, London 1952.
Tooley, Michael J. Ed., *Gertrude Jekyll, Artist, Gardener, Craftswoman*, Michaelmas Books, Durham 1984.
Tunnard, Christopher, *Gardens in the Modern Landscape*, Architectural Press, London 1938.
Verey , Rosemary, *Classic Garden Design*, Viking, London 1984.
Watkin, David, *The Rise of Architectural History*, Architectural Press, London 1980.
Watkin, David, *Thomas Hope and the Neo-Classical Idea*, London 1968.
Whistler, Laurence, *The Imagination of Vanbrugh and his Fellow artists*, London 1954.
Woods, May and Warren, Arete, *Glass Houses: A history of Greenhouses, Orangeries and Conservatories*, Aurum Press, London 1988.

Index

Numbers in italics refer to illustration page numbers